D1226401

Handbook of Sports and Recreational Building Design
Volume 1

HANDBOOK OF SPORTS AND RECREATIONAL BUILDING DESIGN

Volume 1 Outdoor sports

Second edition

THE SPORTS COUNCIL
TECHNICAL UNIT FOR SPORT

Edited by Geraint John and Kit Campbell

Butterworth Architecture
An imprint of Butterworth-Heinemann Ltd
Linacre House, Jordan Hill, Oxford OX2 8DP

ℛ A member of the Reed Elsevier group

OXFORD   LONDON   BOSTON
MUNICH   NEW DELHI   SINGAPORE   SYDNEY
TOKYO   TORONTO   WELLINGTON

First published 1981
Second edition 1993

British Library Cataloguing in Publication Data
Sports Council
    Handbook of Sports and Recreational
    Building Design. – Vol. 1: Outdoor Sports. –
    2Rev.ed
    I. Title   II. John, Geraint
    III. Campbell, Kit
    725.8

ISBN 0 7506 1293 2

Library of Congress Cataloguing in Publication Data
Handbook of sports and recreational building design/edited by
    Geraint John and Kit Campbell. – 2nd ed.
    p. cm.
    'The Sports Council. Technical Unit for Sport.'
    Contents: – v. 1. Outdoor sports.
    ISBN 0 7506 1293 2 (v. 1)
    1. Sports facilities – Design and construction –
    Handbooks, manuals, etc. I. John, Geraint. II. Campbell,
    Kit. III. Sports Council (Great Britain). Technical Unit for
    Sports.
    GV413.H36   1993   v. 1   92–35106
    725.8–dc20   CIP

Whilst every effort is made to ensure the accuracy of the
information in this publication it is provided without liability
on the part of the Sports Council.

Typeset by Scribe Design, Gillingham, Kent
Printed and bound in Great Britain

Volume 1   Outdoor sports

A note about the Sports Council   vii
Foreword   ix
Preface   xi
Contributors to Volume 1   xiii

Part I   Overview
 1 Outdoor sport and recreation   3
 2 Whole life costs   6
 3 Facilities for people with disabilities   9
 4 Planning for sport and recreation   12

Part II   Briefing guide
 5 Planning obligations for sport and recreation   17
 6 Briefing guide   20

Part III   Surfaces for outdoor sport
 7 Surface selection   25
 8 Grass pitches   30
 9 Bound and unbound mineral surfaces   37
10 Sheet and in-situ synthetic surfaces   39
11 Synthetic turf   41
12 Specialist surfaces – general   44
13 Athletics – track and field   45
14 Bowls – crown and flat   47
15 Cricket   50
16 Tennis   53
17 Children's play and recreation facilities   55

Part IV   Ancillary work
18 Floodlighting   59
19 Fencing and rebound walls   62
20 Equipment   63
21 Ancillary work   64

Part V   Sport-specific facilities
22 Stadia   67
23 Pavilions and clubhouses   94
24 Golf courses   102
25 Golf clubhouses   106
26 Artificial ski centres   113
27 Motor sports   119
28 Multi-use games areas (MUGAs)   121
29 Air sports   128

Part VI   Water recreation
30 Rowing   133
31 Sailing   136
32 Canoeing   151

33 Angling facilities for people with disabilities   154
34 Marinas   156
35 Water skiing   162
36 Personal watercraft riding   164

Part VII   Sports data
37 Introduction   169
38 Archery – target and clout   171
39 Athletics – track and field   174
40 Baseball   180
41 Basketball   183
42 Bicycle polo   186
43 Bowls: Lawn bowls   188
44 Camogie   190
45 Cricket   192
46 Croquet   194
47 Crown green bowls   196
48 Curling   198
49 Cycle racing   200
50 Cycle speedway   205
51 Eton fives   207
52 American football   208
53 Association football and five-a-side   211
54 Australian football   216
55 Gaelic football   218
56 Rugby league football   220
57 Rugby union football   222
58 Handball   224
59 Hockey   226
60 Mini hockey and six- or seven-a-side hockey   231
61 Hurling   233
62 Korfball   235
63 Lacrosse: men   237
64 Lacrosse: women   239
65 Lawn tennis   241
66 Netball   244
67 Petanque   246
68 Polo   248
69 Riding and equestrianism   250
70 Roller hockey   258
71 Roller skating and speed skating   260
72 Rounders   262
73 Shinty   264
74 Softball   266
75 Stoolball   269
76 Tchouk-ball   271
77 Tug of war   273

Index   276

A note about the Sports Council

The Sports Council was incorporated by Royal Charter in 1972 and its main objectives are to increase participation and excellence in sports and physical recreation, to increase the quantity and quality of sports facilities, to raise standards of performance, and to provide information on sports and sports facilities.

Back Row 1 Rita Bonomini 2 Dean Sanger 3 Jennifer Millest 4 Peter Clapp 5 Lyn Taylor 6 Christopher Harper 7 Eifion Roberts 8 Peter Ackroyd 9 Gordon Stables **Front Row** 10 David Bosher 11 David Butler 12 John Davies 13 Patricia Smith 14 Geraint John 15 Robin Wilson 16 Veronika Mhatre-Rolvien

Foreword

This handbook is the result of many years of hard work by our Technical Unit for Sport, working closely with a number of authors, all experts in their various subjects. When the first edition of four volumes was published in 1981, it was the largest and most ambitious undertaking of its kind. It has established itself as a major national and instructional reference work. Now this new, completely revised edition continues the tradition.

Much progress has been made since the Sports Council began its work in 1972, but much work remains to be done. New facilities constructed to the right standards are continually needed, together with the need to modernise and update the existing stock of sports buildings. We need to respond to the demand for sports and recreational facilities, and time and resources are wasted if these resources are not well designed and well built.

That is why I unreservedly welcome the publication of this new edition of the handbook covering, as it does, a wide range of sports and recreational buildings with the emphasis on provision for both the general community and for excellence. Properly designed buildings, offering a wide range of uses, capable of withstanding prolonged wear and tear, and providing value for money in operation and construction are essential if we are to meet the leisure needs of·the future.

Sir Peter Yarranton
Chairman, Sports Council

Preface

This is a new edition of a book which has established itself as the definitive practical handbook for architects, clients and providers of sports and recreational buildings. The original edition, which was written in 1981, has been substantially revised, rewritten and updated. Like its predecessor, this book aims to provide practical advice and guidance on the design of new facilities and the conversion, adaptation and upgrading of existing buildings.

In short, this publication is designed to be the new edition of the major textbook on the subject. It is a new statement bringing together a wide range of reference works, including those which have been written since the first edition, to make the book as comprehensive as possible. New material has been added as appropriate. Because of the quantity of information, the book has been split into two volumes, with Volume 1 covering outdoor facilities and Volume 2 indoor. This two volume format is a change from the four volumes of the previous edition.

Dimensions and specifications are given for some 80 sports in the two volumes.

This book would not have been possible without the help and encouragement of a wide range of people involved in the sport and recreational field.

Individual authors and sources are credited within the book, but thanks are also due to colleagues in the Sports Council working closest with the Technical Unit for Sport, namely the Facilities Unit, the Information Centre and the Research Unit, for their contributions. Mention must also be made of the help given by the Sports Council's regional officers, staff in the National Sports Councils and others who have given their time and assistance.

The relevant Governing Bodies of Sport and other sports organisations have made a significant contribution in helping to ensure the accuracy of the information contained in this book.

Geraint John
1993

Contributors to Volume 1

Peter Ackroyd Dip Arch RIBA MILAM is a Senior Architect in the Technical Unit for Sport of the Sportts Council.

Donald Adie Dip Arch RIBA DipTP MRTPI is an architect and town planner and Director of Greater London Consultants.

Stephen Baker BSc PhD is the Senior Research Officer of the Sports Turf Research Institute.

David Bosher is the Environmental Services Engineer in the Technical Unit for Sport of the Sports Council.

Bruno Broughton BSc (Hons) PhD MIFM is an independent Fisheries Management Consultant and Organiser of the Angling Federation.

Kit Campbell BArch MSc RIBA ARIAS MRTPI MILAM is an architect planner and Principal of Kit Campbell Associates, Leisure Recreation and Tourism Consultants, Edinburgh.

David Carpenter is a Senior Sports Development Officer in the Sports Council and is responsible for tennis development.

Cynthia Coombe is a former member of the Technical Unit for Sport of the Sports Council.

Peter Cranstone is Vice President of the Personal Watercraft Association.

Peter Dury NDT FAPFLM AILAM is a sports ground manager and Head of the Sports and Landscape Development Unit of Nottinghamshire County Council.

Roger Dyer Dip Arch (Birm) RIBA is an architect in private practice in Dyer Associates, Architects and Designers, in London.

Mike Earle is an architect and Director of Design and Project Management at Sports Partner.

Roger Evans is an Advisory Agronomist with the Sports Turf Research Institute.

Ken Farnes is an architect Director of Atkins Lister Drew Ltd, Urban and Regional Planners and Landscape Architects, and a Union Cycliste Internationale Commissaire.

Mike Fitzjohn is a Senior Research Officer in the Sports Council.

Ian Fytche is a Development Officer in the Sports Council Facilities Unit.

Christopher Harper is a Senior Architect in the Technical Unit for Sport of the Sports Council.

Martin Hawtree BA (Hons) MCD PhD is principal of Hawtree Golf Course Architects and Consultants and Honorary Secretary of the British Institute of Golf Course Architects.

Colin Jepson is Manager of the Bowls Division of En-tout-cas plc.

Geraint John is Chief Architect and Head of the Technical Unit for Sport of the Sports Council.

Jim Meikle ARICS is a Partner in The Davis Langdon and Everest Consultancy Group

Michael Nussbaum is a former Director of the National Childrens' Play and Recreation Unit in London.

Barry Odell is the British Water Ski Federation's Development Officer.

David Payne is Head of the Facilities Unit of the Sports Council.

Carel Quaife is the National Development Officer at the British Canoe Union.

John Sills is an economist and former member of the Central Policy Unit of the Sports Council.

Gordon Stables CEng MICE MIHT FBIM is the Civil Engineer in the Technical Unit for Sport of the Sports Council.

Neil Thomson BSc(Hons) MA DipArch RIBA is an architect and Principal of Neil Thomson Associates, Architects and Designers, London and Malvern.

Graeme Tipp LRSC FPRI is a polymerics scientist and Director of Materials Science Consultants.

Chris Trickey BSocSci(Hons) MIOG is the Technical and Research Manager of the Lawn Tennis Association.

Vic Watson LRSC FPRI is a polymerics scientist and Director of the Centre for Sports Technology.

Nigel Weare is a national rowing coach at the Amateur Rowing Association.

Jean Wenger is the Technical Director of the National Playing Fields Association.

Robin Wilson Dip Arch RIBA is a Principal Architect in the Technical Unit for Sport of the Sports Council.

Part I Overview

1
Outdoor sport and recreation

John Sills

Outdoor sports can take many forms, and exist in many different environments, **1** and **2**. They can be team-based or structured around the individual; they may be situated in urban areas, on the fringes of towns, in the countryside and on the coastlines. Each activity and location will have its own special characteristics, its own requirements, but all are testimony to the wide ranging benefits that sport can bring. Participation in sport can improve the individual's health and sense of well-being; promotion of sporting excellence can help foster civic and national pride. Sport can bring social and economic benefits to communities – whether it is school children from inner cities discovering new interests and challenges in the countryside or the generation of income by the sports

industry and related services. Many commentators have extolled the virtues of sport and the part it has to play in national culture. President John F Kennedy expressed it as well as any in 1962, when he said, 'Our own history, perhaps better than the history of any other great country, demonstrates the truth of the belief that physical vigour and health are essential accompaniments to the qualities of intellect and spirit on which a nation is built.'

In an era when people the world over are becoming more conscious of the environmental consequences of modern life, the simple pleasures of outdoor sports, the interaction with the environment, can help to nurture that awareness. Of course, sporting activity can sometimes come into potential conflict with conservation

1 *A rugby union game: amateur sport in winter in the open air*

2 *Cambridge University rowing training*

and other interests, but through good management and good facilities, the problems can be minimised, the benefits brought to the fore. The challenge for the providers of sporting opportunities in the future will be to offer the quality of experience and the compatibility with other concerns that increasingly affluent and sophisticated populations will demand.

Participation in outdoor sports generally increases as people's disposable income rises, their mobility improves (especially through car ownership) and health consciousness gains ground. It is expected that leisure time (at least in western societies) will expand in the coming decades, and this may lead to further increases in sports participation. However, sport will face intense competition from other activities, and must be prepared to embrace this challenge. It is often a time-consuming activity compared with others (particularly those based in the home) and, therefore, must offer the participant easy access, high quality facilities and good ancillary services (for example: car parking, public transport, bars and restaurants, childcare, and access for the disabled).

Let us take the UK as an example of the trends in participation. Outdoor sports participation grew in the 1990s, but the overall changes mask a considerable contrast between different groups in society and different sports. Between 1983 and 1988, participation by men rose from 7.5 million to 8.1 million, which represented 41.7% of men. Growth in participation has been heavily concentrated in men over 25 years of age; in fact the rate of participation amongst 13–24 year olds actually declined. Women's participation declined slightly from 5.1 million to 5.0 million, with only women of over 60 years registering an increase. The participation rate of

women was 29.75% in 1988. This overall decline in women's outdoor participation (which disguises some increases, such as walking in the countryside) contrasts greatly with a massive increase in indoor participation: a reflection of the growing appeal of sports such as aerobics, dance and swimming.

A general trend can be observed towards participation in individual rather than team sports, although many of the traditional team sports such as football (soccer), rugby and hockey remain vibrant, and in many parts of the world are growing in popularity. The success of individual sports in the UK is partly a reflection of the time factor referred to above: an individual is able to be much more flexible about when he or she participates. This reinforces the point about facilities needing to be conveniently sited and of a high quality.

Sport and recreation in the countryside has witnessed a strong growth in participation over the last decade, although this is thought to have stabilised in recent years. Its advantages include: the chance for town dwellers to enjoy open space, fresh air, and the beauty of the surroundings; the opportunities available to people of all ages or either sex; and the flexibility of choice between organised and informal recreation. The English Countryside Commission estimates that around 75% of the English population visited the countryside at least once in 1990, and that more than 35% of the visits involved playing or watching sport (which includes walks over 2 miles, or 3.2 km). A General Household Survey for 1986 estimated that around 10 million people a year participated in countryside sports, the biggest of which were walking, fishing, cycling, water sports and horse riding.

4

Clearly the popularity of countryside sports – which should increase with people's mobility – brings economic benefits to local communities as well as personal benefits to the participants. But it can also generate problems: traffic congestion at popular times, erosion of the landscape, threats to wildlife, temporary noise disturbance in the case of activities such as motor sports and shooting. As a result, sport and recreation finds itself opposed by conservation and other similar interests at times. Few of the problems are insoluble when all interests work together to manage the demand and supply for sport in the countryside. The Sports Council promotes the theme of 'sustainable development' of sport and its facilities in the countryside. If well-managed, sporting activity can address environmental concerns and thus thrive.

One area of sport which has been the subject of concern regarding erosion and tree cover in recent years is winter sports – in particular skiing, which has boomed in popularity, often in countries (such as Britain) which have no great tradition of mass-participation. The boom has greatly enhanced the tourism potential of many alpine areas in Western Europe, but is storing up environmental problems for the future, according to critics. The winter sports are responding to these fears: for example, Lillehammer, in Norway, the venue for the 1994 Winter Olympics, has drawn up environmental targets for its facilities-building programme, which will aim to preserve equilibrium in a largely unspoilt region of great ecological interest. In all outdoor sports the key to future developments will be to ensure a balance between environmental and recreational interests.

One of the most important ways of ensuring that the countryside does not become overburdened is to improve sport and recreational opportunities in urban areas and their periphery. In most economically developed societies a majority of the population lives in cities and towns. It makes sense, therefore, to provide sporting facilities where they will be accessible to a large number of people. The interests of sport and the environment coincide to a large degree in this respect. The preservation of open space, which is often under threat from commercial development, is vital for the quality of life in urban communities, and also provides opportunities for outdoor recreation. The recreational purpose can act as a protection against overdevelopment, which would result in the open space being lost for the long term.

At the same time, however, designers and planners of outdoor sports facilities need to be mindful of the less obvious ways in which the environment can be affected.

The local impact of floodlighting and noise from a sporting event or its spectators is clearly recognisable, but the environmental effect of transport used by participants and spectators alike also needs to be taken into account when planning the development of facilities. The longer term environmental consequences of the manufacture, usage and disposal of artificial sports surfaces are not immediately obvious, but they could be significant globally. All buildings associated with outdoor sport will affect the environment through the materials used for their construction and the energy requirements they have once in operation. All these factors, and others of a similar nature, should be given serious consideration in the planning, design, operation and maintenance of outdoor sports facilities. The aim should be to make them as 'environment-friendly' as possible.

The development of sport and recreational facilities can act as a spur for urban regeneration. Derelict land can be reclaimed; disused railways can provide routes for walkers, joggers, cyclists and horse riders; old mineral workings can be transformed into centres for a range of activities, including water sports, which are otherwise fairly inaccessible for most of the population. New facilities such as golf courses can act as a focus for the development of amenities in previously neglected areas on the urban fringes. In all these examples, it is clear that the interests of sport should be seen as part of a whole: one interest among many, including private commercial investors, working towards mutual benefit. The UK government recognised this in 1991, with the publication of its planning guidance note on sport and recreation. It is appropriate to end with a quotation from this document, which emphasises the importance of planning for the provision of sporting facilities. It is a message which could be applied to any country:

> Sport and recreation are important components of civilised life ... It is part of the function of the planning system to ensure ... that adequate land and water resources are allocated both for organised sport and informal recreation. It is part of planning authorities' responsibilities to take full account ... of the community's need for recreational space ... and to resist pressures for the development of open space which conflict with wider public interest.

In a world where people are becoming more concerned with the quality of life for themselves and future generations, sport and recreation will have an important contribution to make, but also responsibilities to live up to.

2
Whole life costs

Jim Meikle

1 Introduction

The planning and design phases of any building project involve a multitude of decisions. Many of these may have physiological, social, political and environmental consequences; nearly all have economic consequences also. In money terms, the big decisions tend to be made early: where to build and when; whether to build new or refurbish existing; how much money is available; and so on, **1**.

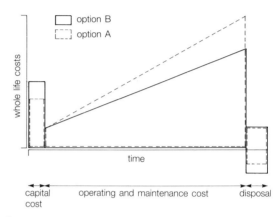

2

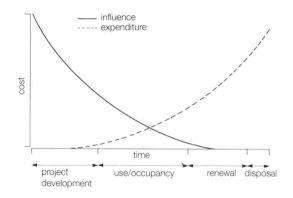

1

As decisions are made, each succeeding one tends to have a narrower impact on total costs. The facility owner and his professional advisers (most notably the designer) make many of the key decisions. They are made early in the process when both the widest range of choices and the least amount of information are available. If 'value for money' is to be achieved then the right decisions will be the ones which achieve the best balance between initial and operating costs and revenue, assessed over the lifetime of the facility. This is the purpose of life cycle, or whole life, costing.

2 The technique

Life cycle cost analysis is a technique. It is an aid to, rather than a process of, decision making. The technique may be used in two ways: to determine the consequences of making a decision, or to allow an informed choice to be made from among options. Life cycle costing generally considers only those factors which can be measured in money terms.

Life cycle costing allows both present and future costs to be compared on a common basis. **2** illustrates two

design options, one of which has low initial costs but high operating costs (option A) and another with higher initial costs but lower running costs (option B). There is a trade-off implied here between capital costs and running costs. By carrying out the analysis it is possible to identify such a trade-off – if it exists. It should not be assumed, however, that spending more now leads inevitably to lower overall costs and improved value for money. Costly assets often need to have a lot spent operating and maintaining them.

Identifying and quantifying all relevant costs and revenues (cash flows) over an asset's life is what life cycle costing is all about. To assess the whole life cost of an asset it is necessary to add together cash flows now to cash flows at some time in the future. Money declines in value over time, however, so that its value now is more than its value in the future. All payments and receipts (now and in the future) therefore need to be converted to today's money, ie its present value.

If £1 is invested today at a 10% rate of interest it will accumulate to £1.10 after the first year, £1.21 after the second year, and so on. Put another way, £1.21 in two years' time has a present value of £1. The rate at which future amounts are discounted is made up partly by inflation and partly by the real rate of return over and above inflation. For capital investments such as those involving a sports facility, the rate at which future sums are discounted is often the rate at which the finance is borrowed. The higher the discount (or interest) rate, and the further into the future the analysis seeks to forecast, the less significant are sums of money in present day terms. As an example, at an annual interest rate of 10%, £11 receivable in 25 years is worth only £1 today.

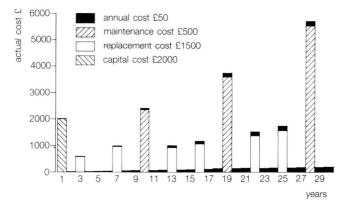

3a

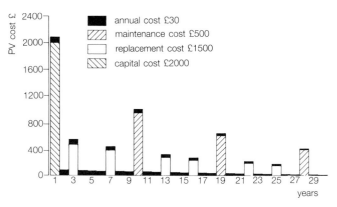

3b

Another example could be a piece of equipment costing £2,000 which is cleaned annually at a cost of £50, is overhauled every 3 years at a cost of £500, and undergoes major replacement of its component parts every 9 years at a cost of £1,500. The unit is installed in a facility built to last 30 years and the annual rate of inflation is 5%. The stream of payments over the 30 year period is indicated in **3a**.

If the payments are discounted to today's values at a real discount rate of 5% (ie after the effects of inflation have been removed), the profile looks very different, **3b**. It is clear that, after about 20 years the present value of even relatively substantial future amounts is becoming quite small.

The total costs over the operating life of the asset can now be added together, **4**. This of itself provides a fairly meaningless result but can be used to compare alternatives so that informed choices may be made. This is where the life cycle costing technique is most useful.

3 Applications

A life cycle costing approach to appraising investment in sports facilities is particularly appropriate. For example, some surfaces may require replacement sooner than others with considerable economic consequences. Additionally, certain types of materials may have to be maintained more frequently. The consequences of higher than normal maintenance levels and the presence of maintenance personnel may also be disruptive to use and have a discouraging effect on users.

Life cycle costing may also help answer the questions 'When should we refurbish an existing facility?' and 'When should we decide to build a completely new facility?' Such questions are not easily answered and really depend on a detailed appraisal in each case. Some facilities, for example, may have inherent characteristics which may make refurbishment the most desirable or indeed the only option. However, if, for example refurbishment costs are beginning to rise above 75% of newbuild costs, then the newbuild option should seriously be considered.

Assuming the need for an improvement in the level of provision has been identified – to be met by refurbishment or newbuild – the owner needs to set key criteria relating to capacity, performance standards and so on. This is important prior to detailed analysis as the more comparable the different options being considered, the more robust the technique is for the basis of selecting them.

The owner and his advisers must consider the period over which an analysis is to be carried out. This can be related to the expected duration of the owner's interest in the building (his time horizon); it can also be based on expectations of changing consumer requirements and fashion. Many capital investments – in the retail sector, for example – are based on life expectancies of less than 10 years. Analysis periods can also be based on expectations of obsolescence. This may affect the whole facility or only part of it. Generally, the results from life cycle cost analysis comparisons are not sensitive to changes in the appraisal period over about 40 years.

The owner and his advisers must identify the options to be examined, bearing in mind that life cycle costing is applicable to options at the level of detailed specification as well as at the level of complete buildings. The stream of costs and incomes associated with each option are then calculated and converted to today's money so that the options can be compared and a choice made.

Cash flows which must be considered include:

- Capital costs, finance charges and professional fees at the project development stage

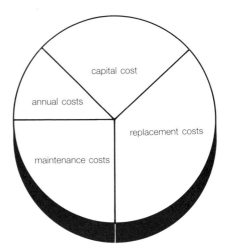

4

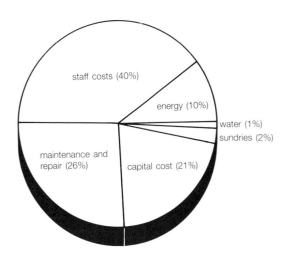

5

- Staff and administration costs, annual maintenance and cleaning, routine replacement costs and when these might be incurred, energy costs, water charges, and other consumables, such as chemicals
- Major repairs and replacement (eg boiler plant, sports surfaces) and when these are likely to occur
- Revenue income
- Any costs or income arising from the eventual demolition or disposal of the facility.

For example, for a 20 m (approx 22 yd) swimming pool over a 30 year period, a typical cost breakdown, 5, shows that capital costs amount to only about one fifth of total costs over the life of the facility. The largest proportion is accounted for by staff costs, but note that maintenance, repair and replacement costs may amount to more than the initial costs of the facility.

3
Facilities for people with disabilities

Neil Thomson

1 General considerations

1.1 Change

The last two decades have seen a significant change in the social position of people with disabilities and this has led to generally beneficial legislation. Regulations and guidelines relating to access within the built environment are being continually improved and extended. Thus, designers are being encouraged to design for the whole community rather than just the average man or woman. New legislation is also beginning to look at the need to improve existing as well as new buildings and facilities.

A consideration of the needs of people with disabilities should now be a natural part of any design and planning process and of subsequent management and maintenance policies. The following recommendations and comments are not intended to repeat regulations or to provide comprehensive guidance but simply to serve as a reminder of some of the more important points to be considered. Designers are advised to consult *Sports and Recreation Provision for Disabled People*, edited by Neil Thomson, as well as the current edition of the Approved Document M 'Access and Facilities for Disabled People' in the UK Building Regulations, for more detailed guidance. For the specialist provision for spectators in stadia, reference should be made to publications by the Football Stadia Advisory Design Council (FSADC): *On the Sidelines* and *Designing for Spectators with Disabilities*.

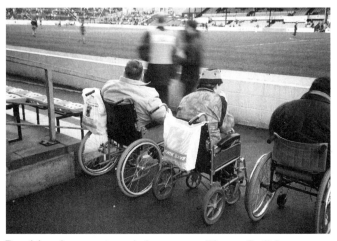

Provision for spectators is important. Photo: G. John

1.2 Sport for all

Sport is an activity which can be enjoyed by people of all ages and abilities, whether by participation or through spectating. All sports facilities and spaces should therefore be designed to cater for all potential users whatever their degree of mobility or impairment. Everyone can experience difficulties in coping with the built environment in certain situations. A well designed barrier free environment will benefit everyone and not just those who are conventionally labelled as 'disabled'.

Very few sports and recreational activities are exclusive to so-called able bodied people. It is now accepted that blind and partially sighted people, wheelchair users, people with deafness or hearing impairment, limbless people and those with other mobility restrictions, and people with learning difficulties, all participate in water sports, field and track events, outdoor pursuits and indoor games. This ranges from casual leisure activity to serious international and Olympic competition.

1.3 Consultation

A programme of consultation with people with disabilities at all critical stages in the planning and design process is perhaps the most important requirement. Even with close adherence to the latest regulations and guidelines, mistakes can still be made by a designer working in isolation.

Consultation should take place with organisations of disabled people interested in sport, and with the local authority's Access Officer who can be a key figure in obtaining planning approval. National bodies (such as the British Sports Association for the Disabled in the UK) can be approached who will either advise directly or put forward more local or specialised groups. Local groups will often have particular needs and preferences which should be taken into account in the design of local community facilities.

2 Differing needs

The needs of people with different disabilities and who use different mobility or sensory aids can vary enormously. There is not space here to describe properly these needs but the following notes might provide some useful pointers.

2.1 Wheelchair users

These can range from being independently mobile athletes to elderly people needing to be pushed at all times. Three common constraints determine basic design requirements:

- Lower level and limited reach – determines heights of controls.
- Width of wheelchair – wider than standing person – determines door and gate widths.
- Can only go where wheels can go – determines need for lifts and shallow ramps to negotiate level changes.

2.2 Ambulant disabled

People who are able to walk but who may depend on other mobility aids, or be unable to manage steps or door handles and other fitments. Most improvements made for wheelchair users will be beneficial but sometimes different provision is required, eg ramps as well as steps.

2.3 Deaf and hard of hearing

There are many variations in hearing quality and amount of hearing loss. Good acoustics are necessary for people who are hard of hearing to distinguish speech from background noise. Good lighting is necessary for deaf people to lip read, through ticket office screens for example.

Good communication is perhaps the most important issue; clear consistent signposting and visual information and warnings are essential. Use of induction loops and amplifiers should be considered for users of hearing aids.

2.4 Blind and partially sighted

The majority of people with visual impairment have some sight and good lighting, large clear signs and colour contrast are important. Avoidance of hazards is essential, especially projections between waist and head height, loose obstacles, barriers and columns in circulation routes. Changes in surface textures on the ground can indicate hazards. Provide raised letters and braille on signs.

Sound clues are useful for orientation. Good acoustics and clear audible information announcements and warnings are essential. Consider producing raised tactile maps for large buildings and outdoor areas. Allow for guide dogs to accompany some blind people. Sports facilities should be well serviced by public transport as blind people obviously cannot drive. Safe comprehensible external routes and footpaths are essential.

2.5 People with learning difficulties and other special needs

Buildings and spaces should be easily comprehensible, and good signposting and avoidance of hazards will benefit everyone. Facilities such as toilets and changing rooms should allow for accompanied use.

3 External areas

3.1 Site, vehicle access and parking

Whenever possible, sites for sports facilities should be selected to be level rather than hilly or undulating, and to be well served by nearby public transport.

There should be generous parking provision and at least 5% of bays should be clearly marked as reserved for disabled users. Reserved bays should be as close as possible to any building or facility entrance and never more than 40 m (44 yd) away. There is a case for grouping them separately from the main car park as this lessens the risk of unauthorised use. The surface should be tarmacadam or similar and be well drained but virtually level, and should preferably be level with adjoining footpaths, or be well provided with ramped kerbs.

There should be good vehicle access to the site and a clearly marked drop-off point for cars and coaches should be provided adjacent to the main entrance, preferably with a weather protective canopy.

3.2 Footpaths and ramps

If changes in level along external routes are unavoidable then ramps should be provided which should not normally be steeper than 1:20. Ramps should never be steeper than 1:12 and if more than 1:20 then steps should also be provided alongside; handrails should be provided to both sides of the ramp and steps.

Footpaths and ramps should be a minimum width of 1.2 m (approx 4 ft), and preferably a minimum of 2 m (approx 6 ft 6 in), to allow for wheelchairs to pass safely. Surfaces should be firm, smooth and slip-resistant. Jointed surfaces such as paving slabs are not recommended but where provided should be laid flush on a well consolidated base.

Ramps should have a 100 mm (approx 4 in) kerb on all exposed edges. Level areas at least 1.8 m (approx 6 ft) long should be provided at every 10 m (approx 33 ft) in length and at the top and bottom of any ramp.

If footpaths are level with vehicle and activity areas they should have clearly marked edges with colour and texture contrasts. If there are raised kerbs, ramped kerbs should be provided at crossings, with a maximum 1:10 gradient and a contrast in colour and surface texture. Seating should be provided at regular intervals and all routes should have good external lighting.

3.3 Signposting

All external areas should have clear and consistent signposting with a minimum of wording. Signs should indicate all accessible routes, entrances, activity areas and facilities.

3.4 Outdoor sports and recreational areas

All outdoor activity areas can normally be made accessible to disabled users. Athletics tracks, for example, need no adaptation for wheelchair racing so long as there is suitable level access on to the track and the track has a synthetic surface. Stands, terraces, and viewing or resting areas should all be provided with a sufficient amount of level area with good unobstructed views. Toilets and changing areas should all be accessible: see Volume 2, Chapter 57 for details of the design of changing areas.

Many other kinds of outdoor activities can be enjoyed by people of all abilities if proper care is taken at the design and planning stage. Accessible fishing platforms can be provided on river banks and canal sides; ramped mounting platforms can be provided in riding schools; adventure play areas can be designed to stimulate children with very limited mobility and with learning difficulties; countryside nature trails can be provided with tapping rails and listening posts for blind people; bird-watching hides can be designed with ramped entrances and wheelchair height viewing slots, to mention but a few examples.

4 Changing rooms, toilets and showers

Open plan and team changing rooms with bench and transfer seating are adequate for many disabled users, although some family sized unisex changing rooms which incorporate shower, WC and basin should also be provided. These are obviously appreciated by families as well as people with disabilities who may have helpers of the opposite sex. The Approved Document M (current edition 1992) of the UK Building Regulations shows examples of an accessible shower compartment and dressing cubicle. However, a combination of accessible open changing and shower areas, and family changing rooms which combine the activities of showering and changing, is more likely to be appropriate.

Access from changing areas to activity areas should be level and as short as possible. Shower areas should have level access and incorporate handrails, folding seats and controls at a height accessible from wheelchairs. Toilets in changing areas should incorporate at least one designed for wheelchair use.

All public buildings should incorporate at least one unisex wheelchair accessible toilet compartment designed to BS 5810, preferably adjacent to the main entrance area. Babycare facilities should also be provided for parents and carers of both sexes.

5 Signposting

Clear and consistent directional signposting is essential to all users of sports facilities and especially for people with sensory disabilities. Of particular importance are signs for accessible routes, toilets, lifts and any special services for people with disabilities. Notice boards giving details of current and special events and programmes should be prominently displayed, well lit, and at a height readable by people in wheelchairs.

6 Activity areas

Detailed guidance on the design of particular areas can be found in *Sports and Recreation Provision for Disabled People* edited by Neil Thomson.

7 Social areas and spectator facilities

Social areas such as restaurants, snack bars and licensed bars have gained significantly in importance and must be accessible to all visitors with disabilities. In viewing galleries, rails should be positioned so as not to interrupt views for people in wheelchairs. All spectator areas should include provision for wheelchair users, and be accessible without steps.

References

British Standards Institution, BS 5810: 1979 *Code of practice for access for the disabled to buildings.*

HMSO, *The Building Regulations 1992*, Approved Document M 'Access and Facilities for Disabled People' HMSO, London (1992)

Football Stadia Advisory Design Council, *On the Sidelines: Football and Disabled Supporters*, FSADC, £12.50, 32 pp

Football Stadia Advisory Design Council, *Designing for Spectators with Disabilities*, FSADC, £15

Thomson, N. (ed.) *Sports and Recreation Provision for Disabled People*, London: Architectural Press, Disabled Living Foundation and Sports Council, 1984.

4
Planning for sport and recreation

Mike Fitzjohn and David Payne

1 Introduction

The purpose of the chapter is to provide a summary checklist of relevant considerations in planning for sport and recreation; it is necessarily wide ranging, seeking to embrace planning from the national/strategic to local facility levels in a worldwide context. It is important to stress, however, that irrespective of context, the planning process for sport and recreation is no different from any other form of planning.

Why plan?

At its simplest a plan sets out a considered way forward to guide future development. There are many reasons why a planned approach to the development of sport and recreation is necessary and beneficial. These include:

● Political and social systems which support intervention to help ensure that resources are owned and distributed equitably amongst the population. In short, a planned approach will help to create and develop opportunities for people to participate – the philosophy which underpins 'Sport for All'.
● To set clear directions and accommodate change. A planned approach will present a clear view of key longer term goals, thereby enabling short term changes to be evaluated in a broader context.
● To make clear to others what is important in sport and recreation and to indicate courses of action which they should pursue to implement the plan.

3 Whose plan, and who does the work?

If the plan affects the interests of several organisations, it will often be sensible for them to come together at the outset in order to prepare it jointly; this will improve the 'ownership' of the plan and help ensure its successful implementation. Whether or not the plan has such multiple sponsors it will be necessary to give early consideration to who might do the work. If the sponsoring agency has sufficient resources of money, time and staff expertise it may wish to carry out the work itself. Alternatively it may wish to place a contract with a consultant, which will have the advantage of bringing an independent view to the task. A third approach is to combine the independent and technical skills of consultants with the practical and detailed knowledge of the sponsor's staff jointly to carry out the work.

4 Setting objectives

The decision to prepare a plan will have been triggered by a perceived problem, eg a shortage of stadia, insufficient water space or the need to improve sports centres. One or more objectives should be derived for the plan; they should be as clear and precise as possible. They might include such issues as:

● Whether the plan is designed to cater for high level performers and competition, for community participation, or both
● Whether there is a need for additional new provision or for improving existing provision
● Whether the plan should deal with built facilities, improved management (especially for countryside issues), other relevant matters, such as the needs for coaching staff, or a combination of these
● The specific sports, specific geographical areas and specific people for which the plan is designed.

5 Context

No plan can be produced in a vacuum; there will be a wide range of factors, most external to sport, which will need to be considered and which will affect the plan. They might include such matters as:

● Climate and geography: particularly for outdoor facilities
● Political priorities: eg the wish to bid for an Olympic Games, or other major international competitions
● The state of the economy and the availability of financial, human and material resources
● Demography: eg size, distribution, age structure, ethnic groupings, role of women
● Natural resources: their availability for sport and recreation, and the convergence/divergence with other policy goals for such resources
● Other policy goals, opportunities and constraints: eg health, planning, agricultural diversification
● Relevant legislation: eg education, recreation, health and safety
● The existing framework of national, regional and local plans: the plan will need to be consistent with broader scale plans, and also set a clear framework for more detailed plans.

It will be necessary to examine recent trends, the current position and likely future trends in each of these factors.

In the light of this analysis it may also be necessary to modify the objectives.

6 Sporting background

Having examined the external environment it will then be necessary to consider the more detailed sporting background. This might include such matters as:

- Sporting structures: history and traditions
- Sectoral mix: public, voluntary and commercial; partnerships and relationships amongst the three
- Client markets: the 'public' generally or specific groups
- Identification of requirements: eg surveys of need, consumer preferences
- Existing participation rates: how many, who, what, when, why?
- Existing facility provision: eg condition, costs, competition
- Related resources: management, coaching and administrative staff availability and skills
- Market trends: eg short term 'fads' or long term interests, conventional versus leisure pools
- Constraints and conflicts: competing claims on resources, eg other land uses in the countryside.

As with the external environment, past and future trends will need to be analysed and, as a result, it may be necessary to modify objectives.

7 Preparing the plan

A wide range of techniques, from the simple to the sophisticated, are available for analysing the assembled material and developing the plan. However, all such techniques are based on one of two broad approaches:

- A 'standards' approach, such as 1 facility per 50,000 population. This has the advantage of clarity and simplicity, but is likely to miss local nuances and detail.
- A 'local assessment', essentially based on a more sophisticated modelling of local factors which affect the demand for and supply of facilities. This approach is more sensitive to local circumstances, but is more costly of resources than the first alternative.

8 Key planning concepts

In preparing the plan there are a number of key planning concepts which are likely to feature. These include:

- Multiple use: the ability to integrate the planned use with both other sporting uses and other land uses, eg agriculture or nature conservation in the countryside.
- Accessibility: both physical, eg for people with disabilities and for relevant transport modes, and social, eg for potential users who may, for whatever reason, find it difficult to identify with the planned provision.
- Environmental considerations: the aesthetics of the built environment and sustainable uses of the natural environment.
- Whole life costs: both of buildings, and their costs in use, eg management, staffing, pricing structures.
- Location and site suitability: this should be determined

by the planning process outlined above, and not simply by considerations of land availability and cost.
- Liaison and consultation: the chances of any plan proving effective in achieving its objectives and acceptable to relevant interests will be greatly enhanced if those most directly affected by it, eg sports users or the local community, are genuinely involved in its preparation rather than presented with a fait accompli.

9 Developing alternatives and choosing the optimum

In many cases it will be possible to identify more than one plan which relates the identified needs to the objectives set and the resources available. In such instances it will be necessary to choose the optimum solution. This will in part be a technical process, involving greater detailing of the options in order that they can be more thoroughly evaluated, and in part a political process involving the community, its elected representatives and other relevant interests.

10 Implementation

Depending on the scale of the plan, implementation will vary from achieving national political and policy change at one extreme to the detailed briefing of the architect/designer at the other. The speed with which any plan can be implemented will be crucially dependent on the resources of finance, manpower and materials.

11 Monitoring and review

Once implemented it is important that performance is monitored against the objectives established at the outset. Again dependent on scale, such monitoring may involve the implementation of policy, the achievement of management objectives (such as for natural resources in the countryside), the performance of buildings and the satisfaction of users. In the light of such monitoring it may be necessary to amend the objectives, modify buildings or management regimes and possibly recommence the planning process with a view to making additional provision to meet unmet demand.

12 References and further advice

The Sports Council and related organisations have published many detailed reports on planning for sport and recreation at the national, regional and local levels. The reader seeking specific advice is advised to obtain such publications. See for example:

The Sports Council, *Sport in the Community: Into the 90s*. The Sports Council, London (1988).
Regional Councils for Sport and Recreation, *Regional Recreation Strategies*. Regional Councils for Sport and Recreation, (1985–1991).
The Sports Council, *District Sport and Recreation Strategies – A Guide*. The Sports Council, London (1991).
The Sports Council, *The Playing Pitch Strategy*. The Sports Council, National Playing Fields Association and Central Council of Physical Recreation, London (1991).

Part II Briefing guide

5
Planning obligations for sport and recreation

David Payne

1 Introduction

Sport and recreation facilities and open space can form an important part of housing, major office, or retail developments. To secure their provision as part of these developments it may be appropriate for local authorities to enter into what is known as planning obligations.

Planning obligations are part of the process of creating and maintaining good standards of sports and recreational provision. How large a part they may play depends on the buoyancy of local economic conditions, local planning policy and the development interests involved. In all cases, however, a community benefit or increment is being introduced into a scheme, the cost being passed on to the landowner or property investor.

2 What are planning obligations?

A planning obligation is a contract made between a local authority and an applicant for planning permission to secure the use or development of land in ways which cannot be enforced through planning conditions as part of a planning consent. Increasingly, local authorities are preparing development briefs which guide planning applications and describe the responsibilities they expect developers/applicants to accept. For example, where provision of sports and recreational facilities are being made, it is becoming commonplace for land to be provided free or at less than the full housing land value; alternatively community buildings, children's playspace and equipment may be constructed at no cost to the local authority and transferred to it. In England and Wales the mechanism for apportioning the costs of these 'extra facilities' and making arrangements for their future management is normally Section 52 of the 1971 Town and Country Planning Act, Section 33 of the Local Government (Miscellaneous Provisions) Act of 1982, Section 106 of the 1990 Act, or local acts. Broadly similar legislation applies in Scotland and Northern Ireland.

3 Why are planning obligations important?

Planning obligations are important because:

- They are a flexible and positive way of achieving several objectives: eg, obligations can be used for cash transactions, land swaps, the construction or re-location of sports facilities and phasing the creation of new facilities

- If the obligation relates only to planning matters, the goods or services received are not capital assets under the 1989 Local Government and Housing Act; obligations are thus outside the strict capital control regime introduced by the Government in 1989
- Improvements to off-site facilities can be achieved: eg, the improvement of a school sports hall or the extension of an existing sports or youth centre.

4 What are the ground rules and tests to apply?

4.1 Ground rules

Section 12 of the 1991 Planning and Compensation Act states that anyone with an interest in land may enter into a planning obligation enforceable by the planning authority:

- by agreement between the local authority and the developer; or
- by the developer making a unilateral undertaking.

A unilateral undertaking is most likely to be used where there are unresolved issues between the local authority and the developer and the case has gone to a planning appeal. An Inspector, if upholding the appeal, may also accept the developers' undertaking. The unilateral undertaking will then be enforced by the local authority in the same way as one reached by agreement. In practice unilateral undertakings are likely to be rare.

Planning obligations may:

- Restrict development or the use of land
- Require specified works to be undertaken on the application site, or other land in the applicant's ownership
- Require land to be used in a particular way
- Require payments to the local authority periodically, or at one time.

The 1991 Planning and Compensation Act allows developers to apply to the local authority to discharge or modify agreements after five years on the basis that they no longer serve a useful purpose.

4.2 Tests

Planning obligations should be sought only where they are necessary to the granting of planning permission, relate to planning issues and relevant to the proposed development. The question then becomes one of interpretation and what is reasonable. The tests of reasonableness are whether what is required:

- Is needed to enable the development to go ahead, for example, the provision of adequate access or car parking
- Will contribute to meeting the cost of providing such facilities in the near future
- Is otherwise so directly related to the proposed development and the use of land after its completion that the development ought not to be permitted without it. This can entail, for example, the provision of car parking in or near the development, or reasonable amounts of open space or social education, recreation, sporting or other community provision, the need for which arises from the development.
- Is designed in the case of mixed developments to secure an acceptable balance of uses; or to secure the implementation of local plan policies for a particular area or type of development
- Is intended to offset the loss or impact on any amenity (or resource) present on the site prior to development, eg protecting the interests of nature conservation.

4.3 Planning Policy Guidance Note on Sport and Recreation

The Department of Environment Planning Policy Guidance Note (PPGN) on Sport and Recreation (PPGN17 September 1991) relates the more general guidance to sport and recreation. Sport and recreation facilities may legitimately be provided in conjunction with major retail and office developments, as well as in schemes to reclaim commercial docks, or re-use mineral workings. PPGN17 also accepts that facilities may be provided off-site and that alternative provision for recreational land may be secured by a planning obligation when recreational land or open space is lost. In the case of small developments the guidance allows for contributions to nearby sport and recreation provision.

In the case of new housing projects, which up until now have been the single biggest source of planning obligations to benefit sport and recreation, the re-issued PPGN3, *Housing* (March 1992) suggests 'it will be essential that proposals for ... (new) housing settlements include adequate community facilities. Developers will be expected to contribute towards the cost of such facilities, and to meet most or all of the costs of providing new infrastructure.'

This guidance is much more important and detailed than any previously published national planning guidance from central government. Sport and recreation interests have benefited from this approach, which

- Specifically lists sport and recreation as a necessary community element for a wide range of types of development, stating that development should not go ahead without such provision
- Increases the emphasis on the community benefits approach to development, with developers' contributions being important
- Accepts contributions for off-site provision as legitimate
- Accepts compensatory ideas, discussing the possibility of providing alternative facilities or recreational land where they are lost
- Raises the importance of the statutory plan, stating that local plan policies should give a clear indication of the types of development, or area, where it is envisaged they will be used.

5 Examples of planning agreements for sport and recreation

Planning agreements for sport and recreation have included:

- Playing pitches, pavilions and a community centre provided in conjunction with a new housing area
- Land for a leisure village in a major town
- Bowling green and club house, with new campus offices
- Provision of a site for a swimming pool in association with a large retail and commercial use scheme
- Contributions to off-site swimming/leisure pool.

6 The process of drawing up planning obligations

6.1 Identify deficiencies and needs

Identifying needs and deficiencies should be part of a district wide sport and recreation strategy. The Sports Council has described how to produce such a strategy in *District Sport and Recreation Strategies – A Guide* (1991). Playing field needs may be identified by conducting a playing pitch assessment, as demonstrated in the Sports Council's report *The Playing Pitch Strategy* (1991).

There will be a need to pay particular attention to the possible impact of growth, for example new medium and large scale housing developments. This might include analysis of on-site needs for open space and built facilities. For large housing schemes an ability to analyse the impact on demand for existing facilities generated by the residents of new housing development will be required.

6.2 Develop a team approach to negotiation

Expertise in sports facility planning, design, management, and landscape must be brought to bear. Valuation skills may also be important in assessing the scale of provision which is affordable by the applicant as well as relevant in sports terms. The existence of a team approach may assist in the subsequent monitoring of obligations.

6.3 Include policies in development plans

Local plans (in shire counties) and Unitary Development Plans (UDPs) Part IIs (in Metropolitan areas) should establish the overall role of planning obligations in the development process. Structure Plans and UDP Part I policies may also help set the context for their use. The particular importance attached to development plans is reflected in Section 54A of the 1990 Planning Act, which states that where an Authority is required to have regard to the development plan, decisions are to be in accordance with the plan unless material considerations indicate otherwise. PPGN1 makes clear the need for local plans to contain policies if obligations are normally to be sought in particular circumstances. *Sport and Recreation* (PPGN17) advises on the types of developments and circumstances where sport and recreation may be secured in conjunction with other uses.

6.4 Prepare development briefs as supplementary guidance

In some circumstances the production of a development brief has proved an appropriate means of setting out local authority requirements at site level. The development brief is seen as a legitimate form of Supplementary Planning Guidance in PPGN12, *Development Plans and Regional Planning Guidance*.

The most relevant circumstances where Supplementary Guidance may be used are when further detail which would overburden the local plan is required, or where there is a need to seize a particular opportunity not foreseen during local plan preparation. More specific situations might include:

● Where detailed requirements of a large development site are to be worked out and related to the particular characteristics of the local environment (eg an area of high landscape quality or of particular historic value)
● Where land for a large new sports facility is needed and where its locational requirements in respect of adjoining uses, and other detailed siting matters, require to be specified
● Where contributions of finance, land or other resources are required from a number of landowners, developers or other agencies
● Agencies to secure the successful implementation of sports provision on a particular site
● Areas where the rationalisation of existing sports facilities is intended
● Areas where management measures to reconcile objectives between sport, informal recreation, nature conservation, landscape protection and other objectives are required, often in a countryside location.

6.5 Consider requirements lists

The listing of sport and recreation requirements in a separate non-statutory document should be considered. This could also be regarded as Supplementary Planning Guidance, having the status of a material consideration in development control decisions if subjected to public participation and Council resolution.

The aim of such a document is to give developers and others an early indication of the full range of infrastructure and services likely to be required as a result of their proposals. It may contain assessments of provision for open space, sport and community buildings, including detailed advice on matters such as:

● How 'open space' is to be calculated
● How the assessment of need for built facilities is to be undertaken
● What constitutes land usable for formal outdoor sport
● How commuted maintenance payments are to be calculated
● Requirements for built sport facilities, pitch drainage and landscaping
● Approaches to the phasing of the building of sports facilities
● The likely approximate costs of the above provision
● Standards required to be reached before land and buildings are adopted/handed over to the local authority.

6.6 Develop a code of practice for negotiations

This should list procedures to be adopted by the local authority for negotiations, publicity and drawing up of agreements. A code of practice may incorporate a listing of requirements relating to sport and recreation, but place more emphasis on the process of negotiation, the roles of the different parties, and issues of public scrutiny and access. A code might give information on:

● How local plan policies will be interpreted by an authority
● How authorities will communicate their requirements on individual schemes to the developer or applicant
● The relationship between the processing of the planning application, the detailed drafting of the obligation, and committee decisions
● Any arrangements for publicity
● Questions of appeals, and how draft obligations may relate to them
● Responsibilities for the legal drafting of obligations
● Arrangements for paying legal and other investigative costs.

6
Briefing guide

Kit Campbell

1 Introduction

Until relatively recently only a limited number of factors had to be taken into account when considering the needs of outdoor sports. Pitches had either a grass or mineral surface with fairly simple drainage, usually laid to a herringbone pattern, for example; bowling greens were always natural grass; water sports facilities were often rudimentary; and most sports pavilions had only limited facilities. In the past two decades, however, higher levels of demand, the development of new drainage and other construction techniques and greater acceptance of synthetic surfaces have made providing for outdoor sport significantly more complex and expensive than before.

Apart from the range of activities to be accommodated, the key factors which should be considered by intending providers at the outset are:

- What standards of participation and performance are proposed?
- What intensity of use is proposed?
- What ancillary facilities will be required?

2 Standards of participation

2.1 Competitive sport

Competitive outdoor sport can take place at international, national, regional, county, district and local level. For some activities – for example football – this has implications for the size of pitch or playing area. For others, such as golf, it can determine the detailed construction methods used. In most instances providers should consult the appropriate governing bodies of sport not only to establish their most up to date requirements but also to determine the likelihood of different standards of play at a particular location.

The UK and many other countries have a network of small local clubs, particularly for the pitch sports. Increasingly many of these clubs will find it difficult to generate the funds they will need to provide synthetic surfaces, upgrade natural turf pitches and modernise or replace pavilions and clubhouses. The answer will sometimes be for two or more clubs to amalgamate, possibly on a new site, using the money gained from selling off pitches or other land no longer required. This may create a more viable unit and opportunities for the addition of other sports or social facilities or the employment of coaching, development or other staff. In such

circumstances the apparent loss of playing fields can lead to a significant improvement in facilities for sport.

In summary, intending providers should:

- Consult with appropriate governing bodies of sport
- Determine the anticipated standard(s) of participation in advance of designing the proposed facility
- Consider amalgamating small facilities to create larger and more viable units
- Always take a long term view.

2.2 Non-competitive informal recreation

Non-competitive outdoor recreational activities do not have predetermined standards for facilities and so determining the most appropriate scale or standard of facility is not easy. In many instances the choice is not up to the provider: most inland water areas cannot easily be enlarged, for example. On the other hand, nearly all participants in countryside activities have access to personal transport. If any of the facilities on offer do not match their requirements they will be likely not to use them. It follows that it is particularly important to get specialist advice when planning non-competitive facilities. Finally, in view of increasing interest in and concern for the natural environment and in order to avoid damage to habitats or landscapes it will often be necessary to consult environmental agencies.

In summary, intending providers should:

- Obtain specialist advice before initiating the use of natural resources for recreational purposes
- Determine the anticipated standard(s) of participation in advance of designing the proposed facility
- Consult appropriate conservation or environmental agencies.

3 Intensity of use

3.1 Competitive sport

Many outdoor sports facilities are being far more intensively utilised than a few years ago. This has occurred in two main ways: through more use per day or week and as the result of extending the traditional season. Many football pitches which were at one time used for one or two games per week in winter and 'rested' during the summer are now used all year for two or three games per week. This means that the sward cannot recover properly from normal wear and tear. The result is a need for significant extra maintenance or a general decline in pitch quality. At the same time, as players' skills develop they demand higher and higher quality facilities.

There have been three main responses to these trends: the development of new construction techniques for grass pitches; the provision of floodlighting; and the development of a wide range of artificial surfaces. Floodlit synthetic grass pitches can be used for thirty or forty games per week. Providers should not assume, however, that one synthetic pitch can substitute for 15 or 20 grass pitches. At 14:30 on a Saturday afternoon a synthetic grass pitch has exactly the same capacity – one match – as a natural turf pitch.

Providers should also always take account of training needs as well as match play. The higher levels of use which will result often make it sensible to consider providing an artificial surface rather than a natural turf one. Floodlit pitches may also make it possible for mid-week leagues to be instituted; they can help to reduce the traditional peaking of demand for pitches at the weekend. Some sports such as tennis and hockey now prefer synthetic surfaces while others such as rugby will probably always require natural turf pitches for matches. Even so, artificial surfaces can be used for some training in sports such as rugby.

In summary, intending providers should:

- Take account of the needs of both training and match play and establish the performance standards required of facilities and surfaces
- Consider the relative costs and benefits of natural and artificial surfaces before making a decision
- Take account of the likely intensity of use when choosing a surface and specification

- Consider providing floodlighting in order to boost the intensity of use of those facilities able to withstand high levels of use.

3.2 Non-competitive informal recreation
Natural-resource based facilities have only a finite capacity to absorb use and recover from wear; if they do not do so eventually the resource will be destroyed. In some cases relatively minor and unobtrusive modifications will result in use capacity being increased. Providers should always consider carefully how damage to natural facilities can be minimised.

4 Ancillary facilities
Nearly all forms of outdoor sport and recreation require ancillary accommodation. Any of the following may be required:

- Changing accommodation and showers
- Social accommodation
- Staff or management accommodation
- Equipment storage facilities
- Grounds or other maintenance equipment storage
- Fuel storage
- Car parking

Where several pitches are located on one site it may be possible to stagger match start times. This can make it possible to reduce the amount of support accommodation and allow a greater proportion of the total project budget to be spent on high-intensity-use artificial surfaces.

Part III Surfaces for outdoor sport

7
Surface selection

Gordon Stables

1 Introduction

1.1 The importance of the sports surface

The success of an outdoor sports facility depends greatly on the suitability of the surface for the activities which are to take place on it. The performance of the surface in its interaction with balls and players is the prime factor in determining whether the playing conditions are perceived as good or bad. It is most important that the surface is considered very carefully when cost plans are prepared. The wrong choice of surface or substrate can significantly affect the effectiveness of a facility and the cost of remedying the wrong choice is likely to be prohibitive in the short term.

It is generally accepted that the move away from some traditional materials has taken place because the alternative synthetic surfaces can provide savings on land costs; improved standards of facility; a reduced need for scarce ground staff skills; reduced down time for maintenance; greater intensity of use and improved standards of play.

Nevertheless, synthetic surfaces often entail a higher capital cost than those they replace. Unlike a sports hall, where the cost of the floor surface is a relatively small part of the overall building cost, a synthetic surface for an outdoor facility represents a more substantial proportion. For example, a sand-filled synthetic turf with shock-pad could represent some 45% of the total cost of a hockey pitch with a macadam base, fencing and flood-lighting. It is therefore most important that surface selection is approached systematically to ensure the best choice of surface.

1.2 Consideration of the supporting structure (substrate)

The substrate will influence, sometimes to a large degree, the performance of the surface it supports. It is therefore essential to give joint consideration of both cost and performance to the combined surface and substrate. All performance tests to assess the suitability of a surface should be carried out with the surface laid on the substrate to be used in the final installation.

Specialist surfacing companies should be consulted at an early stage in design on the standard of finish for the substrate on which their products are to be laid and the required edge fixing details. Incorrectly specified substrates and edge details may cause surfaces to fail or not meet specified standards of surface regularity.

Unlike indoor surfaces, outdoor structures can be severely affected by climate. The substrate therefore needs to be designed to prevent frost heave and settlement from ground shrinkage or poorly compacted fill and provide adequate drainage for porous surfaces.

The substrate should be laid in accordance with the latest edition of the appropriate British or European Standard Code of Practice or other nationally applied specification, eg the Department of Transport Specification for Highway Works.

Most artificial surfaces are relatively thin and when laid closely follow the profile of the substrate. The substrate will therefore need to be finished to the same level and surface regularity tolerances required for the completed installation.

1.3 Surface evenness and regularity

Most sports require a flat surface lying in a single plane which may be level or inclined within recommended or specified limits. Two examples of exceptions to this are the crown bowling green with its rounded profile and the cycle velodrome with its heavily banked track (see Chapters 47 and 49). Athletics tracks have particularly demanding level and gradient requirements specified by the International Amateur Athletics Federation (IAAF) which must be met if the track is to be used for major competitions. Governing Bodies should therefore be consulted to confirm any level requirements at an early stage in design. Where there are no detailed requirements, a degree of flatness suitable for a multi-sports area can be obtained by applying the following standards contained in BS 7044 Part 4, AMD 7426 Jan '93:

- The overall surface slope in any direction should not be greater than 1:100
- Any localised bumps or hollows shall be such that when measured using a straight edge and slip gauge there shall be no gaps greater than 10 mm (0.4 in) under a 3 m (10 ft) straight edge or 3 mm (0.12 in) under a 300 mm (1 ft) straight edge
- The surface level shall not deviate at any point from the finished plane by more than plus or minus 25 mm (1 in) when measured by standard surveying methods.

Notwithstanding these requirements there should be no ridges, bumps, hollows, joints, seams or textural variations which might cause a ball to be deflected from its true path. If the deviation from the finished plane is checked on a 10 m (33 ft) grid a 'flatter' surface would be obtained by limiting the difference in level between adjacent grid points, after taking design gradients into account, to a maximum of 25 mm (1 in) rather than the total of 50 mm (2 in) permissible under BS 7044 Part 4.

2 The choice of a surface

The selection process
The process of selecting the most appropriate surface for a particular facility comprises two distinct parts

- the clear specification of the client's requirements; and
- an examination of product test results against the client's requirements.

For an outdoor facility, the sports surface and substrate are vitally important to the quality of play and a major element of expenditure. It is therefore essential to have a systematic approach to the selection process to ensure that all aspects of use are included. A short-list of potentially suitable products can be made using the following methodology:

- Confirm that the surface is for outdoor use. This may seem obvious, but some surfaces can be used both indoor and outdoor while others can only be used for one or the other.
- Identify the activities for which the surface is to be used; one specific sport (eg athletics), multi-sport (eg hockey and soccer) or both sports and non sports use (eg concerts and Town Shows).
- Prioritise the activities: for example should hockey take priority over soccer or vice versa?
- Decide upon the standard of play to be designed for: eg the Sports Council's Hockey Handbook differentiates between International and Club standard.
- Classify the surface as Medium Duty, Heavy Duty or Spike Resistant in accordance with BS 7044:Part 1:1990 or other appropriate standard.
- Consider the regular or prolonged use of the facility by participants: for example, in top level training if that is a priority activity.
- Extract from the current National and Governing Body Standards the performance limits relevant to the planned use of the facility: eg ball bounce, roll and spin, surface friction, shock absorbency, spike resistance, smoothness, permeability and durability.

At this stage, companies whose products are under consideration should be asked to provide the results of tests carried out by independent Test Houses in accordance with either the Sports Council's *Specification for Artificial Sports Surfaces*, BS 7044 Part 4 (1991) for multi sports surfaces or Governing Bodies' specifications for individual sports in order to verify the performance of products in relation to the qualities required, together with any special maintenance requirements. Whenever possible, visits to similar installations should be made by the client, his consultant and the key users to assess how satisfactory the preferred choice of surface and substrate has been in use, the performance of the Contractor, the effectiveness of design detailing and the practicality of maintenance. The latter is particularly important. Local repairs of a minor nature should be within the capabilities of staff at the facility. It should also be possible to carry out repairs without the need to remove large areas of sound material with associated high costs.

The standard and level of use and life expectancy of the facility should be clearly specified by the client and guaranteed under contract.

2.2 Range of activities

Sports activities
The choice of a surface for a single dedicated sport is relatively straightforward. However, although no surface can be equally satisfactory for a range of different activities, many surfaces are provided for multi sports use. In this case there has to be compromise between the various sports performance parameters which should be selected in favour of the most important activity whether this is training or competition at recreational or international level. It is fundamental to surface selection to identify the level of use and standard of play of all the various anticipated activities and then decide an order of priority from which the most appropriate sports performance parameters can be determined.

The choice of a particular surface can itself influence the pattern of demand on a facility by:

- Creating opportunities for new activities
- Encouraging use by the Sports Council's target groups, especially women and ethnic groups
- Changing the balance of popularity between the various activities.

Consideration should also be given to the growth in interest in sports from other countries, eg petanque and kabadi, and how they can be accommodated through surface selection.

Many sports traditionally played on natural turf can be played on synthetic turf provided that the specification reflects the particular requirements of the sport. The performance requirements of natural turf cricket wickets and winter sports pitches are totally different, however, and this applies to any synthetic alternative.

Non-sports activities
Some outdoor facilities may be considered by their managing authorities for uses other than sport. However, it is the aim of the Sports Council to ensure that the sports activities do not become secondary to alternative uses which may not be compatible with or even destroy the performance requirements for sports activities. It is vitally important that the possibility of such uses is taken into consideration in the surface selection process.

3 Qualities of a sports surface

3.1 General
The characteristics required of a sports surface are those which enable one or more sports to take place in accordance with Governing Body or other requirements, with a certain intensity, frequency and for a defined period of time, using appropriate equipment and taking into account the health and safety of users and impact on the environment.

3.2 Sports performance characteristics
These relate to the interaction of balls or wheels and players with the surface.

Ball/surface interaction
- *Height of ball rebound*. This varies according to the needs of sport, hence the need to prioritise activities.
- *Spin*. This is of particular importance in tennis and cricket where the response of a spinning ball to impact with the surface provides an essential subtlety to the game.

- *Ball roll.* The rate at which a rolling ball loses speed is dependent upon the rolling resistance of the surface and affects the distance of travel. Not only does this requirement vary between different sports, but hockey, football and bowls use different test methods.
- *Surface texture.* Neither the surface texture nor any minor irregularities should affect the direction of roll or rebound of a ball.

Wheel/surface interaction
- *Rolling resistance.* This is important for roller skating and other wheeled sports. However in these activities the weight of the person will bring into play other factors to a greater degree such as the need for a surface of high stiffness.

Person/surface interaction
- *Slip resistance and traction coefficient.* For most sports the level of friction between the players' shoe soles and the surface needs to be high enough to prevent accidental slipping but not so high as to restrict foot movement either in the direction of movement (slip resistance) or when turning (traction). A capacity for controlled sliding is required in some sports but not in others: eg, some surfaces which give a satisfactory controlled slide for tennis may be too slippery for netball in which foot movement is limited by the rules of the game. Frictional qualities of some surfaces can be reduced considerably when wet. This can cause problems for players, particularly if the surface is wet or dry in patches, but they are minimised if the wet slip resistance value is within 30% of the dry value. In sports where sliding contract between the player and the surface is likely, the friction should be low enough to prevent friction burns and the surface smooth enough to avoid severe skin abrasions.
- *Force reduction/impact absorption.* The dynamic interaction between the surface and a player running, landing or falling is very complex. Various Governing Bodies including the Fédération Internationale de Hockey (FIH), IAAF and the (English) Football League have specified requirements for their individual sports and BS 7044 likewise for a multi-sports surface. For most sports, a moderate level of stiffness is desirable but for those involving bodily contact with the surface, as in hockey or football, an energy absorbing surface is required to reduce the force of impact and potential for injury. Nevertheless it is the responsibility of the owners and operators of facilities to satisfy themselves on the safety of a surface for the sports to be played.

3.3 Material characteristics
- *Durability.* The surface must be able to withstand abrasive wear resulting from the intended activities including the penetration and tearing action of spikes in a surface classified as spike resistant. It should also resist and adequately recover from indentation from portable equipment, maintenance vehicles and impact loads from dropped equipment or during the course of play at both high and low temperatures.
- *Ageing.* The surface should retain its sports performance qualities throughout its anticipated life unchanged by the effects of sunlight, ozone, and the full climatic range to which the installation will be subjected. It should remain structurally and dimensionally stable without delamination, curling, buckling, shrinking, stretching or loss of joint integrity to an extent which detrimentally affects its use.

3.4 Other properties
- Surfaces (other than natural turf and unbound hard porous) should not transfer their colour to other materials such as balls and clothing.
- Surfaces should not contain any substance known to be toxic or carcinogenic when in contact with the skin or released as vapour or dust during normal use.
- A small source of heat such as a cigarette or match should not cause the surface to burn or ignite or damage it sufficiently to cause a ball to deviate from its true path. The propensity of the surface to contribute to a larger fire should be considered in the context of the flammability of surrounding materials and means of escape.
- The colour, tone and light reflectance of the surface should be considered under both natural and artificial lighting and in conjunction with the background and specific sports requirements.

3.5 Standards and specification
Tests for most of these properties (together with specification limits intended to provide a reasonable compromise between the optimum conditions for sports performance and the best conditions to reduce each type of injury, plus reasonable resistance to wear and ageing) were previously included in the Sports Council's Specification for Artificial Sports Surfaces and Artificial Grass Surfaces for Association Football. These have been revised and updated and the References at the end of this chapter should be consulted.

European Standards (Comité Européen de Normalisation (CEN)) at present in preparation are expected to cover tests and limits for all the above properties. They may include additional tests and limits, for example ball rebound speed, behaviour under a rolling load, impact strength, structural and dimensional stability and delamination. These are not included in the Sports Council's Specifications or BS 7044 but are among the tests carried out in some other European countries.

Meanwhile, further work on surfaces for specific sports is continuing and specifiers are advised to check with the Sports Councils and Governing Bodies to obtain the latest possible information.

4 Line markings

4.1 General
Line markings are necessary for most outdoor sports. For specific Governing Body requirements or recommendations on dimensions and line widths and colours see individual Data Sheets in Part VII.

In some cases sports surface companies will carry out markings or recommend specialist contractors. Details of line marking products and companies are also available from the Sports Council's Information Centre.

It is essential that the method selected should be capable of marking the surface without damage. Three types of marking are available:

- Inlaid lines
- Paint or powder applications
- Tape or moulded plastic lines.

4.2 Inlaid lines
This method is usually the most complex but also the most permanent. This can be inconvenient if changes occur in Governing Body rules on dimensions and

markings, alternative layouts are required or movement occurs in the surface distorting line marking. The inlaid line may be the same material as the surface with different pigmentation but problems with jointing and pile lie on some synthetic turf pitches have led to painted markings being favoured.

Advantages
- May be maintained in the same way as the surface without damage
- Line widths constant
- If the same material as the surfacing, the qualities would be the same, in particular slip resistance.

Disadvantages
- Cannot be removed when not required
- Increases the number of joints and hence joint related problems
- Colours may be restricted by manufacturers' list.

4.3 Paint or powder applications
These can be applied by brush, spray using a template or machine with a wheel or pressure jet marker. The first two methods are little used on natural turf except, for example, on the relatively small detailed markings for cricket.

Wear and discoloration will entail occasional relining according to the intensity of use.

Characteristics, price, and availability of marking materials vary greatly as do drying times and durability – it is advisable to seek a guarantee covering the life expectancy of the markings. These factors should be clarified with surfacing and line marking companies and taken into account at the time of surface selection.

Careful selection of the material can provide temporary or permanent markings for lines and more complex patterns. For example high build chlorinated rubber paint can provide a semi permanent line on non-sand-filled synthetic turf until the surface has bedded down when permanent lines in a polyurethane paint can be provided.

Advantages
- Easily applied by one person
- Wide colour range available
- Curves as easy to produce as straight lines
- More durable than tapes on hard surfaces
- May be used on virtually all surfaces including natural turf
- Choice of temporary, semi permanent or permanent markings
- Any shape can be produced for logos.

Disadvantages
- Play may not be possible immediately after application
- Application of some materials is weather dependent
- Line width may vary if equipment not properly maintained
- Continued re-painting may build up a line into a ridge of unacceptable thickness.

4.4 Tape or moulded plastic lines
Self-adhesive tape is not suitable for natural and synthetic turf, rough or granular surfaces. On other surfaces, subject to the manufacturer's advice, it may easily be laid for short term use and then removed. Non-adhesive tape is commonly used on unbound mineral surfaces where it is fixed by long clout headed galvanised nails. These should always be inspected before play commences and any necessary refixing carried out to prevent injury to players. An alternative on the market is a perforated plastic line, formed as an inverted channel, which is laid into two parallel slots cut into the court surface and rolled in during the final surface preparation.

Advantages
- Subject to manufacturer's advice, self-adhesive tape is easy to lay and remove for one-off events
- Standard widths and wide colour range of tape available
- Play immediately available after laying
- Better definition on unbound surfaces than paint or powder

Disadvantages
- Not as flexible in application as paint or powder
- Limited number of surface types on which they can be used
- Tapes may be damaged or disturbed during use.

4.5 Colour
In most cases, fewer outdoor sports are played on one particular area than will be found indoors. However, it is just as important that markings should be clearly identifiable to players and officials. A basic rule to follow is to provide white markings for the priority sport and yellow for the second most important. Other activities should then be provided with markings which give a good contrast between these lines and the surface under all light conditions. Some floodlighting, particularly sodium based, may reduce the colour contrast between the colours of the surface and line markings. Reference should be made to the Chartered Institution of Building Services Engineers (CIBSE) Lighting Guide: LG4 – Sports, paragraph 7.3 and table 7.1.

Governing Bodies should be consulted on their preference before making a final colour selection for a multi sports area.

5 Portable sports surfaces
Compared to indoor sports, there is relatively little demand for portable or roll-out surfaces. The description 'portable' or 'roll-down' surface is a loose one. In fact, with the exception of cricket, the surface areas required are such that the weight often makes laying, lifting and storage a laborious, time consuming and therefore expensive process. Although most manufacturers aim to produce a comparatively lightweight material, the preference for a surface which will lie flat without special fixings and not ruck in use will always entail some degree of self-weight.

The quality and nature of the surface on which the portable surface is laid may have a significant effect on its performance which should not differ from that of a permanent specialist installation.

Australia saw the development of portable natural turf cricket pitches grown and nurtured in specially designed containers which are then manoeuvred and placed by crane. This enabled the recognised Test Grounds to be used for Australian Rules Football one week and First Class Cricket the next without any break in use to prepare the cricket pitch area in the normal way. Similar proposals may be considered in the future for synthetic turf outfields for cricket.

6 References and further advice
British Standards Institution, BS 7044 *Artificial Sports Surfaces*. Part 1 Classification and General Introduction: Part 2 Methods Test: Part 4, AMD

7426, Specifications for Surfaces for Multi Sport Use. BSI, London (1989, 1990, 1991, 1993).

Football League, *Commission of Enquiry into Playing Surfaces* (1989).

Fédération Internationale de Hockey, *Handbook of Requirements for Synthetic Hockey Surfaces Outdoor*. FIH, Brussels (1992).

International Amateur Athletics Federation, *Performance Specification for Synthetic Surfaced Athletics Tracks (Outdoor)*. IAFF, London (1990).

The Sports Council, *Artificial Turf Pitches for Hockey*, The Sports Council, London (1990).

Millest JA, *Surface Judgement*. The Sports Council, London (1988).

8
Grass pitches

Jean Wenger and Stephen Baker

1 The development of grass pitches

The construction of grass playing fields can appear to those without previous experience to need little more than close mowing of a grassed area such as parkland open space. Many playing fields were initiated in this manner. Only when games have regularly to be cancelled is it realised that simple mowing, rolling and the occasional scattering of seed and fertiliser are insufficient.

A few locations with especially free draining soils, if reasonably level, will convert successfully. The vast majority of sites, however, have soil containing high proportions of clay and/or silt and require regrading to achieve satisfactory levels. Many need substantial cut and fill operations to produce a level terrace of suitable size for pitches.

The selected site is rarely in the ideal location and many playing fields have been slotted into the space left over after layouts for housing and industrial developments have been established. Pitches planned in this way often have problems as the site may have been excluded from more profitable development owing to poor drainage, difficult levels and other expensive construction considerations.

The 1980s saw significant developments in grass pitch construction. Improved fertilisers, herbicides and grass strains have significantly increased the carrying capacity and playing qualities of pitches as well as their appearance. Perhaps more significant have been the improvements in the areas not visible, an example being sports field drainage. Techniques have been developed for the design of drainage systems which take account of the specific soil conditions at a site, the anticipated rainfall and the required rate of its disposal.

2 Planning and layout consideration

2.1 Assessing the need for pitches

In 1991 the Sports Council, National Playing Fields Association (NPFA) and the Central Council of Physical Recreation (CCPR) jointly published *The Playing Pitch Strategy*. This details the assessment of playing pitch requirements and development of local policies. It includes 'supply' or pitch related issues (land resources, planning provision and use) together with 'demand' or sports related issues. Most importantly it makes suggestions for key actions required for adequate provision throughout all user sectors.

The strategy recommends a three point approach:

1 The adoption of the NPFA minimum standard of 2.43 ha (6 acres) of outdoor playing space per 1000 people as a global measure of the land required for a given population. Depending on the population profile of the locality concerned, the strategy suggests that the total open space requirement should be met by an aggregation of space within the following ranges:

- Youth and adult use: 1.6–1.8 ha (4.0–4.5 acres).
- Children's use: outdoor equipped playgrounds 0.2–0.3 ha (0.5–0.7 acres) plus casual or informal play space within housing space 0.4–0.5 ha (1.0–1.25 acres).

2 Because of different circumstances in different towns, the undertaking of a detailed local assessment of a facility requires the use of the more detailed supply and demand methodologies produced by the Sports Council and its Regions, as detailed within the Strategy document.

3 On the basis of local research the formulation of local standards of facility supply per 1000 population for demographically cohesive areas.

2.2 Site selection criteria

The selection of a site for pitches should take account of the following factors:

- *Proximity to user groups, ease of access by public transport and car, plus sufficient land for parking.* A site with boundaries adjacent to property and roads may require special treatment to remove nuisance factors and dangers from exiting balls.
- *Site shape and orientation.* A rectangular shape on a north/south orientation ensures minimum wastage of space and will prevent players being blinded by the setting sun.
- *Site area.* An area which is ideally not be less than 2.43 ha (6 acres), even in rural areas where the population may be less than 1000, allows efficient planning. A rectangular shape can provide the following community facilities; senior and junior football pitches (or hockey), cricket table, two tennis courts, three rink bowling green, children's playground, pavilion and car park.
- *Existing site levels in relation to the desired finished levels.* In order to minimise construction cost, where possible a site should be selected that does not require major regrading.

- *Existing subsoil and topsoil depths and physical, chemical and biological properties*, including how well tipping and/or reclamation was controlled on reclaimed land. Topsoil of at least 150 mm (6 in) consolidated depth is essential and ideally should be a light loam, free from stones; importation of additional topsoil and sand may otherwise be necessary.
- *Services*. A land drainage discharge point, mains water and electricity supplies are required although sites with main services (water and electricity) passing underneath potential playing areas should be avoided. Sites with overhead power lines should be discounted.
- *The site's natural drainage capacity*, **1**. The subsoil and topsoils should be assessed for drainage capabilities before any commitment is made to develop the site. In order to maximise winter pitch usage land drainage systems will probably be required unless the site is naturally sandy (at least 75% sand for light usage and at least 90% sand for heavy usage) and has no water table problems. Sites subject to flooding or with rock close to the surface should be considered only in conjunction with land reclamation schemes.

2.3 Internal planning considerations

Pitch layouts require careful analysis to ensure that their orientation and surround clearances for safety and maintenance are satisfactory. There will normally be unused areas which may benefit from screen planting to reduce the prevailing wind and improve the environment. The inclusion of training areas and fitness circuits will often be an advantage. Dogs should be kept away from playing surfaces and ideally from the whole site and existing footpaths should, where possible, be diverted around pitches.

3 Construction

3.1 Factors to be considered for all sites

The establishment of a satisfactory facility whether on a virgin site, reclaimed land/waste tip or upgrading of an existing playing field will require consideration of a wide range of factors, including:

- The quality of the construction operations
- The quality and composition of the grass seed mixtures and suitability of the fertiliser programme
- The implementation of maintenance operations necessary fully to develop the grass sward
- The allowance of sufficient time for root establishment prior to first usage.

The design of a grass playing surface requires specialist knowledge and it is strongly recommended that the services of an experienced sports-turf consultant be obtained. He or she should prepare tender documents to allow comparable quotations to be sought from specialist contractors. The consultant's services should be retained to assist in the selection of the successful tenderer, to inspect the work and approve interim and final payments.

With the increasing devolvement of local authority resources away from in-house departments, more use is being made of advisers and contractors. The importance of experienced consultants providing good specifications is becoming more and more apparent. Apart from ensuring a common basis for quotation comparison it is the only way of providing local authorities which have no dedicated in-house facilities with current constructional developments.

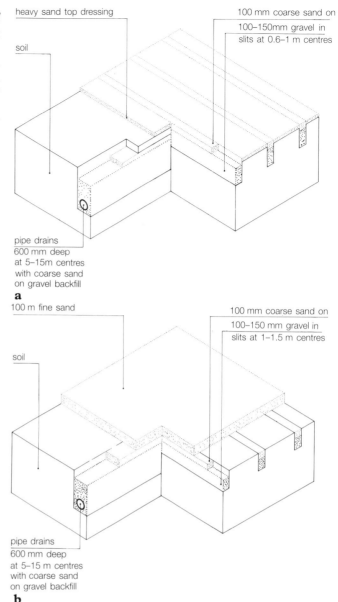

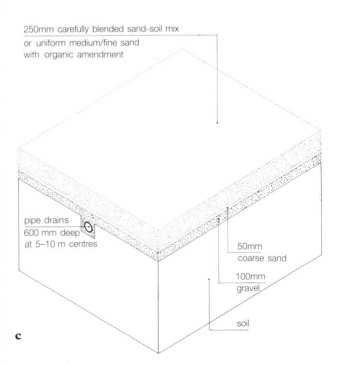

1 *Potential methods of upgrading the drainage of sports pitches through slit drainage or the use of sand-dominated rootzone layers*

Adequate inspection should be provided for all stages of the work and each operation checked and approved before the contractor is allowed to proceed. A good specification and drawing does not necessarily guarantee a good result.

3.2 Reclamation sites

Land suitable for playing fields is a scarce resource and every opportunity should be taken to use the site most accessible to the community. Playing fields may be constructed on reclaimed land quite satisfactorily, albeit at increased cost. Sites available for reclamation are often subject to flooding or household and industrial tipping. Where land drainage techniques can resolve the problem, areas subject to flooding are often the most suitable. The reclamation of tip or filled sites is more problematical and will require analysis of their tipping history, toxicity and liability to subsidence. Some can support sub-surface combustion for many years and many major sites may also produce substantial quantities of gas requiring disposal. Professional advice should be sought in all cases.

Landfill sites will normally be capped with a 450–600 mm (18–24 in) layer of subsoil often of a high clay content. This seals in the waste material but presents construction problems as no topsoil exists and drainage will be poor. A drainage system will normally be required and often a semi-rigid system is preferable to avoid problems resulting from subsidence.

Many sites include deleterious material close to the surface such as glass or other scrap. Care must be taken to ensure that this is not disturbed and brought within the topsoil. Such sites will require substantial work and every care should be taken to avoid using heavy machinery as further compacting of the soil layers will increase drainage problems.

3.3 Gradients and grading

To facilitate drainage it is usually desirable for a playing field to have a slope between 1:60 and 1:80. The main fall should if possible be across the pitch rather than in the direction of play. Fine turf areas, except bowling greens and croquet lawns, should also be given a cross-fall.

The maximum slope acceptable to players depends on the standard of play and the level of competition. On public pitches it is inadvisable to accept a slope of more than 1:30 owing to the fatigue caused to players and the variable run of the ball. Facilities for other sports such as tennis, athletics and cricket have differing requirements. The extent of any grading required and the amount of terracing will be determined by the proposed layout of the pitches and other facilities.

Grading operations fall into three categories, **2**:

- The adjustment of very minor surface irregularities within the depth of the existing topsoil but still leaving a sufficient depth to support a good grass sward, ie at least 100 mm (4 in) on any part
- Minor grading involving the stripping and replacement of topsoil over individual high and low areas
- Major grading on steeply sloping sites necessitating the stripping of all the topsoil and movement of the subsoil to produce correct levels. This is usually carried out on the cut and fill principle. The importance of expert advice and the preparation of a carefully worded specification cannot be over-emphasised so far as this aspect of construction is concerned.

2 *Grading work using a D8 and box grader. Photo: Sports Turf Research Institute.*

3.4 Pipe drainage

Unless land is naturally free-draining and likely to remain so when subject to compaction through use as a sports field, the installation of a pipe drainage system will be necessary to reduce the incidence of waterlogging during the winter months.

There are several aspects of pipe drainage which need to be considered:

- The necessity for a suitable outfall.
- The gradient of the pipes – normally at least 1:200 with a maximum of 1:80. Falls should preferably be uniform and must not become less steep along the line of the drain as this will slow down the rate of flow and can lead to silting up.
- Drain spacing – this would usually range from 3 m (10 ft) for a heavy soil to 10 m (33 ft) for a light soil.
- The backfill of the drain trenches – normally an 8–10 mm (approx 0.3–0.4 in) hard gravel blinded by a coarse sand, should be placed to within 150 mm (6 in) of the surface. This allows for the possibility of future slit drainage, **3**.

3.5 Subsoil and topsoil cultivations

Subsoil cultivations are usually essential on compacted and heavy soils. The main purpose of the operation is to improve drainage by the shattering and fissuring of the subsoil, the maximum effect being achieved under dry conditions. The exception to this requirement is where slit drainage is installed.

In major grading schemes, where over-compaction has occurred, subsoiling after topsoil replacement may also be necessary to shatter the subsoil whether or not it was cultivated prior to topsoiling. On very stony sites, however, subsoiling after topsoiling is not always practicable as it may cause unacceptable upheaval of the surface.

The topsoil should be ploughed, disked, graded and chain harrowed as necessary to produce a smooth surface with even falls and a fine tilth ready for seeding. Ameliorants and fertiliser should be mixed into the topsoil as required during seedbed preparation.

3.6 Topsoil

The nature of the topsoil and its condition are of paramount importance as they will determine the kind of sward which will eventually be established. Ideally, true

3 *Installation of slit drainage. Photo: Sports Turf Research Institute.*

4 *The importance of good drainage – compare the waterlogged, pipe drained area with the sand rootzones to the left and rear. Photo: Sports Turf Research Institute.*

uncontaminated topsoil with good drainage characteristics which is not too stony should be used. There should be an average depth of at least 150 mm (6 in) and at no point less than 100 mm (4 in). The subsoil should be sufficiently permeable to enable surface water percolating through the topsoil to drain away reasonably quickly. Any deficiencies in the topsoil should be made good during the work of construction prior to seeding. Such physical ameliorants as may be necessary should be determined by mechanical analysis and, if the depth of topsoil is found to be inadequate, additional soil imported from an approved source. If the deficiency is known in advance the purchase of suitable sand may be more appropriate. A chemical analysis of the existing topsoil and any imported soil should be carried out to check on the need, if any, for lime and as a guide to fertiliser requirements. If there is any possibility of toxic chemicals being present in the soil this should also be evaluated.

If grading is carried out requiring the removal and replacement of topsoil, great care must be taken to ensure that no subsoil is picked up with the topsoil. The mixing of subsoil with topsoil, particularly if it contains silt or clay, is frequently the cause of serious drainage difficulties and poor growth which can only be rectified at considerable expense and loss of use.

When replacing topsoil after grading or when spreading additional materials, laying drains or carrying out any other work, compaction should be minimised by using the lightest possible machinery and equipment. It is also essential to avoid working on the soil when it is too wet as this results in damage to the soil structure which neither cultivations nor chemical treatments can rectify fully. The adverse effects are reflected in growth and drainage for a long time. Surface cultivations are needed to eliminate compaction from the topsoil and to break down thoroughly all lumps so as to produce a fine tilth for seeding. The final seed bed should be free from mounds and depressions.

3.7 Getting water through to the drains

Even when a pitch has been constructed with a pipe drainage system, compaction resulting from play generally means that water can pass through the surface layer only relatively slowly. Unless the site possesses a very sandy, free-draining soil it is usually necessary to consider improving surface drainage. This can be achieved either by installing a by-pass system in the form of slit drainage

or modifying the surface layer with larger quantities of carefully selected sand so that it remains permeable even when subjected to high levels of compaction, 4.

The most common form of slit drainage is based on excavated slits, where the soil is excavated with a trenching machine and the spoil removed leaving channels typically 50–75 mm (2–3 in) in width. These channels are filled with either sand or a layer of sand over a suitable rounded drainage aggregate, usually around 5–8 mm (approx 0.25 in) in diameter. A number of factors are important:

- The slits must be close enough to prevent ponding in the area of the soil between them. The spacing therefore should vary from about 0.6–1.0 m (approx 2–3 ft).
- The sand in the slit must have a high permeability, give adequate moisture retention for plant growth, remain stable if the grass is lost and not filter into the underlying gravel. Detailed recommendations on sand sizes for slit drainage as well as for other applications are available from the Sports Turf Research Institute (STRI).
- There must be good contact between the slits and the backfill of the drain trenches. A minimum overlap of 25 mm (1 in) is recommended.
- The drainage design rate can be calculated using the slit and drain spacings, the width and depth of the slit and the permeability of the fill material. The design rate should be related to rainfall intensities in the area.
- It is essential that a layer of sand is placed over the slits to prevent them being capped by soil. This can be achieved by adding a 25 mm (1 in) layer of sand before the slits are installed or heavy top dressing of about 100–150 tonnes (100–150 t) per pitch per year for three years after construction. With both methods future sand dressing of about 50 tonnes (50 t) per pitch per year will also be required.
- In soils of high clay content which are subject to shrinkage in dry weather there can be settlement of the material in the slits. Ideally there should be irrigation to prevent excessive drying but as a minimum requirement there should be a supply of sand available to top up the slits if settlement occurs.

There are other forms of slit drainage which are sometimes used in conjunction with excavated slits to produce a very intensive pattern of permeable bands in the soil which may be as close as 200 mm (8 in) centres. With sand injection, deep bands typically 15–20 mm (approx 0.5–0.75 in) in width are formed using a cutting blade (but with no excavation) and sand is added to the resulting fissure. In sand grooving, narrow slits are inserted to a depth of 75–100 mm (3–4 in). The principal use of sand grooving is to restore continuity between the soil surface and existing slits which have been capped by soil.

The main alternative to slit drainage is the use of a rootzone dominated by sand-sized particles or even pure sand. If the materials are properly selected the rootzone will remain free draining and well aerated even under the effects of play. If sand is mixed into an existing or imported soil it is important that adequate quantities are added, usually to dilute the silt plus clay fraction to below 10%. It is essential that the composition of sand-soil mixes should be checked by laboratory analysis of particle size and hydraulic conductivity.

Pure sand constructions are of two main types:

- Sand carpet construction, in which a layer of 100–150 mm (4–6 in) of uniform, medium-fine sand is placed over the natural soil, which should be intensively drained with a system of slit and pipe drains. The sand layer gives considerable advantages in terms of drainage and aeration but the grass roots can still utilise reserves of moisture and nutrients held in the underlying soil.
- Suspended water table construction, which has a profile consisting of 250–300 mm (10–12 in) medium-fine rootzone sand overlying a 50 mm (2 in) coarse sand blinding layer and 100–150 mm (4–6 in) of gravel. This type of construction can sustain very high drainage rates but does have major management implications in terms of the fertiliser programme and irrigation.

In the selection of the type of construction system for a pitch there must be close consideration of the natural soil, local rainfall, projected levels of use, expectations of quality and the intensity of management. Detailed guidelines on pitch selection are currently being prepared by the Sports Council's Pitch Prototype Panel following an extensive programme of research by the University College of Wales, Aberystwyth and the STRI.

3.8 Fertilisation
In the early life of new sward, particularly during the first 12 months, it is important to ensure good root growth and produce a thick turf quickly. For the successful and rapid establishment of a hard wearing grass sward and to ensure its future maintenance, appropriate fertiliser mixtures should be applied as follows:

- Before seeding – a pre-seeding compound fertiliser, eg 11:6:9, $N:P_2O_5:K_2O$ applied at a rate of circa 500 kg/ha (approx 450 lb/acre).
- After seeding – in the first 12 months (whether from an autumn or spring sowing) generous fertiliser treatments of a nitrogenous nature supplying up to 250 kg/ha (approx 225 lb/acre) of nitrogen with phosphate and potassium applied in proportion to the nitrogen using a ratio of 4:1:3 of $N:P_2O_5:K_2O$.
- Annually thereafter – type of fertiliser and frequency of application according to circumstances, with nitrogen a principal requirement at a rate of up to 200 kg/ha (approx 180 lb/acre). On sand constructions greater frequency of application will be necessary although the

5 *The differential slip wear machine – developed at the Sports Turf Research Institute, to examine the wear tolerance of different grasses and cultivars. Photo: Sports Turf Research Institute.*

overall annual amount need not be greater. Slow release forms of nitrogen fertiliser could also be considered.

3.9 Grass seeds mixtures
Seed mixtures for pitches should produce a playing surface which will withstand wear and tolerate mowing and as a result provide an acceptable surface of good appearance. Grass species and cultivars (varieties within a species) vary greatly, and so the seed mixture should be chosen with care to ensure that the constituent grasses are suitable for their intended use. Price should only be considered after the potential mixtures have been limited to those which contain appropriate cultivars. For winter games pitches perennial ryegrass is the main species which is used but smooth-stalked meadow-grass can also be considered if there is a long establishment time. Highland bent is sometimes incorporated into the seed mixture when a pitch is used in the summer as a cricket outfield.

Much knowledge of grass cultivars and mixtures has been gained through trials carried out by the STRI over many years, 5. The annually published *Turfgrass Seed* booklet obtainable from the STRI summarises information on amenity grass availability. The reliability of cultivar description is ensured by seed certification. For some species, certified seed is the only category which can be purchased. For others, there are both certified and commercial seed, the latter being an inferior grade not certified as to cultivar; certified seed will obviously be preferable for most situations.

It is important to use seed of satisfactory analytical purity and germination. The Seeds Regulations, revised in recent years to conform with European Community procedures, lay down minimum standards for these qualities, in respect of each species; there are, however, no minimum standards applicable to mixtures, apart from the average of the individual components' standards.

A purchaser can verify the analytical purity and germination of any seed by a test at an official seed testing station but this is expensive and time consuming, particularly for a mixture with several components. Details in the UK can be obtained from:

England and Wales   Official Seed Testing Station
                                       Huntingdon Road
                                       Cambridge CB3 0LE

Scotland	Department of Agriculture & Fisheries for Scotland Agricultural Scientific Services East Craigs Edinburgh EH12 8NJ
Northern Ireland	Official Seed Testing Station 50 Houston Road Crossnacreevy Castlereagh Belfast BT6 9SH

It is sometimes assumed that the more generous the seeding the better will be the results. High rates of seeding seldom show real benefits and it is better to spend the money on ensuring that good quality seed is used and that soil cultivations and ameliorants are adequate. Of particular importance is the proper preparation of a fine tilth for the seed bed. Poorly prepared ground with inadequate removal of compaction and/or large lumps at the surface are often the cause of seed failures, particularly of the finer species. It is sometimes in the hope of compensating for this condition that high rates of seeding are employed.

If turf is used it should be selected to contain the desired grass species and varieties. It is important to ensure that the turf has been grown on a relatively sandy soil so that it does not seal the surface of an otherwise free draining construction.

3.10 After maintenance

However well the construction and seeding or turfing operations are carried out, the ultimate result will be seriously endangered if the immediate after maintenance is neglected.

The contract must clearly state the maintenance for which the contractor is responsible before handing over so that the client can make such advance arrangements as are necessary to avoid any hold up of essential maintenance work.

The client must therefore be in a position to carry out the required maintenance work as soon as the contract has been completed. Failure to keep the new grass properly mown can be particularly disastrous. Important too is the application of fertiliser to ensure that the initial growth is maintained.

4 Turf reinforcement

4.1 General principles

There has been considerable interest in combining some of the advantages of artificial turf, notably in wear resistance, into natural turf surfaces. Accordingly, a number of turf reinforcement materials have come on to the market in recent years. There are two main groups. First, various plastic mats and polypropylene needle-punched geotextiles act to spread surface load, prevent smearing of the underlying soil, retain surface levels and, in some cases, protect the growing point of the grass plant. The second form of reinforcement is designed primarily to increase the stability of sand constructions and includes polypropylene fibres and small mesh sections which can be mixed through the sand rootzone.

There has been an extensive programme of research at the STRI to study the potential of turf reinforcement, **6**. The results have been variable. At best the reinforcement materials give substantial protection to goalmouth areas; at worst some of the continuous surface mesh materials

6 *Installation of a trial to examine methods of turf reinforcement on a sand rootzone. Photo: Sports Turf Research Institute.*

are potentially dangerous because of problems of footlock. More detailed guidelines on turf grass reinforcement are given in the Natural Turf Pitches Prototypes Advisory Panel Report No. 2.

4.2 Non-woven fabrics

There are also a number of filter membranes or fabrics used primarily for civil engineering purposes. Available in different strengths, these membranes are made up of a very large number of fine pores which permit the passage of water but not fine sand. The main situations under which such filter membranes are used are:

- The insertion of a membrane between the formation surface and the foundation layer of a hard porous pitch where ground conditions are difficult. This prevents the soil from being forced up into the foundation and obstructing the free flow of water. A 50 mm (2 in) layer of hard ash or coarse sand is normally used in similar circumstances.
- The covering of waste tips before soiling and seeding to prevent broken glass and similar dangerous materials from working up to the surface. Normally it is necessary to cover a tip with a thick layer of soil or screenings before the topsoil can be spread.
- The bottom of bunkers on golf courses.

5 References and further advice

Baker, S W, Sands for Sports Turf Construction and Maintenance, *Journal of the Sports Turf Research Institute*, **58** (1990).

Baker, S W, Regional Variation of Design Rainfall Rates for Slit Drainage Schemes in Great Britain, *Journal of the Sports Turf Research Institute*, **58, 57** (1982).

Baker, S W, Reinforcement Materials for Winter Games Pitches, *Natural Turf Pitches Prototypes Advisory Panel Report No. 2*, Sports Council, 26 (1987).

National Playing Fields Association, *Gradients for outdoor sports facilities*, NPFA, London, 3 (1983).

National Playing Fields Association, *Gradients for Sports Facilities*, NPFA, London (1983).

National Playing Fields Association, Drawing No 3, *Space Requirements Markings and Orientation of the More Popular Outdoor Games*, NPFA, London (1987).

National Playing Fields Association, *Sports Ground Maintenance*, NPFA, London (1989).

National Playing Fields Association, *Hard Porous (Waterbound) Surfaces for Recreation*, 2nd edition, NPFA, London (1989).

National Playing Fields Association, *Cost Guide and List of Main Contractors and Suppliers of Outdoor Sports and Play Facilities*, NPFA, London, revised annually.

The Sports Council, The National Playing Fields Association and The Central Council of Physical Recreation, *The Playing Pitch Strategy*, The Sports Council, London (1991).

9
Bound and unbound mineral surfaces

Jean Wenger

1 Introduction

Bound and unbound mineral surfaces can be used to provide pitches or courts for a variety of sports including basketball, football, hockey, netball, and tennis. They can be classified into two broad categories:

- Coated macadam, asphalt and concrete
- Unbound hard porous surfaces.

2 Coated macadam, asphalt and concrete

These surfaces, although hard and abrasive, continue to serve as the initial training ground for both incidental and professional play. When specifically designed (or, more commonly, adopted by children using quiet access roads and parking areas in housing areas) they provide one of the most durable and economic surfaces available.

2.1 Coated macadam and asphalt

As general surfacing for children's play and games areas these materials are still highly regarded with much experimentation in the use of colours and graphics to further stimulate activity. However they are no longer recommended for use beneath or immediately adjacent to children's playground equipment over 600 mm (2 ft) high. Surfacing specially designed to absorb the impact of falling children now provides safer landing areas.

Apart from asphalt, the coated macadams are available in pervious or impervious form. All designs should however employ gradients of approximately 1:80 to ensure continuing disposal of water throughout their life. In time grit, mud and atmospheric pollution will block the interstices of pervious surfaces.

As training areas they provide valuable all weather facilities for a wide range of sports. They provide the only surface currently recommended for netball by the All England Netball Association (AENA) and continue to be used as competition surfaces for five-a-side football, tennis and other minor team games, especially those common to school physical education programmes. Developments in hockey now encourage training on these surfaces in preference to grass in preparation for playing on synthetic surfaces.

The binders of many proprietary products, especially those for tennis courts now incorporate latex to reduce softening in warm weather and are colour coated to improve performance and reduce ball scuff.

2.2 Concrete surfaces

No-fines concrete surfaces are now laid infrequently and have largely been replaced by synthetic surfaces. Their construction with single size aggregates allows rapid water percolation through the interstices which gave them significant advantages over coated macadam and asphalt. However, silting up of the interstices in the same way as pervious macadam can occur and is then more serious as generally no gradient to shed water is provided.

Concrete surfaces are not normally used on large games areas because of problems of shedding surface water and the need for frequent construction joints.

3 Hard porous (waterbound) surfaces

The origins of hard porous (waterbound) surfaces for recreational purposes go back to ancient Greece where they were used for several Olympic sports. Their use was revived over 60 years ago in response to the increasing performance needs of sports authorities, players and athletes. They required a surfacing material that could sustain intensive wear yet offer a more sympathetic and tactile surface than those other surfaces then available, namely coated macadam and asphalt.

Hard porous (waterbound) surfaces are suitable for many sports except those games involving a direct hand to ball contact. Sports such as basketball and netball result in an unacceptable migration of fine particles between the ball and the player's hand which reduces the necessary ball control. They are therefore used primarily for athletics, football, hockey and tennis.

Hard porous (waterbound) surfaces are normally composed of suitably graded hard limestone, granite, basalt, crushed brick, whinstone, or blaes (burnt red shale). These materials have taken over from the graded cinder and clinker from power stations on which many athletics records were set in the past, including the first four minute mile. Cinder surfaces gave excellent drainage qualities but were dirty and extremely abrasive. With changes in power station fuel grades they are no longer so readily available.

The surface consists of mineral particles which form a stable playing surface by a combination of their moisture holding capacity and variations in their size and shape. They are in the main quarried materials which are sometimes provided with additional binders to increase their cohesiveness. The particle size should not normally exceed 5 mm (approx 0.25 in) and ideally be not larger than 3 mm (approx 0.12 in). They come in a range of pastel colours, the more common ones being pink, red, grey and yellow. The surface finish is usually 40–50mm (approx 1.5–2 in) thick and laid over a free draining base at least 150 mm (6 in) deep but is determined by local site conditions.

Hard porous (waterbound) surfaces are normally marketed by trade name. Their proprietary nature is such that they are often retained by specific sports grounds construction companies. Owing to the differing minerals contained within proprietary products mixes should not be made without carefully ensuring compatibility. If the material source is limited to specific proprietary quarry seams their geographical location can make haulage a significant factor in the overall cost of a pitch.

Today the dominance these surfaces held up to the start of the 1970s has waned and many have been replaced by synthetic products oriented towards specific sports or greater usage capabilities with lower maintenance requirements. In comparison with synthetic surfaces they have had their competitiveness reduced significantly in recent years by increasing labour and related maintenance costs. Their main handicap, however, is that they do not provide a true all weather surface. They become unplayable during thaw conditions after frost and many cannot be used during or after heavy or prolonged rainfall. Careful construction and improved modern drainage techniques can significantly reduce this problem but it will always remain owing to the nature of the materials involved.

Hard porous (waterbound) surfaces nevertheless still offer a remarkable provision opportunity for low cost, intensive use and long lasting pitches (more than 20 years). Multi-use pitches, training surfaces and a number of specialists sports such as tennis are still being installed by client bodies able to provide the regular maintenance they require.

Regular maintenance is required and primarily consists of luting, brushing and drag matting. These may need to be done once daily or as an additional operation that is necessary between major sport changes. Rolling and occasionally scarifying are also required to maintain the surface in good condition. Most of these operations are carried out by specialised machinery of a weight that will not over compact the surface.

There are now several companies able to provide this specialist ancillary equipment which can be operated from the same power unit, allowing substantial savings in maintenance time and delivering improved pitch quality. With large areas it is possible to provide basic maintenance operations in the order of 6000 sq m (approx 7200 sq yd) per hour. It should be noted that where intensive use is maximised especially with the provision of flood lighting such maintenance operations may be required more than once a day.

The order in which games are played can increase the time between maintenance operations. For example the surface of multi-use areas will last longer and perform better if junior or small ball games are played before senior games, football or training activities.

As the term 'waterbound' implies, moisture is a critical factor. It is equally important to ensure that excess water is removed quickly and that the surface does not dry out in warm weather. On exposed sites, especially in coastal areas, such problems may be exacerbated by wind erosion of the top surface leading to the need for regular re-dressing.

Irrigation is the key solution and all pitches will benefit from a specialised system. This may be by travelling sprinklers or pop-up units: the latter are far more suitable for areas of tennis court size upwards. They may be automated and include evening/night programming. Significant amounts of water are required, over 22,000 litres (approx 5000 gallons) requiring at least a 50 mm (2 in) main feed pipe for a hockey pitch. Discussions should always be held at the design stage with the water supply company. Pitch construction therefore requires carefully designed and installed drainage systems. Interceptor drains should be laid to prevent water from surrounding areas reaching the pitch.

Foundations will vary according to site and the type of installation machinery. They are normally laid to a depth of 125 mm (5 in) in Department of Transport Type 1 stone graded 10–25 mm (approx 0.5–1 in) blinded with a further 25 mm (1 in) layer graded 3–10 mm (approx 0.1–0.5 in). This foundation should be positively linked into the drainage system. The hard porous stone (waterbound) material is then laid to a consolidated depth of 32–50 mm (1.25–2 in) depending upon the proprietary surface selected.

The junction between hard porous (waterbound) surfaces and other surfaces, especially grass areas, requires careful detailing. A paved perimeter is advantageous, if only to the main access points. This restricts mud, grass clippings etc. from reaching and contaminating the surface and subsequently reducing the surface's drainage capacity and cohesive nature.

Raised edging kerbs are commonly used to contain the material and separate it from other surfaces. It is necessary to prevent possible trip points or restrict unnecessarily the movement of water off the pitch. Equally mud and other materials from abutting areas need to be prevented from coming on to the pitch. Raised edgings to the lower sides of gradients should be designed to allow water to drain away without the build up of fines that will themselves increasingly restrict the movement of water.

Marking hard porous (waterbound) pitches is understandably an ongoing operation owing to the continual maintenance of the playing surface. On small areas such as tennis courts plastic marking tapes are occasionally used but for most pitches and courts repeated applications of proprietary paint compounds provide the best solution. Tapes and machinery do not normally work well together. The permanent marking of game line positions on surrounding boundaries or concrete edgings will significantly reduce the time involved in resetting out and marking individual pitches.

4 References and further advice

British Standards Institution, *BS 5696: Play Equipment Intended for Permanent Installation Outdoors.* BSI, London (1979).

British Standards Institution, *BS 7044: Artificial Sports Surfaces*, BSI, London (1990).

Department of Transport, *Specification for Highway Works*, Part 3. HMSO, London (1986).

National Playing Fields Association, *Cost Guide and List of Main Contractors and Suppliers of Outdoor Sports and Play Facilities*. NPFA, London (revised annually).

National Playing Fields Association, *Facilities for Athletics.* NPFA, London (1980).

National Playing Fields Association, *Gradients for Outdoor Sports Facilities*. NPFA, London (1983).

National Playing Fields Association, *Notes on Choosing Hard Tennis Courts*. NPFA, London (1985).

National Playing Fields Association, *Kick-about Areas*. NPFA, London (1985).

National Playing Fields Association, *Impact Absorbing Surfaces*. NPFA, London (1987).

National Playing Fields Association, *Hard Porous (Waterbound) Surfaces for Recreation*. 2nd edition. NPFA, London (1989).

10
Sheet and in-situ synthetic surfaces

Graham Tipp

1 Introduction

The earliest synthetic materials to be used as outdoor sports surfaces emanated from the flooring industry when, in the 1960s, it began to take an interest in the growing leisure industry. Gradually the market became more selective and products were specifically formulated to meet the particular requirements of sport.

By the 1990s, the market had become very sophisticated, with a wide range of products for different sports and a number of well-developed standards and specifications covering different aspects of their installation and performance.

2 Prefabricated systems

2.1 Sheet rubber systems

One widely used form of pre-fabricated surfacing system utilises polyurethane (PU) resin as a binder/adhesive in combination with granulated rubber. The components are mixed in carefully metered quantities and blended with rubber particles, without heating, to form a 'pudding-like' mixture. This is poured into a mould where it cures under slight heat and pressure, to emerge as a block or slab of rubber. The slabs are cut into tiles or sheets or, if continuous lengths of material are required, sliced from a rotating cylindrical 'log'.

Other forms of rubber are used to prepare sheet surfacing systems, by continuous vulcanisation processes. Some are two-layer materials with a cheaper, more compressible material as their lower layer and a higher quality, pigmented grade on the surface to give the necessary durability.

2.2 Textiles

Some early sports surfaces were little more than 'outdoor carpets' and textiles still form an important group of products for sports use. With the exception of synthetic turf (dealt with in Chapter 11) the most commonly used are non-woven (needle-punched) nylon or polypropylene carpets. Whilst the majority are intended for indoor applications, they have found application as outdoor bowls carpets, golf greens, or even athletics surfaces.

2.3 Plastics sheeting

Plasticised polyvinyl chloride (PVC) has been very successfully used for tennis courts but is probably most frequently encountered outdoors as cricket wickets.

2.4 Plastic tiles

A number of systems are offered in which a complete sports surface is assembled from interlocking moulded tiles. These can be easily laid to improve the appearance and playing characteristics of a surface that is failing to drain properly, or one that has become cracked or pitted.

Interlocking tiles surfaced with a series of vertical polyethylene 'needles' are used as an artificial ski-slope surface, but the more commonly encountered ski-slope system is based on polymer brushes, set in a net-like grid of metal channels.

2.5 Installation

Sheet materials are delivered to site in roll form, ready to be adhesive-bonded to a macadam or concrete base. To avoid the adhesive forming an impermeable barrier, special machines have been developed which dispense the adhesive in a series of parallel ribbons, leaving sufficient area uncoated to maintain porosity, **1**.

PVC sheeting has the advantage over rubber that it can be jointed, either by solvent bonding, or by thermal fusion (welding), to give a particularly strong seam. Textile products may be loose-laid in small areas, or more usually adhesive-bonded to the base and to a seaming tape in order to form durable joints. Interlocking tile systems would always be loose-laid, but might require perimeter restraint in certain applications. Occasionally

1 *Dispensing parallel ribbons of adhesive to maintain porosity*

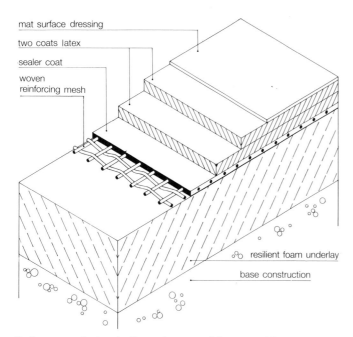

mat surface dressing
two coats latex
sealer coat
woven reinforcing mesh
resilient foam underlay
base construction

2 Latex surfacing built up in several layers, with a reinforcing mesh and foam underlay

these prefabricated systems are laid over a supplementary layer, to confer additional shock absorption.

3 In-situ systems

The versatility of PU means that the liquid chemical components may be blended directly on site, most frequently as a resin binder in conjunction with rubber particles. The mixture is blended in a cold paddle mixer and dispensed onto the base, where it is spread and consolidated to the required thickness and surface regularity. In large areas this may be done using sophisticated, laser-controlled paving machines.

PU is not the only way in which a rubber can be formed from liquid components. Latex systems were amongst the first sports surfacings to be formulated for site use. Latex systems 'cure' through loss of water and as they do so, they undergo shrinkage. To avoid problems of dimensional instability, latex systems are therefore usually built up in a series of thin coats to the required thickness. Some incorporate reinforcing fabric for improved dimensional stability, **2**.

4 Colour

Rubber crumb can be produced in virtually any colour but many products utilising recycled rubber are black. Colour may be added to these by spraying or pouring a layer of coloured liquid rubber onto the surface. Some of these coatings reduce porosity and this factor needs to be considered at the design stage.

5 Marking

The most durable marking paints are again based on polyurethane, but acrylic and polychloroprene systems are also used. Marking a court or a pitch is a skilled operation requiring meticulous care and the permanent marking of a new court or pitch should be carried out by a specialist contractor.

Occasionally, temporary line-markings are needed to supplement the more commonly used marks. The manufacturer of the surfacing should always be asked for guidance on the selection of temporary marking paints.

6 Standards

Many standards have been published by different authorities around the world, covering synthetic sports surfaces. Some individual sports' Governing Bodies publish requirements for surfaces to be used in international competitions.

More general requirements for surfaces for multi-sports use may be found in BS 7044 *Artificial Sports Surfaces*. Part 4, Specification for surfaces for multi-sports use, lists a series of performance requirements for dimensions, safety, playing performance and durability and Part 2 describes methods of test for these parameters, both in the laboratory and on site.

7 Quality control

A specifier must not only select the right surfacing for the particular application, but also ensure that the required standards are achieved. This is done by following a strict programme of quality control.

The basic principles of such a scheme are:

● The Contractor submits with his tender reference samples of his system, supported by independent test certificates showing that it meets the parameters specified.
● As work proceeds, samples are removed to check conformity with reference samples.
● The finished job is checked, using BS 7044 or other test procedures, to demonstrate that the requirements and standard of workmanship have been met.

8 References and further advice

Tipp, G and Watson, V J *Polymeric Surfaces for Sport and Recreation*. Applied Science Publishers Ltd, London (1982).
British Standards Institution, BS 7044: *Artificial Sports Surfaces*. BSI, London (1990).

11
Synthetic turf

Gordon Stables

1 Introduction

Synthetic turf was developed for outdoor use but was first laid as a sports surface indoors at the Houston Astrodome, Texas, in 1966. Since then, a large number of both indoor and outdoor installations have been completed worldwide. The first synthetic soccer and hockey pitch in the UK was laid at Caledonian Park, Islington in 1971 and followed by a similar area at Mabley Green, Hackney in 1973. From this tentative start, the development of different products and construction types accelerated and by 1989 the 200th pitch had been installed, all but a tiny handful of them outdoors.

Although synthetic turf has been provided for five-a-side or kick-about areas, most emphasis has been on its use for eleven-a-side hockey and football because:

- It provides a perfect surface for top level training and competition, particularly for hockey
- It can be used in virtually all weather conditions
- Its potential for intensive use meets the demand for team games where there is a shortage of suitable open space.

It has been used for netball and lacrosse and the growing popularity of American Football will no doubt further increase the demand for synthetic pitches. More recently synthetic turf surfaces have been developed for the summer games of tennis, bowls and cricket. In Scotland they have also been used for shinty and are being considered for hurling, camogie and Gaelic football in Ireland.

2 Governing body acceptability

The initial research into and recommendations on the use of synthetic turf for football, usually referred to as the Winterbottom Report, was published by the Sports Council in 1985. More recently the *Commission of Enquiry into Playing Surfaces* by the (English) Football League in 1989 recommended that the use of synthetic turf be banned in Division 1 with effect from Season 1990/91 and only a limited extension of its use in the lower Divisions permitted. The Commission's Report included revised performance standards for all new pitches, superseding those of the Winterbottom Report and required a full review of all artificial surfaces by the end of Season 1992/93. However, many Football League clubs have provided synthetic turf training areas and this increasing tendency for top soccer players to train on synthetic turf coupled with advances in technology and revised performance standards may yet produce a greater degree of acceptance by football administrators.

Greater progress has been made in hockey where the International Hockey Federation (FIH) now requires its use in all major FIH tournaments including Olympic and World Cup Competitions, resulting in an increasing demand for similar facilities in the UK. In order to achieve unified standards on installations used for major international competitions under its direct supervision and act as a guide to organisations installing surfaces for hockey, the FIH published its *Handbook of Requirements for Synthetic Hockey Surfaces Outdoor* in 1987. This has now been superseded by the third edition (1992) which includes both amended and additional standards.

3 British experience

In response to this increasing demand and in order to monitor the performance of synthetic turf the Sports Council installed pitches at Bisham Abbey, Crystal Palace and Lilleshall National Sports Centres. The three original carpets have now been replaced after reaching the end of their useful lives which averaged slightly over ten years.

Although essential for the specialised training of national teams, the study of the performance of these relatively new materials is equally important in determining advice to facility providers. This is particularly necessary because climatic conditions and types of use in Britain are different from those in the USA where these surfaces were first developed. The refurbishment of existing pitches will be an increasing area of work during the 1990s.

4 The manufacture of synthetic turf surfaces

There are many combinations of carpet materials and manufacturing processes from which to select. The principal material groups are:

- Polyamides   Nylon 6 and 6,6
- Polyesters   Polyethylene terephthalate
- Polyolefines   Polythene and polypropylene

Carpets are not necessarily made from a single material – polyester, for example, is used in backing other materials where particularly good dimensional stability is required.

Polyester has an inherently high resistance to degradation by natural light while polypropylene and polyamides require the addition of photo-stabilisers in the manufacturing process. Photo-stabilisers can be affected by other chemicals and so advice should be sought from the manufacturer before applying weedkillers or insecticides. The quality of daylight varies considerably around the world and a product which performs satisfactorily in the UK may be quite unsatisfactory in sunnier climates. Polyamide piles have very good resilience and resistance to abrasion and unlike polyolefines and polyester can absorb approximately 4% water.

Synthetic turf is manufactured by most of the techniques readily available in the carpet industry, the most popular in Europe being tufting, weaving, needling and knitting. All require a secondary backing process to provide dimensional stability or ensure that the pile is strongly bound. There are benefits for most sports if the surface finish of the carpet is non-directional. Some manufacturers have overcome this potential problem by crimping the fibres to produce a curly pile. They have also produced fibres with a waxy finish which are claimed to reduce the problem of friction burns without making the surface too slippery.

4.1 Synthetic turf products
Synthetic turf products fall into three broad categories:

- *Non-filled pile products:* these are typically dense and heavy with pile heights of 10–13 mm (approx 0.4–0.5 in). Crimping of pile yarns and mixed pile heights have been helpful in reducing the effects of pile lie in manufacture. Non-filled pile pitches require an irriga-tion system, ideally located outside the carpet area, to wet the surface for hockey and cool it during hot weather. The 1966 Astroturf was a non-filled pile carpet and, more recently, these have been preferred to filled pile products by the FIH for its major tournaments.
- *Filled pile products:* these generally have longer, more open pile than the non-filled products. The particulate filling improves person/surface and ball/surface inter-action. The weight of filler holds down the carpet and the pile stabilises the particles. Typically the particles are 0.2–1.0 mm (approx 0.008–0.04 in) in size and rounded. Shape is important because angular particles become interlocked and the surface gradually hardens. Sand is the most common filler used and may amount to 25–40 kg/sq m (approx 45–75 lb/sq yd) depending on pile height but other materials which can be coloured have also been used: for example, rubber granules, synthetic polymer beads and elastomeric coated sand. Although now recommended by the FIH, irrigation systems are not generally required in the UK.
- *Non-pile products:* these have been produced for sports where harder, more uniform surfaces are required, for example tennis and bowls, but have also been used instead of the piled products as an economic alterna-tive for other sports.

5 Installation
Carpets are delivered to site in rolls up to approximately 100 m (330 ft) long and varying widths depending upon the origin of manufacture. They are generally laid across the width of the playing area to facilitate the stretching of non-filled carpets and reduce the effect of balls track-ing along the joints. Consideration should be given to laying rolls in alternate directions to reduce any problems of pile directionality in the surface and produce the striped appearance of newly mown turf.

All carpets need to be seamed to produce a full playing surface because of the relatively narrow roll widths. The nature of the carpet construction needs to be considered when deciding between mechanical or chemical bonding of adjacent rolls. Woven and knitted materials have a selvedge and can be stitched whereas the edge of a tufted material may fray. Chemically bonded (glued) seams must be resistant to weather and capable of withstanding damage from sports shoes in order to minimise joint failure through peeling. The quality of seam in tension must be high when the carpet has to be stretched before fixing.

Synthetic turf can be fixed in position by:

- *Edge fixation after stretching.* The whole surface is seamed and fixed down one edge and tensioned by winches to remove any rucking and reduce the poten-tial for thermal movement before being fixed on the free edges. The edges are turned over a perimeter board and fixed with large-headed galvanised nails or gripped under the metal cover of purpose made precast channels.
- *Chemical bonding (glued).* The carpet may be bonded to the underlying layer either along the seams or by ribbons of adhesive over the whole area to maintain free drainage through the carpet.
- *Sand filling.* 25–40 kg/sq m (45–75 lb/sq yd) is worked into the pile to approximately 80–90% of its height according to the performance characteristics required of the carpet.

5.1 Gradients and drainage
The FIH specification (1992) for hockey surfaces requires a piled carpet/shockpad combination having a minimum porosity equivalent to a rainfall intensity of 600 mm/hr (24 in/hr) with surface gradients not exceeding 1% in any direction. It also requires the base to be 'capable of accepting and disposing of draining water at least at the same rate as the surface.' This can be achieved with either a level or sloping porous base with an under pitch drainage system or a non-porous cambered profile base draining to channels at the pitch edges, both systems discharging to an outfall. The latter option was used for the 1992 Barcelona Olympics because of its better water retention in the non-filled pile carpet during play. Water retention is not a problem with sand-filled pile carpets and a base with a minimum poros-ity related to maximum anticipated rainfall intensities is recommended. For example a minimum base porosity of 150 mm/hr (6 in/hr) is required for club standard hockey in the UK.

5.2 Shock pad, base and sub-base
Synthetic turf needs an accurately laid base and care should be taken to engage a contractor with sufficient expertise to meet specified standards.

The choice of base and sub-base materials and construction will be dependent on the existing ground conditions. The base may be

- *Concrete, macadam or unbound stone.* An energy absorb-ing layer (shock pad) is generally needed between the synthetic turf and the base construction to modify their properties and provide specified performance charac-teristics, in particular for ball bounce and shock absorption. It may be provided as an integral part of the carpet, laid separately in sheets or formed in situ. Foam materials should be of closed cell manufacture to avoid damage by water and frost: polyurethane is better than latex in this respect. Rubber particles bound with a resin such as polyurethane used in sheet form may have a profiled construction. Alternatively these polymer products may be laid in situ and, mixed with other materials such as small pieces of lava and stone, laid 40–50 mm (approx 1.5–2.0 in) thick as part of the base construction.

- *Unbound particles restrained by a geotextile envelope.* These bases can be tuned for different playing characteristics – a stiff geotextile with interlocking particles gives a high bounce for tennis and cricket while a softer geotextile with round particles provides a lower bounce for hockey and soccer. A shock pad may not be required over a dynamic base if the particles are rounded or include a proportion of rubber granules of a similar size. Pitch levels are probably better maintained if the upper layers of the mobile base particles are semi-restrained in a needle punch textile or three-dimensional polyamide matting.

All shock pads need to be permeable and dimensionally stable. Some polymeric products have been known to curl and alter in size with changes in moisture content.

5.3 Line markings
Line markings can be permanent or temporary. Permanent lines produced during manufacture or cut and fixed in situ can be distorted by carpet movement and may wear differently from the main carpet pile. Lines of temporary paint or powder can be used until any initial movement of the carpet has stopped and then permanent painted lines applied. Temporary paints or powders can also be used to provide lines or logos for one-off events.

6 Carpet life and maintenance
It is usual to require a 5-year guarantee from the contractor that the synthetic turf will perform to a specified standard. In order to sustain any claim under such a guarantee, the site manager must operate and maintain the surface in accordance with the manufacturer's instructions which should be supplied under the contract. Maintenance will normally include:

- Keeping the surface clear of litter and leaves using methods and equipment agreed with the contractor
- Topping up/regrading of filler in a filled-pile carpet with material to the original specification
- Keeping oil, food, glass and other foreign matter off the surface
- Occasional rolling of dynamic bases
- Irrigating non-filled pile surfaces
- Snow removal with a rubber-bladed plough not less than 10 mm (approx 0.4 in) above the surface and attached to a machine agreed with the contractor
- Repairs to damage carried out quickly.

7 Levels of use

7.1 Urban areas
Whether a pitch is to meet the competitive needs of hockey or provide for intensive community use, the justification for the high capital outlay for a synthetic turf surface must take into consideration other available surfaces including natural turf, land availability/cost and potential hours of use.

Some figures from the London Borough of Islington help to put the arguments for such a surface into perspective. Twenty years ago the population of Islington was approximately 200,000 with a density almost four times the average for all the London Boroughs. Consequently open space was

in short supply. Areas of at least 0.8 ha (approx 2 acres), sufficiently large enough to locate a soccer pitch, equated to only 0.16 ha per 1000 residents compared with 2.2 ha per 1000 residents for Greater London. At that time the population of Islington had the potential to generate 250 soccer teams which would have needed some 40 to 60 natural turf pitches. However Islington could provide only three which were supplemented by one synthetic turf pitch and seven smaller hard porous areas.

By 1991 the population of Islington had fallen to 169,000 which still required the provision of some 35 to 50 pitches. In order to overcome this deficiency, the Borough Council responded by increasing its provision of artificial surface pitches to two synthetic turf and two hard porous pitches supplemented by smaller hard porous areas and the retention of one natural turf pitch. It is in this situation, common to many inner-city areas, that the 'thirty-games-a-week' potential of synthetic turf all weather surfaces in particular can be realised and provide opportunities for sport which would otherwise not be available.

7.2 Rural areas
Synthetic pitches can also be an appropriate form of provision in rural areas, particularly if linked with a local secondary school. There are examples at Beith and Ellon in Scotland where successful full size synthetic pitches have been provided in village communities and used for a wide range of activities including rugby and athletics training. There is also a case for less than full size pitches and multi-courts suitable for tennis and other sports as well as football and hockey. The specification of the base and shock pad for such multi-purpose pitches is inevitably a compromise between the needs of different sports but can provide a pitch which, although not ideal for some of the activities for which it may be used, will still result in a successful facility.

7.3 Maximising use
Achieving maximum use does not depend simply on the synthetic turf alone. It also requires the provision of fencing; floodlighting; sufficient changing accommodation for players both on the pitch and those ready to use it in the next session; enlightened management; a flexible attitude to traditional playing times by staff and users; and programmed use for schools and other groups during daytime off-peak periods. Where sufficient land is available and there is a substantial local population it may be desirable to consider complexes with two or three synthetic turf pitches, particularly when it will be possible to employ sports development and coaching staff.

8 References and further advice
British Standards Institution, BS 7044: *Artificial Sports Surfaces*, BSI, London (1990).

Crawshaw, G H *Textile Sports Surfaces and Artificial Grass*, Elsevier Science Publishers Ltd, Oxford (1989).

Fédération Internationale de Hockey, *Handbook of Requirements for Synthetic Hockey Surfaces Outdoor*, FIH, revised and updated edition (1992).

Football League, *Commission of Enquiry into Playing Surfaces*, Football League, Lytham St Annes (1989).

Tipp, G and Watson, V J *Polymeric Surfaces for Sport and Recreation*, Applied Science Publishers Ltd, London (1982).

Winterbottom, Sir W *Artificial Grass Surfaces for Association Football – Report and Recommendations*, The Sports Council (1985).

12
Specialist surfaces – general

Gordon Stables

Although there has been a continuing tendency towards the provision and installation of multi-sports areas and surfaces, there are several sports which require exclusive facilities. These vary from a specially profiled crown bowling green in either natural or synthetic turf to cricket wickets.

It is not the intention here to include specialist surfaces where they relate solely to facilities for top-level training and competition. For example, the principles of the installation of synthetic turf for international hockey are no different from those for synthetic turf generally and are covered in Chapter 11.

In addition to the continuous research and development work carried out by manufacturers to provide improved new surfaces and the development of standards through the Sports Council, the BSI and now CEN, many Governing Bodies of sport set their own performance standards. It is advisable, therefore, to confer with the relevant Governing Body whenever it is intended to introduce a specialist surface.

Amongst the most popular outdoor sports requiring exclusive facilities are

- Athletics (Track and Field)
- Bowls
- Cricket
- Tennis

The next four chapters of the Handbook give details of suitable surfaces for these sports.

13
Athletics – track and field

Vic Watson

1 Introduction

Although there are many examples around the world where competitive athletics events are held on cinder or grass surfaces, it is difficult to envisage a major athletics competition taking place on anything but a synthetic surface. Since the installation of the first synthetic track in Europe at Crystal Palace National Sports Centre in 1968, athletics clubs and local authorities have come to recognise the advantages of such facilities:

- the track can be used in all but the most severe weather conditions throughout the year
- there are low maintenance requirements
- the consistent physical properties enhance athletics performance.

Modern synthetic surfaces for athletics are high performance systems formulated to be durable and designed to offer the best combination of dynamic properties for athletes. Obviously the surface requirements of sprint-event athletes are different from those of the long-distance eventers. The technology exists to vary the dynamic characteristics of the surface to favour one type of event over another. Clearly with major athletics meetings involving all disciplines, such 'tuning' of the track to favour one particular group of athletes would not be acceptable. For this reason, all current commercial surfacing systems offer a balance of dynamic properties which represents a compromise between the needs of the different athletes using the facilities. The performance requirements now stipulated by the IAAF are based on the needs of all athletes.

2 Baseworks

All synthetic surfaces rely on a good standard of base construction. It is an essential pre-requisite for the successful installation of the surface and for its long term performance. The base should be adequate for at least 25 years without showing signs of structural movement or losing its water shedding capability, 1. It is impossible to lay down precise recommendations for base construction because every site will be different geotechnically. The exact depth and type of base required therefore has to be determined by experts. The orientation of the facility and the precise details of the layout for all events also need input from experienced consultants. It cannot be stressed too highly that advice from independent experts should be sought at an early stage in any project.

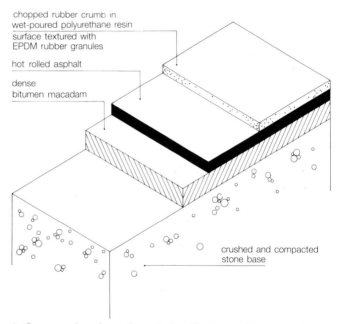

chopped rubber crumb in
wet-poured polyurethane resin
surface textured with
EPDM rubber granules

hot rolled asphalt

dense
bitumen macadam

crushed and compacted
stone base

1 *Cross-section through typical athletics track construction*

3 Surfacing

There are two principal types of synthetic surface:

- systems prefabricated in the factory and delivered to site as rolls of material which are adhesive bonded to the base
- systems fabricated on site by machine mixing and laying the raw material ingredients.

3.1 Prefabricated sheet

The sheet is made from a rubber compound, usually polychloroprene, processed by calendering, curing and rolling. It is invariably non-porous and has an embossed or textured finish to improve traction and slip resistance. By producing the surfacing material in the controlled conditions of a factory, its performance properties should be very uniform. Also because the thickness of the sheet can be controlled very accurately, possible problems due to thin areas on the completed facility are avoided. However, the installation of the material requires a high degree of skill and accuracy. The sheet must be bonded to the base of the track with adhesive. The butt joints must be soundly executed, both between adjacent sheets of surfacing and between the surface and the perimeter edges of the track or runway. The durability of the surface is only as good as the integrity of the bond between itself and the base. Furthermore the material will obviously conform to any contours and irregularities in the base to which it is bonded. It is therefore vitally important that the base fully conforms to the stipulated gradients and levels requirements.

3.2 In-situ systems
The second main group of surfacing systems comprises those products which are fabricated on site from raw materials. There are three principal sub-divisions:

- Cast elastomers
- Resin-bound rubber crumb
- Composite systems.

For all such systems, the compatibility of the raw material ingredients is of vital importance. All reputable installers of in-situ surfacing systems should ensure by constant monitoring and testing that each component does not have an adverse effect on another forming part of the same surfacing product. It is advisable to have a consistent supply of each ingredient and test data to confirm the performance of each combination. Because the end properties of such systems are very dependent on the nature of the raw materials delivered to site, their mixing, laying and the operation of a comprehensive quality control scheme are pre-requisites to a satisfactorily completed facility. All reputable installers willingly submit to independent quality monitoring by experienced test laboratories.

Cast elastomers
These products are laid as free-flowing liquid polyurethane. The cast polyurethane resin is prepared by mixing two components, one a liquid polyol and the other an isocyanate, in the correct proportions. It also incorporates chopped rubber crumb. This mix is applied to the base of the track, either in one layer or as a multi-layer build-up, to the full thickness required and given a textured finish by broadcasting specially formulated coloured ethylene propylene diene modified (EPDM) rubber granules on to the surface. Following cure, the excess surfacing granules are removed.

All cast elastomer systems are non-porous and hence it is of paramount importance that the stipulated gradients and levels requirements are met, otherwise water ponding may occur in low areas. The final surface is largely free from joints, and should adhere well to the base. Such surfaces are strong and durable, provided they are correctly formulated using compatible raw material ingredients, properly mixed and installed under satisfactory environmental conditions.

Resin-bound rubber crumb
These products comprise a principal layer of polyurethane resin-bound rubber crumb, finished with a texturised surface coating of polyurethane paint. The crumb is mixed with a one-component moisture-curing polyurethane resin in the correct proportions. This very viscous mix is then spread by paving machine on to the base of the track, with the thickness controlled by screeding bars. After cure, two coats of a coloured polyurethane paint containing a fine rubber aggregate are spray applied to this rubber base mat in order to give the finished surface the correct traction and slip resistance.

These systems have many of the advantages of the cast elastomers, although they are probably a little less durable. One advantage is their porosity which means that even areas slightly out-of-tolerance for levels will not water pond. In particularly high wear areas, for example at the end of javelin runways and the high jump take off points, it is common to reinforce the surface with cast resin material prior to spray applying the finishing coats. These systems probably comprise the most widely installed group of synthetic surfaces for athletics.

Composite systems
As the name implies, these systems are a hybrid of the cast elastomer and the resin-bound rubber crumb products. They are sometimes known as 'sandwich' or 'double-decker' systems. They are formed from a base mat of resin-bound rubber crumb, typically about 9 mm (approx 0.3 in) in thickness. After cure, the open textured mat is grouted with a very fine rubber crumb and then a cast elastomer layer is applied as the top surface. The appearance of the finished facility is exactly as for a cast elastomer system, but the surface requires less of the expensive cast polyurethane resin.

4 Testing
Whatever surfacing system is chosen, it is most important that quality control of its installation is undertaken by independent experts. It is also recommended that the completed facility is tested for the requirements now stipulated by the IAAF. These include:

- levels and gradients
- thickness of synthetic surface
- force reduction
- modified vertical deformation
- friction
- colour uniformity
- drainage.

All of these parameters have limits set by the IAAF at a level which will permit top quality international athletics to take place with comfort and safety for the athletes.

5 References and further advice
International Amateur Athletics Federation, *Performance Specification for Synthetic Surfaced Athletics Tracks (Outdoor)*, IAAF, London (1990).
Tipp, G and Watson, V J *Polymeric Surfaces for Sport and Recreation*, Applied Science Publishers, London (1982).

14
Bowls – crown and flat

Roger Evans and Colin Jepson

1 Natural turf greens

1.1 General
The successful establishment of a natural turf bowling green requires careful programming to take advantage of optimum weather conditions which in the UK are late autumn for turfing or, more occasionally, late summer/early autumn for seeding. Spring or summer turfing and seeding can be carried out but require adequate attention and watering to prevent drought damage during initial establishment.

Although greens for crown and flat bowls are different in profile and ditch detail, and may differ in size and plan shape (see Chapters 43 and 47), there are many constructional aspects applicable to both types. They include:

- drainage
- designed soil mix
- surface levels and regularity
- grass cover
- water supply
- ditches.

1.2 Drainage
Greens should be constructed on a drainage layer 150 mm (6 in) deep of 8–12 mm (approx 0.3–0.5 in) sized hard aggregate blinded with 50 mm (2 in) sharp sand. This leads infiltrated water to perimeter perforated pipe drains in the case of a crown green while flat green drainage is supplemented by additional drains of the same type laid diagonally across the green below the drainage layer.

1.3 Designed soil mix
Rarely is the natural soil suitable for direct re-use. The normal procedure is to ameliorate some of the top soil with a suitable sand to produce a mixture which is free draining but will maintain a healthy hard wearing turf. It should be laid to a minimum firmed depth of 110 mm (approx 4.5 in).

1.4 Surface levels and regularity
Finished levels should be carefully set out. The final levels of the completed flat green should preferably be within + or – 6 mm (0.25 in) from the mean green level and the difference between adjacent spot heights on a 3 m (10 ft) grid should preferably be below 6 mm (0.25 in). Levels should be set out on a 3 m (10 ft) grid of level pegs or boned in screeding battens at 3 m (10 ft) centres. The profile of the crown green should be set out with

level pegs at 3 m (10 ft) centres along the contours shown in Chapter 47. However, maintenance of these levels is not critical for a crown green provided there are no sudden changes in level which prevent the bowls from running smoothly across the green.

1.5 Grass cover
Whether turfed or sown, the grasses should be a suitable mixture of bent and fescue cultivars. Advice can be obtained from the STRI which publishes *Turfgrass Seed* annually.

Turf and seed should be ordered in advance to ensure availability at the critical time of laying or sowing. Turf should be free of weeds and weed grass and have a grass cover no longer than 12 mm (0.5 in). Seed should be sown at a total rate of 35 g/sq m (1.25 oz/sq yd) in two transverse passes. Both turfed and sown greens should have a double layer of turf laid along their perimeters to ensure stability of the extreme edges.

1.6 Water supply
A sufficient supply is needed to maintain a healthy grass sward at all times. This can be provided from permanent pop-up sprinklers installed outside the perimeter of the green or portable rotary impact sprinklers which can be placed strategically on the green. The turf is close cut during the playing season to a height of 6–8 mm (approx 0.25–0.3 in) and can be susceptible to drought conditions. The supply may need to be supplemented until the sward becomes well established.

1.7 Ditches
These may be the traditional form of treated wooden boards or special units made of precast concrete (PC) or glass reinforced concrete (GRC). The flat green ditch, **1**, is surmounted by a bank, which can be turfed, paved or walled. If turf is not used, the vertical face must be covered with a striking surface to protect the bowls from damage. Requirements for the crown green ditch are less rigid but include a striking board along the outer ditch edge, **2**. The bottom of the ditch for both green types is covered with a 50 mm (2 in) depth of pea gravel, rounded pebbles or similar hard inert material which will not damage the bowls.

2 Synthetic surfaced greens
Introduction of synthetic surfaces for outdoor bowling was a logical progression from the rapid development of indoor surfaces during the 1970s. Much of the

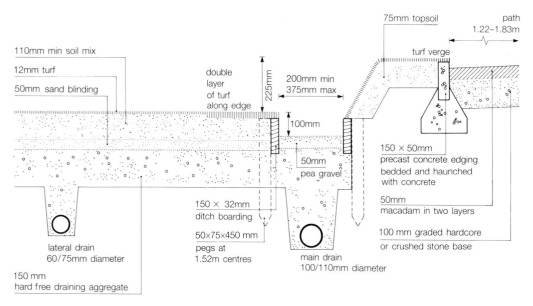

1 *Details of flat bowling greens with traditional ditch and bank boards*

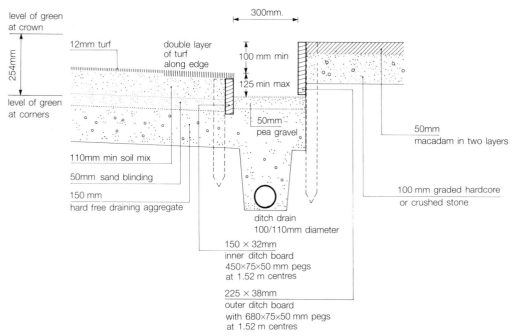

2 *Details of crown green bowling greens with traditional ditch and bank boards*

experience gained on indoor synthetic surfaces has been transferred back to the outdoor green.

Though relatively small in number compared with traditional turf greens, the lack of experienced green-keepers and rising cost of turf maintenance suggest continued future growth in the number of artificial greens. Generally flat greens have been installed but two crown greens are now in use. As with other sports, the synthetic surface can sustain longer and more intensive use leading to an increase in membership for clubs and the possibility of increased revenue and potential savings on annual maintenance costs for green operators. Principal factors affecting the synthetic bowling surface for both green types are rolling resistance, wear and resistance to set, indentation or permanent deformation. The green should be neither 'too slow' nor 'too fast' (flat green speeds of 12–15 seconds are suitable), give the correct amount of bias and be comparable with a good turf green.

Although some artificial greens have been constructed with a short pile synthetic grass (for the two crown greens in use this is sand filled) the most commonly accepted surfaces to date are non-bladed synthetic textile products with a needle punch polypropylene underlay. Whichever surface is chosen the product should be non-directional. This has been proved to be a major criterion as a directional pile can lead to varying playing characteristics. Machine sewn seams are generally more durable and weather resistant than glued seams. On flat greens the seams should be at right angles to the line of play to minimise the effect of the seams on rolling bowls. In New Zealand carpets have been successfully laid with the seams running diagonally at an angle of 45° across the green enabling it to be used in two normal directions (E–W and N–S) like a natural turf green.

Maintenance of the artificial green is confined to regular vacuuming and sweeping or occasional washing down. Periodic rotation of surface panels may help in obtaining maximum potential life which should certainly be in excess of 10 years.

Various methods of providing a suitable substrate for the synthetic outdoor surface have been used. Mesh reinforced dense concrete incorporating a drainage system through the slab or a porous bituminous macadam are most commonly used, the latter being particularly suitable for crown green construction.

In all cases, the provision of a stable sub-base and suitable drainage system for water removal from the structure is essential to enhance playing conditions and prevent frost heave. Care must be taken with the detailing of all joints in a reinforced dense concrete base to ensure that surface levels are not affected by differential or thermal movement. Whichever base construction is used it is absolutely vital that the surface of the base is finished to extremely high tolerances because any deviation from design levels is invariably reflected through the surface element and can cause unsatisfactory bowling characteristics. There should be no abrupt changes in level, such as may occur at joints and cracks, on the base of either flat or crown greens whatever their construction. However, the surface regularity for a flat green with either base may be expected to be better than its natural turf counterpart. In order to achieve these standards, the construction to finished base levels should, whenever possible, be undertaken by an experienced contractor.

The initial construction cost of an artificial bowling green is comparatively high but the advantage of immediate use upon completion, the potential for intensive and extended use with no restrictions to allow recovery of the surface or costly day to day maintenance make it an attractive proposition.

3 Other details applicable to both natural turf and synthetic greens

3.1 Orientation
There is no preferred orientation for crown greens, where the game is played in any direction, or natural turf flat greens, where the line of play is changed through 90 degrees on a regular basis to minimise wear. However on a synthetic flat green where the line of play is limited by the direction of carpet lay, a north/south orientation is preferable to east/west to avoid the problems associated with bowling towards a low setting sun in the evenings.

3.2 Shelter screening
All types of green benefit from some type of shelter screening. Close boarded fences and hedges are both suitable but very careful consideration should be given to any tree planting. Shade, falling leaves and the effect on rainfall and ground moisture from trees can cause problems on all types of bowling green.

3.3 Floodlighting
Floodlighting can be considered to extend the use of both natural turf and synthetic greens. It is unlikely that the length of season would be extended on a natural turf surface but the hours available for evening play could be significantly increased. Floodlighting could make a synthetic green an all year round facility subject, of course, to certain weather conditions and winter competition from indoor bowls.

4 References and further advice
Evans, R D C Bowling Greens: their History, Construction and Maintenance, Sports Turf Research Institute, Bingley (1992).

15
Cricket

Peter Dury

1 Performance standards

Problems of inexperienced or insufficient ground staff have caused concern in cricket circles over reduced standards of pitch preparation and maintenance at school, public and club level. Considerable developments in both natural and non-turf cricket pitches have taken place over the past decade designed to assist in the provision of suitable pitches for all levels of play.

Performance standards have been developed for both natural and non-turf cricket pitches by measuring the performance levels of natural turf pitches. Much of this work was based on research carried out in the 1960s by Stewart and Adams of the Soil Science Research Unit (SSRU) at the University of Wales, Aberystwyth. They developed the rebound bounce test for measuring pace, 1, and the Adams and Stewart Soil Binding (motty) test for determining the strength of a soil which focused attention on the importance of clay particles in bonding together the structure of a pitch.

Nottinghamshire County Council, the STRI, RAPRA Technology Ltd and the Sports Council co-operated in extending this research to methods of testing and identifying suitable performance characteristics for both turf and non-turf cricket pitches. Much of the work of identifying what constitutes a 'good' pitch was carried out by Nottinghamshire County Council in conjunction with the National Cricket Association (NCA) and Nottinghamshire and Warwickshire County Cricket Clubs. The parameters identified included bounce in play, stability of surfaces, evenness, rebound bounce (for pace), stiffness and durability. Suggested performance standards for artificial cricket pitches are listed in Table 15.1.

2 Baseworks

Whether the surface is natural or artificial, the base plays a major role in determining its playing quality. Disintegration and 'layering' of the base often produces air pockets which can absorb much of the ball's energy and produce an unpredictable bounce. In addition to layering, the thickness and stability of the underlying layers, root depth, thatch, herbage and pitch smoothness are all factors which affect performance.

3 Natural turf pitches

If a natural turf surface is being considered, the soil on site should be analysed to determine its suitability for the

Table 15.1: Suggested performance characteristics for assessing pitch playing quality

Property suggested	Performance	Test method
Ball rebound (in play)	Balls pitching 2–3 m (approx 6–10 ft) in front of the popping crease should pass stumps between half and full stump height	Assessed through use of the pitch
Ball rebound (for assessment of pace of wicket)	Below 10%–slow pace 10–15% – medium pace Above 15% – fast pace	BS 7044 Pt 2, Section 2.1 Method 1
Spin	Ball should bounce a distance not greater than 700 mm (approx 27 in)	BS 7044 Pt 2, Section 2.1 Method 4
Surface evenness	Localised bumps and hollows should not be greater than 3 mm (0.12 in) at any point using a 3 m (10 ft) straight edge	Suitable method in BS 8203
Surface stability	There should be no breaking up of the structure or individual particles	Visual inspection
Stiffness	Pitch: the force corresponding to an energy input of 2.5 J should be 2.5–5.5 kN with a maximum surface deflection of not more than 25 mm (1 in)	BS 7044 Pt 2, Section 2.1 Method 5
	Underlay: the deflection under a load of 932 g should be not less than 25 mm (1 in) nor more than 75 mm (3 in)	Nottinghamshire County Council SFAL Method (1992)

1 *Rebound bounce test*

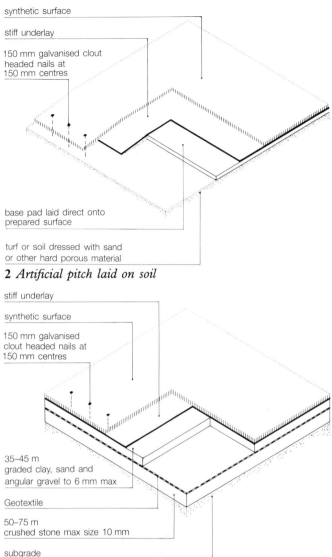

2 *Artificial pitch laid on soil*

synthetic surface
stiff underlay
150 mm galvanised clout headed nails at 150 mm centres
base pad laid direct onto prepared surface
turf or soil dressed with sand or other hard porous material

3 *Artificial pitch laid on unbound particulate base*

stiff underlay
synthetic surface
150 mm galvanised clout headed nails at 150 mm centres
35–45 m graded clay, sand and angular gravel to 6 mm max
Geotextile
50–75 m crushed stone max size 10 mm
subgrade

production of a good pitch. If not it will be necessary to import an appropriate clay loam with a clay content ranging from 25% to 35%. Many of the top pitches in the UK have been successfully reconstructed using imported clay loam up to 300 mm (12 in) deep. For pitches where covers are not available, such depths of clay loam are not recommended although it is important to have a depth of not less than 100 mm (4 in).

Irrigation and good drainage are essential for the establishment and maintenance of good pitches. The water supply should be located close to the pitches to avoid the need for long hose connections. The pitches should, if soil conditions require it, have perimeter drains to collect water from the blanket of free draining material laid under them as a sub-base and discharge it into a field drain system or other suitable outfall.

A recent development on natural turf pitches has been the use of synthetic fibres to stabilise the soil particles for the bowlers' approach and delivery stride areas. Synthetic fibres are also being used to stabilise full length pitches in Nottinghamshire. Whilst extremely useful on soils which have poor binding qualities, they are no replacement for a good clay loam although they can be used in conjunction with such a material to provide improved stability and durability.

4 Artificial pitches

Artificial pitches have become increasingly popular in recent years mainly because they can now be designed with bounce characteristics and, where a client wishes, playing characteristics similar to natural turf. This removes one of the main criticisms of artificial pitches by cricketers who require consistent conditions on the day but appreciate the subtle variations caused by changes in climatic conditions and moisture content within the pitch structure.

There are three main types of artificial pitch construction:

- *Surface and underlay components laid directly onto an existing soil*, **2**. They usually comprise a single or double stiffened underlay which is laid directly onto closely mown turf or a bed of sand or hard porous material. Such pitches have the changeable characteristics of natural turf, particularly where the underlay and surface materials allow water to penetrate readily through their structure and affect the firmness of the ground beneath.

- *Surface and underlay components laid onto an unbound particulate base*, **3**. Typically this comprises a shallow crushed stone raft 50–75 mm (2-3 in) deep, preferably with particles no larger than 10 mm (approx 0.4 in), laid under a hard porous material with particle size in the range from clay/silt to an angular gravel of no more than 6 mm (0.25 in). In some situations a geotextile membrane is used to separate the two types of material in order to prevent migration of particles. On top of the hard porous material a stiffened underlay should be laid to prevent disturbance of the particles by the impact of the ball. In some pitches the bowlers' run ups are supported by a rubber matting beneath the synthetic turf whereas in others the stiffened underlay extends the entire length of the pitch. Where a rubber matting is used it should have a similar stiffness to the other parts of the artificial pitch. Where a stiffened underlay is not used, the surface has to be removed from time to time and the base re-levelled and made true.

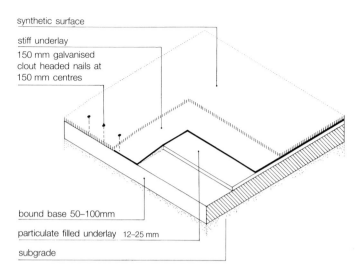

synthetic surface

stiff underlay

150 mm galvanised
clout headed nails at
150 mm centres

bound base 50–100mm

particulate filled underlay   12–25 mm

subgrade

4 *Artificial pitch laid on bound base of macadam or concrete*

● *Surfaces laid onto a bound base of macadam or, more usually, concrete,* **4**. They can be sub-divided into two types:
   (a)   Those with an underlay, sometimes containing a particulate infill, surfaced with a stiffened pad and synthetic turf.
   (b)   Those where the surfacing material constitutes both surface and underlay.

All of the above construction types are usually surfaced with a woven or needlepunch synthetic turf although a smooth polyurethane surface is occasionally used on a concrete base. Surfaces laid directly onto concrete invariably have a much higher bounce than a natural turf pitch or a surface laid with an underlay component. Where the underlay incorporates particulate material, bounce characteristics similar to natural turf can be produced.

When laying a synthetic pitch, it is important that the ground on which it is to be constructed is adequately drained. Expert advice should be sought to ensure long term stability of the pitch. Prospective purchasers are also advised to select a surface that has a proven 'track record' in its resistance to spiked footwear. While some surfaces will show a high degree of resistance, prolonged use of spikes in areas of high wear will inevitably damage the surface to some degree. This can be minimised on piled surfaces by filling the pile with particulate material in the area of the bowlers' run up, delivery stride and follow through but not the area where the ball would normally pitch.

What of the future? Having gone some way towards providing artificial wickets with the playing characteristics of natural turf, there has been some speculation on the possibilities of providing synthetic outfields to increase the range of uses at major cricket grounds. Some of the currently available surfaces might be accepted at club level but further research will need to be carried out to find an acceptable synthetic replacement for turf outfields.

5 References and further advice

Dury, P L K and Millest, J *The Non-turf Cricket Pitch,* The Sports Council, London (1990).

Evans, R D C *Cricket Grounds,* Sports Turf Research Institute, Bingley (1991).

Nottinghamshire County Council, *Cricket Pitch Research,* Nottinghamshire County Council, Nottingham (1978).

Nottinghamshire County Council, *Cricket Pitch Research Supplement,* Nottinghamshire County Council, Nottingham (1979)

Nottinghamshire County Council, *Cricket Pitch Research,* Nottinghamshire County Council, Nottingham (1985).

Nottinghamshire County Council, *To Play Like Natural Turf,* Nottinghamshire County Council, Nottingham (1985).

Nottinghamshire County Council, *Sports Facility and Amenity Landscape Standards,* Nottinghamshire County Council, Nottingham (1987).

Nottinghamshire County Council, *Sports Facility and Amenity Landscape Standards: Methods of Test,* Nottinghamshire County Council, Nottingham (1992).

The Sports Council, *Specification for Artificial Sports Surfaces: Pt 3 Surfaces for Cricket,* The Sports Council, London (1984).

16
Tennis

Chris Trickey

1 Introduction

In addition to traditional surfaces such as natural turf and water-bound loose particle courts (shale, clay, etc.) a wide range of outdoor surfaces are used for playing tennis. They can vary significantly in their playing characteristics, the effect of adverse weather on usage, maintenance requirements and cost of construction

The choice of surface and the required construction specification will depend on whether the courts are to be built from new or existing courts upgraded. There are also many different trade names for basically similar surface materials and it is important that specialist advice is sought at the outset.

2 Grey-green, gritted bituminous

This is a porous bitumen-bound surface finished with a grey-green coloured natural grit. It is traditionally constructed by spraying or mixing the stone aggregate base with bitumen emulsion on site. The surfacing grit, much of which remains loose, allows a degree of slide.

The main advantages of this type of surface are its modest costs, unobtrusive appearance and the fact that it can be laid without the use of heavy machinery making it very suitable where site access is difficult. Grey-green is ideal for domestic installations but not suitable for clubs or heavy-duty use.

3 Porous macadams

3.1 Standard bitumen macadam

Many thousands of courts have been built employing a straight bitumen macadam surface, although generally this surface has now been superseded by modified bitumen macadams.

The quality of the hot macadam can be variable and it may contain 'cut-back' oils which makes it more readily workable on site but leaves the surface with a pronounced tendency to soften in warm weather. The bitumen-bound surface is usually laid in two courses and difficult to colour-coat immediately, this process normally having to be postponed to the following season.

3.2 Modified bitumen macadams

During the 1970s new additives were introduced which removed many of the shortcomings of straight bitumen macadams. The macadam mix no longer needed to contain cut-back oils and this has significantly lifted the temperature threshold at which the surface softens. Sometimes the term 'non-softening' is used to describe this type of surface. It is, however, misleading: all bitumen-bound surfaces soften to some extent in warm weather. The absence of the oils also enables the surface to be colour-coated within 10–14 days of being laid.

Well-specified and installed modified bitumen macadam courts should be porous and frost resistant and may be constructed with a single or double course of macadam.

3.3 Colour coating macadam courts

Acrylic-based paints containing slip-reducing agents are most commonly used to colour coat macadam courts. A range of colours is available, although red and green or two-tone green are generally the most common combinations. Apart from the obvious aesthetic improvement, painting a court will produce a slightly faster surface. However it may reduce the foot-surface traction and slip resistance. These should be tested in accordance with BS 7044 or an existing court inspected.

4 Porous concrete

The porous no-fines concrete surface is laid in-situ in rectangular bays with 36 of them making up an average size court and safety surround. Construction joints must be designed and built to good concrete practice if they are not to cause problems. The bays themselves should be a minimum of 75 mm (3 in) thick. The concrete is laid over a sub-base in two layers, one immediately following the other so that they become monolithic. The lower layer employs aggregate of 14–19 mm (approx 0.5–0.75 in) and the top layer 3–6 mm (approx 0.12–0.25 in) of clean chippings.

The cement can be pigmented, when the final surface may then be left unpainted, or painted with an acrylic colour-coating which gives a better appearance. By their nature the bays will expand and contract slightly with changes in temperature and moisture. They may also develop hair-line cracks but these will barely be perceptible and will not hinder play.

Porous concrete courts can be laid to fine tolerances of level, although differences between adjacent bays may subsequently result from ground movement. The surface is 'all-weather' and very hard-wearing; the foothold is very safe and the surface gives a consistent game.

5 Synthetic turf

Synthetic turf surfaces for tennis are of two types, particulate filled or non particulate filled, the former far outnumbering the latter.

5.1 Particulate filled

There are numerous particulate filled synthetic turf systems, all superficially similar but differing substantially in their detailed specification. Most, however, use green polypropylene fibres (other colours are available) which are tufted with varying tuft spacings and sand as the particulate filling.

The sub-base is usually porous macadam. In the early days of the introduction of the surface it was hoped that the carpet could be laid directly on an unbound granular base but this has not proved satisfactory because of problems with levels and frost disturbance. The carpet can also be laid on suitable existing hard porous surfaces. The surface is rapid-draining but takes somewhat longer to dry than other more traditional 'all-weather' surfaces such as porous macadam.

The sand filling should be hard and clean to assist drainage. Silica sands are favoured for this purpose. Adjacent rolls of carpet are joined by means of a backing tape and appropriate outdoor adhesives.

Play lines are very short lived when painted onto the particulate filled surface. Most products therefore employ 'cut-in' lines using carpet of similar specification, or lines woven or tufted into the carpet.

5.2 Non particulate filled

Non particulate filled synthetic turf for tennis is not often laid out of doors, but hybrids between the two systems with shorter pile and a small addition of sand are seen.

6 Impervious acrylic

Impervious acrylic is the surface most widely used throughout the tennis playing world and many major championships are staged on such courts. Tight tolerances of surface levels and high standards of specification and workmanship are essential for successful installation. The surface is impervious, the courts being laid with a crossfall to assist rainwater to run off, and formed by multiple applications of coloured acrylic materials. There is a wide choice of colours and most systems incorporate a cushion layer or layers to improve player comfort. Play lines are painted on the completed surface. The structure supporting the surface must be strong, carefully consolidated and protected from water ingress to prevent settlement or frost damage. A base of concrete or two layers of asphalt are usually laid to achieve an impervious and sufficiently level surface for the acrylic layers. The court should be long-lasting and can be easily and economically resurfaced.

7 Polymerics

A polymeric tennis surface is usually an elastomeric mixture of natural or synthetic rubber granules in a binder of polyurethane. It may be cast in situ or supplied in prefabricated sheet form and glued to the court base. Polymeric courts can be constructed with either porous or impervious surfaces and have a degree of cushion, providing a softer, more comfortable footing than the harder surfaces such as porous concrete or macadam.

The surface is not affected by frost or ultra-violet attack and does not soften in hot weather. Surfaces can be finished in a variety of colour combinations and are 'all-weather' and virtually maintenance free. A polymeric court must have a conventionally engineered base of open-textured bituminous macadam or concrete for a porous construction and hot-rolled asphalt for an impervious surface. Play lines are normally applied using a compatible polyurethane paint.

8 Plastic tiles

These surfacing systems consist of prefabricated plastic tiles which link together to form the playing surface. The tiles vary in size from system to system but usually provide a flat, open lattice-like surface supported by small plastic legs. They are manufactured in various colours to enable two colour courts to be constructed. Small white tiles are inserted to provide play lines. The tiles have the advantage of easy installation where access to the site may have become restricted. The tiles, which are perforated and raised off the surface on their legs are normally laid on macadam or concrete bases and are particularly suitable for resurfacing old hard courts provided they are sound and level. Alternatively, they can be laid on an impervious sub-base, always assuming there is sufficient gradient on the sub-base to shed the water. A complete court can be installed in two days.

The court requires very little routine maintenance and is 'all-weather', although some systems have had a tendency to be slippery when the surface is wet.

9 Hard porous waterbound surfaces

This group of surfaces, which includes the traditional shale courts, are now seldom constructed in the UK. However the Lawn Tennis Association (LTA) has recognised the importance to top UK players of practice facilities with surface types likely to be met in major competitions abroad. The Sports Council has provided three clay courts at Bisham Abbey National Sports Centre to meet this need. There is no unique specification for the base but the surface materials were imported from France. The main requirements are

- a stable base which is free draining but retains sufficient moisture to keep the surface bound together
- a surface of finely crushed limestone (Calcaire Broyé) laid to a 50 mm (2 in) consolidated thickness and topped with a 5 mm (0.2 in) consolidated layer of powdered red brick
- a surface irrigation system to keep the top layers bound together.

There is little experience of clay court construction in the UK. Maintenance requires many of the traditional ground keeping skills: watering and rolling being the key to compacting the surface which should approach brick hardness. The surface layers are damaged by winter frosts and have to be totally broken up, re-levelled and compacted every Spring before the May-September playing season can begin. Daily maintenance, including watering, is very similar to that for shale courts.

10 References and further advice

Trickey, C *Tennis Courts*. Lawn Tennis Association, London (1991).
Indoor Tennis Centres. Lawn Tennis Association, London (1992).

17
Children's play and recreation facilities

Dr Mike Nussbaum

1 Introduction

Play is crucial to any child's healthy development. Through play children learn and develop socially, physically, intellectually, creatively and emotionally (the SPICE acronym) and their needs must be the key consideration in the planning of play facilities. A well designed play area will attract children because it offers challenge, adventure, fun or a quiet area in an environment which is as safe as possible and child-friendly. It is important too that access is easy and safe for children as well as parents/carers and that they are encouraged to stay.

Children are the greatest users of the outdoor environment and when relatively young will move away from the

confines of home or garden, if they have one. For flat or apartment dwellers the need for well designed play opportunities of various kinds is even more essential. Often the environments created not just in inner city areas and on housing estates, but in villages and very rural areas, are hostile and potentially dangerous. More room and consideration may be given to the car than to children and even walking on grass or playing games may be prohibited.

Sadly, therefore, much provision is of poor standard and/or badly maintained and often ill conceived in its development. Because planning for children is not given priority good play opportunities tend to be the first to suffer when finances are restricted. There is also a tendency to concentrate purely on equipped provision (fixed equipment playgrounds) rather than, for example, areas where children can play as well as a variety of supervised play opportunities.

What is required, (and in the UK is reflected in guidelines issued by the Department of Education and Science with the National Children's Play and Recreation Unit) is a greater awareness and understanding of the role of play in a child's life. Following from that is the need for clearly thought out policies for play that express children's wide ranging needs at different stages of their development. Strategies to implement policy that realistically allow for availability of resource and lead-in times for specific projects are crucial.

There is a need for a variety of provision which will include staffed as well as unstaffed facilities. Briefly this may involve:

- Play space for young children (principally those under 5 years of age), situated within 50 m (55 yd) of home and accessible without encountering traffic.
- Local play space/community open space: playspace designed mainly for children over 5 years of age and located within easy reach of family homes (not more than 400 m (440 yd)). These play spaces should be accessible without crossing major roads.
- Neighbourhood playspace or park, perhaps serving a whole neighbourhood, say within a radius of 1 km (1094 yd). Such areas are designed for use by all age groups from small children with their parents or carers to the elderly and are able to accommodate a whole range of activities for children of different ages. Such a playspace or part may well have a staffed play provision, eg a play centre or adventure playground. All of these playspaces may have specific fixed equipment

Climbing play structure

available, appropriate to age and chosen for play value with sensitive layout and any necessary impact absorbing surfaces.

- Ball game or kick-about areas in the form of small non-turf areas and larger grass areas for casual play and informal activities.
- A range of staffed play provision: the guidance and encouragement of sympathetic adults, playworkers, in a variety of settings is very important. These settings may include:
  - Adventure playgrounds
  - Playcentres in school buildings or community centres
  - Play provision within sports or leisure centres
  - Holiday playschemes
  - Play buses.

Any of these staffed play opportunities will offer a wider range of experience for the child than an unsupervised site and the quality of the experience will be enhanced by the relationships with other children and playworkers. The provision can be either 'open access' where children can choose to stay or to leave or 'care schemes' where they cannot leave until collected by a specified parent or carer.

2 Playwork
Playworkers enrich and extend the play experience for children and perhaps do not yet receive the recognition, status or training opportunities they need. However the picture is changing. In the UK, the Children Act 1989 recognises the importance of a range of good play opportunities as a part of support to children and families. Guidance on the Act from the Department of Health clearly states this and emphasises the importance of good and varied training opportunities for playworkers.

3 Participation
One key element in the planning of play space or supervised provision is the participation whenever possible of children and their parents or carers. This should be at the earliest stage and involve commenting on design and management, the layout and nature of equipment or the type and function of staffed provision. A continuing involvement once a playspace or staffed play provision exists is also important.

4 Monitoring, evaluation and review
Any play policy and strategy for implementation should include monitoring and evaluating the use of a play space or supervised provision and include issues of appropriateness to local requirements. Circumstances change with time, populations and age groups differ and therefore such monitoring and evaluation needs to be accompanied by a review process that allows change to occur.

5 Children are the future
Any very brief summary of children's play, its importance and what needs to be provided, can only indicate the key principles. It is essential to understand the need for a variety of good play opportunities and child-friendly environments as part of shaping the future.

Adventure playground. Photo: National Playingfields Association

6 References and further advice

Coffin, G and Williams, M, *Children's Outdoor Play in the Built Environment*, National Children's Play and Recreation Unit, London, (1989).

Department of Education and Science/Welsh Office/National Children's Plan and Recreation Unit, *Playground Safety Guidelines*, DES, London, (1992).

Heseltine, P and Holborn, J *Playgrounds: the Planning, Design and Construction of Play*, Mitchell, London, (1987).

Heseltine, P, Holborn, J and Wenger, J *Playground Management and Safety*, National Playing Fields Association, London, (1989).

Macintyre, S at al, *Safety First Checklist: the site inspection system for play equipment*, Mig Communications, California, (1989).

Ministry of Defence: Defence Work Services, *Children's Play Areas: Guide for Property Managers and Designers* (Defence Work Functional Standards 01), London, HMSO, (1991).

Moore, R (ed), *Play for All Guidelines: Planning, Design and Management of Outdoor Play Settings for Children*, Mig Communications, California, (1989).

Rennie, G *Playground Safety*, The National Centre for Play, Edinburgh, (1989).

Part IV Ancillary work

18
Floodlighting

Jean Wenger and David Bosher

1 Introduction

Floodlighting of appropriate sports areas may be considered for two main reasons:

- to extend the hours of use in order to allow the full potential of the playing surface to be achieved
- to allow a greater percentage of the working population to participate in the outdoor sport of their choice.

It is essential that the level of any sporting activity is not restricted when carried out under floodlights. Great care should be taken to ensure the lighting meets the necessary standard and will continue to do so throughout the life of the installation, 1 and 2.

2 Planning considerations

As sporting facilities are installed for the benefit of the local communities, often within residential areas, proper care must be taken at the design stage to ensure that the lighting scheme does not result in any significant loss of local amenity. Attention should be given not only to the impact of floodlighting installation at night but also its day time appearance.

Unfortunately one aspect often conflicts with the other. Lower structures are often better from the point of view of day time appearance but higher structures can achieve more satisfactory playing conditions and greater control at night. This control may be achieved by means of additional louvres, skirts, adjustment in mounting height, and careful selection of floodlights and lamps.

Whilst there is no specific legislation covering spill lighting, or indeed day time appearance of such installations, it is important to ensure that the location of the pitch to be floodlit is carefully selected. It is also generally considered that the degree of spill lighting should be restricted to a level not exceeding that produced by a normal, residential street lighting scheme.

Planning permission will be required for floodlighting installations. Any proposed floodlighting scheme or enquiry should therefore be accompanied by a location plan detailing properties and roads which may be affected.

3 Lighting design

A lighting engineer should be engaged to prepare a detailed specification for the proposed installation giving the required standard of lighting, illumination levels,

1 *General multi-use floodlighting installation*

2 *Major stadium floodlighting installation*

uniformity, available mounting positions and height restrictions, plus any ground and access problems. Horizontal illumination levels and uniformity ratios should be included as performance requirements in all contract documents and only maintained levels of illumination should be used.

Design work should be carried out in accordance with the recommendations of the Institution of Electrical

Table 18.1 Recommended maintained illumination levels (in lux) and uniformities (see Note (1))

Handbook Reference	Activity	Recreational or Training	Club/County	National/ International
38	Archery (Target)	100/0.25	750/0.8	750/0.8
	(shooting zone)	50/0.25	200/0.5	200/0.5
39	Athletics	100/0.5	200/0.7	500/0.7
41	Basketball	75/0.5	200/0.7	500/0.7
43	Bowls: Lawn	100/0.5	200/0.7	300/0.7
47	Crown Green Bowls	100/0.5	200/0.7	300/0.7
49	Cycle Racing	100/0.5	200/0.7	500/0.7
50	Cycle Speedway	100/0.3	200/0.5	400/0.7
52	American Football	75/0.5	200/0.7	500/0.7
53	Association Football (2)	75/0.6	200/0.7	500/0.7
56	Rugby League Football	75/0.5	200/0.7	500/0.7
57	Rugby Union Football	75/0.5	200/0.7	500/0.7
59	Hockey (3)	300/0.7	300/0.7	500/0.7
60	Mini Hockey	200/0.5	300/0.6	ND
65	Lawn Tennis (4)			
	Over Court	300/0.7	500/0.7	500/0.7
	Over Playing Area	250/0.6	400/0.6	400/0.6
66	Netball	75/0.3	150/0.5	500/0.7
70	Roller Hockey	150/0.5	300/0.6	500/0.7

Note (1): The recommended levels do not include lighting for television broadcasting and for these requirements refer to Volume 2, Chapter 11 – Facilities for the Media, CIBSE Lighting Guide: LG4 - Sports, and CIE Guides 67 and 83.

Note (2): there are specific requirements by FIFA and UEFA for international matches and competitions and many domestic leagues and competitions have specific requirements (such as FA Cup, FA Trophy, Football League, GMVC etc.) Refer to the *Guide to the Artificial Lighting of Football Pitches*, FIFA/Philips Lighting BV and *Digest of Stadium Criteria*, FSADC.

Note (3): The FIH recommend 250 lux for ball training and club competition. Refer to the *Guide to the Artificial Lighting of Hockey Pitches*, FIH/Philips Lighting BV.

Note (4): The ITF have produced recommendations. Refer to the *Guide to the Artificial Lighting of Tennis Courts*, ITF/Philips Lighting BV.

Engineers (IEE), Chartered Institution of Building Services Engineers (CIBSE), Institution of Lighting Engineers (ILE), The British Standards Institute (BSI) and Local Authority Planning Authority recommendations or restrictions. This will enable competitive quotations to be obtained without specifying particular lamp or column manufacturers. It will also allow the lighting engineer to calculate illumination levels on a (computer generated) grid. This grid should be extended to include, where appropriate, neighbouring properties and roads.

Alternative manufacturers' lamp types and fittings will require differing mounting heights, numbers of structures, and final spacings. This often results in schemes of an equivalent standard with differing numbers of structures and floodlights. It is therefore very important to judge the standard of any scheme by illumination levels, quality, uniformity, overall efficiency and operating costs and not simply by the number of columns or floodlights. Many floodlighting schemes rely upon high efficiency discharge lighting with some loss of colour rendition. Such lighting may not be acceptable to certain levels of play and it is wise therefore to specify a light source with the appropriate colour rendering characteristics.

Table 18.1 gives the recommended minimum maintained illumination levels and standard of floodlighting for each of the main sporting activities described in Part VII. Illumination levels are expressed as the Average Horizontal Illumination Level measured at ground level with the Uniformity expressed as a ratio of the minimum to average value. Maintained illumination levels should be calculated using the minimum depreciation factors given in Table 18.2.

Guidance on standard layouts and budget costs is available from the NPFA which also produces a simple guide covering initial installation costs and comments on running costs. Floodlit leagues of some sports sometimes publish their own requirements and ask for a survey each year to confirm that the floodlighting still meets the required standards.

4 Structures

There are many differing types of supporting structures available and in order to simplify and regulate the standards to which they are designed several current standards and codes of practice are available covering lighting columns and high masts. Lattice towers are now rarely used for new sports lighting projects.

Columns and masts are more acceptable visually and usually easier to maintain. Hinged columns or 'raise and lower' masts are preferable because all cleaning, relamping and repairs can be carried out at ground level therefore significantly reducing future maintenance contract costs. This is important in order to maintain illumination levels throughout the life of the scheme.

Columns up to 20 m (approx 66 ft) should be designed in accordance with British Standard BS 5649 parts 1–9. Masts over 20 m (approx 66 ft) high should be designed in accordance with *Technical Report No. 7* published by the IEE. It refers to all relevant British Standards and codes of practice. These specifications are the recognised standard within the Lighting Industry and their use will ensure compatibility between competitive offers.

Some specialist manufacturers may offer a comprehensive design service but it is important that local wind loads and soil conditions are taken into consideration

Table 18.2: Minimum depreciation factors
(Reproduced from Table 6.1 of the CIBSE Lighting Guide LG4: Sports)

Cleaning Interval Months	Pollution Category High	Medium	Low (1)
6	0.91	0.92	0.96
12	0.86	0.88	0.94
18	0.83	0.85	0.92
24	0.81	0.83	0.91
36	0.79	0.82	0.90

Note (1): the pollution category definitions are:
High   Large urban areas and heavy industrial areas
Medium   Residential and light industrial areas
Low   Rural and open country areas

during the design process. Most local authorities structural engineers have within their Technical Services Departments detailed knowledge of wind loadings for their area. It is wise to obtain their advice before preparing a specification. They may also be able to advise on local soil conditions for the design of foundations.

5 General electrical design and installation

To ensure the satisfactory performance and safety, all installations should comply with the current regulations of the IEE (Currently the 16th Edition).

Floodlighting normally requires a 3 phase supply and it is important to ensure the design allows for voltage reductions which will occur with long supply cables. Most manufacturers' designs are based on full supply voltage and unless the optimum supply voltage is available for the required loading a significant reduction in illumination levels may occur. Some manufacturers include the means within their equipment to compensate for this and it should always be confirmed prior to commencing a contract.

Careful consideration should also be given to the floodlighting control point. For larger schemes two or three switching levels may be included to allow for training. Further facilities are available to allow the floodlighting of areas behind columns or masts for training by means of motorised crossarm units. They allow the floodlights to be rotated through 180 degrees. Following training the operation of a switch returns the floodlights to the original aiming position.

6 Civil/groundworks

Unless otherwise specified at the outset competitive floodlighting quotations usually assume normal soil conditions. It is therefore necessary to carry out a soil survey to determine the type of ground and foundation required to support the proposed structure.

In addition main supply cables will need to be buried in cable trenches normally 450 mm (approx 18 in) deep throughout the route from the switchroom to each floodlighting structure. Care must be taken to avoid existing electrical/water/gas services which may exist along these routes. This can normally be achieved by forwarding marked up plans to each of the supply companies for their comments and a meeting with each representative on site.

7 Commissioning

The capital cost of floodlighting is considerable. Allowance should therefore be made within the contract for the full testing and commissioning of the scheme along with a detailed illumination survey carried out in accordance with the recommendations of the CIBSE Guide. Certain sports leagues may require a minimum number of point readings.

8 Maintenance

All floodlights require regular cleaning at intervals in order to maintain illumination levels throughout the life of the installation. Discussions between the client and lighting engineer will be necessary to establish the required maintenance factor based upon the frequency of cleaning, hours of use and lamp replacement periods. Ideally a separate maintenance contract should be taken out to carry out the cleaning and maintenance of all flood lights on a rotation period as set down in the relevant maintenance plan.

9 References and further advice

British Standards Institution, BS 5649 *Lighting columns*, Part 1 1978 Definitions and terms: Part 2 1978 Dimensions and tolerances: Part 3 1982 Specification for materials and welding requirements: Part 4 1982 Recommendations for surface protection of metal lighting columns: Part 5 1982 Space for base compartments and cableways: Part 6 1982 Specification for design loads: Part 7 1985 Method for verification of structural design by calculation: Part 8 1982 Method for verification of structural design by testing: Part 9 1982 Specification of special requirements for reinforced and prestressed concrete lighting columns: BSI, London.

Chartered Institution of Building Services Engineers, *Lighting Guide: LG4 – Sports*. CIBSE, London, (1990).

Commission Internationale de l'eclairage, *Guide 67 – Photometric Specification of Sports Lighting Installations*. CIE, (1986).

Commission Internationale de l'eclairage, *Guide 83 – Lighting of Sports Events for Colour Television*. CIE, (1989).

Fédération Internationale de Football Association, *Guide to Artificial Lighting of Football Pitches*. FIFA/Philips BV, (1991).

Fédération Internationale de Hockey, *Guide to Artificial Lighting of Hockey Pitches*. FIH/Philips BV (1990).

International Tennis Federation, *Guide to Artificial Lighting of Tennis Courts*. ITF/Philips BV (1991).

National Playing Fields Association, *Floodlighting of Outdoor Facilities*. NPFA, London, (1993).

19
Fencing and rebound walls

Gordon Stables

Fencing around sports areas may be provided:

- for security and to protect the facility from abuse when not in use
- to control access during hours of use
- to contain balls within the playing area particularly if it is sited near a road, private property or areas of water.

By far the most common system is chain-link fence. It should be manufactured by specialist contractors using heavy gauge, top quality galvanised and/or plastic coated components. It can be supplied in a range of heights and is fixed with corner, intermediate and straining posts to suit all purposes by specialist contractors. The maximum mesh size for tennis courts is 50 mm (2 in) square. A rectangular welded mesh panel which is stronger and more durable than chain-link is recommended around goal areas.

Nevertheless, fencing behind goal areas is particularly likely to be subjected to regular, heavy impact loading from balls which can distort and lift the bottom edge. This is unsightly and allows balls to escape from the playing area. It can be prevented by strengthening the bottom of the fence with strainer wires and steel angle sections or providing ball rebound boards. These measures are necessary wherever goals are located including at the sides of large areas which are sub-divided into smaller areas for five-a-side soccer or mini hockey.

If rebound walls are provided, they should be 1–1.2 m (3–4 ft) high, robust and weatherproof with a flush inside face and no dangerous projections. They should be of such a colour as to be clearly distinguishable from the playing surface and enable fast moving balls to be seen under floodlit conditions. Although usually of a permanent construction, movable timber wall sections are available which can withstand body impact when linked together. Any gaps at ground level under fences or rebound walls should not exceed 5 mm (0.25 in) to prevent injury to users from their feet becoming wedged in the gap.

All the clips, fixtures and fittings to the fences and rebound walls should be robust and devoid of any sharp or jagged edges. Ideally they should be rounded or recessed to avoid dangerous protrusions into the playing area.

Main access gates should be a minimum of 3 m (10 ft) wide for maintenance or resurfacing machinery. They should be positioned where they will not cause danger or interfere with play, eg away from goal areas. Ball rebound boards/walls should be integral with and continuous across gates, with vertical gaps kept as small as possible and no sharp edges or fixings protruding on the playing face.

Reference and further advice
The Sports Council, *Floodlit Multi Use Games Areas*. TUS Data Sheet 29. The Sports Council, London.

20
Equipment

Gordon Stables

Two of the major benefits of synthetic surfaces are their ability to sustain intensive use over long periods with minimum maintenance and the wide range of different activities for which they can be used. Consequently, at the planning stage consideration has to be given to the equally wide range of equipment to be purchased and installed as permanent fixtures or stored and moved on and off the playing area as required.

Whatever the surface material, it is vitally important that portable equipment is chosen or modified so as not to damage the surface when in place or in the course of being moved. If portable equipment is to be left in place for long periods of time, the surface may become indented and consideration should be given instead to designing the facility around permanently fixed equipment. Small areas for five-a-side soccer and mini hockey, for example, may be designed with recessed goals with the goal line flush with the end rebound walls, fixed goal posts and robust removable cross bars.

Sockets can be provided for post fixings for most sports but advice should be sought before installing them in synthetic turf surfaces where free standing net supports for tennis and netball may be more appropriate. Where sockets are provided they should have cover plates with similar slip resistance characteristics to and flush with the playing surface in order to avoid danger to users. They must also be designed not to allow any penetration of water into the surface or base where it could cause long term damage.

References and further advice

The Sports Council, *Floodlit Multi Use Games Areas*. Data Sheet 29. The Sports Council, London.

21
Ancillary work

Gordon Stables

In order to maintain the required slip resistance, traction or porosity of a sports surface it is essential to minimise the likelihood of mud or grass cuttings being taken onto the surface through careful design. All access routes to the playing area, whether from the public highway, car parks or changing/social facilities, should be surfaced with a hard, clean, well drained surface of paving slabs or blocks, concrete or macadam.

Inevitably, outdoor surfaces become dirty from airborne pollution and use. They should be cleaned only in accordance with the surfacing manufacturer's/installers' instructions, provided at the time of installation, in order to sustain any claims which may have to be made under a Contract Warranty. Regular sweeping or washing down of small areas by site staff is relatively simple and specialised machinery is available for hire for synthetic turf or larger polymeric areas.

The area required for storing equipment should not be underestimated. A full sized hockey/soccer pitch used for multi-sport activities may require storage for a pair of full size goals for both hockey (3.66 × 2.13 m or 12 × 7 ft) and soccer (10.97 × 2.44 m or 36 × 8 ft) and three pairs of goals for both five-a-side soccer (5 × 1.22 m or 16 ft 6 in × 4 ft) and mini-hockey (3.66 × 2.13 m or 12 × 7 ft).

Reference and further advice

The Sports Council, *Floodlit Multi Use Games Areas*. TUS Data Sheet 29. The Sports Council, London.

Part V   Sport-specific facilities

22
Stadia★

Geraint John

1 Historic development

The stadium was first produced by the ancient Greeks to fulfil a religious and social need. It was one of a group of buildings in which culminating rites were performed. At Olympia in Greece a huge sanctuary of temples and altars to various deities housed the periodic fetes which accompanied the celebrations of the most ancient and most revered worship, and made this spot the rendezvous for the whole Greek world.

The competitions, which varied in number and nature, began at sunrise with foot races for single runners, pairs or teams of six. Those were followed by wrestling (palms open); boxing and the pentathlon, which comprised contests with discus, javelin, a foot race, jumps and wrestling. All these contests were held in the stadium.

The stadium was the foot racecourse in cities where games were celebrated, and it was eventually used for other athletic performances. It was usually straight at the end used for the starting-place and semi-circular at the other, **1**, and always approx 185 m (600 ft) long, although the actual foot unit varied in length in different states. It was sometimes planned with its length skirting the side of a hill so that the seats could be cut out of the hill slope, as at Olympia, Thebes, Epidauros, and Delphi; or it was constructed on the flat, as at Athens and Ephesus. The stadium at Athens, begun in 331 BC and reconstructed in AD 160 is reported to have accommodated 50,000 spectators.

What is so remarkable about the stadium is its basic similarity to what we know as the same building type today.

The Romans spurned many of the competitive physical sports of the Greeks, although small stadia for foot races formed part of the Roman Thermae, which included pools and gymnasiums. They preferred public displays of mortal combat as they were considered to be good training for a nation of warriors. The oval amphitheatre, with its rising tiers of seats, may be regarded as a compound of two theatres, stage to stage, thus making an auditorium around an elliptical arena, **3**. In addition to their normal purposes, they were also used for naval exhibitions and water-pipes for flooding some of the arenas still exist. The arena, a Latin word meaning sand or beach, was so called because of the sand with which it was strewn to absorb the blood of the combatants. Amphitheatres were a triumph of Roman art and engineering for a combination of theatre and competition. The finest examples include the Coliseums in Rome and Pula.

★The contribution of Harry Faulkner Brown in the preparation of this chapter is gratefully acknowledged

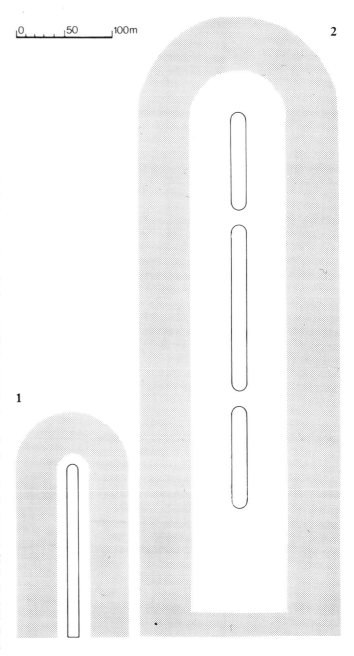

1 *The plan of the Greek stadium was determined by the arena. Rows of spectators were parallel to it. Stadia were sited in valleys to allow raked seating following the ground shape. In Athens the stadium (331 BC) was reconstructed in AD 160 and again in 1896 for the first modern Olympic games.*
2 *The world's largest stadium, the Circus Maximus in Rome, was built for horse and chariot racing. It seated 255,000 spectators in three tiers parallel to the arena*

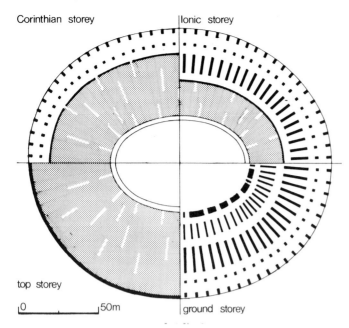

Corinthian storey | Ionic storey

top storey | ground storey

0 ————— 50m

3 *Roman amphitheatres were for displays of mortal combat and were really two theatres (back to back) with viewing tiers of seats forming a continuous grandstand round a central stage or arena (a Latin word meaning sand), so called because sand was used to absorb the blood. The Coliseum (AD 70) has an elliptical arena with seating for 50,000 spectators in four tiers supported on massive raking vaults forming ambulatories, unlike Greek theatres which were excavated to form an auditorium*

The Spanish bull-ring is a direct descendant of the Roman amphitheatre. The Roman circus was derived from the Greek hippodrome. The most notable example was the Circus Maximus, in Rome, an enormous leisure building – an all-seated 255,000 spectator stadium for horse and chariot racing, **2**. It was perhaps the largest stadium ever constructed. Its major phase of construction was begun in 46 BC, and the structure was about 660 m long by about 210 m wide (approx 722 yd × 230 yd). The Roman arenas and hippodromes used engineering skills to create structures above ground, using vaults.

At the end of the classical period the stadium as a building type disappeared and in medieval times competitions on foot or horseback were held in open meadows with temporary staging for spectators. Edifices for jousting at the lists were not of a permanent nature.

It was not until the Industrial Revolution in Great Britain and Europe in the 19th Century that spectator sports revived, and the stadium re-emerged to cater for the leisure needs of the industrial society. This was largely in the form of football and rugby grounds, and baseball in the USA. Although cricket had remained a popular spectator sport since earlier times, no significant cricket spectator facilities were built until this time. Substantial spectator grounds for bull-fighting and horse-racing had also been developed.

It was not until the Olympic games were revived in 1896 that the re-emergence of the athletics stadium was seen. The early Greek stadium at Athens was restored for the first Olympic games. With accommodation for about 50,000 people, it follows the same long, narrow shape used by the early Greeks.

The first new purpose built Olympic stadium was built in London in 1908. The stadium accommodated 100,000 spectators, and all the events were accommodated in the central arena. This was followed by the construction of the stadium in Stockholm.

4 *The 1936 Berlin Stadium was converted into a football stadium for the 1974 World Cup, with a column-supported roof*

a

b

5 *The Aztec Stadium in Mexico stacked the tiers for spectators and eventually covered most of them with a cantilevered roof. Photo a: John Adams; photo b: Allsport.*

1.1 Building forms: Olympics

With certain notable exceptions, the occasion of the modern Games seems to encourage a country, its architects and its technologists sometimes to produce vast edifices, often the result of national pride rather than suitability for athletic competition. Nevertheless, it has set the pattern for stadia throughout the world. In Rome, Mussolini tried his hand at the 'nouveau/Greco/Romano-

6 The Olympia Park in Munich of 1972, designed by Gunter Behnisch and Frei Otto, had perhaps the most exciting roof for a stadium since the Coliseum

style'. In 1936 the games were staged in West Berlin, and the stadium which was built expressed, in quite a marked degree, Nazi despotism with all its overwhelming monumentality, **4**. It seated 100,000 and was an extension of a former 60,000-person stadium built in 1913. In 1948 the games were held at Wembley in a stadium which was then already 25 years old. Later, the Finns built a stadium with accommodation for 70,000, not to glorify their country but dedicated to two of their principal athletes. When the next games were held in Melbourne in 1956, the Australians extended their cricket ground so that it could accommodate 100,000 becoming the largest cricket ground in the world. In Rome in 1960 there could be seen the type of development which was to set the pattern for the future. The athletics stadium was in one part of the city and some distance from it Nervi built an elegant football stadium with a sports hall, the Palazzetto, close by, with yet a larger sports hall with spectator accommodation on the outskirts of the city.

The Tokyo games in 1964 caused the Japanese to demolish the stadium which they had built for the 1940 games (which did not take place) and to rebuild the entire edifice. But it is in Mexico in 1968 that we see probably the best example so far of a large football stadium, the Aztec Stadium, **5a**, **b**, built to accommodate 105,000 seated spectators.

The games came back to Germany in 1972, and, with a conscious desire to erase the memories of the heavy monumental architectural expression of the previous Berlin Stadium for the 1936 games, a delightfully elegant roof was thrown over one side of the Munich athletics stadium, **6**. The only major stadium of note in Great Britain was built at Wembley in 1923 and it still houses principal spectator events. It has been considerably modernised in the 1980s and 1990s. Barcelona's Olympic Stadium is also a modernisation of a much older facility.

1.2 Football and sport specific stadia
Stadia or Sports Grounds emerged for specific sports, eg cricket, rugby, baseball and football (soccer and American football). The most common type in Europe was the soccer or football stadium. In many countries, particularly in Great Britain, this created stadia in which spectators were close to the central pitch and a good atmosphere with the crowd. Many of these grounds were developed and modernised 'piecemeal': a number of present stadia have developed in this way, **7**. In the USA the period 1960–1977 saw thirty new stadia built, to cater for American football and baseball. Notable examples are the Oakland Coliseum, the Shea Stadium in New York and the Busch Stadium in St. Louis **8**.

2 The modern stadium
There has been a noticeable change in the facilities required in stadia. In many cases they have been given over to multi-purpose use and, in Europe and the United States, to highly specialised dual-purpose uses.

7 *The Mound Stand at London's Lords Cricket Ground, by Michael Hopkins and Partners, is an example of piecemeal modernisation. It is also an exceptionally fine work of architecture, demonstrating that stadium architecture can be both sensitive to place and history, and beautiful*

In examining the types of existing stadia and the needs which this building type must satisfy, it is necessary to examine the design criteria. To begin with, it is important to try to determine what is·meant by a stadium. A stadium is considered as being a pitch, track for athletics or team competition area with a central space, surrounded by rising, stepped tiers for the accommodation of standing or seated spectators, with coverings that do not, however, cover the field to enclose the whole building.

2.1 European and American developments
In Europe (excluding Great Britain) there has been a tendency for a city to establish its own municipal stadium sometimes for the use of a number of sports clubs. This has been supported by football clubs running their own football pools or lotteries and ploughing back the profits into the game. Often athletics tracks surround the pitch and the conditions for viewing football, ie the spectator/player relationship, is thereby impaired in comparison with a single use stadium.

In North America, there are several different approaches, eg dual-use or stadia for baseball or football; double stadia for baseball and football. There is a move towards single sport purpose-built stadia.

3 Safety in stadia
Provision for the safety of spectators is vital. There have been a number of stadium disasters of many different kinds in recent history which emphasise the importance of this aspect.

In 1964 in Lima in Peru 340 people were killed and 500 injured in a soccer match after the referee disallowed a goal by the home team.

At the Ibrox Stadium in Glasgow in 1971, 66 people died as a result of massive surges on a gangway and staircase towards the end of a football match.

In December 1979 at the Riverfront Coliseum in Cincinnati, fans surged forward before a pop concert and were trapped by the tunnel effect of a large crowd attempting to enter a small space. 11 deaths and a number of injuries resulted.

At the Lenin Stadium in 1982, 340 people were reported to be killed in a crowd crush.

In 1985 a fire in the Bradford Football Ground resulted in 56 deaths.

In 1985 at the stadium in Mexico University, crowds tried to enter the ground through tunnels after the kick-off, but the gates were locked. Ten people died and 70 were seriously injured.

8 *Pilot Field Stadium at Buffalo, New York, fits successfully into its urban surroundings. Photograph by courtesy of HOK Sports Facilities Group, copyright Patricia Layman Bazelon*

The death toll in the Heysel Stadium in 1985 was 38 and 100 were injured when fans rioted.

On April 15 1989, 96 people were crushed to death at the Sheffield Hillsborough Stadium.

More than 40 soccer fans were trampled to death and 50 fans seriously injured in Johannesburg in January 1991 after fighting broke out during a friendly match, when the referee allowed an own goal.

Disasters like these have as much to do with management as design: they are inter-linked.

3.1 Developments in community use

There is much interest in developing football grounds as multi-sports complexes. One effective scheme has been built at Bristol where an indoor bowling rink has been housed at ground level under the stand. At the Sheffield Hillsborough ground, a training hall was built adjacent to the stand. It can be used out of season and in the evenings for large social events, especially since the toilet and refreshment facilities of the stand can be used in conjunction with the training hall. Arsenal in London has a sports hall used by the community. However, training grounds separate from stadia also have potential for community use.

Several courses would appear to be open to football clubs. One is that they might rationalise their position and, wherever possible, jointly use a single stadium. Inter-Milan and AC Milan, for all their deep rivalry, share the giant San Siro stadium, modernised for the 1990 World Cup.

A further alternative is to build additional sports facilities alongside the stadium, not necessarily in emulation of the ancient Greek example (but nevertheless there is a parallel), so that a large number of sports clubs could use all the facilities. This scheme has been developed to some extent both in the United States and in Europe, **9**. Planning guidance in the UK suggests that any available land needs to be used profitably to fund the stadium redevelopments, and also that new stadia should be of benefit to the whole community.

3.2 The future

Some examples in the United States show that by providing additional facilities in conjunction with the stadium the whole family can be encouraged to participate. There are television rooms, small cinemas, saunas, hairdressing suites and plenty of activity space for children.

The fundamental fact about combining other sports and entertainment with a stadium is that by its very nature the structure of a stadium is inflexible. The large cantilever roof, **46**, which is so highly desirable that it has almost become mandatory, requires a substantial structure at frequent centres. It is difficult to inject large covered sports halls or swimming baths under the structure, and one must therefore consider additional accommodation being separate from, but possibly attached to, to the stadium. If this is done, and if space permits, it would seem that allying sports facilities with the stadium is an extremely desirable one.

9 *A site developed with supporting indoor and outdoor facilities*

The stadium is not usually a profitable venture and often needs to be subsidised. There are too few sports facilities which can make a substantial subsidy to the stadium, and if idle stadia are to become well-used and profitable it would seem that the emphasis in the additional accommodation should be on entertainment and commerce as well as sports facilities. Also, if finance is to be raised to assist the improvement of stadia, the marriage of sport with entertainment and the arts should be explored, with perhaps some commercial development to provide extra help.

The ideal situation could be a balance between the users of the stadium and the local authorities with their subsidised sports facilities on one side, and commerce providing the experience and finance for commercial development and entertainment on the other. The whole complex could then become one enormous multi-purpose community centre with the concourses, lavatories and refreshment facilities at the stadium providing some of the needs for large events.

4 Facilities for spectators with disabilities

The importance of sport for people who are disabled, both as participants and spectators, is now well established.

The UK Building Regulations state that the number of places for wheelchair bound disabled people should be 20 or 1% of the total number of seats available to the public, whichever is the greater. In Italy the standard is one place per 400 people, ie 2.5 places per 1000.

10 *An example at Sheffield, England, of good provision for people with disabilities to view the arena. Photo: Geraint John.*

Where possible these places should be covered or have protection from the weather, and be distributed at various locations in the stadium.

4.1 Dimensions and detail

A wheelchair space means a clear space with a width of 900 mm (36 in) and a depth of 1.4 m (approx 5 ft) accessible to a wheelchair user and providing a clear view of the event, 10.

The eye level of disabled people must be taken into account when designing rails, and glazed screens. Each area, however, should ideally measure 1400 × 1400 mm (55 × 55 in) to allow for a wheelchair and seat for an accompanying person. The spaces should not be all together, but generally dispersed among the seating. In the USA, a demountable seat has been designed to accommodate wheelchairs.

Entrance routes should be obvious and not arduous for disabled people. In contrast to almost every other building type, a 1992 study in the UK recommended *separate* entrances for spectators who are disabled.

Changes in level should be kept to a minimum and designed to blend into the landscape and building.

Other factors which need to be taken into account are:

- Ramps, not kerbs and steps
- Ramps should not be steeper than 1:20 and have a clear width of at least 1200 mm (47 in). Ramps may be steeper, up to a 1:12 slope, but then they must have landings. In the UK details are set out in the approved Document of the Building Regulations.
- Adequately wide doors, gates and corridors
- Adequate adjacent parking
- Information signs
- Toilet provision
- Access to refreshment areas and other amenities.

Complementary to carefully planned escape routes for spectators who are disabled is a well rehearsed management procedure for an emergency.

Arrangements should be made with management for stewards to marshal disabled spectators and to supervise their safe exit. BS 5588, the primary reference in this subject in the UK, stresses the importance of staff training and programmed fire drills. For example, discarded wheelchairs could be a real hazard to escape routes.

4.2 Other safety factors

In addition to the design criteria mentioned in this section, there are many other factors which need to be considered:

- Good co-ordination between security and emergency services, and club and stadium management. Good communication with the control room.
- Efficient devices for addressing the crowd.

5 Stadia briefing guide

5.1 Design of building volume

General Data

Status of commission	Feasibility study	Former studies or schemes, board resolutions, local authority requirements
Finances	Establish financial constraints, capital ceilings, revenue effect	Income present and projected must be estimated
Programme	Planning timetable, building commencement date, target date for completion of project, close season considertions	Can determine phasing, and financing

Objectives

Compactness	To provide good visibility of central area from every part of the stadium	Check viewing distances, need for proximity and whether a running track should be incorporated
Cafe/Restaurants/Catering	For participants, spectators and disabled	
Convenience	So that it is well located for all types of transportation, accessibility to stadium from neighbourhood and movement within stadium easy and unrestricted	
Comfort and safety	So that a civilised, safe and inviting environment is provided	
Flexibility	So that the arrangement of spaces within the stadium and their relationship to each other should enable management to use the stadium for a variety of purposes and so that a phased development is possible	
Economics	In initial capital expenditure and recurring maintenance costs	

Client's requirements	Statement of all accommodation	Spectator, participant, media, management
Movement	Bus, car and pedestrian, rail	Public and private vehicles into and close to stadium
Capacity	Seated (and standing where appropriate)	Careful assessment with trends considered
Services	Present and future	To serve phased development
Phasing	Options, flexibility, expansion	To consider unknown pattern of use and finance
Safety and control	Determine police and stewarding requirements	

Site considerations

Investigation and survey	Old site, old stadium, new site	General land use and historical records, accurate topographical and mining survey
Accessibility	Access, egress, crowd safety, pedestrians, cars, coaches, disabled	Convenience and safety
Constraints	Boundaries, roads, buildings, miscellaneous	Check with planners and deeds of property
Orientation	Sun penetration, micro-climate	For the benefit of pitch drying and spectator and player comfort
Site difficulties	Identify	Stability of sub-soil, water table, other abnormalities
Site advantages	Is there potential for shared use with other users?	Other sports, entertainment, commerce
Car parking	On site, near site, remote from site	Check with planners
Relationship to adjacent buildings	Consider visual and practical implications	Consult planners and local services

5.2 Accommodation

Spectators

Capacity	Determine proportion of types of seats (and standing places where applicable)	To give flexible arrangements
Filling and emptying stadium	Fill slowly, empty in 8 minutes or less	Requirement of National Criteria
Seating area	Determine location and type and gangways	Requirement of National Criteria
Toilet facilities	Convenient to spectators and catering amenities	Ratio acceptable to licensing authority
Restaurants and refreshments	Disposed around ground convenient for spectators	Determine management policy
First aid rooms for spectators	One per small stadium, several in convenient locations in large stadium. Perhaps central major facility	
Concourse	Spectator concourse for ease of movement and access to toilets and refreshments	Unrestricted where possible
Disabled people	Consider spectator facilities for disabled people together with refreshment facilities	

Participants

Playing field/ central area	Size of pitch, protective measures for pitch, ancillary pitch. Athletics facilities.	Check with Club, especially manager, covers against weather. Consider warm up facilities for athletes
Areas for trainers and reserve players	Seats at edge of pitch with no obstruction to the view of spectators	'Dug-out' trainer's bench, protected from spectators

Team rooms	Changing, showers, baths, massage, toilets and treatment rooms and kit store and laundry	Check with manager and trainer
Access from changing to playing field	Tunnel or protected access segregated from spectators	Separate corridors from team rooms joining before exit near edge of pitch
Referee, umpires and linesmen	Changing, showers, toilets	Near team rooms

Media

Press	Location, number of seats for reporters and photographers	Scale depends on local, national or international requirements
Radio	Location, number of cabins for announcers	Scale depends on local, national or international requirements
Television	Location, number of cabins for announcers and interview studios	Scale depends on local, national or international requirements
Media support facilities	Catering, rest rooms, interview and briefing/conference rooms	

Management

Administration section	Size and location	Offices for general and team managers, secretary, accounts and development association
Directors	Suite and box	Board Room, guest rooms and toilets with immediate access to box
Vice Presidents/ Sponsors	Club and seating area	Closely associated with each other
Ground staff	Changing rooms, toilets, stores for equipment and supplies	At any part of the ground, but check with manager
Private viewing boxes	Number, location and type	Preferred location at front of first tier
Public restaurants/ catering	Size and location	See management strategy or policy
Private car parking	Directors, shareholders, team cars and visiting team Parking also required for television vans	Limited by location of stadium

5.3 Building services

General

Type of system for heating	Central boiler plant or local unit. Consider emergency back-up facilities	Direct-fired warm air or radiant systems find most application in small, low-cost schemes, low pressure hot water in larger schemes should be near main load centres so that distribution runs are short
Location of plant	Basement, ground level or roof	
Fuel	Gas, oil, coal, electricity, solar energy	Solar energy is still at the development stage and can only be a secondary system
Space requirements	Fuel storage, meters, heating plant, ventilation, plant, domestic water plant, main switchboard, emergency lighting, workshop area, spares storage	
Thermal considerations	Levels of structural insulation, zoning heat energy	Separate circuits can aid control and save energy, and are often necessary for performance in different areas
Fire requirements	Sprinklers, fire alarms, emergency lighting, hose reels etc.	

| Cleaning | Water and power supplies. Storage of materials. | Convenient and appropriate concealed locations for cleaning equipment at different areas |
| General installations | Power points, clocks, GPO and internal telephones, public address, electric score-board, tv security monitoring, alarms | |

Ancillary

General

Apart from the following ancillary building services, lighting, heating, ventilation and acoustics of internal spaces are not specialised	Standards for playing, television and international matches	Determined principally by needs of colour television. Discuss with television company their requirements for television for colour outside broadcasts
Floodlighting Illuminated indicator board	Conspicuous location, adequate size lettering	One end or both ends
Pitch heating	Electric, hot water, hot air	Economics need to be evaluated
Stands heating	Under seat radiation, slab warming by hot water or air	If economically feasible
Concourse	Heating, ventilation and lighting for comfort, relief at intervals and participation in refreshments	
Telephone exchange	To meet management and media needs	Varies with standards of competition
Communications	Crowd control by management and police Public telephones at distributed locations	Check with police

11a shows a diagrammatic approach to access by the different user divisions of the stadium. **11b** shows the circulatory routes for players, performers and competitors.

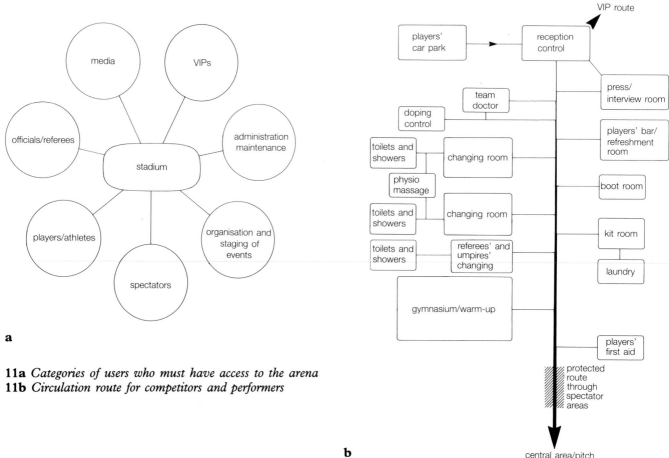

a

b

11a *Categories of users who must have access to the arena*
11b *Circulation route for competitors and performers*

6 Types of stadia

6.1 General

The design of a stadium is dictated very largely by the anticipated type of activity, or activities, and by the number of spectators to be accommodated. The outcome can be seen as a real and easily recognisable response to needs.

Later considerations will attempt to identify the varying factors. At this point it is worth investigating the various types of stadia and some of their characteristics. The intention of this examination is to limit consideration to the activities of athletics, football (American and soccer) and rugby (union and league). Tennis and cycling, cricket and baseball have their own particular requirements.

6.2 Football, rugby and athletics

The plan of all stadia is determined first by the regulation size of the activity and auxiliary areas, ie the pitch or track on which the activity takes place and its necessary surrounding areas for linesmen, plus the need to place the first row of spectators for adequate viewing. The activity space is bounded by the first row of spectators. The outer edge of the plan of the stadium is determined by the desired capacity. Pitches are rectangular for football and rugby, 12a, b, while for athletics the rectangle is increased by semi-circular ends, 12c. A football pitch can be inscribed within an athletics track. There is a conflict between the best viewing conditions for athletics and those for football, however, in a joint use stadium.

With the exception of different sized rectangles, there is no conflict or difference between stadia for rugby and football, with the possible exception of the preferred spectator positions. These are along the touchlines rather than the goal lines for rugby, with less emphasis on this aspect in football. However, an athletics stadium has preferred spectator positions along the straight, and particularly on the home straight and sprint lane side. Further differences lie in the intensity of interest of spectators. For football and rugby, it is assumed to be sustained for the duration of the game, with a very short mid-game interval. The more relaxed involvement at athletics meetings, when the intensity of interest is spasmodic and occurs principally at the end of an event, is usually extended over a much longer period.

Participant requirements are also different – football and soccer need changing rooms, showers and massage rooms for the teams and officials, perhaps 40 persons, whereas athletic events can attract about 1000 participating athletes. The athletes also require warming-up and assembly areas (perhaps under cover) near the stadium.

a
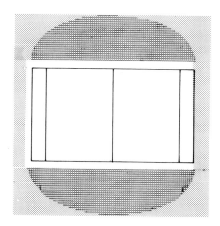

b
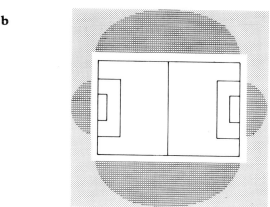

c
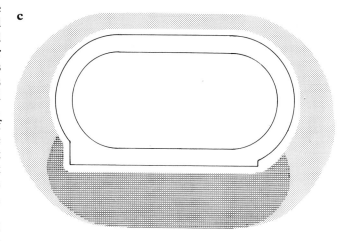

12 *Changes in the needs of sports and spectator activities have produced new shapes for arenas. There are clear differences in preferred locations for spectators viewing rugby a, football b, and athletics c.*

7 Design aims

7.1 Zones of stadium design

Stadium design can be broken down into four main zones, as shown in 13. These zones can be helpful in considering a plan of safety.

- Zone 1 The central playing area and secondary safety area.
- Zone 2 The spectator viewing areas and internal circulation area.
- Zone 3 The zone outside the spectator and internal circulation areas, but inside the perimeter fence. This is the temporary safety zone.
- Zone 4 The zone outside the perimeter fence. This is the permanent safety zone.

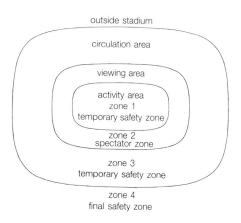

13 *Design for safety may be aided by dividing the entire area into four main zones*

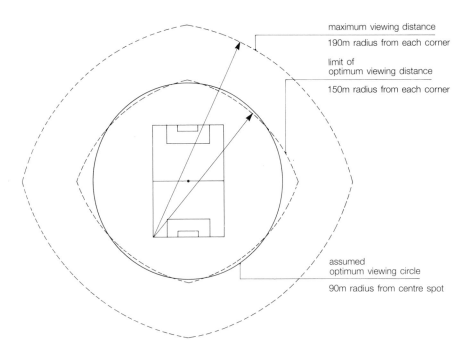

maximum viewing distance
190m radius from each corner

limit of
optimum viewing distance
150m radius from each corner

assumed
optimum viewing circle
90m radius from centre spot

14 *The absolute maximum viewing distance for football is 190 m (approx 208 yd) but the practical maximum is about 150 m (164 yd). An optimum viewing circle can be assumed at 90 m (approx 98 yd) from the centre spot for both football and rugby*

For smaller stadia where spectators will exit directly onto the exterior from the spectator areas Zones 3 and Zones 4 can be combined. Such small stadia will not justify a perimeter fence and temporary safety zone.

7.2 Objectives
By clearly outlining the objectives at the beginning, a better understanding of the problem is possible. Six broad objectives are normally desirable:

- The stadium should be compact and designed to provide good visibility of the central area Zone 1 from every part of the spectator viewing areas at all times.
- The whole stadium should be safe for users.
- The stadium should be convenient for users: specifically, it should be well located for all types of transportation; accessible from the neighbourhood and movement within the stadium itself should be easy and unrestricted.
- Spectator and participant accommodation should to be comfortable so that a more civilised and inviting environment is provided.
- The stadium should be flexible in use, ie the arrangement of spaces within the stadium and their relationship to each other should enable management to use the stadium for a variety of purposes. The objective of flexibility also impinges on the design of the structure, which should be developed so that extensions can be added conveniently in an easy, logical and economic way as needs change and finance becomes available.
- The stadium should be economical in initial capital and recurring maintenance costs.

7.3 Compactness
There are two interesting aspects about this objective which affect the design. The first is the limit of viewing distances, the second is the influence of preferred viewing locations related to the activity arena.

In all activities involving spectators, the relationship between spectator and performer is crucial, eg in a theatre it is vital that the action can be clearly heard and seen. For full appreciation the audience should be able to distinguish facial and bodily expressions and must therefore be close enough to the stage to be able to identify the subtleties of the acting.

A central pitch or an athletics field, though much larger, is similar and the arena of activity is just as much a stage as in a theatre. An appropriate relationship between audience (spectators) and actors (participants) is vital.

Viewing distances
The limit of viewing distance is determined by the ability of the spectator farthest from the activity to be able to distinguish the smallest moving object: in the case of football and rugby, this is the ball; in athletics, it is usually the runner, particularly as he or she approaches the finish line, though the javelin and other events are important.

The human eye can just distinguish objects subtending an angle of one minute of arc at the eye. Its physiology is such that it can only differentiate, to any degree, objects subtending an angle of at least four minutes of arc at the eye. This results in a maximum viewing distance for football of 189.7 m (approximately 190 m or 208 yd). This is much too great for good viewing since the perception of ball and body movement is poor and must be regarded as the absolute maximum. A better limit is about 150 m (164 yd). This figure is based on a study of a number of football stadia. Viewing distances can be applied to the extreme corners of the pitch, **14**, from which arcs can be described. Their average configuration suggests a circle struck from the centre spot at a radius of 90 m. It is described as the 'circle of optimum viewing' and is used to test a number of examples, **15** to **25**.

Preferred viewing locations
The other factor is the desire spectators have for preferred viewing locations. This can change substantially the plan of the stadium. Spectator accommodation which is in rows parallel to the side lines or touchlines and close to the pitch is self-obscuring. Unless care is taken with sight lines, spectators near a corner of the pitch will have difficulty in seeing the other corner on the same side because the view will be obscured by adjacent intervening spectators. Failure to provide an unobstructed view encourages them to stretch and strain and so generate dangerous pressures within the crowd. Viewing can be much improved by setting back the first row of specta-

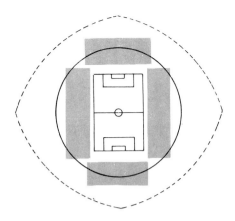

15 *Rectangular arena with separate rectangular stands, parallel to the edge of the rectangular arena but without using the corners for viewing, are quite common*

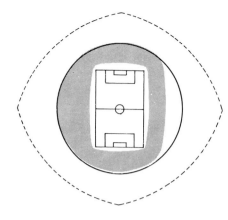

18 *Curved grandstand parallel to quadric arena with curved corners and west side extended back to limit of optimum viewing. If the area of accommodation is too large the advantage of viewing to the east with the sun behind can be achieved*

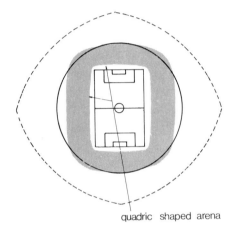

quadric shaped arena

16 *Curved grandstand parallel to quadric arena with curved corners (football). The ancient Greeks curved the seats of the arena in plan with about a 3 m (approx 10 ft) chord of a 200 m (approx 219 yd) arc. A number of modern stadia have adopted this improvement to give a quadric-shaped arena, for instance the Aztec Stadium in Mexico*

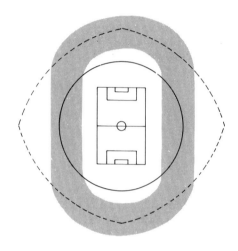

19 *Wembley Stadium*

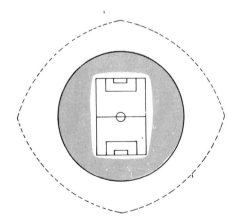

17 *Curved grandstand tiers parallel to quadric area following optimum viewing circle. A quadric shape is preferred for the arena. The consequence is that step and seat lines, being parallel, are also quadrics in plan. The most economical plan then becomes a series of concentric quadrics with the external limit a giant quadric, as in Mexico. A more desirable plan shape can be achieved by limiting the extension to the optimum viewing circle. This gives a very good relationship of spectator to player, and various seating arrangements are possible*

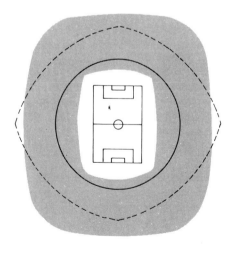

20 *The Aztec Stadium, Mexico City, also has a large arena but is quadric in plan. Most of the spectators' space (105,000 seats) is not within the circle of optimum viewing and too much is not within the maximum viewing distance. The stadium, built in 1966, was designed exclusively for football competitions; the spectator area has subsequently been roofed.*

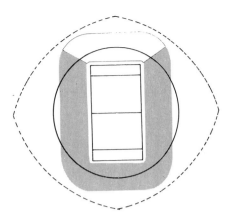

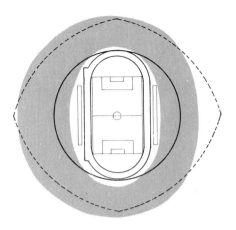

21 *The Welsh National Rugby Stadium in Cardiff. When fully developed the stadium will have the majority of the spectator space within the optimum view circle. Pitches for rugby are larger than for football; but if it is assumed that for viewing purposes the two different balls are dimensionally similar, then the optimum viewing circle applies equally to both*

24 *The Olympic Stadium in Munich was designed primarily for athletics. The perimeter closely follows the lines of maximum viewing distance with the depth of seating at a maximum along the sprint lanes and finish line*

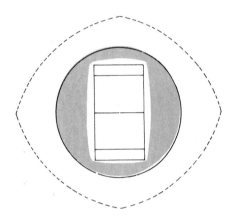

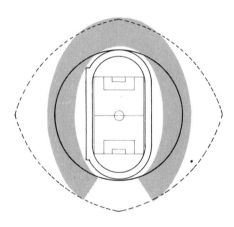

22 *Curved grandstand tiers parallel to quadric arena following optimum viewing circle for rugby. To gain advantage from viewing distances, tiers may become necessary to achieve an optimum spectator/player relationship*

25 *At the Dusseldorf Stadium (see also **9**) most spectators are outside the circle of optimum viewing for football*

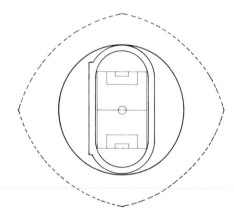

23 *Athletics and football; viewing for athletics alone is straightforward but the track cuts the circle of optimum viewing for football. It can be seen that the two segments left can still accommodate many spectators*

tors and curving the rows in plan as in the ancient Greek stadia. Each of these is helpful individually and together they become very beneficial. The resultant shape is a quadric or oval plan. The minimum distance recom-

mended by FIFA from the touchline to the wall or moat of the spectator area is 6 m (approx 20 ft); from the goal line it is 7.5 m (approx 25 ft).

Another factor affecting good viewing is orientation. An attempt should be made to give both teams, as nearly as possible, identical lighting conditions. In the Northern hemisphere League Football is generally played on winter afternoons or at night. The pitch or arena should therefore lie with its long axis running north/south. Naturally spectators prefer to view the game with their backs to the sun, thereby suggesting an asymmetric plan with the bulk of spectator accommodation to the west of the pitch, **18**. It is in this stand that the majority of the ancillary accommodation is usually best located. Seats for directors, the press, television reporters and crowd controllers are usually here. It is also logical to house the suites for the team manager and players below this stand.

Many single-storey stadia of large capacity have been built. At the University of Michigan football stadium in Ann Arbor, Michigan, built in 1927, for example, in a single tier there is capacity for 101,000 in 90 rows. Binoculars would be necessary in almost half the stadium for ideal viewing. Overlapping the tiers of spectator accommodation is an obvious method of reducing substantially the maximum viewing distance, **32**, and several multi-tiered grandstands have successfully improved the spectator/participant relationship.

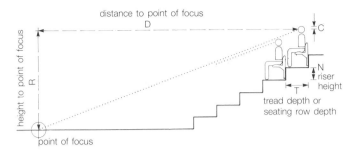

26 *Illustration of terms for calculating a suitable rake; see also* **34**

The following guide lines are suggested for C values:

- 150 mm (6 in) is an ideal standard capable of giving excellent viewing conditions
- 120 mm (approx 5 in) should be the optimum standard arrived at for most spectators, giving very good viewing
- 90 mm (approx 4 in) should be regarded as the working minimum as a viewing standard
- 60 mm (approx 2 in) is a standard which means that good viewing can only be achieved between the heads of spectators in the row in front. In very large stadia, there may be some positions where this is the best

7.4 Sight-lines and rake of spectator tiers

The rake of spectator tiers is determined either mathematically or graphically in section, where the principal factors are the assumed constant of 'the crown', ie the distance from the eye to the top of the head which is known as the C value, and the following variables:

- the tread depth or seating row depth
- the point of focus (the middle of the innermost athletics track or the near touchline in football or rugby)
- the height of the spectator's eye in the first row, **26**.

In determining the rake, the lines of sight from the eyes of spectators in each row to the focus should be clear of, or at worst tangential to, the top of the head of the spectators in the row in front. This will give a profile which is parabolic, with the rake increasing with the viewing distance. In some countries, this is considered to be uneconomic to construct and unsafe for crowd movement – the stairs in gangways become unequal and therefore unacceptable. Nevertheless the parabolic approach is acceptable in some countries and was used at the Munich Olympic Stadium.

A straight rake with the necessary elevation between steps will be satisfactory. However a series of straight rakes tangential to the theoretical parabolic curve is practical and widely used, **27**. The effect of lowering the eye level of the front spectator is quite significant. A number of illustrations of comparative sections of existing stadia shows how varied solutions can be, **28** to **33**.

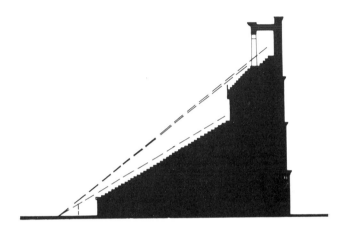

28 *Section through the Coliseum, Rome*

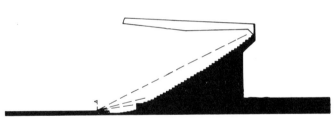

29 *At Dortmund a few rows of perimeter standing terraces are divided from a long curved seating tier. Many seats fall outside the circle of optimum viewing; overlapping tiers would have helped*

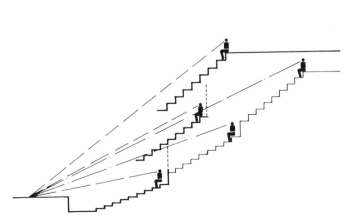

27 *Three straight tiers approximately tangential to the theoretical curve in a single tier is economical in cost but not in space. Separating and overlapping the tiers reduces plan area. Angle of rake must not exceed 35° to the horizontal*

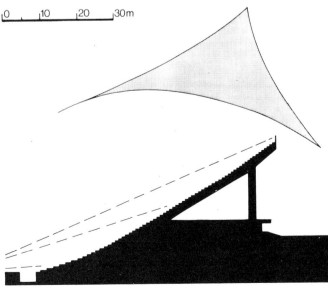

30 *The stadium at the Olympia Park, Munich (see also **6** and **43**) is an example of a single very long curved tier*

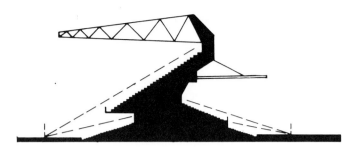

31 *At Cardiff Arms Park overlapping tiers are arranged to bring the highest spectators closer. The National Stadium is on the left; the Cardiff Rugby Club Single tier stand is tucked under the larger structure – an interesting solution to two adjacent fields*

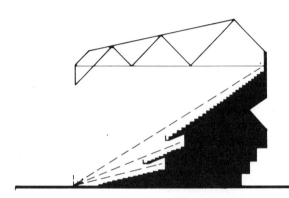

32 *To economise on the distance from the arena to the periphery of the stand, overlapping straight tiers are used at Chelsea*

33 *In a circular multi-storey tiered stadium in San Diego, the distance from the arena is not satisfactory*

standard which can be achieved from some seats, but wherever possible these should be kept to the minimum.

Riser heights
Viewing standards will be affected by the riser height of each seating row.

The following calculation, **34**, is used to determine the riser height:

$$N = \frac{(R + C) \times (D + T)}{D} - R$$

Where:
N = riser height
R = height between eye and point of focus
C = viewing standard, ie the C value

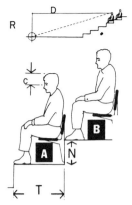

Note that the figures R, D & T for position **A** are used to determine the riser height N for position **B**

34 *Calculation of riser height*

D = distance from eye to point of focus (typically the near touchline)
T = tread depth, ie depth of seating row

'8 Seating

In the move towards all-seated major stadia, it is important to give some consideration to the seat where spectators will spend some time.

The time for sitting in the seat will vary with the stadium type. The following are some examples:

Cricket	All day, perhaps even more than one day
Football	1.5–2 hours
Rugby	1.5–2 hours; for seven-a-side tournaments perhaps all day
Pop concerts	3 hours or more
Athletics	Sometimes all day, eg Olympics
American Football	3–4 hours

The need for comfort will vary. Multi-purpose stadia need to be quite flexible in this matter.

Outdoor stadia seats need to be weather-resistant, robust and comfortable to sit on. Suitable materials include aluminium, some timbers and the most common material for modern stadia, some form of plastic. This latter material has the greatest potential for moulding and shaping for comfort.

Fire retardance also needs to be taken into account. With plastic, additives can be introduced but they often limit colour choice and sometimes will add only delay to fire resistance.

The design of a plastic seat is as critical as the material itself, regarding fire resistance. Double skin forms avoiding edge material details which can catch fire easily are also important.

The life of a seat should be considered as about twenty years.

Colours are important and can add to management of the stadium by colour blocks. The colour of a seat can also be important when the stadium is partially empty. One approach is to use a varied pattern of colours which give a random effect and help to reduce the feeling of emptiness when the stadium is partially full.

35 *Fold-up type seat*

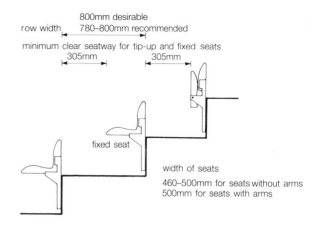

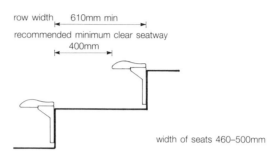

36 *Spacing between fold-up types seats (top) and between benches (bottom). Benches without backs allow closer spacing but are less comfortable and are becoming less acceptable for that reason*

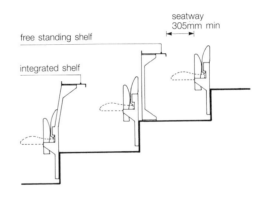

37 *Two options for press box seating: integrated writing shelf or free-standing shelf*

Some colours will also withstand loss of colour by ultra violet rays better than others and designers must take this into account.

The seat must be designed to drain and not hold water.

The seat must be easy to clean. This is important to deter vandalism, as users will respect a clean seat. Cleaning around and under the seat must be easy. Fixing must be designed with this in mind: in general, the fewer floor fixings the better.

The fixings must be corrosion resistant and robust. Spectators will occasionally stand on seats, or rest their feet on them from behind, exerting considerable force.

In existing stadia, the floor construction will limit the fixing choices available, particularly in older facilities. This can be an important factor in re-equipping an existing stadium with seats, because of the large number of fixing points involved.

8.1 Forms of seating
The quality of the seating will vary depending on the use, but also to produce a range of seats available in the stadium. Standards of comfort demanded by users tend to be rising.

Better quality seating will be on individual seat basis probably with backs.

In this case the seat will inevitably be designed with a seat which folds back when not in use, **35**. This increases the seat gangway, providing greater convenience and greater safety. VIP seating will require even higher standards in selected areas.

Cheaper seating can be provided by the use of benches or seats with no backs. This can result in a more economical spacing between rows of seats, **36**.

8.2 Comfort and event usage
Upholstered versions of standard seats are widely available, while some clubs may wish to upgrade their existing standard seating with the addition of back pads and cushions or full covers.

Armrests cannot usually be added to existing standard seats.

If the stadium is to be used for events other than football – for example, pop concerts, American football, public gatherings – it may be worth considering higher grade seats in sections where customers will sit for a longer period than 90 minutes, perhaps at higher admission prices.

8.3 Press box seating
Several ranges of seats can be supplied with integrated writing shelves or tablets for use in the press box, **37**.

However, it is necessary to consult with regular press box users to determine how much space they may need for computers, monitors, telephones, fax machines or other equipment, **54**.

Note that the requirement for a minimum seatway of 305 mm (12 in) applies in this case to the distance between the rearmost projection on the shelf and the front of the seat, **37**.

9 Safety

9.1 Convenience of location and parking
A stadium made convenient for users should be easily accessible with inviting approaches and unconstrained routes. The convenience of access depends on many factors, the principal ones being the capacity and location (urban, suburban or rural).

a

b

38 *Car parking requirements may pose an enormous problem. San Diego Stadium, a, shows one type of solution on a green-field site. In an urban location this would not be possible and Cincinnati Stadium, b, shows an example of a stadium built over a vast car park*

39 *An external (or internal) ambulatory should permit spectators to walk unimpeded around the entire stadium and give access to evenly disposed turnstiles (zone 4)*

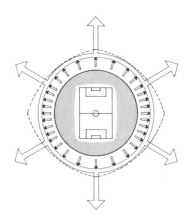

40 *Exits should allow the ground to be cleared in not more than eight minutes*

a

b

41a, b *Sydney football stadium showing an unusually elegant flowing structure. Architect Philip Cox; structural engineer Ove Arup and Partners. Photo a: Ove Arup and Partners; photo b: Allsport*

A new or rebuilt stadium in an urban location is a difficult planning problem. One of the first decisions to be taken in conjunction with the local authority planners is whether or not public transport is close by, and if not, whether it can reasonably be changed to cope with a regular large surge of spectators, perhaps every second Saturday in the case of football. In a tight urban area a further decision is needed at the outset on car parking, **38**. Should or could the area accept a massive car park? A German guideline suggests one car space to every four spectators. For more general use, and in countries where car ownership may be lower, FIFA recommends that 10,000 car spaces should be provided for a stadium of 60,000 spectators; this is one car space per six spectators. FIFA also recommends that 500 bus places should be provided for 60,000 spectators, ie one bus space per 120 spectators.

42 *Stadio Sao Paulo, Napoli. Photo: Allsport/Olympia*

44 *Saddle Dome, Calgary shows an elegant and functional structure, clearly expressed externally. Photo: Geraint John*

43 *Stadium at Olympia Park, Munich, designed by Gunter Behnisch and Frei Otto. Photo: Allsport/David Cannon*

45 *In hot climates shelter against the sun will be needed for spectators, as in this elegant stadium in Australia*

An alternative approach is to limit the access for vehicles to team members, directors and shareholders and the media, restricting the number to say 200, with general car parking in a series of locations disposed in an annular arrangement some distance from the stadium with a park and ride system from those beyond reasonable walking distance. If spectators are expected to walk to the stadium from their car park space, it should be no further than 1 mile (1.6 km).

As pedestrian traffic approaches the stadium there is much to be said for segregating it from vehicular traffic and immediately surrounding the building there should be a clear circulation space (Zone 4) to allow spectators to walk unimpeded around the entire stadium, 39. Clearly visible on the perimeter of this ambulatory there should be regularly spaced turnstile positions, sufficient in number to admit spectators at a rate fast enough to avoid large admission queues and yet slow enough for their comfortable distribution within the ground, 40. The turnstiles should in addition control the dispersal of spectators within a stadium to their chosen sections. Experience has shown that one turnstile should be provided for every 800 spectators. Ticket sales can be provided by separate booths external to Zone 4.

9.2 Comfort

Comfortable stadia are needed. Designers should concentrate on warmer, less windy, better-equipped buildings. Toilet and refreshment facilities, although used for a very short time must be to a high standard.

Protection from the weather has had a considerable influence on the design of stadia, 41 to 44. In some countries a sunshade is necessary, 45. In Europe shelter from the wind and rain are high priorities, 46. Completely covered spectator accommodation is advisable, particularly where seated.

Covering the spectators has a marked effect on the plan of the stadium. Athletics stadia are generally used in the

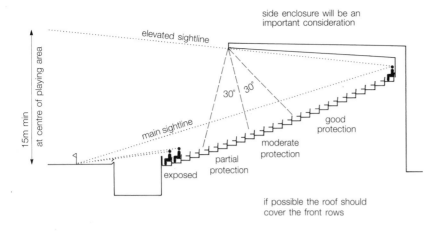

46 *In northern Europe protection against rain and wind are the priorities. The diagram indicates general standards, but prevailing winds will have a major effect and must be taken into consideration*

47 *Crystal Palace stadium in south London is minimally covered. Photo: Bill Toomey*

summer and there is not the same necessity for protection from the weather. This is clearly demonstrated at Crystal Palace, London, **47**, Sheffield, Don Valley and Munich, **43a**. Cantilevered roof structures are preferred since it is unacceptable for columns to obstruct the spectator areas. Column-free grandstands are possible without a cantilevering roof if a wastage of viewing space is accepted at the corners. A column at each end of a grandstand supporting a deep truss parallel to the touchline has been used at Aston Villa football club and Ibrox Stadium in Glasgow.

9.3 Flexibility

It is very difficult within a compact layout to accommodate space for anything other than the areas needed for

the proper functioning of the stadium itself. However, if additional facilities for recreation, entertainment and commerce are built adjacent, the stadium toilet, refreshment and ancillary areas can be used in conjunction with them.

A possible different use of the stadium could be achieved by erecting a stage on part of the arena with a limited amount of spectator seating and back-up facilities in a proper relationship with each other. This could have particular appeal for pop festivals and large scale entertainment, particularly if the seating in the curved corners was so adapted.

Covering a natural grass pitch for spectators for pop concerts is possible on a short-term basis (say two days

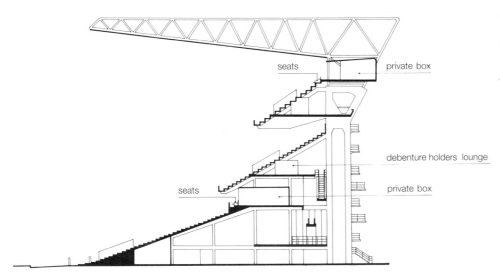

48 *The north stand at Twickenham Rugby Football Ground, near London, showing the location of private viewing facilities*

at the most, although new systems being developed may be able to cope with more). This cover system should be stored adjacent to the stadium.

Such multi-purpose use must also consider the capacity of toilets, refreshment facilities and other amenities to cope.

9.4 Economy

The cheapest stadium is not necessarily the best. It might not suit the exact requirements of the site or the client, nor fit into a comprehensive development scheme, which of course should be considered from the outset. The stadium is very much exposed to the weather and careful choice of materials will be vital if maintenance costs are to be kept to a minimum. An economic solution would be for a stadium to be located, where possible, in a natural bowl in the ground needing minimum excavation. Part of the superstructure can then be erected as necessary. This was done at the Olympic Stadium in Athens and the Don Valley Stadium in Sheffield.

Naturally, a single tier is more economic than a multi-tiered solution, but if a cantilevered roof to cover the full depth of tiers from the arena to the farthest spectator is a necessary requirement, the smaller it is the lower the initial capital cost. A multi-tiered solution goes some way to meet this if there is a substantial overlap in tiers. The North Stand at Twickenham, London is an example, **48**. It also accommodates private boxes at intermediate levels.

9.5 Floodlighting

Present requirements need to meet three standards. The first is that the floodlighting scheme should be designed to allow football, athletics, or other relevant sports, to be seen adequately by the spectators. The second is that the amount and quality of light is suitable for colour television. The third is that the level of lighting be up to the very high standards required by FIFA for international football competitions or the International Olympic Committee, where appropriate.

The merits of corner tower systems and sidelighting systems must be considered. The favoured system at present is to mount lighting along the front edge of the stadium roof, if the roof is high enough on both sides. However this solution may not be so suitable for athletics. Manufacturers of floodlights now have a great deal of reliable information on this matter.

9.6 Stadium roof structure

The roof structure of a stadium is often architecturally one of the most important features, **49**.

49 *The roof becomes very large when covering spectators surrounding an athletics field in Dusseldorf*

The reasons for providing a roof are:

- To protect spectators from rain and snow, eg in Europe, North America and other inclement parts of the world where much of the activity takes place in winter.
- Protection from the sun in hot countries. The roof is obviously an expensive feature and in many parts of the world, stadia are largely open, but increasingly spectator comfort universally requires some sort of cover.
- In some parts of the world, particularly the USA, stadia are entirely covered, including the pitch or central area itself, **50**. This presents a choice in the state of current technology of playing surfaces: most stadia want a natural grass surface but permanently covered stadia must use some kind of artificial surface. The technology of moving grass in and out is as yet unproven.

Movable roof structures for stadium roofs are possible technologically, but expensive. Examples include the Toronto Skydome, which has an ingenious system of sliding roof, and the Montreal Olympic Stadium which had a movable roof pulled up on a cable structure from a very high tower although this solution has been troublesome.

9.7 Translucency of stadium roof

The translucent stadium roof has developed largely because of the problems of overcoming the shadows cast

50 *The Georgia Dome at Atlanta, USA – a recent American example of a completely covered stadium. Designers: Heeny*

by large grandstands. The difference in light value between shade and sunshine causes a real problem for TV cameras.

There was no doubt another reason: there is also an aesthetic appeal of translucent grandstands to give spectators a pleasant feeling of being outdoors.

Examples include the Munich Olympic Stadium, **43b**, Twickenham Rugby Stadium in London, **51**, (North and South stands), Split Stadium in Yugoslavia, **52** and the Don Valley Stadium in Sheffield.

9.8 The effects of wind, sun and weather on the form of the stadium

Roofs over the spectators are provided for protection from wind, sun, rain and snow. However the design of these roofs must be considered from the following points of view:

● The effect on the health and conditions of the grass pitch
● Wind effects within the stadium which may affect both spectator comfort and conditions for play
● Wind effects on the structural design of the roofs.

There are at present no formulae for calculating satisfactory conditions. Therefore it is recommended that designs be studied using models and wind tunnel testing.

The health of the grass pitch has to be considered. It seems that the extensive roofs and increase in size of the Milan Stadium for the World Cup in 1991 created unanticipated problems for the central pitch. The pitch at the Sheffield Bramhall Lane Stadium was moved because of the shadow created by the new stand. Good

conditions demand adequate sunlight and wind conditions. Watering can be provided artificially.

Rudolf Bergermann has written that closed roofs arranged in a circle normally achieve a calming effect on the air inside the stadium: with smaller stadia, eg Turin, unwanted strong winds can occur owing to openings and the 'jet effect'.

The roof should ideally project as far as the front row of spectators. This will not give complete cover: the various levels of protection are suggested in **46**.

9.9 Covered stadia

The use of artificial grass for the central field has meant the development of covered multi-purpose stadia in the USA, Canada and Japan.

The most economical permanent cover is some kind of lightweight membrane. This can be either air-supported, eg the Tokyo 'Big Egg' stadium in Tokyo, or a membrane structure supported by cables.

The 80,000 seat Pontiac Silverdome (1975) demonstrated the effectiveness of large air-supported roofs. A small internal pressure differential (approximately 0.25%) maintains the inflation of a Teflon-coated fibreglass fabric, which can also be provided with a double skin to improve insulation. Steel cables maintain the roof profiles and support the fabric in case of collapse, as happened twice at the Metrodome in Minneapolis (once during construction in 1981, and once in 1982 when workmen were clearing snow from the roof and a large crane bucket punctured the skin). Both were safely repaired. There are arguments for and against fabric roofs, with capital cost savings against longer-term revenue costs and environmental problems.

a   b

51a, b *The south and north stands at Twickenham Rugby Football Ground showing the translucent roofs. Photos: Action-Plus/Tony Henshaw and Husband Design Group*

52 *At Split in Yugoslavia a translucent roof of tinted "Lexan" sheeting has been provided to minimise contrast with the bright sky when events are being televised. Photo: Helen Heard*

Covered stadia with permanent roofs include the Louisiana Superdome with a capacity of 80,000 spectators which has a solid opaque roof, and the Houston Astrodome which has a translucent domed roof.

Montreal and Toronto have created stadia with roofs which can be opened. This is an expensive technical solution but may point the way to future developments of large stadia; but see 9.6 above.

9.10 Perimeter fences between spectators and playing area

There is great controversy over perimeter fences. Inadequate access through such fences has been a contributory factor in accidents and tragedies, eg the Sheffield Hillsborough disaster in 1989.

The purpose of these fences is to prevent spectator access onto the playing area. By and large they will be applicable only to stadia catering for football, although in France they are also found in stadia for Rugby.

Design criteria must include:

- The fence must be robust and capable of withstanding crowd pressures and unclimbable.
- The design should permit the best vision possible through the fence.
- There must be adequate provision for escape through

the fence. This can be achieved in several ways, but whichever method is used it must be as foolproof and as safe as possible.

● Gates must be provided in the fence, with a minimum width of 1.1 m (3 ft 6 in) clear opening, at regular frequencies and in proper locations central to access.
● There are several versions of open fences now possible. These open in emergency, but the following need to be checked:
  (i) Will the fences withstand the loads of crowd pressure?
  (ii) Is the opening mechanism reliable and 'fail safe'?
● Ideally, in a multi-purpose stadium the fences should be removable, eg Wembley. Arguably they are needed only for 'high risk' games.
● After the Sheffield Hillsborough disaster the Inquiry recommended that all fences have adequate escape gates onto the pitch, and these gates must remain open during an event. This requires permanent supervision at each gate.

It is unlikely that permanent perimeter fences which cannot be dismantled will be satisfactory for stadia used for athletics.

9.11 Moats
In the same way as a perimeter fence places a physical barrier between the spectators and the players, moats, **53**, provide a separation by using a sunken area into which spectators must descend before they can then attempt to climb the opposite wall onto the pitch. It is relatively easy to design the pitch side of the moat to be unclimbable and also to police the moat with security staff so that crowd invasion is easily controlled. The moat may serve a further purpose in providing a circulation route around the stadia for officials and security staff to gain access to any part of the viewing terrace easily and quickly. It can also provide a vehicular circulation route for ambulances and emergency vehicles and is used in the Olympic Stadium in Barcelona for circulation by the media. In the past some have even been designed to be filled with water but this is not recommended. The one inconspicuous advantage of the moat is that whilst controlling crowd movement and giving good access for the management of the stadia it does both of these without impeding the spectators' view of the pitch. Its aesthetic qualities are therefore far superior

to those of a perimeter fence. Use of a moat can mean the central playing area is more remote from the spectators by the width of the moat and therefore there may be most justification for their use in larger stadia. In designing a moat a number of design parameters must be taken into account:

● It may be important under emergency circumstances to allow access across the moat onto the playing area and therefore a method of bridging it should be incorporated, either on a permanent or temporary basis.
● A method of gaining access to the pitch for service vehicles must be found by either a bridge, ramp or adjustable platform. In some situations heavy vehicles may be necessary, particularly where the stadium is used as a concert venue when large quantities of stage building materials will be used.
● In addition to allowing the spectators to cross the moat onto the pitch in certain circumstances, access can also be provided for the spectators into the moat if it is to be used for public circulation. In these circumstances correctly designed stairways must be provided at regular intervals around the circumference of the moat to provide egress into the moat and from the moat to the outside of the stadia. This route can be either underneath the tiers of seating or at the corners.
● Dimensions of the moat should be such as to make it impossible for spectators to jump across from the front row of the terrace as well as provide a wide enough escape route if it is to be regarded as a means of egress. In addition to the above requirements, if it is to be used for vehicular access around the stadia by the police, ambulance and other service vehicles, the moat should have a minimum of 2.5 m (8 ft 3 in) clearance.
● The moat may be used to help clean the spectator terraces. An air blower or sweeping of debris and refuse forward can be used with the moat containing rubbish skips so that the waste is deposited directly into the container. The front balustrade should have openings designed at the base to accommodate this.
● Access for players, performers and police onto the pitch should be provided by way of tunnels or covered crossing points directly into dug-outs for the teams, if this is appropriate.
● Kiosks for the sale of refreshments can be provided in the moat under the terrace so that spectators descend into the moat via staircases during the interval.
● FIFA requires the moat to be a minimum of 2.5 m (8 ft 3 in) wide and 3 m (9 ft 9 in) deep with protective barriers on both sides. It should not be filled with water.

A third category which may be a combination of a perimeter fence and a moat can also serve as a barrier. The principle here is to design a moat perhaps only 1.5 m (4 ft 10 in) deep which, when combined with a 1 m (approx 3 ft) high fence on the pitch side will present a significant deterrent to crowd invasion but still provide good access around the perimeter of the pitch for official use. Alternatively the first row of seats can be lifted above the playing area by 1.5 m (4 ft 10 in) or 2 m (6 ft 6 in) which will act as a deterrent but only to the less motivated pitch invader. This is the 'bull ring' method and is often used in the USA where the change of level hides the large number of players, officials and others at the side of the pitch. It does have the disadvantage of hampering the design of sight lines from the seating tier behind, particularly in large stadia.

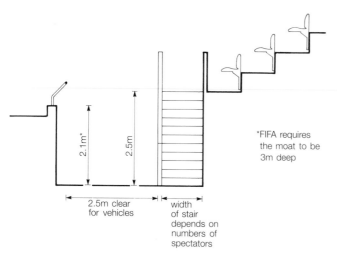

2.1m*

2.5m

2.5m clear for vehicles

width of stair depends on numbers of spectators

*FIFA requires the moat to be 3m deep

53 *Typical 'moat' section to separate spectators from the pitch*

10 Ancillary accommodation

10.1 General
As a rough guide to some of the additional accommodation and other factors to be considered in a stadium, listed below are some of the needs for International and major league football stadia.

10.2 Sponsorship and hospitality boxes
The introduction of private facilities for sponsors is a feature of modern stadia which helps to finance new developments. The principle is simple.

The sponsor buys a box and facilities for a defined period, providing capital and revenue for the stadium. There are a number of types. The favourite sizes are units catering for 10–18 people, but it would be wise to consider partitions which can be opened up to provide a range of accommodation options and sizes. Each box is provided with some kind of kitchen facilities, sometimes within the box but usually also served from a central kitchen. Toilet facilities can be provided individually or collectively, but in both cases to a high standard. Access will need to be private and secure.

The main factors to be borne in mind when developing such facilities are:

- It is an advantage if the access is planned so that they can be used even when events are not taking place. This can provide full use and income.
- A careful balance must be preserved particularly with glass-fronted suites, so that the atmosphere of crowd participation is not damaged. Current opinion seems not to favour a glass fronted box which separates the viewer from the pitch, but to have a private balcony in front of the box, so that spectators sit in the stadium environment, **48**. Variations include access from the boxes onto the grandstand seating itself. This gives greater flexibility of numbers.

10.3 Illumination of stands
Stands, approaches and entrances must be adequately illuminated for evening and winter games. Emergency lighting is essential.

10.4 Toilet facilities
There should be toilet facilities for women and toilets and urinals for men, some of which are to be outside the entrance control turnstiles. The remainder inside the stadium should not be more than 60 m (approx 65 yd) from the spectator stand exits. Some of these can be portable and provided for big events.

10.5 First aid
First aid rooms consisting of a treatment and rest room (15 sq m (16 sq ft)), store room (2 sq m (22 sq ft)) and two toilets, are required for every 20,000 spectators. A central facility can be considered with the other first-aid rooms as outposts, plus drug testing and physiotherapy treatment rooms for players.

10.6 Indicator board
An illuminated indicator board(s) is needed to announce the opposing sides, their teams and the results of other matches.

10.7 Car parking
Sufficient car parking spaces are required close to the stadium connected by public transportation – a 'park and tube stadium'. All car parks should be well-illuminated.

One car space for every four spectators has been suggested (leaving space for coaches on the same basis) with a maximum vehicle distance of 1500 m (approx 1640 yd) from the stadium plus set down/pick up space for coaches.

Spectators must be able to walk unimpeded around the main stadium (outside the control barriers).

10.8 Directors' and guests' box
Guests, VIPs and directors should be seated in a convenient box with at least 100 seats for a major stadium, with a lounge and toilets adjacent. In national stadia, important politicians and Royalty need security of access.

10.9 The pitch
The pitch should be constructed with a 1% gradient. A private ancillary pitch (50 × 90 m (approx 55 yd × 98 yd)) and a covered warming up area close to the changing rooms are required for World Cup and major international competitions. Good drainage is essential. Under pitch heating needs to be considered.

10.10 Team changing
Each team must have at its disposal a changing room (40 sq m (approx 430 sq ft)) and a massage room (10 sq m (108 sq ft)) common to both. The referee and linesmen need a changing room (20 sq m (216 sq ft)) with two showers, at least one WC and one urinal.

10.11 Ancillary services
The fire-brigade, police force and security service each require a room as headquarters. These rooms must be accessible from the concourse and connected with the pitch and spectator stands. Ideally the control room should overlook the pitch. The police room should be linked with CCTV facilities.

In addition, there must be a covered area or supplementary rooms at the disposal of the police and security services to discuss their plans of action.

10.12 The media: radio, TV and press
Press seats with desk tops, **54**, must be provided in the west grandstand (main grandstand). The number of seats should vary according to the importance of the match. For example a World Cup game can require:

- Preliminary round — 400 seats
- Quarter final — 500 seats
- Semi final — 700 seats
- Opening ceremony and final round — 1200 seats on each occasion

Behind each goal line there should be about forty places for photographers. These seats should be planned in such a way that the spectators' view is not obstructed by the photographers.

All TV and radio requirements should be discussed with the national company. Fixed camera platforms for television and film teams have to be provided at positions which have to be agreed with the television companies. Example requirements are:

- Five platforms for television teams
- Eight platforms for film teams

While only one or two cabins are needed generally, the following number of announcers' cabins for radio and television companies must be available at major stadia for international events:

54 *Press facilities are needed in all stadia. Photo: Geraint John*

- Radio: 24 cabins per match (but 40 cabins for the final round)
- Television: 10 to 30 cabins per match until the semi-final; for the final round: 40 cabins.

The following working facilities must be available for the press and they should be favourably situated in the stadium with regard to the press seats mentioned above:

- Preliminary round   Office for 100 persons
- Quarter-final   Office for 150 persons
- Semi-final   Office for 250 persons
- Opening ceremony and   Office for 350 persons
  final round

The necessary space should be divided up into various work areas and consist of desks, 50% of which must have a telephone extension.

For radio and television one or two studios are necessary, which should each accommodate four to six persons to be interviewed and a team of engineers. Each room should measure 40 sq m (430 sq ft). In major stadia, a 100 sq m (1076 sq ft) room in the vicinity of the Press office will be suitable for press conferences.

A telephone exchange, teleprinters, dark room and appropriate wash rooms and toilets must be provided.

11 Requirements for football World Cup

The following is a summary of the FIFA Requirements for the 1998 World Cup which is likely to last between 28 and 35 days.

11.1 Stadia capacity

- for the group matches   30–40,000
- for the opening match,   60–80,000
  semi-finals and finals

Each spectator shall be allotted an individual, numbered seat. The VIP grandstand and working area for the media must be under cover.

11.2 Special requirements

Each stadium shall have a field of play measuring 110/105 by 75/68 m (120/115 × 82/74 yd) and laid with natural turf. Moreover, a minimum space of 7.5 m (approx 8 yd) shall be allowed behind the goal-lines and 6 m (approx 7 yd) along the touchlines:

- To ensure the players' safety
- To accommodate substitutes' benches for photographers
- To allow enough space for ground advertising
- For television cameras

Covered benches shall be provided for:

- Technical staff and officials accompanying each team and for substitutes (seating capacity on each bench for 20 persons)
- Officials supervising the match (three persons)

These benches shall be placed at ground level and not in dug-outs.

The stadia shall have one set of main floodlights and one reserve set which comply with television requirements (1500 lux) plus a modern loudspeaker system.

There shall be a choice of training grounds near the teams' hotels each with a pitch measuring 110/105 m by 75/68 m (120/115 × 82/74 yd) and laid with natural turf in good condition.

11.3 Doping Control

The organising National Association shall provide a dope-testing centre fitted out with modern equipment and qualified personnel.

This centre shall be capable of carrying out the analyses stipulated in the Doping Control Regulations.

A dope-testing room shall be provided close to the players' dressing rooms in each stadium and include:

- A room for the dope-testing officials
- A rest room
- Toilets
- Showers
- A refrigerator.

12 References and further advice

BS 5588: *Fire precautions in the design, construction and use of buildings:*

     Part 1 1990 Code of practice for residential buildings:

     Part 2 1985 Code of practice for shops:

     Part 3 1983 Code of practice for office buildings:

     Part 4 1978 Code of practice for smoke control in protected escape routes using pressurization:

     Part 5 1991 Code of practice for firefighting stairs and lifts:

     Part 6 1991 Code of practice for places of assembly:

     Part 8 1988 Code of practice for means of escape for disabled people:

Part 9 1989 Code of practice for ventilation and air conditioning networks:

Part 10 1991 Code of practice for shopping complexes: BSI, London:

Football Stadia Advisory Design Council, *Football stadia bibliography*, 1980–1990, FSADC, London (1991) £37.50, 172 pp

Football Stadia Advisory Design Council, *Stadium public address systems*, FSADC, London (1991) £12.50, 24 pp

Football Stadia Advisory Design Council, *Designing for spectators with disabilities*, FSADC, London (1992) £15

Football Stadia Advisory Design Council, *Digest of stadia criteria*, FSADC, London (1992) £12.50, 92 pp

Football Stadia Advisory Design Council, *On the sidelines: football and disabled supporters*, FSADC, London (1992) £12.50, 32 pp

Football Stadia Advisory Design Council, *Stadium roofs*, FSADC, London (1992) £12.50

Football Advisory Design Council *Seating: Sightlines conversion of terracing seat types.* Football Stadia Advisory Design Council, London (June 1991). Gives guidance to football clubs and architects on viewing standards for seated spectators, the conversion from terracing to seating and examines the different seat types available.

Football Association, *Crowd safety memorandum: the safety of spectators. The control of crowds at football matches.* Football Association Handbook 1990–91. Football Association, London (1990).

Ford, AJ Home Office Science and Technical Group: Police Science Development Branch (1990) *Guidance notes for the procurement of CCTV for public safety at football grounds* (Publication No. 4/90). London: Home Office, 1990.

Home Office *The Hillsborough Stadium disaster. Inquiry by Rt. Hon. Lord Justice Taylor: Final report.* HMSO, London (1990). Concluded the investigation into the Hillsborough disaster with recommendations on the future of football, including all-seater stadia, the establishment of an Advisory Design Council, and a revision of the Green Guide. Includes recommendations on safety at sports grounds, crowd control and hooliganism, the Football Spectators Act 1989 and the advantages and disadvantages of a national membership scheme.

Home Office, Scottish Office *Guide to safety at sports grounds.* HMSO, London (1990). Gives guidance to ground managements, local authorities and technical specialists such as engineers in order to assist them to assess how many spectators can safely be accommodated within a sports ground used for a sporting event. Also outlines measures for improving safety at existing grounds and covers aspects such as stairways, terraces, barriers, temporary stands, crowd behaviour and perimeter fences.

Inglis, S *The football grounds of Europe.* Willow Books, London (1990). A guide to over 150 grounds in Europe, including every major World Cup and club venue from 33 countries. Looks at the history, design, and architectural development of the grounds and highlights the main features of modern stadium design, particularly the need for increased levels of safety and comfort.

Luder, O (Ed) *Sports stadia after Hillsborough* (Papers presented at the Sports Council/Royal Institute of British Architects Seminar, 29 March 1990). RIBA/Sports Council in association with the Football Trust, London (1990). Papers look at safety issues raised after the Hillsborough disaster, such as the structure of football, the role of regulatory bodies, stadia design, planning and commercial development. Examples are drawn from Wembley, the Ibrox stadium, Italy and the World Cup and the development of stadia in America.

Home Office, *Safety of Sports Grounds Act 1975*, Chapter 52, (Revised edition). HMSO, London (1988). Revision of 1975 Safety of Sports Grounds Act. Omits certain provisions which have now been repealed by the Fire Safety and Safety of Places of Sport Act 1987. Covers safety certificate for large sports stadia.

Shields, A and Wright, M (Ed) *Arenas: a planning design and management guide.* Sports Council, London (1989). Covers all aspects of the design, construction, facilities, costs and management of a modern arena. Includes case studies, products and services guide, bibliography and major sporting events.

Stadia, *Spaziosport*, Volume 8, No 1, (March 1989). Reviews stadia design for the FIFA World Cup from 1978–1986 and the evolution of stadia design. Describes and reviews stadia design for 1990 World Cup in Italy.

The Stadiums of the 1990 FIFA World Cup, *Spaziosport*, Volume 9, No 2 (June 1990). Describes the organisation of the 1990 FIFA World Cup, including issues such as safety, transport services, television facilities. Provides detailed information and diagrams of the twelve stadia used for the event.

23
Pavilions and clubhouses

Peter Ackroyd

1 Introduction

This section relates primarily to playing field pavilions and small clubhouses serving a few pitches for soccer, cricket, rugby and hockey but which could be adapted to other uses. It is intended only to offer an initial guide which is relevant also for outdoor changing provision in local sports centres. Reference should also be made to the sections dealing with sport-specific facilities in both Volumes of this Handbook.

2 Planning considerations

At the outset it is normally desirable to discuss the following points with the local authority and others:

- Multiple use by more than one sport and midweek community activities offers economies and may be

more likely to attract support from grant aiding bodies. Different sports should therefore consider joint projects whenever possible. This will offer the best means of achieving maximum benefit from available resources.

- Location and accessibility
- Aspect and orientation
- Quality of design and choice of structure, 1-3
- Security to counteract vandalism
- Environmental and energy conservation issues
- Site service points for water and electricity, drainage outlets or septic tanks and cesspits, water table level in all seasons. These could affect costs substantially
- Car parking: provide a maximum of one space per two changing places, plus additional spaces for spectators
- Future developments must be considered to allow for an economic link-up, whilst retaining the largest land area for play
- Capital cost and management: the way a facility is to be managed can affect the design. There is little point in spending large sums of money on a pavilion unless it can be utilised effectively and this means well

1 *Christchurch Bowls Club, Dorset, by S Wernick & Sons Ltd. Photo: Paul Reeves Photography*

2 *Southgate Cricket and Hockey Clubs pavilion, Walker Cricket Ground, London Borough of Enfield (Architects: Colin Stansfield-Smith of Emberton Tardrew and Partners). Photo: Richard Einzig*

3 *Charing Sports Club, Kent. The tea and social room roof and canopy reflect the shape of a cricket cap. This clubhouse is also designed to be used by football and hockey teams, tennis players, for social functions and mid-week daytime purposes. The clubroom has also been extended under the canopy. (Architect and photo: Peter Ackroyd)*

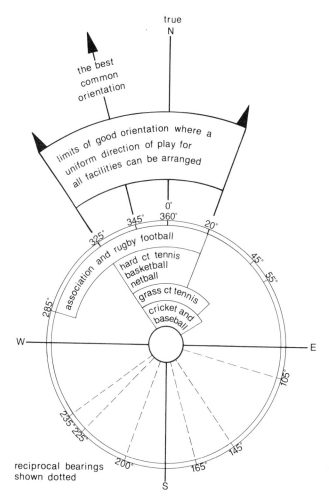

4 *The National Playing Fields Association's pitch and pavilion orientation diagram. Another important consideration is the direction of the prevailing wind; sheltered viewing should be provided if possible. Architectural detailing related to weather protection should be carefully considered to prevent the penetration of damp through doors, windows and junctions*

Notes:

(a) For the purpose of this chart the seasons for the various recreational facilities have been taken as follows:

1 September to 30 April	*Association football, Rugby football*
All the year round	*Hard court tennis, Basketball, Netball*
1 May to 15 September	*Cricket, Baseball, Grass court tennis*

(b) Hockey pitches may be sited in any direction as in this game the ball seldom rises sufficiently for the sun to be a nuisance

(c) Pavilions should avoid the SW to NW aspect (225–315°)

managed. Revenue costs must also be considered at an early stage. Extra capital expenditure may reduce running costs.

3 Aspect

Diagram **4** provides an indication of the correct orientation for pavilions serving some typical outdoor games. A low setting sun can seriously affect the viewing of games where the spectator facilities are positioned to face the geographical arc south-west to north-west. In practice such close examination of sun angles will be required only for precise placing of canopies which need to act as solar louvres, **3**.

Another important consideration is the direction of the prevailing wind; sheltered viewing should be provided if possible. Sports pavilions are often located on exposed sites and natural shelter should be considered wherever possible.

4 Choice of structure

Before starting design work it is worth considering modular unit construction. There are suppliers on the market who have expertise in buildings suitable for sports pavilions. Designs have improved and are now much more secure, robust, durable and attractive, **1**.

Some manufacturers of factory-produced, prefabricated timber-framed systems are able to provide a finished building which does not have the 'hut like' appearance of the past. Natural cladding materials and the latest standards of thermal insulation and fire resistance are available in some of the up-market systems available. This is an important consideration, particularly when it comes to the choice of internal finishes to reduce long-term maintenance costs.

It should also be remembered that not all timber systems can extend their frames to the spans and heights needed in the larger games rooms and small sports halls.

Some advantages of system building are:

● May cost less than traditional construction, but this depends on location, local building trade situation, transport charges and ease of access to the site

● Modular units can be erected quickly, often in a matter of weeks

● Bolted together buildings are movable and are therefore suitable for temporary accommodation

● Timber linings and structure produce a warm looking interior, **5**.

5 *Bruce Castle Park pavilion by John Hirn Construction. Photo: Richard Bryant*

The disadvantages are:

- Standardised designs may not meet particular requirements of a project. Modifications to layout and specification may be costly
- Basic costs, such as laying the base and connecting services, are not always included. There should be one complete contract covering all works
- Standard finishes in wet areas are often poor
- Timber exteriors are prone to vandalism.

Other lightweight structural forms include:

- Portable, secure plug-in cabins, **6**
- Mobile units
- Log cabin construction, 7
- Tented structures.

Portable or mobile cabins are suitable for changing rooms, offices, bars, showers and toilets. Fully equipped cabins can be rented, leased or purchased and are ready to plug in, by flexible pipe connections, to existing or new services and drainage manholes. Cabin units can be used singly or coupled in pairs or groups.

5 Accommodation and design criteria

The range of accommodation required in pavilions may extend from changing rooms only to facilities serving many teams, their visitors and relations and a number of other functions, particularly social and day-time uses. The following schedules of accommodation are suggested as a general guide to help sponsors and their professional agents establish the brief for a project. The appropriate long-term range of facilities needed, the pattern of use and number of people likely to use the accommodation, are just some of the basic factors to be decided. To assess the space needed for games and indoor sports mentioned in this section, see Part VII of this volume. For further details of non-sports uses and for larger clubhouses, see References.

The minimum size for a pavilion to accommodate two teams of 12–15 players with showers, toilets and other basic facilities is 40–60 sq m (approx 430 sq ft–646 sq ft). This is approximately 1.7–2 sq m (approx 18 sq ft–22

6 *Securra changing units. Photo: En-tout-cas plc.*

7 *Double skin log wall construction. Photo: A G Stuart Ltd*

sq ft) per player, although this area will be reduced as the number of teams increases.

5.1 Changing

Units of 12–15 players per team at a minimum of 0.75 sq m (8 sq ft) up to 1 sq m (approx 11 sq ft) each player. Allow a minimum of 450–500 mm (approx 18–20 in) per seat along slatted timber benches, with easy cleaning open space beneath and two coat hooks per place. In multi-team rooms lockers may be preferable for security. Part M of the Building Regulations, 1992 edition, requires dressing cubicle(s) for people with disabilities.

Some form of background heating of about 25° C is required which can be operated on a flexible basis considering intermittent use. Electric convector heaters of 'green house' type under seat heating tubes may be suitable. Avoid sharp corners on heaters – recess if possible, and if not, provide grille guards.

Good permanent ventilation is essential in buildings with intermittent use. Vents should be provided at high and low level to ensure thorough cross ventilation, of about 10 air changes per hour, to prevent condensation damage and to keep the interior fresh. Poor ventilation results in condensation and rapid deterioration of internal finishes.

For normal playing fields, the total electricity supply for the pavilion and changing rooms could be fitted to a time switch which gives say two hours supply on pressing a central button. One press would cover soccer matches and two or three presses cricket matches. This prevents electrical appliances being left on from one week to the next.

Changing rooms are a facility for which multi-purpose use should be considered, eg table tennis, weight-training, play groups and as an overflow social space for special occasions. The multi-use may provide added

amenities, but it should be remembered that such a scheme will require more carefully selected finishes, types of heating, storage and sound insulation. Movable seating or clothes racks could be used for this purpose but there will also be storage implications, **8**.

Ladies powder room, vanitory unit and hairdryers should be provided where appropriate.

A drying room or space might be required, linked to changing areas.

5.2 Toilets

For each 15 changing spaces, provide one WC and two urinals and two wash basins (men); and two WCs and two wash basins (women).

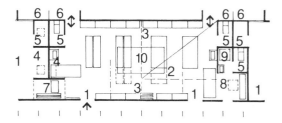

8 *Arrangements for multi-purpose twin changing rooms/indoor activities room: 1 Multi-purpose changing room for 30–34 players; 2 Changing room subdivided for 24 players; 3 Sliding-folding partition; 4 Wash hand basin/fold-down couch bay; 5 Top lit and vented WCs with children's platform and slip-over seat; 6 Showers/dry-off; 7 Equipment store and stow-away for changing benches and playgroup trunks; 8 Alternative arrangement with referees' room/equipment storage; 9 Referees' shower; 10 Table tennis room with light point and ceiling hooks for lighting frame*

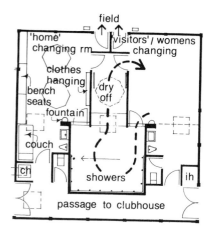

9 *One-way circulation from two changing rooms into the central shower and back through a shared dry-off area. Players arriving and leaving after re-changing use a 'clean' passage from and to the clubhouse. There is a separate 'dirty' field entrance direct from each changing room. These must be secure and protected from vandalism, but they allow the changing rooms to be used without always opening up the whole building. Enfield St George's Recreation Centre. Architect: Peter Ackroyd*

Where cost permits, cantilevered or solid back to wall types of WC should be considered, as they allow floors to be cleaned quickly and easily. Stainless steel slab urinals are recommended for public toilets.

5.3 Showers and drying areas

Provide 3–4 showers per 12 changing spaces, open plan 1 sq m (approx 11 sq ft) each, with 0.76 m (2 ft 6 in) between nozzles. Large drainage outlets help to prevent clogging. A plunge bath may now be considered to be unhygienic.

A dry-off area is essential, located between showers and changing, with drainage outlet to reduce water taken into the changing area. Step up to drying area and changing spaces. Provide towel rails in preference to hooks, **9**.

Part M of the Building Regulations 1992 requires shower compartment(s) with unobstructed approach for people with disabilities.

Extractor fans should be provided to remove clouds of steam. All fittings must be anti-corrosive, robust and switched centrally, or on light switches.

Individual showers could be fitted with automatic timers to give 30 second–1 minute supply of hot water at each push. Foot controlled shower activators help to reduce vandalism. All pipework and mixer valves should be concealed where possible, or run at high level.

5.4 Wet areas

Non slip tiles are essential for shower and dry off floors. These may be of a ceramic type, or non absorbent sealed granolithic composition. Covings between floor and wall are essential for ease of cleaning. Check ease of cleaning in showers and toilet/urinal areas. Ensure a good fall to drainage outlets.

Water heating in small pavilions by electric heaters giving instant hot water is probably the simplest and most flexible system considering intermittent use. These heaters may be prone to vandalism but some types are designed to counter this. Alternatively a central industrial type instant heater with thermostat will be less prone to damage but is more expensive both initially and to run

on an intermittent basis. Space will have to be allowed for a central boiler.

The cold water tank has to be accommodated usually in a roof area. Most shower systems need a minimum head of water. Alternatively, pumps must be fitted. The size of cold water tanks will depend on the type of system and is covered by appropriate building regulations and byelaws. The local water authority should be contacted for detailed guidance.

Pipes should be lagged and anti-freeze put in waste water pipes. Frost thermostats could be fitted to switch on small electric heaters at low temperatures when pipes are at risk of freezing. With few or no windows, heat losses will be small.

A means of hosing down 'wet' areas and power cleaning other rooms is essential with associated taps and power points, which must be the earth proving type – substantial sockets with metal cover flaps and earth leakage contact breakers.

5.5 Officials' changing

Allow 1–3 places, one shower and a dry off area.

5.6 Circulation space

Access to changing rooms eg lobby, entrance and other areas varies between 0 and 10% of total area. A Cleaners' store or cupboard fitted with slop sink is best accessed from general circulation space.

5.7 First aid provision

Could combine with officials' room or provide at least a secure cupboard. Refer also to TUS Datasheet 60.8 and Volume 2, Chapter 58.

5.8 Refreshment/social space

Variable from nil to vending machine space, to small kitchen area to kitchen plus club room with bar. Allow minimum of 10 sq m (approx 107 sq ft), **10**.

5.9 Grounds store

Locked area for toxic materials, fertilisers and equipment. This area is vulnerable to vandalism. Its size will depend

10 *Social focal point in Nottingham Rugby Football Club. Photo: Richard Bryant*

on the type of machinery and the number of pitches, but 6 sq m (approx 65 sq ft) may be adequate, although tractors, mowers or large equipment will need more space. Posts and playing equipment may also need to be stored. Where a tractor and gang mower is to be stored a 'drive through' arrangement is particularly useful.

5.10 Steward's/groundsman's flat
Viability (revenue income) and vandalism issues may suggest advantages of live-in accommodation for permanent staff, **15**.

6 Layout and circulation
Some of the considerations for the layout and performance specification are as follows:

- Layouts should be planned for flexible use and other weekday activities.
- Segregate wet areas from any cross circulation and entry/exit points to the field, preferably by placing shower areas as an integral part of the changing rooms, **9**.
- It is preferable to have two separate changing units with own showers and toilets, but services on the same side of the building. The simplest layout is two units side by side with a central entry/exit point as shown in **9, 11 & 12**.

- A small changing room for officials could also act as a first aid room, **12**.
- A covered porch area outside to include boot scraper and brushes could be considered. This can also act as shelter for spectators.
- Several home teams can share a changing unit if suitably sub-divided by seating but each visiting team should have its own changing room. Staggered start times for matches may make better use of pavilions, but the clothes storage equipment will need to be increased and self-service lockers may also be needed.
- A small open kitchen unit area in a corridor or lobby could be useful. Kitchens require external screened bin areas. Bar areas require secure stores and screened lockable external 'empties' areas. These areas must be accessible for deliveries and collections, **12, 13 and 14**.
- Public toilets for general use by spectators should preferably be a separate provision with own external access, but can be incorporated, **12**.
- Throughout the pavilion, inadequate thermal insulation may result in cold walls, condensation, smells and general unpleasantness. The minimum Building Regulation Standards may be adequate in some situations.

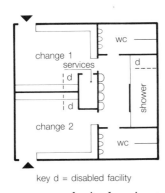

key d = disabled facility

11 *Type-layout: two team basic changing pavilion*

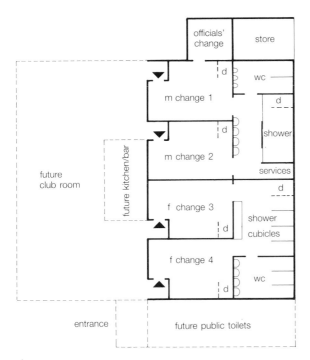

12 *Type-layout: four team (both sexes) changing pavilion with attached groundsman's equipment store*

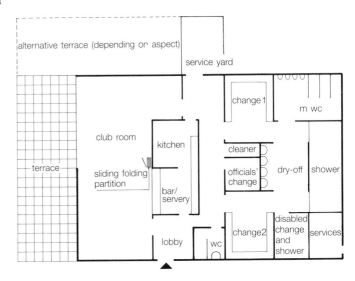

13 *Type-layout: changing (single-sex) and social pavilion/clubhouse*

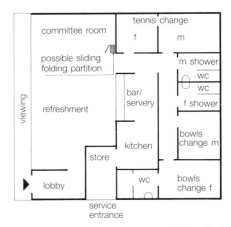

14 *Type-layout: Tennis and Bowls pavilion. It is also stressed that the above layouts should not be taken as standard plans, but rather as a selection and progression of possible arrangements, graded by size and range of amenities offered. They are intended to aid sponsors in deciding the scope of the pavilion appropriate to their needs*

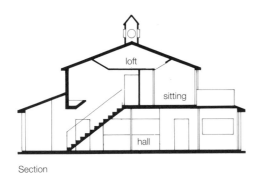

Section

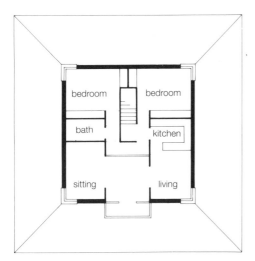

First floor–Manager's flat

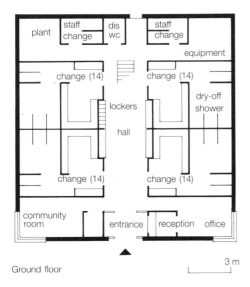

Ground floor

3 m

15 *Preston Sports Club changing facility with roof space staff flat. Architect: Sir George Grenfell-Baines*

It is stressed that the layouts shown in **11–14** should not be taken as standard plans, but rather as a selection and progression of possible arrangements, graded by size and range of amenities offered. They are intended to aid sponsors in deciding the scope of the pavilion appropriate to their needs.

7 Security

Security in isolated pavilions should be a major consideration in design. The intended contents could also affect the level of security, eg a full bar requires greater protection than basic changing rooms. Protection needs to be tailor made for each risk and the local Crime Prevention

16 *Eastcote Cricket Club. In many situations, anti-vandal window shutters are also necessary. Photo: S Wernick & Sons Ltd*

Officer and Insurance Surveyor will be able to advise, preferably, at design stage.

The advice of Rex Barnett of the Prudential Assurance Company, is acknowledged in the preparation of this section.

7.1 Construction

Brick or stone walls are preferable to wood but should allow ease of cleaning off graffiti and repair of wilful damage. Roofs are often vulnerable: a pitched, tiled roof is recommended. Access should not be possible on to roofs without ladders, eg no parapets below 3 m (10 ft). Lightweight roofs are suitable only for buildings housing rollers and minor tools. Plastered wall finishes are unsuitable because they invite graffiti and vandalism.

7.2 Vents and drainpipes

Vents and drainpipes should be exposed as little as possible, vents being sited 2.4 m (8 ft) above ground or more.

7.3 External doors

Doors and fittings must be robust with a minimum of five lever Mortice Dead Locks manufactured to BS 3621. (Look for British Standard Kite Mark).

Doors should be at least 44 mm (1.75 in) thick and steel plate facing doors should be considered. Roller shutters secured with high quality padlocks are an alternative.

7.4 Windows

There should be as few windows as possible. Those that are necessary should be narrow, less than 0.5 m (approx 1 ft) deep and sited at least 1.8 m (6 ft) above ground level. Opening windows should have catches limiting the opening to 150 mm (6 in). Window locks should be fitted to all opening windows.

Unbreakable glass should be considered and external tight fitting shutters should be included, **16**.

7.5 Grilles and bars

If bars are to be fitted, these should be a minimum of 19 mm (0.75 in) solid steel bars at not more than 125 mm (5 in) centres and if external, grouted into the brickwork.

Internal bars can be flattened and secured to the woodwork with at least two screws. All bars should be vertical. Grills should be secured to the surrounding woodwork with a good quality padlock.

7.6 Alarms

Alarms of the 'Police informing' type are expensive and can only be justified where high value stocks are held, eg licensed facilities. Audible alarms are much less effective and rely on neighbours or passers-by informing the Police.

Full protection can mean that all doors and windows are contacted or foiled. Full perimeter protection is not normally practical. Partial protection of a limited area is therefore recommended, eg bar area and gaming machines.

In the UK, alarm companies should be members of the National Supervisory Council for Intruder Alarms (NSCIA) and alarms should conform to BS 4737. At least three quotations should be obtained as security is a highly competitive business. The local Police Crime Prevention Officer should always be consulted.

The NSCIA companies have been approved after capitalisation has been checked and the quality of the service installation and back-up service has also been cleared as satsifactory.

7.7 External lighting

External lighting is a good deterrent – no thief likes to be lit up at work. Low pressure sodium bulkhead lamps in vandal resistant housings are suitable and economical in use.

8 Common mistakes

The following check list gives some of the most frequent mistakes to be avoided:

- Cross circulation
- Poor sight lines, incorrect sequence of changing rooms for each sex, door should be positioned to avoid overlooking
- Too many windows
- Inadequate ventilation and background heat

- Inadequate storage space, may need to include:
  - bar crates and empties
  - litter receptacles
  - playing equipment
  - groundsmen's equipment and materials
  - cleaning equipment
  - kitchen stores and refuse
  - valuables store
  - water storage
  - spare storage for other users
- Internal fixtures and fitments frequently lack robustness. Savings in initial costs are usually more than offset by heavier repair bills
- Spectating areas at ground floor level are low cost but give limited viewing
- Slippery floors in showers
- No means of hosing down wet areas or cleaning other areas
- No heating in changing rooms
- Inadequate thermal insulation of walls/roof
- Plastered wall finishes.

9 References and further advice

BS 3621 1980, *Specification for thief resistant locks*.

BS 4737 1977–1988, *Intruder alarm systems*, Parts 1–5.

National Playing Fields Association publications and cost guides.

Scottish Sports Council Information Digest FD8 *Pavilions and Clubhouses – briefing guide* (1982).

The Sports Council, East Midlands Region, *Playing Field Pavilions*.

The Sports Council, *TUS Datasheet 60.8: Designing for Safety in Sports Halls: Part 8: First Aid Provision*. The Sports Council, London (1991).

Building Regulations 1992, Part M, Changing facilities for people with disabilities.

24
Golf courses

Martin Hawtree

1 Description of the game

Golf basically involves striking a ball not less than 42.67 mm (1.5 in) in diameter, as few times as possible with one or other of a set of 14 (maximum) iron or wooden headed clubs having variously angled faces, over a course measuring between 4572 and 6400 m (5000 and 7000 yd) divided into 18 holes between 90 and 510 m (98 and 558 yd) long. Holes are traditionally measured in yards but nowadays the metric equivalent is normally added. Play is from a tee along the fairway, to the green where the ball must be putted into a hole 10.8 cm (4.25 in) in diameter and marked by a flag. Along the way there are hazards such as sand bunkers which the player tries to avoid. In match play, scoring is by holes won or lost (up or down). In medal play all strokes are added together. Handicaps, based on past performance, theoretically enable players of differing abilities to compete on equal terms. Two or four play together, sometimes three.

2 Golf courses

2.1 Standard scratch score and 'par'

Golf courses are graded by a 'standard scratch score' (see Table 24.1) calculated from total length with marginal allowances for special circumstances and is the score which a scratch player (a player who received no strokes from his opponent) is expected to return over a measured course.

Table 24.1 Standard scratch score

Metres (Yards)	Standard Scratch Score
4573–4755 (5003–5202)	65
4756–4983 (5203–5451)	66
4984–5212 (5452–5702)	67
5213–5441 (5703–5952)	68
5442–5669 (5953–6202)	69
5670–5852 (6203–6402)	70
5853–6035 (6403–6602)	71
6036–6218 (6603–6802)	72
6219–6401 (6803–7002)	73
6402–6584 (7003–7203)	74

Individual holes are allotted a par, the minimum number of strokes normally needed to reach the green plus two putts.

Par is fixed by the Club in relation to length and playing difficulty within the following ranges:

- Holes of 229 m (250 yd) and under: Par 3
- Holes between 201–457 m (220–500 yd): Par 4
- Holes of 402 m (440 yd) and over: Par 5

The total par does not necessarily equal the standard scratch score. A predominance of holes towards the lower end of these brackets would produce a lower standard scratch score.

A notionally ideal layout would have four par 3, four par 5s and ten par 4s. The lengths provided within each

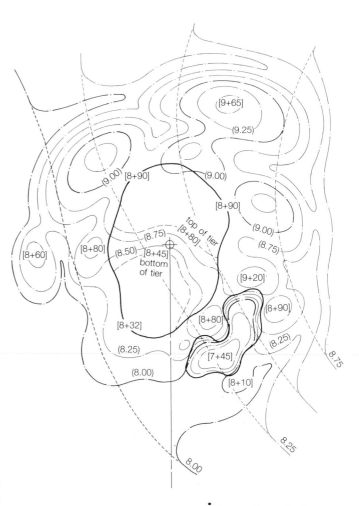

1 *A detailed green plan showing existing and required contours so that anyone familiar with elementary levelling can set out and construct the formation desired*

group should vary widely, the par 3s and par 5s being well separated. Par 3 holes over 210 m (230 yd) and Par 4s below about 293 m (320 yd) are not popular. But both overall length and distribution of individual lengths will be a compromise between site factors and the game's traditional requirements, **1**.

2.2 Length

A total length between 5800 and 6520 m (6345 and 7133 yd) is very satisfactory (professional tournaments may take 6400 m (7002 yd) or more).

Ladies' tees are set forward to produce perhaps 5000 m (5470 yd). A reduction of 15% is normal.

Total length and the form of the layout will, however, be determined primarily by acreage, boundaries, contour and natural features which can be used to enhance design. As area reduces, so total length comes down until it is necessary to change the category of the proposal.

A rule of thumb guide to potential length might be as shown in Table 24.2.

Table 24.2 Potential length of courses

Hectares (Acres)	Holes	Metres (Yards)
20–28 (49–69)	9	2000–2800 (2187–3062)
36 (90)	18	5120–5304 (5601–5803)
40 (99)		5304–5486 (5803–6002)
44 (109)		5486–5669 (6002–6202)
49 (121)		5669–5852 (6202–6402)
53 (131)		5852–6035 (6402–6602)
57 (141)		6035–6218 (6602–6802)
61 (151)		6218 + (6802 +)
73 (180)	27*	8100 + (8856 +)
91 (225)	36†	11 000 + (1203 +)

*3 loops of 9 holes, each of 2700 m, gives a length of 8100 m.

†2 loops of 18 holes, each of 5500 m.

There are, however, other considerations. For example, 6200 m (6783 yd) on a flat featureless site might be considered undesirable (without expensive landscape changes) on grounds of possible tedium. Less length with one of the shorter forms of layout could be a better solution. A hilly site might produce a low total length to avoid frequent uphill holes which are unpopular. The budget may also require avoidance of areas deficient in topsoil or drainage. Neighbouring roads, houses or public parks will need safety margins which make 1 ha (2.5 acres) unusable for golf for every 300 m (329 yd) of boundary affected.

A good layout will retain and use the maximum number of natural features while providing a sequence of holes, varying in length, interest and direction, comfortably separated for safety and planting space. It should also offer at least one alternative starting point, preferably No. 10 tee with the 18 green in full view of the clubhouse and a practice ground nearby.

What size of complex is chosen must depend upon a thorough market survey and analysis of the site. Today new private courses tend to be coming closer to public courses in their philosophy with the attempt to provide multi-facility complexes. Pay-as-you-play will now look for 18 + 9 + 9 or 18 + par 3 + driving range. Many private developments will look for a driving range and at least one other facility if space permits, **2**. At the very least an area for practice and tuition should be provided.

3 Design

Golf originated on the links of the eastern seaboard of Scotland. The sand, whins and varied contours of that type of land still strongly influence design but are often softened inland by the needs of maintenance.

Five design elements are available:

- Sand: in bunkers, natural or artificial
- Contour: the use of slopes, moundwork and hollows requires and develops extra skill and judgement in the player
- Grass: varying heights of mowing ranging from rough (50–100 mm (2–4 in)) through semi-rough, fairway (25 mm (1 in)), and tees to greens (5 mm (0.2 in))
- Planting: the use of trees and shrubs for landscape and wild-life interest as well as influence on play
- Water: the creation of pools or the use of streams or lakes for landscape effect and as potential hazards, **3**.

The conflicts between power and precision should also inspire the planning of each hole, so that prudence can be balanced against daring, stimulating the personal stock-taking which makes this game so different from others needing only instinctive reflexes. Golf has been described as a 'contest of risks'. The type of hole planned to induce that atmosphere is called 'strategic'.

Both layout and design should emphasise informality. A strong element in the total enjoyment of the course by the player is its natural beauty. But enjoyment of deep rough or artificial water hazards will be limited if they lead to frequent delays and lost balls. Similarly, bunkers multiplied simply to punish bad shots are monotonous. This type of design is called 'penal'. A third approach, though the notion is implicit in 'strategic' is called 'heroic'. But however dramatic the heroic shot across water, sand, or trees, the wise designer will provide a safer option, easier to play though possibly needing one more stroke.

In this way, the player is called upon to assess his abilities and sometimes to try and surpass them. Variety in design changes the nature of the problems from hole to hole and the degree of muscular control and thought demanded. These factors, allied to the perambulation of some 6 km (approx 4 miles) of agreeable scenery in the context of companionship and competition, correspond to the recreational needs of a steadily increasing number of men, women, and children of all ages and abilities.

4 Small areas

Where space is limited, land expensive, or contours difficult, a smaller scheme may be appropriate.

4.1 A 9-hole course

This is simply one half of a full course with all the same needs of layout, feature, and interest. Wherever possible, provide for its extension to 18 holes.

4.2 An executive course

This type of course consists of 9 or 18 holes with a higher proportion of par 3 holes and shorter par 4s to reduce the area required and speed the play of the round while still providing full-scale golf.

4.3 A par 3 course

This course only provides short holes, generally between 90–180 m (approx 98–197 yd) long. This is still full-scale golf in a sense, though smaller greens are sometimes specified: 12 ha (approx 3 acres) would provide a 9-hole layout comfortably.

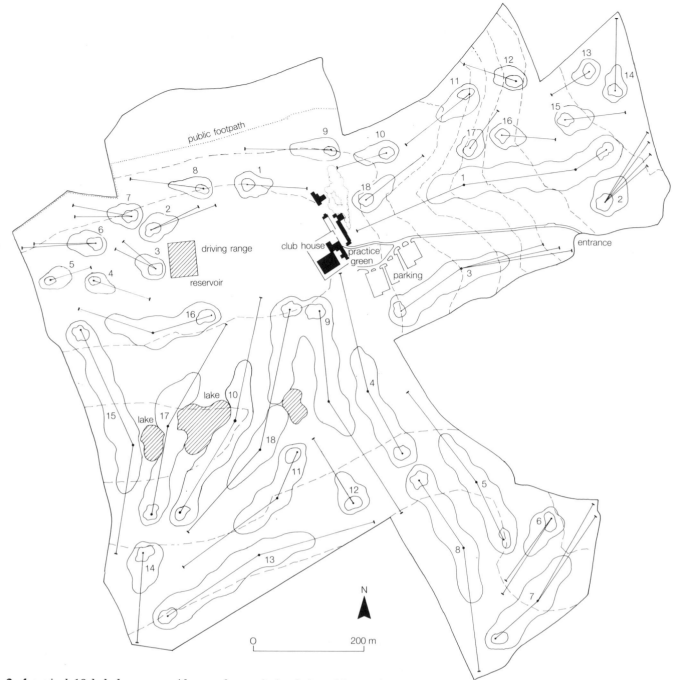

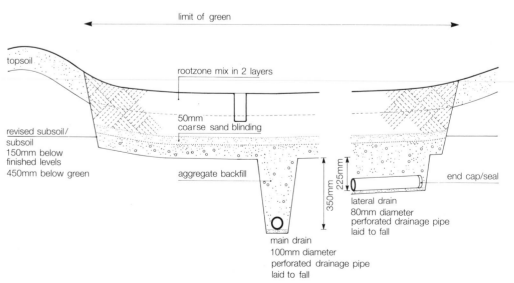

2 *A typical 18-hole layout provides two loops of nine holes with practice ground and a clubhouse overlooking the 9th and 18th greens. A par 3 Course or intermediate 9 holes are very useful adjuncts and make up the modern concept of a golf centre*

3 *Drainage factors are more important as play increases. The proportion of sand and peat in greens should be determined by laboratory tests, and specialist advice should be sought for the design of the green construction*

4 *A modern green mower can complete mowing within a few hours and therefore keep ahead of play and avoid disturbing players*

4.4 A pitch and putt course
This type of course consists of holes under 90 m (98 yd), with 70 m (approx 76 yd) being the normal maximum. For this reason, and because it attracts beginners and children, safety considerations should be stringent.

4.5 The driving range
This is a flat or descending area 220–275 m (approx 240–300 yd) long by 100–150 m (110–164 yd) wide. Play is from a one, two or three-tier platform with fixed mats and sometimes devices to tee up balls automatically. the platform may be covered with a roof and divided into bays 3 m (approx 3 yd) wide, or it may be in the open. Balls are bought by the bucket and collected later by the range staff. A range with associated par 3 and/or pitch and putt facilities is more successful than one providing practice alone. It could equally be associated with a full-scale 18 hole course but proximity to an urban centre is desirable. The range is excellent for all classes of player wishing to practise.

5 Capacity
When planning the capacity of a new golf course, it should be noted that there is usually a maximum of 8 players per hole or 144 players simultaneously on 18 holes. This gives a total of 36 four-ball games starting at 5 minute intervals over a period of 3 hours. In practice, 6–minute intervals should always be allowed, with an estimated 2.5–3 hours for a singles game and 3.5–4 hours for a four-ball game. Here, the lower figures operate when the course is relatively clear, **4**.

5.1 Green fees
Municipal courses near London record 60,000 rounds a year and more. In the provinces 35,000 to 40,000 are expected in populous areas. Few courses support more than 50,000 rounds without showing signs of wear. Thus, play may need restriction in a wet winter.

5.2 Membership
Playing members

9 holes	150–200
18 holes	350–400
36 holes	850–1000

6 Cost
The NPFA produces a pamphlet with guides to cost annually. Further information and advice on design can be obtained from the British Institute of Golf Course Architects.

7 The need for expert consultancy
These notes will be helpful in setting out the main parameters and factors in the design of a golf course. However, it is recommended that specialist expertise be employed for the final design. Advice from bodies like the British Institute of Golf Course Architects (BIGCA) should be sought.

25
Golf clubhouses

Roger Dyer

1 Background

Golf courses originated and existed for some while without the need for clubhouses. The increasing popularity of the game caused golfers to formulate and observe rules and this in turn led them to band together socially and to run competitions, creating a membership or club.

The majority of clubhouses therefore serve a limited number of members – a group of people who provide their own facilities without the need to operate at a profit. At most clubs the public may also use the facilities of the course and building, but only at certain times at the discretion of the club and on a daily fee basis.

A slightly different type of clubhouse came to be required when local authorities started building public golf courses which did not have a membership but were open to all on payment of a 'green fee' allowing either one round or a day's use of the course.

Recently a further type of golf clubhouse has emerged in which investors are developing golf courses with the object of producing a financial return on capital. This return is generally achieved either by housing developments fronting on to the course, by building additional social and sporting facilities into the clubhouse or by developing an hotel and country club linked to the course.

No matter which of these three types of clubhouse is being considered, it is important to decide on the management structure before embarking on design. The management structure is increasingly attracting much discussion and change. Member clubs are usually run by committees elected on a yearly basis, with the day-to-day administration handled by a secretary who is often part-time. However, the popularity of the game is creating increased pressure on clubs which are now beginning to

MANAGEMENT OF COURSE AND PAVILION

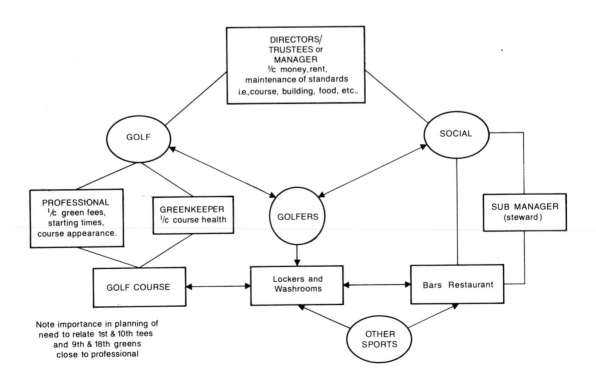

1 *Typical management structure for a course and clubhouse*

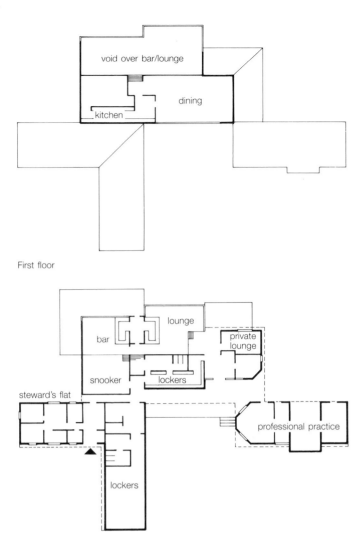

First floor

Ground floor

2 Kenilworth Golf Club, an example of a larger clubhouse

realise that their facilities require professional management. The importance of social income for viability has also made it important for golf club management to be concerned as much with social as golf matters. Many member clubs are therefore beginning to give more power to a full-time manager whilst ensuring continuity of policy by a committee involving a limited number of members. This arrangement is typical of American clubs.

Traditionally local authorities have paid little heed to the need for a membership structure. This has led to groups of golfers forming clubs in order that players can gain a handicap – only properly constituted clubs can offer this important facility. These clubs usually enjoy rights of access to their local authority course at certain times, for example for their monthly medal competition. Many have developed social facilities on or near the course. With increasing pressures on local authority budgets many are realising that golf courses can be more profitable if they have a membership structure. This in turn is putting more emphasis on the provision of social facilities and their effective management.

Finally, proprietary or commercial golf and country clubs places great emphasis on the provision and effective management of high quality social facilities.

2 Facilities

Common to all three types of enterprise is the fact that a clubhouse exists only to provide two main facilities for the golfer: a changing area comprising lavatories and a social area which is basically a pub. Management structures should therefore mirror this split and **1** sets out a typical management structure allowing for a well-integrated social side. It also illustrates the possibility of incorporating other sports and leisure facilities in a commercial club.

Increasing family participation in golf means that the basic facilities offered by many public and private clubs will no longer be adequate, **2**, **3**, **4** and **5**. The first requirement will often be higher catering standards, but increasingly additional sports and ancillary facilities will also be necessary to enable the whole family to enjoy the club. The facilities which will be most likely to be provided will include creches, small swimming pools, tennis courts, squash courts, multi-purpose studios, fitness areas, snooker room, saunas, sunbeds and extensive high quality social facilities. Examples of this type of provision may be seen in commercial club form at the St Pierre Golf and Country Club at Chepstow, part of the developing chain of Country Club Hotels owned by Whitbread plc; and in local authority form at the Shipley Park Leisure Centre at Derbyshire.

3 Schedule of accommodation
Table 25.1 sets out minimum clubhouse requirements for a members' club based at an 18-hole course assuming a normal requirement for social facilities. Any further accommodation required for a country club can be added to this basic list. If additional sports facilities are provided it will be necessary also to increase the amount of changing, showering, social and other ancillary accommodation.

Table 25.1: Sizes of basic accommodation

Golfing facilities	Size
Entrance	25–50 sq m (269–538 sq ft)
Men's locker room	50–150 sq m (538–1615 sq ft) upwards depending on locker policy
Men's toilet	25–40 sq m (269–430 sq ft) depending on extent of social and sporting facilities
Ladies' locker room	30–35 sq m (323–377 sq ft) upwards
Ladies' toilet	20–25 sq m (269–538 sq ft)
Professional's shop	50–55 sq m (538–592 sq ft) upwards depending on club storage requirement
Manager's office	15–25 sq m (162–269 sq ft)
Additional desirable golfing facilities	
Greenkeeper's flat/house	65–85 sq m (700–915 sq ft)
Professional's flat/house	65–85 sq m (700–915 sq ft)
Social facilities	
Lounge with bar	55–110 sq m (592–1184 sq ft)
Kitchen/stores	20–40 sq m (215–430 sq ft)
Beer store	20 sq m (430 sq ft)
Steward's flat	65–75 sq m (700–807 sq ft)
Additional desirable social facilities	
Dining room	40–55 sq m (430–592 sq ft)
Separate men's bar	40–75 sq m (430–807 sq ft)
Ladies' lounge	25 sq m (269 sq ft)
Multi-purpose room (Cards, meetings etc)	35 sq m (377 sq ft)

One 18-hole course will support approximately 600 members before complaints occur regarding overcrowding. A typical division of these 600 members is 450 men, 80 women and 70 social and junior members.

For everyday use, the range and size of clubhouse facilities required depend less on the total number of members than the rate at which the course can be used. At the minimum, four players can tee off every six minutes and therefore changing facilities will be subjected to a maximum of four players coming in and four going out every six minutes. These calculations give a clue to clubhouse size.

107

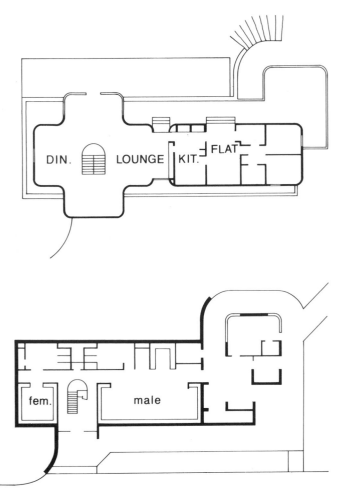

3 Lilley Brook Golf Club, Cheltenham. Existing levels were exploited to provide views over the course and access to ground level from both floors

3.1 Entrance area

The entrance foyer required is very variable in size and in the case of a minimal building serving a public course is not entirely necessary. In the case of a private club the anticipated members' use of the building will influence the size as will the number of rooms which circulate directly off the entrance.

The foyer area is in many ways an appropriate place for honour and notice boards, always difficult but necessary items to accommodate, as well as a public telephone and instructions to visitors. It should be emphasised that first impressions are gained at this point and an inviting, clearly signed area is necessary.

3.2 Men's locker room

The area required for this room is based upon the capacity of the course. An 18-hole course will be full when it is being played by about 120 players (four balls every six minutes for three hours) or 150 if allowance is made for evening players. The maximum number of people likely to be using this room at any one time on a competition day would therefore be no more than 40–50.

Allowing 1 sq m (approx 11 sq ft) per person this gives a minimum area of 50 sq m (538 sq ft) assuming no lockers are required. This will be the case at many public courses and those private clubs where golf bags are kept

out of the locker room – an increasingly common practice. If bags are kept in lockers in this room, however, each locker, together with an attached seat plus circulation space, will occupy approximately 0.5 sq m (approx 5 sq ft) and therefore a total requirement of 200 lockers will translate into a room size of 100 sq m (1076 sq ft) plus the basic area of 50 sq m (538 sq ft).

Ideally any drying area should not be enclosed as this encourages the accumulation of old clothes, shoes, and other items. Consideration should be given to a drying rack which has a draining recess and hot air heater to encourage quick drying. This drying area can then double up as extra hanging space when not being used to dry wet clothes.

Access to the course from the locker room should be past or though the professional's shop. In larger clubhouses consideration should be given to a shoe and club cleaning and storage area linked to the professional's shop and under his or her control.

The appearance of locker rooms is determined largely by floor and wall finishes. In the past a popular practical and spike resistant floor finish was conveyor belting. This has limitations where a fitted appearance is required or where under-floor heating is used; the colour choice is also very limited and it shows dirt badly. Spike resistant carpets and squares are now available at reasonable cost and have proved to be a suitable alternative. Applied wall finishes can be kept to an absolute minimum if lockers are used to line walls.

3.3 Men's toilet

The normal rule of thumb figures for sanitary fixtures are one WC and one urinal for 25 men and one basin for 15 men. However, a maximum of 50 players expected at any one time will require the use of these facilities at a much greater rate than normally expected and it is not unreasonable to double this standard, ie 4–5 WCs, 4 urinals and 4–5 basins for 50 people. In addition at least 4 showers will be required.

3.4 Ladies' locker room

Similar detailed requirements apply as for the men's locker room, although proportionately more hanging space and handbag lockers could be provided. Ladies' competitions will create the need for a more generous area allowance than the membership structure might suggest.

3.5 Ladies' toilet

Approximately 3–4 WCs and basins will normally be quite adequate although this once again will depend upon the strength of the ladies' section in the club. Two showers should also be provided. Basins should be vanity type with the whole area 'softer' in appearance than the normal utilitarian type of room found in many clubs. A powder room may also be desirable.

3.6 Professional's shop

The location of the professional's shop should allow good views from it over the course. It is often freestanding and at courses where the professional collects green fees and controls starting times it should be adjacent to and be provided with a window giving an unobstructed view of the first tee.

Display space is important, and long wall lengths are desirable. Height to swing a club is also an asset and better still if it is linked to an undercover practice area.

Depending on the skills of the professional a work room facility may also be required. Generally it can be fairly minimal providing a vice, bench and space for a club can be accommodated. Similarly an office and trolley storage facilities can be incorporated.

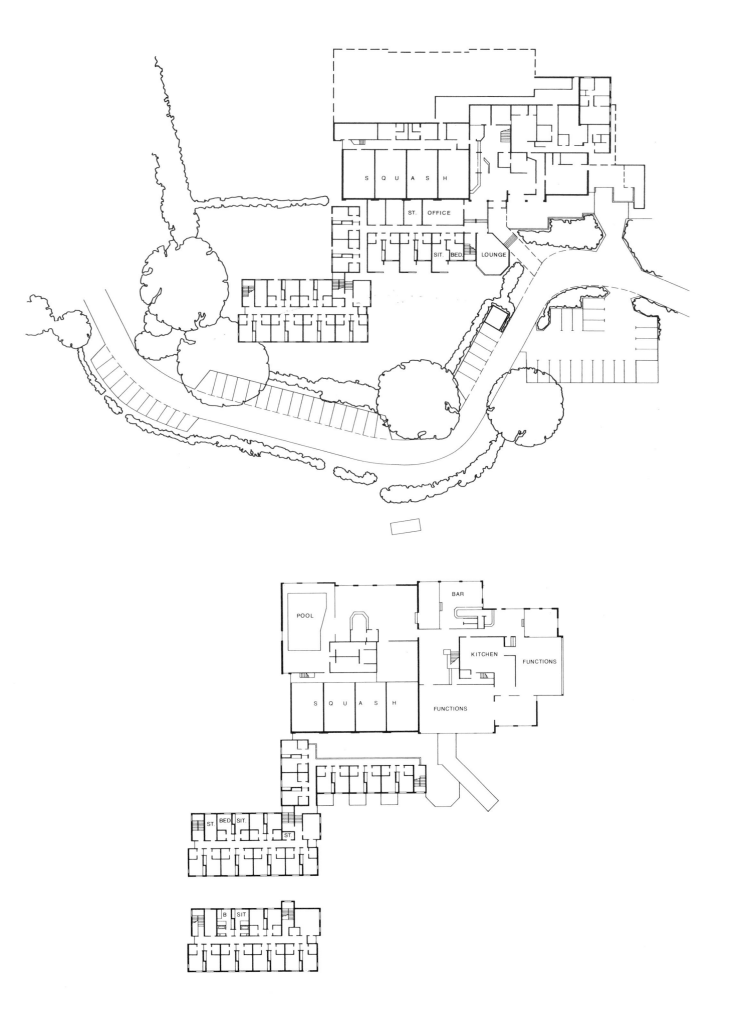

4 *Meon Valley Golf and Country Club which includes a pool, squash courts, and bedroom suites, in addition to the standard clubhouse accommodation*

5 *Meon Valley Clubhouse*

A storage area under the supervision of the professional will be needed for clubs if a policy decision is taken to exclude them from the locker room. Generally speaking bags will take up less space if stored horizontally but less wear and tear will occur if they are stored vertically.

3.7 Manager's or secretary's office
This room should be capable of accommodating the occasional meeting and interview as well as space for a typist. It will also be used for the storage of permanent records and day-to-day papers. A fireproof safe is desirable.

Surveillance of all points of access of the course is an advantage, particularly on the public course, and close proximity to the professional's shop is also desirable.

3.8 Greenkeeper's flat/house
The greenkeeper's well-being is essential in any properly run club, whether public or private, and provision of living accommodation contributes to this end. Similar accommodation to that of the steward or manager should be provided, although perhaps on a slightly increased scale. There is some advantage in providing greenkeeper's accommodation adjacent to the course so that immediate attendance to problems is possible.

3.9 Professional's flat/house
Similar considerations apply as for the greenkeeper. However, it can be argued that there are obvious disadvantages to the professional in being constantly accessible.

3.10 Lounge
The minimum size suggested will be suitable only for normal day-to-day use and cannot accommodate large competitions or visiting groups unless linked to other rooms. If no other rooms are provided then this room should be at least 100 sq m (1076 sq ft) at which size integral dining on a snack basis can take place. Views over at least the finishing hole are essential as well as a pleasant internal environment.

3.11 Kitchen/stores
The minimum size of 20 sq m (215 sq ft) together with minimum storage facilities will allow 'pub' type snacks to be prepared and served. More extensive menus will demand extra space. This room should be located to serve the lounge and any bars as well as any outside terracing.

3.12 Beer store
This area is the minimum necessary to serve a one or two bar building, although if beer deliveries are infrequent it should be increased in size. It is not necessary to provide traditional cellarage as beer will be artificially cooled.

3.13 Steward's flat
A flat or house with three bedrooms, living-dining room, bathroom and kitchen is essential to enable a family to be accommodated. The position of the flat is crucial for ease of running the bar and kitchen facilities. Also of importance is the degree of privacy offered to the steward.

It is conceivable that this facility could be omitted in the case of a public course. However, it is unwise to leave the clubhouse unattended and better service can be provided by having the steward permanently in attendance.

3.14 Dining room
This area will accommodate 50 people and, for flexibility, should be separated from the main lounge only by a movable screen or change of floor level. At a public course a coffee shop type of service may be acceptable and the area can then be reduced to about 40 sq m (430 sq ft). This emphasises the need to agree the style of catering at a very early stage.

3.15 Men's bar
The smaller size will provide a small snug bar while the larger size can accommodate a snooker table if required.

3.16 Ladies' lounge
This facility can act as a focal point for the lady membership, particularly when the main club facilities are fully occupied with competitions or visiting societies. It may not be necessary for a public course.

3.17 Multi-purpose room
This is a useful facility which can provide the key to the flexibility of use often required of the clubhouse, particularly if separated by a removable screen from the dining room or main lounge. It can be used to accommodate card and committee meetings and will also suffice for small golf societies and TV viewing. The area indicated will hold 6 to 8 sets of four person dining tables.

A children's and/or young golfer's room may be desirable if provision is to be made for more than a minimal club.

4 Services

4.1 Heating
Assuming that all energy sources are available, the main problem with choosing the type of heating for a new clubhouse will be the demands of flexibility and response. A clubhouse lounge will more often than not be empty at 11:30 on a Sunday morning, but by 12:30–13:00 it will be full and by 15:00 empty again. The heating system must be capable of maintaining the empty clubhouse at 18–21°C (approx 65–70°F) but virtually shutting off when the building is full.

Owing to their lack of quick response, therefore, radiators are not suitable for some areas although they may be used for areas where large numbers of people do not accumulate. If the system is set at say 16°C (approx 60°F) the amount of 'topping up' required by an additional quick response system is limited. Furthermore continuous heating of the fabric of the building, eg underfloor heating, enables lower temperatures to be accepted and has definite advantages in locker and toilet facilities in terms of comfort.

Hot-air heating, normally by ducted means, will provide the quick response required in public areas. It can also be used for supplying cooler air directly from the outside in summer.

4.2 Lighting
In many ways the problems of heating are also those of lighting – flexibility and fitness for purpose are paramount. Lighting for locker rooms, toilets and other ancillary areas can be by fluorescent fittings. In the social areas tungsten lighting almost invariably will be the only method of providing the flexibility and 'atmosphere' required.

Various types of tungsten architectural fittings are available to create the highlights and drama which are essential to an interesting and popular interior. These same fittings can be separately switched or controlled by dimmer switches to suit various functions.

4.3 Cooking and supplies
The quality of the cooking will be a major contributing factor to the success of a club building but is often left entirely to the steward with little or no attempt by the club to influence the quality of food. For any new building part of the brief should consider the type of menu to be served for this will affect the type of dining environment the architect should design as well as the size of the kitchen and stores.

The cooking equipment required generally consists of one or two large ovens, at least six cooking rings, grill and frying units, a boiling still and warming cabinets for food. In addition to this the kitchen will need an extractor fan, two sinks with draining facilities, a garbage disposal unit and dish washing machine. Plenty of working-top surfaces will also be required together with storage space for non-food items such as cutlery and linen.

5 Storage
A dry and canned goods store, a large refrigerator and a large deep freeze unit will all be required. Supplies other than food consist mainly of beer and liquor – the amount of storage depending not only to a great extent on the club's throughput of these items but also on the frequency of deliveries from the brewery.

There are no specific requirements for underground storage as beer is cooled either in the cellar store or at the counter. However, there are limitations to the horizontal distance that the beer store can be from the pumps. Ideally it should be as short as possible; although 24 m (approx 80 ft) is possible, 12 m (approx 40 ft) is considered a normal maximum. Care should be taken to insulate beer runs and keep them away from heating sources. Most breweries will advise and help on these practical matters.

6 Internal decorations
Furnishing and lighting are two of the most neglected areas of clubhouse design and will continue to be so unless their importance to the attraction and consequent profitability of the new clubhouse is more widely appreciated. Furnishing can be superficially likened to the wrapping of an article – it can increase the chances of it being sold if it is attractive. This is a very real analogy which has been realised by the brewers in their increased standards of public house furnishing and also by the restaurant and hotel trade. The lessons for any new building committee are therefore clear.

Furnishings generally should reflect an inviting atmosphere appropriate to the use, eg traditionally club-like in a men's bar. Pictures and trophies are items that will contribute to the lived in, comfortable feeling so essential to a successful clubhouse and a sum of money should be set aside for this purpose in any budget. Items also to be considered which are necessary and yet often forgotten or left until the last moment include TV aerials and outlets, gaming machines (best located near bar), notice boards (a general one in the entrance hall or lounge and golfing ones in locker rooms), honour boards and trophy cabinets. A policy of 'containment' needs to be stated early as window placement by the architect and choice of wall finishes will be affected.

7 External works

Rather like furnishings, external works can make all the difference between an appealing building and an unappealing one. Too often this aspect is ignored and only token efforts are made resulting in a few paving slabs being laid without regard to proper indoor/outdoor use of the clubhouse.

An essential part of any club is the activity on the course – particularly the 1st tee and 18th green. Users of the clubhouse should be able to see these two key areas from social areas and this will help to determine both the siting of the clubhouse and the disposition of its main elements. Views and the sun aspect are of vital importance in increasing the enjoyment of a clubhouse particularly if it is proposed to install a swimming pool.

Other items which have to be considered in detail at the planning stage are the location and capacity of all services (telephone, water, gas, electricity, drainage) as well as possible expansion requirements. Car parking should also be considered in detail and a rule of thumb allowance for parking and circulation is 20 to 25 sq m (approx 24–30 sq yd) per car with a minimum capacity of 100 cars and a desirable capacity of 150. Additional overflow space for large functions should also be provided.

8 Maintenance

Maintenance is increasingly a source of major expenditure on most existing clubhouses; indeed it is often the need to make major repairs which leads clubs to consider a new building.

With a new clubhouse the opportunity arises to seek to minimise maintenance expenditure in the future. Proven materials are now available which make this possible. Unfortunately they tend to be expensive but injudicious choice of finishes can prove to be extremely expensive in the future.

Another aspect in the choice of materials is the near certainty that what is built will need amendment or change in the future. Intelligent anticipation in this respect can allow some materials or components to be chosen for their expendability in the medium future.

26
Artificial ski centres

Kit Campbell

1 The disciplines of skiing

Most skiers do so for fun and enjoyment rather than to compete. Nevertheless the sport of skiing has three major disciplines which each require a different facility:

- Alpine: most recreational skiing plus competitive slalom, giant slalom and downhill
- Nordic: cross-country skiing and ski jumping
- Freestyle: aerial manoeuvres, ballet and mogul skiing

All of these activities can be undertaken on artificial surfaces except for giant slalom and downhill racing. Alpine skiing can also be practised on grass slopes using special skis fitted with rollers or caterpillar tracks although erosion and damage to the grass can result from intensive use or when the ground is wet.

2 The development of new facilities

Ski centres contain two main facilities: the slope itself and essential ancillary accommodation. The planning of new centres should take account of:

- Types of use
- Estimated catchment population
- The size and distribution of existing centres
- Opportunities for school or other educational group or ski club use
- Environmental impact
- Opportunities for phased development

Good road access is essential along with car and coach parking. It is also desirable for the site to be served by public transport as not all users will have personal transport. Users will fall into four main categories:

- Novices wishing to learn the basic principles of skiing.
- Holiday skiers wishing to prepare or improve before a trip to snow slopes.
- Recreational skiers who can already ski but who wish to learn more advanced techniques.
- Competitive skiers involved in race training and instructing.

2.1 Indoor ski slopes

In some areas indoor slopes with 'real' snow, created by the use of new technology and maintained in a refrigerated and well insulated environment, are under consideration.

If the first few such developments are successful at providing actual snow skiing they will attract many users from outdoor artificial slopes. The capital cost, however, will probably mean they can be provided only in areas with a large catchment population.

3 Design

There is no such thing as a standard artificial ski slope design. Any layout should however comply with the minimum safety dimensions given in 1. The key design criteria are:

- Required capacity
- Choice of skiing surface
- Gradients
- Layout
- Phasing and expansion

The design of artificial ski slopes should be undertaken by a specialist. The national Governing Bodies for skiing may be able to recommend experienced consultants.

3.1 Capacity

Capacity is determined more by width and the availability of uplift than overall length. For beginners a slope as small as about 10 m long × 6 m wide (approx 33 × 20 ft) can provide a useful facility while most skiers can improve their skills and technique on slopes which are only 40–50 m long and under 12 m (approx 40 ft) wide. If racing and training in slalom and dual slalom is planned the slope should be not less than about 150 m long and 10–12 m wide (approx 500 × 40 ft) and be provided with floodlights, uplift and changing facilities. All slopes should be at least 10 m (approx 33 ft) wide. The most appropriate length for a slope to include a range of teaching opportunities is around 100 m (approx 330 ft).

3.2 Choice of skiing surface

The skiing surface must be selected before the skiing layout and contours can be designed. There are three main types of surface:

- Mono-filament PVC bristle set in stainless steel channels and fabricated into interlocking mat sections, 2
- Injection-moulded rounded bristle and fabricated into interlocking mat sections, 3

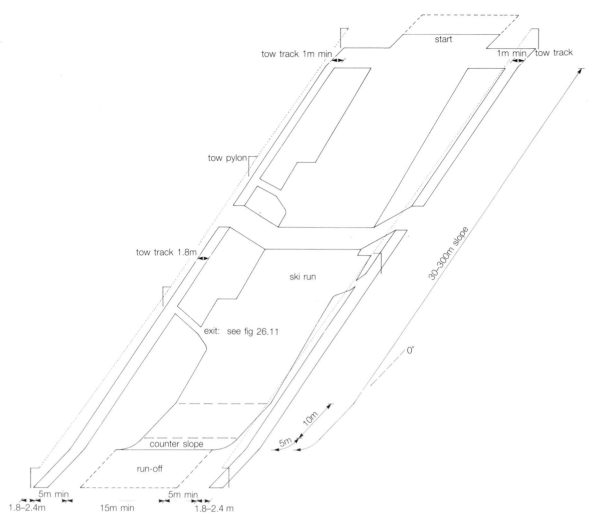

1 *Space diagram. There is no such thing as a standard ski slope but layout and design should comply with the minimum safety dimensions given in this diagram*

- Carpet types fabricated in rolls of woven or injection moulded plastic, **4**

There is no surface which is ideal for all artificial slopes although mono-filament PVC bristle is the most popular surface with many skiers. Development of other surfaces is still taking place and the carpet type surfaces are the safest in the event of a fall and therefore may be particularly suitable for beginner and novice areas. The various surfaces respond differently to the ski and therefore it is dangerous to lay them in a way which will allow users to ski off one surface on to another. If a particular facility has more than one surface they should be in physically separate areas.

Ski slope design should be satisfactory in both technical and visual terms. Most artificial surfaces are white and therefore prominent but their impact can be minimised by careful landscaping.

3.3 Gradient

Advice should be obtained from the manufacturer of the chosen ski surface in relation to gradients. The optimum gradient slope will depend upon the target market and the type of matting to be laid. In general, however, the best gradient for all weathers is usually about 14–18° to the horizontal although slopes can range from 5–25°. Small slopes, aimed primarily at beginners, should have an average gradient of about 14°. This will allow for a shallow, smooth terrain interspersed with areas of reduced gradient. Larger slopes – more than about 200 m (approx 660 ft) long – should contain a range of gradients and contour complexities giving skiers an opportunity to move from difficult to easy terrain. Gradients should average between about 12 and 18° depending upon the length of the slope and may include areas of less than 12° and small sections greater than 18°.

The steeper the slope the less safe it is likely to be because higher speeds will be possible. The rate of wear also increases with gradient. Wear is highest in braking and turning areas and it is common for matting sections to be moved around to distribute wear.

All slopes must have a flat area at the top and an adequate run-out area at the bottom. Many run-out areas have a slight upward slope because this makes it easier for fast skiers to turn and stop. Beginners' slopes should be separated from main slopes for safety reasons, **5**.

Artificial skiing surfaces have been laid successfully on three main types of incline:

- A natural hillside or landscaped incline
- A man-made mound – possibly using spoil from a nearby development and allowing adequate time for settlement
- A ramp or scaffolding

114

2 *Mono-filament PVC bristle. Photo: John Shedden*

3 *Injection-moulded rounded bristle. Photo: John Shedden*

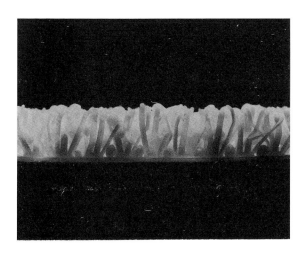

4 *Carpet type surface. Photo: Sports Council*

3.4 Layout
Careful planning will minimise future problems. Key points are:

- The integration of the slope with the surrounding environment and ancillary facilities
- Shelter planting or mounding
- Customer flow between different parts of the complex
- Expansion
- Adequate uplift and floodlighting

5 *Beginners' area separate from main slope (Hemel Hempstead). Photo: John Shedden*

As skiers develop their skill, they seek more variety and challenge, 6. Many will want slopes which mimic the runs found on mountain hillsides and a variety of features such as moguls and small jumps can be introduced to cater for this need. Artificial surfaces behave most like snow when the skier is descending the fall line and least like it when travelling across the slope. Some variety in the shape of runs is desirable, therefore, but bends should be carefully shaped and the slope cambered to retain the grip properties of the surface.

3.5 Phasing and expansion
While financial and other constraints may necessitate the construction of only a small centre initially, long term expansion will be easiest and simplest if all slope contouring and drainage can be undertaken at the outset.

4 Construction of artificial ski slopes
Detailed advice on the laying of ski surfaces for artificial slope should always be obtained from the appropriate governing body and surface manufacturer. In most cases the construction sequence will be:

- Remove topsoil and any rock which might force the finished skiing surface upwards
- Lay drainage: a typical drainage system consists of pipe drains in a herringbone pattern at about 10 m (approx 33 ft) centres discharging into main carrier drain(s) and then into a water course or large soakaway. The drainage system should be designed with substantial spare capacity to meet future demands in slope lubrication such as the installation of a sprinkler system. Particular attention should be paid to providing a cut-off drain at the bottom of the slope and ensuring that the run-out area will be laid over free draining material
- Lay other services, eg pipework for the automatic irrigation system and cableways for floodlighting
- Construct foundations and pylons for the uplift system
- Lay a barrier membrane on the consolidated sub-base to prevent small particles penetrating upwards to the ski surface
- Lay topsoil to a depth of 150–200 mm (6–8 in) and turf or sow a suitable grass mixture
- Complete services installations, including uplift, and ancillary accommodation
- Lay an impervious underlay over the slope
- Lay ski surface: in high winds the surface can be lifted and blown sideways and therefore it must be anchored

6 *The addition of 'bumps' makes a slope much more interesting and exciting. Note the separation of the slope from the tow track and lighting pylons (Hemel Hempstead). Photo: John Shedden*

securely. Individual mats are usually fastened to each other and then the complete surface tensioned and attached to the slope

- A hard wearing surface should be laid in run-off areas around the circumference of the slope. The type selected will be dependent on the type of ski surface chosen and type of anchorage system used; at many slopes it is a similar material to the underlay immediately beneath the skiing surface. The main alternatives for this underlay are:
  - Coir matting off cuts laid on 1000 gauge polythene sheeting. This is not suitable for run-off areas at the edges of slopes because the coir matting will not withstand wear from steel ski edges.
  - Polyvinylidence chloride matting. The long term durability of this material on run-off areas is not yet established.
  - Woven polyvinylchloride (PVC).
  - Woven polypropylene.

5 Mechanical and electrical equipment

5.1 Lighting

Artificial ski slopes attract maximum use during the winter and artificial lighting is essential. All parts of the slope, including uplift facilities, walkways, queuing areas and slope edges must be clearly floodlit.

Lighting systems for recreational and practice slopes should be designed to provide not less than 30 and preferably about 100 lux maintained illuminance with a uniformity ratio of 0:3. Floodlights are normally mounted on columns not less than 4 m (approx 13 ft) high located along the sides of the slope. All luminaires must point down the slope in order not to create disability glare for skiers moving down or across the slope.

5.2 Uplift

Uplift is essential for all slopes longer than about 50 m (approx 165 ft). There are four main types:

- Chairlift: only for longer slopes of about 300 m (approx 1000 ft) or more) or where walkers and other visitors can also use it to ascend a hill, 7, for walking or picnics. Chairlifts are not suitable for severely exposed sites because they are unusable in high winds.
- Platter lift with overhead cable, 8, on which users sit: suitable mainly for slopes of about 75–300 m (approx 250–1000 ft). A separate narrow strip of ski matting must be provided to allow users to 'ski' up the slope.
- Platter lift with waist high cable, 9: similar to platter lifts with overhead cables but cheaper and particularly suitable for beginners.

7 *Chairlift at Hillend Ski Centre. Photo: Sports Council*

8 *Drag (button) lift with overhead cable. Photo: Peter Ackroyd*

9 *Drag (button) lift with waist high cable. Photo: Peter Ackroyd*

10 *Rope tow: particularly suitable for beginners' slopes as they allow skiers to join or leave at any point. Photo: John Shedden*

- Drag lift with cable or rope at waist height which users grip and are pulled up the slope on their skis, **10**.

Drag lifts should be at least 5 m (approx 16 ft 6 in) away from the main slope. They require a narrow strip of

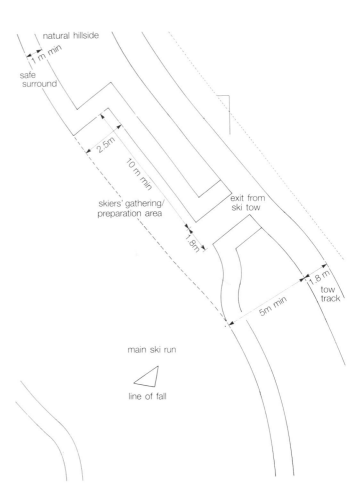

11 *Diagram of tow departure point and junction with main ski run. The margins shown along the edges of the slope are soft surfaced and not less than 1 m (approx 3.3 ft) wide.*

matting which will allow users to be towed uphill on their skis. The exit from uplift on to the slope must be designed with a skiers' gathering area, **11**.

The approach to uplift facilities must be located well away from the bottom of any slope in order to avoid the possibility of those descending the slope running into others waiting for uplift. In the same way, areas where skiers leave uplift and join the slope must be well away from the direct descent line of skiers already on it. It is usually advisable to have a gathering/holding area well to the side of the slope at uplift exit points.

The price and efficiency of uplift facilities varies widely and regular maintenance is essential. Accordingly specifiers should be satisfied that adequate arrangements exist for the rapid repair of imported equipment.

5.3 Slope lubrication
In certain conditions the plastics used for skiing surfaces can become 'sticky' and this makes it more difficult for the skis to slide over the surface and may, in extreme cases, result in injuries to skiers. Water can be sprayed on to the surface to reduce friction and enable skiers to turn their skis more easily. The best systems appear to be those which produce a fine mist of water below knee height.

There are two types of system in common use:

- Static systems where the irrigation pipework runs down one or both sides of the slope and feeds sprinklers fixed above ground level along the length of it.

117

12 *Photo: TUS*

● Pop-up sprinkler systems which are similar but are installed below ground level and pop up only when in use.

Most systems are automatically controlled by an electric timer. Large quantities of water may be required and a large tank and pump will generally be needed. Where automatic systems are installed it is also essential to have a manual override.

6 Ancillary facilities

The scale of ancillary facilities will depend upon the size of slope, the anticipated throughput, the amount of equipment to be stored and the markets it is intended to serve. Even at the smallest slopes the following will always be required:

● Car and coach parking
● Toilet accommodation
● First aid facilities: the minimum requirement is a table, bed or bench, a chair, wash hand basin and medicine cabinets. It must be possible for a stretcher-borne casualty to be carried into and out of the room
● Ski store and workshop
● Ski/boots hire area with boot washing facilities
● Reception and administration areas
● Instructor's changing facilities
● Plant room (serving both indoor facilities and uplift)

At large slopes it may also be necessary to have:

● Changing facilities for users
● Refreshment facilities with kitchen and stores
● Ski shop
● Creche
● Meeting/lecture room
● Bar and storage

Social facilities should be planned with a view over the slope(s); a common arrangement is to have the reception, ski workshop, ski and boot hire, changing and toilets at ground level with social areas on the first floor. Ideally reception should also have a window looking out over the bottom of the slope(s) and be provided with emergency stop switches for uplift facilities. The exit from the building to the slope should be close to the beginners' area and/or uplift at a point where no congestion is likely to occur. All circulation areas should be generously sized for two main reasons: because many skiers will be carrying skis and in order to make it easy to handle users with lower limb injuries.

7 Further information

Sports Council TUS Datasheet 20.
For further information contact:
English Ski Council.
Ski Council of Wales.
Scottish National Ski Council.
Ulster Ski Council Ltd.

27
Motorsports

Ian Fytche

1 Introduction
Over 200,000 people actively participate in motorsports in Great Britain. Of these, it is estimated that 100,000–150,000 people participate in motor car sports whilst a further 50,000–70,000 participate in motorcycle sports. In addition, it is estimated that 500,000 people are indirectly involved in motorsport, for example as marshals, stewards, officials and mechanics.

2 Site requirements
There are, principally, thirteen motor car disciplines and nine motorcycle disciplines. Precise site requirements can be obtained from the relevant governing body. However, the main requirements are outlined below:

2.1 Motorcar sports
- Road racing — Purpose built or modified circuit with sealed surface
- Off road racing — Unsealed surface, usually grass or stubble; uses short oval circuit with 15 m (50 ft) wide track and barriers
- Sprints and hill climbs — Sealed surface venues; sprints require straight flat course over 805 m (0.5 mile) in length (normally an airfield); hillclimbs require steep gradients (normally land)
- Autocross — Smooth grass or unsealed surface circuit of 550–1100 m (600–1200 yd) length
- Rallycross — Longer laps than autocross, combination of sealed and unsealed surfaces, usually located at motor racing circuits such as Lydden or Brands Hatch
- Kart racing — 100–250 cc karts on sealed surface circuits of under 1.5 km (approx 1640 yd) (short course), or over 1.5 km (approx 1640 yd) (long course); usually adapted airfields, or new purpose built circuits, such as Langbaurgh, Cleveland
- Rallying — Variety of stages including public highways, off road areas and race circuits. Single venue and special stage rallies use the above and Forestry Commission and MOD land, airfields, and private estate land
- Trials — Test events for production and modified cars on small, private offroad sites with varied terrain and steep slopes; usually private agricultural land. Classic and four wheel drive trials may also include use of the public highway.
- Autotests — Flat, sealed surface areas of less than 2 ha (2 acres), for example car parks, airfields, industrial sites and supermarket car parks
- Non-competitive trail — Driving of groups of up to six vehicles
- Driving — On green lanes, RUPPs (Roads Used as Public Paths) and Byways; organised by specialist clubs such as the All Wheel Drive Club or Association of Rover Clubs.

2.2 Motorcycle sports
- Road racing — Purpose built or converted circuit with sealed surface
- Grass track racing — Flat oval or kidney shaped grass or stubble course 450–900 m (500–1000 yd) in length; agricultural land
- Sand racing — On sea-shore (beach), with marked out continuous circuit
- Motocross (scrambling) — Off road circuit of 805–3218 m (0.5–2.0 miles) in length often with purpose built jumps and banks; fencing and paddock areas. Use agricultural land, rough land, quarries, and moorland
- Enduros — Long distance time and reliability trial on courses up to 100 km (60 miles) in length; mixture of on and off road sections with stages commonly on Forestry Commission or MoD land
- Trials — Low speed event with skill sections on rough terrain sites including quarries, woodlands and moorlands
- Sprints and hillclimbs — Sealed surface venues; sprints require straight flat course over 805 m (0.5 mile) in length (normally an airfield); hillclimbs require steep gradients (normally land)

- Arena trials — As for trials above, but with artificial obstacles either outdoor or indoor; includes playing fields, small stadia, large indoor arenas
- Non-competitive trail riding — Riding 'trail bikes' along unsealed public highways, green lanes, RUPPs and By-ways.

3 Site planning and layout

Careful site planning is required if planning applications for new permanent facilities are to be successful. Motorsport and recreation have witnessed a gradual loss of facilities over recent years and restrictions on access to established rights of way. The following aspects of site planning should be taken into account:

- Site topography and layout: consideration should be given to the need for obstacles, such as gradients, streams and landscaping features. This will depend on the site land demands, which fall broadly within the following categories:
  - Off road sites with no permanent course layout
  - Off road sites with a permanent or semi-permanent layout
  - Sealed surface venues not permanently laid out as a course or circuit
  - Sealed surface venues with a permanently laid out course or circuit
  - Venues offering a combination of sealed and unsealed surfaces.
- The positioning of pit and paddock areas
- On site facilities: the use and design of additional facilities should be carefully planned, for example:
  - Administration block/clubhouse
  - Changing room
  - Toilets
  - Workshop
  - First aid
  - Car parking
- Location: there are no rules governing proximity to residential or commercial property. However, a number of authorities have adopted 400 m (approx 440 yd) from residential property as a guideline – if natural screening measures are taken it may be possible to reduce this distance.

- Public access: care should be taken to ensure that rights of way crossing the site are not impeded, or that measures are taken to divert rights of way around the site. In addition, there should be physical separation from general public access.
- Security: the site should be secured against unauthorised use.
- Interested parties: all interested parties should be involved in planning new developments, including local authority planning and leisure departments, motorsports organisations and regional offices of the Sports Council.

4 Effective provision

The wide range of motorsports disciplines involved make simple prescriptive planning inappropriate. Some of the common types of arrangements include the following:

- Leasing off road sites: these could be disused or degraded land, land awaiting development, farmland, woodland and parkland. These sites could be leased by local authorities, public bodies or private owners and would be suitable for motorcycle and car trials, motorcycle grass track racing and possibly non-championship motocross. Providing that use would be less than 14 days per year planning permission is not normally required.
- Semi-permanent off road sites: this would involve using land with jumps, barriers and associated facilities, normally for motocross. Arrangements have included leasing local authority land and purchase of land by clubs and Governing Bodies. In some cases public service utilities will lease land. Planning permission will normally be required.
- Sealed surface venues: these may include (a) the use of private roads or the public highway for hillclimbs and sprints; (b) hiring disused airfields or industrial land for sprints, rally cross or karting; and (c) hiring local authority owned or supermarket car parks for autotests.
- Motorsport parks: these may be sites for motor car and motorcycle events and may include sprints, karting and scooter racing. The first type involves the adaptation of a disused airfield (for example at Pembray, Llanelli, South Wales), or the construction of a purpose-designed motor recreation park using local authority or development corporation finance (for example Three Sisters, Wigan, Greater Manchester where the earliest provision has been for karting).

28
Multi-use games areas (MUGAs)

Christopher Harper

1 Introduction

MUGAs vary in size from one, two or three tennis courts to a full hockey and football pitch, **1**. Recommended areas for soccer, basketball, hockey and netball are given in Part VII. Soccer areas can vary in size to cater for junior and adult teams of from four-a-side up to eleven-a-side, with five to seven-a-side being the most common. In dimensioning MUGAs there is always scope for flexibility and improvisation to suit local needs and sites.

The MUGA concept can embrace a wide range of facilities, from a one-tennis-court area in a remote rural village or inner city area, to a many-court-centre capable of catering for large netball or soccer competitions. In most projects, specifications for surfaces and surrounds will depend on finances available. Sponsors are urged to consider the range of options available on surfaces and surrounds and to construct to a good specification. A good standard of facility will attract users and provide value for money.

It is strongly recommended that any area provided for intensive use should be floodlit. The justification for substantial expenditure on an extensive use surface is greatly increased when floodlighting will enable it to be used throughout winter evenings. The inclusion of a

1 *Large pitch at Shene School, London SW14. A football pitch is subdivided for five-a-side soccer and tennis. Photo: C J Harper*

rebound wall, a low maintenance fixture, and floodlighting, giving all the year round intensive use, make MUGAs good value.

2 Planning and management

2.1 Location
Good promotion and management of these areas are required to obtain the best possible use and return on investment. Therefore, it is preferable for the facility to be located where there is an existing management structure with the potential to achieve a high level of use.

MUGAs are best located:

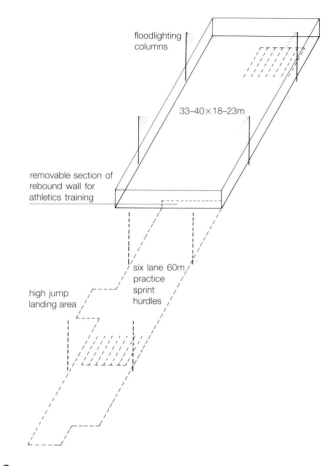

- On a club site to provide an ancillary playing and training facility for other sports
- In local parks and playing fields where more intensive use could be made of tennis courts or other areas. Well lit paths for safe access are essential
- Adjacent to sports and community centres, to extend the range of facilities available and enable increased use of the sports hall for those activities that can only take place indoors by making it possible to play some sports (eg five-a-side football) outdoors
- In rural areas adjacent to village halls, or linked to a junior school where limited management arrangements already exist
- Ideally MUGAs should be located adjacent to a pavilion or changing rooms, or suitable indoor spaces, to give more intensive use of these existing facilities and amenities.

Before an approach is made to the local planning authority, primary and possible other uses should be defined. For example, a soccer area can also accommodate netball, tennis and possibly hockey and basketball. In addition, roller skating, roller hockey, cricket and athletics training might be included.

Planning permission and approval of building regulations will normally be required for new facilities and for floodlighting. Early discussion with planning authorities is advised. Planning considerations include:

a

- The likely intrusions from floodlighting and activity noise levels to adjacent properties
- The need to restrict floodlit hours of use
- Access and car parking requirements
- The need for landscaping or screening in sensitive locations
- Possible basic shelter for players waiting for a game, and/or changing and other ancillary accommodation.

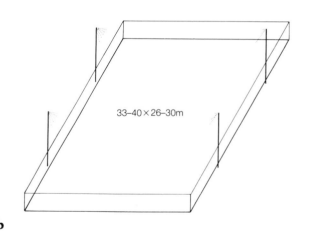

b

2.2 Management
When planning the project, it is essential to consider its management – how it will operate and who will run it.

The location and estimated levels of use will suggest the form of management which is most appropriate to each venue. Some form of promotion will normally be desirable. The options are:

- Positive promotion of an intensive programme of use within the duties of an existing management structure such as a local authority recreation department or sports and community centre; further education programmes; at commercial/industrial sports grounds and soccer clubs. This would assume supervisory or coaching staff on site during hours of use.

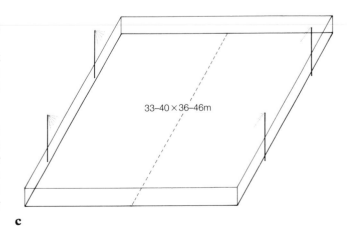

c

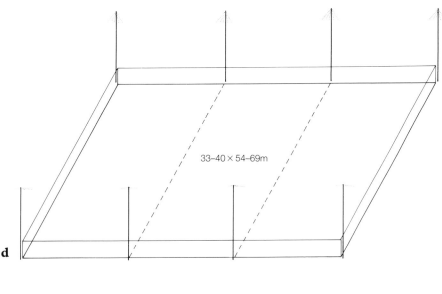

33–40 × 54–69m

d

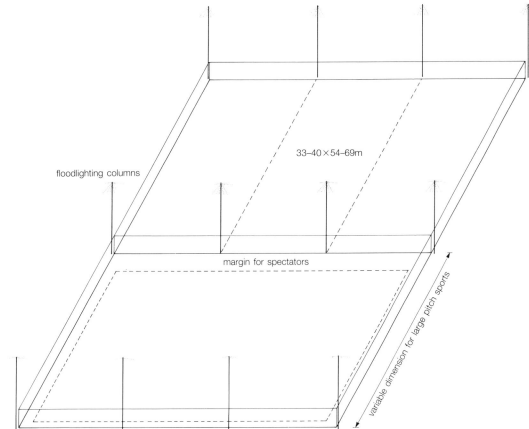

floodlighting columns

33–40 × 54–69m

margin for spectators

variable dimension for large pitch sports

e

2 *A graduated range of MUGA dimensions. Refer also to specific sports dimensions in Part VII:*
(a) Single court pitch area: capable of accommodating five- or six-a-side soccer, netball, tennis, six-a-side hockey, short tennis and basketball to different play standards depending upon the dimensions selected. Roller skating and roller skate hockey can also be considered providing the surface is suitable
(b) Medium pitch area: extra area provides for full width hockey and maximum five- or six-a-side soccer dimensions as well as two competition basketball courts.
(c) Large (double area): twice the size of (a) and twice the capacity. A removable central barrier provides full flexibility enabling the whole area to be used for a team game or separated pitches for different concurrent activities.
(d) Multiple, triple area: consider one permanent and one movable divider or two movable dividers to make the best use of this area
(e) Large multiple areas: this example is half the area of a full size junior football pitch but bigger pitches may be considered. The installation of removable rebound barriers will help to maximise use and ensure viability.

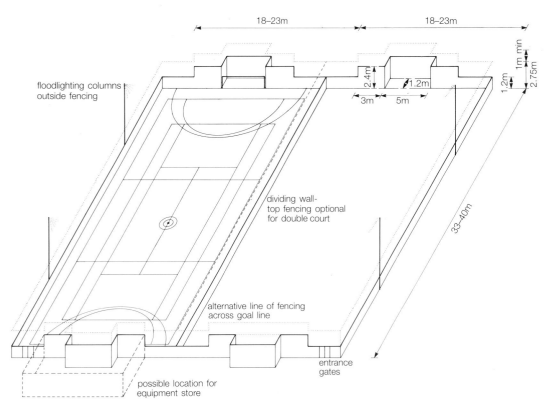

3 *Details of a typical large (double) area MUGA.*

- Peak-time or part-time on-site staff, Monday–Friday evening, Saturday or Sunday morning coaching sessions. This level of management may be appropriate where the location is not adjacent to a full time on-site management structure.
- A booking system through an individual who is responsible for opening and closing the facility and operating the lighting at required times. A key collect and return system operated with approved user groups with metered lights may be adequate.
- Minimum controls or open casual use with limited programmed use.

The first two options will usually be desirable to promote the maximum use of the facility with a balanced programme of activities which cater for a range of age groups among juniors, teenagers and adults.

3 Design

3.1 General description
The play area should be enclosed with rebound surfaces and netting.

It is desirable that the overall appearance should be as attractive as possible. Coloured rather than black surfaces are preferred. Court lines should be clearly marked and maintained to a good standard.

Lines of concrete posts are unsightly, particularly in small-scale developments and steel or possibly oak posts are preferable in most locations. Chain link fencing and weldmesh will soon develop weak spots and breaks if not fitted and fixed to correct specifications. This particularly applies to areas around goals.

Good drainage and adequate maintenance of the surface areas are necessary to ensure maximum use and continuity of programme.

The design of basketball posts and soccer goals, and the storage of netball and tennis posts, are directly related to ease of use and management and specification of these items must be part of the initial planning design brief.

3.2 Scale of provision
A range of dimensions is suggested for different scales of project as shown in **2**.

3.3 Floodlighting
Wherever possible, floodlighting should be included to ensure maximum utilisation. All MUGA projects require a three-phase electricity supply.

Floodlighting schemes must be discussed with the planning authority at an early stage of the development. In some areas, planning permission may be difficult to obtain and in these cases low profile lighting may have to be considered.

Floodlight tubular steel columns are normally used, the height varying from 6–12 m (approx 20–40 ft) and related to the overall requirements of the agreed lighting scheme. Columns can be raised and lowered using hydraulic counter-balance units.

Design features should discourage vandalism eg anti-vandal lenses and the possible use of anti-vandal paint to a height of about 2.5 m (approx 8 ft). The control panel should, if possible, be installed inside a permanent building such as a changing room, clubhouse or sports centre. The advice of the Regional Electricity Board should be sought on the location of a three-phase supply, and lighting specialists should submit a light diagram with their proposals.

Minimum readings of approximately 75 lux should be adequate for recreational soccer and training, with a minimum level of 200 lux for competition play.

Refer also to Chapter 18.

4 *Timber rebound and central dividing barrier with recessed goals at Bury St Edmunds. Photo: C J Harper.*

3.4 Drainage
MUGAs must be drained adequately, with water being shed rapidly from the surface by:

- A totally pervious structure where water passes through the base and sub-base, which may consist of a drainage raft construction. This may also include a drainage system of main and lateral pipe drains, or slits, or a combination of these, to suit the situation; or
- An impervious construction which relies on surface drainage with an adequate cross fall to perimeter drainage outlets (usually along one side of the area).

Cross falls to give some surface run off may be needed with pervious constructions, dependent on site circumstances. Perimeter drainage usually requires a minimum of a single line of surface catchwater open blocks along the length of one rebound side wall, flush with pitch level, with rodding access along its length and connected to drainage soakaway or storm water drains.

3.5 Base construction
Whatever the chosen surface, it is essential that the most appropriate base is selected, since this has a major bearing on the quality of playing surface and its performance and characteristics, 4. It may be designed to have a life several times that of the surface to make future refurbishment economical. Specific information on bases is given in Chapters 7, 9, 10 and 11.

3.6 Surface choice
Surfaces for kickabout areas usually need to be low maintenance, hard wearing with traction and ball rebound properties suitable for the intended sports and other activities. No surface will be ideally suitable for all uses, and compromises will be necessary. Advice on surface selection is given in Chapter 7 and more information on specific surfaces suitable for MUGAs are covered in Chapters 9, 10 and 11. However, all surfaces require some maintenance. The hard porous waterbound (shale type) surfaces are particularly demanding in this respect. They are not recommended for MUGAs, though they can provide good playing qualities where there is a commitment to adequate maintenance.

3.7 Rebound walls
The construction may be:

- Dense concrete blockwork
- Precast concrete units
- Brickwork – semi-engineering standard with bull-nosed top section
- Treated softwood boarding
- Treated exterior quality composite woodchip boards or panels to BS 5669
- Treated exterior quality marine plywood panels with top capping.

Timber surfaces are generally preferred on the grounds of both cost and resilience; they minimise the chance of impact injuries.

The height should be 1–1.2 m (approx 3–4 ft) with additional height around goal areas. The rebound wall can be linked to the construction of the netting surround or built within existing tennis court areas. Where funds are very limited, or as a short term measure in order to make better use of an existing tennis court area, an additional inner layer of heavy-gauge chain link fencing

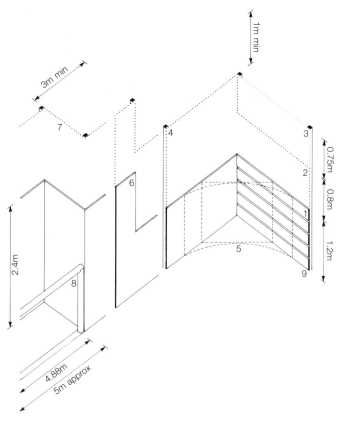

5 Fencing and rebound wall details. 1 Flush robust rebound wall: timber boarded or marine quality plywood fixed to sturdy posts. 2 Heavy-duty galvanised welded mesh fence along sides, particularly at corners. Minimum overall height 2.75 m. 3 Alternative galvanised heavy duty chain link mesh. 4 Essential welded mesh at goal ends. Extra strengthening and straining wires required. 5 Possible splayed or rounded corner units for roller hockey and soccer. 6 Rebound wall raised to 2.4 m around goals. 7 Fence raised to minimum 3.75 m high around goals. 8 Built-in rounded steel goal posts and removable cross bar. 9 Avoid creating a gap where balls (and shoe caps) can get wedged.

with low timber battens or edging could provide a cheaper alternative to a rebound construction, 4.

3.8 Recessed goal areas and dividing walls
Where soccer is the primary use, goal mouth areas should be recessed to give a goal line flush with end walls. The recess also allows for the construction of fixed goal posts (half rounded) with a strong removable cross bar bolted or clamped down, or a more stable fixing for portable goals. Where the site will allow it, rebound walls should be built to offer both sides for use, eg behind end walls, using two adjacent areas, to include complementary smaller training or play areas.

Dividing walls are usually of permanent construction, ideally with netting above rebound surfaces. Movable timber wall sections such as are used in sports halls can also be considered. These are usually 1.2 or 2.4 m (approx 4 or 8 ft) long by 1.2 m high and 0.6 m (approx 4 and 2 ft) in width and can withstand body impact when positioned in series. They can be used to sub-divide any of the areas shown in the diagrams to the required dimensions. A tennis practice wall may also be incorporated on one long side.

Where basketball posts need to be fitted, the detailed design of the surrounds must accommodate them. Modified dimensions may be acceptable in order to provide basketball facilities. Any changes from recommended court sizes should be checked with governing body officials to confirm acceptance in specific locations.

The dimensions of the recesses should provide for soccer goals of up to 4.9 m (approx 16 ft) between posts by 1.2 m (approx 4 ft) in height. Hockey-sized goals 3 × 2 m (approx 10 × 6.5 ft) giving extra height are used for soccer in some locations. Extra high goals may be preferable in larger playing areas to relate more closely to the eleven-a-side game.

3.9 Fencing and access gates
A height of 2.75 m (approx 9 ft) is required for fencing, with an extra height of 3.7 m (approx 12 ft) behind the goals. This extra height should extend at least 3 m (approx 10 ft) beyond each side of the goals to contain balls. The rebound surface can be taken to a height of 2.4 m (approx 8 ft) behind the goals. This should extend 2–3 m (approx 6.5–10 ft) beyond each side of the goal mouth, 5. Welded wire netting around the goal areas is recommended rather than chain link, with additional horizontal support of extra strainer wires, or preferably angle iron, to prevent bulging of the netting.

The main access for larger areas should be double gated for maintenance machinery and is usually located at a mid-point down one side. Additional single gates can be located where required. The path between the site entrance or pavilion and access gate should be surfaced to prevent transfer of mud and dirt to playing surface or changing area. Other important specification notes are:

- Higher fencing may be required to safeguard neighbouring roadways or residential property
- All exposed steelwork and netting should be heavy duty galvanised or coated, with no removable fixing and parts
- Entrance gates may need to be heavy duty
- All clips and fixings should avoid cut metal and sharp edges.

4 Changing facilities/refreshment amenities
Refer also to Chapter 23.

Where there is regular organised training and competition, changing facilities will normally be required although they are not essential. Local toilet provision is needed and drinking water or a vending/refreshments machine should be provided as long as security and supervision is adequate.

5 Storage
Where portable equipment is used, storage facilities will be required adjacent to the playing area. They must be designed to accommodate netball posts, soccer goals and possibly basketball posts and hockey goals. If necessary, a storage structure could be incorporated into the design of a goal recess or wall end.

6 References and further advice
British Standards Institution BS 5669 *Particleboard* Part 1: 1989 'Methods of sampling, conditioning and test'

Part 2 1989 'Specification for wood chipboard'

Part 4 1989 'Specification for cement bonded particle-board'

Part 5 1989 'Code of practice for the selection and application of particleboard for specific purposes.

British Standards Institution. BS 7044 *Artificial Sports Surfaces*. BSI, London (1990).

Chartered Institution of Building Services Engineers, *Lighting Guide – Sports*. CIBSE, London (1990).

Fédération Internationale de Hockey, *Handbook of Requirements for Synthetic Hockey Pitches Outdoor*. FIH (1991).

Football League Commission of Enquiry into Playing Surfaces. Football League, London (1990).

National Playing Fields Association, *Kick-about Areas* (revised). NPFA, London (1985/6). Also various cost guides.

National Playing Fields Association, *Sports Pavilions*. NPFA, London.

Northern Council for Sport and Recreation, *Community Sports Provision in Rural Areas, Appendix 2 – Multi-Games Areas*. Northern Council for Sport and Recreation, Durham.

The Sports Council, *Artificial Grass Surfaces for Soccer, Hockey and Multi-Games Areas (State of the Art)*. The Sports Council, London (1985).

The Sports Council, Research Working Paper 20 – *Kickabout Areas: Providing for Sport in Areas of Special Need*. The Sports Council, London (1981).

The Sports Council, TUS datasheet 40: *Floodlighting – Outdoor Sports*. The Sports Council, London.

The Sports Council, TUS datasheets (individual sports). The Sports Council, London.

The Sports Council, *Artificial Turf Pitches for Hockey*. The Sports Council, London (1990)

The Sports Council, *Specification for Artificial Sports Surfaces:* Part 1: General Principles and Classification; Part 2: Surfaces for General Use. The Sports Council, London.

Winterbottom, Sir W. *Artificial Grass Surfaces for Association Football – Report and Recommendations*. The Sports Council, London.

Playboard, the Association for Children's Play and Recreation Ltd, Britannia House, 50 Great Charles Street, Queensway, Birmingham B3 2LP. Publications advice and support through area offices.

29
Air sports

Mike Earle and Cynthia Coombe

1 Land use planning and environmental management

Air sports clearly have a range of environmental effects. They vary from noise created for those living in towns near aerodromes, or similar facilities, to the erosion of popular hill soaring sites in National Parks. In some cases extra off-site traffic movements can be created. Demands for a range of ancillary buildings including hangarage, training rooms, accommodation for those under instruction, or caravan and camping facilities can also occur. Powers to control or manage wider environmental effects, as well as the crucial issue of the change of use of land to air sports, lie largely with local planning authorities.

2 Gliding

A glider is an aerodynamically efficient unpowered aircraft whose energy comes from gravity. It is, in effect, an aerial toboggan. The sport of gliding has moved on from the gentle hill soaring and controlled descent it once was to an activity which requires considerable skills, knowledge and training. Such requirements reflect the major advances made in glider technology and the technique of glider flying. Today cross country flights have reached distances of around 1500 km (approx 930 miles), while increased performance and speed has led to a higher level of achievement by a greater number of pilots. However, despite such advances, the sport continues to attract large numbers of new participants each year.

When wind blows against an obstruction such as a hill, most of the air is forced up creating a band of rising air.

A glider flying in this band of lift will be able to stay airborne as long as the air is rising at a rate equal to or greater than the rate of descent of the glider. If the wind is blowing at right angles to a ridge, then the glider will be able to soar back and forth in front of the slope, but as soon as the glider leaves the area of lift, it will sink at a rate determined by the glide angle of the craft. Therefore, to travel any distance from an area of hill lift, a pilot must take advantage of other sources of lift.

2.1 Sites and land use planning

Clubs are largely defined and categorised by the size of their site and its location. The types of land used can range from licensed airfields, through private airfield to MoD sites and farmland.

The large site with security of tenure will tend to have better facilities, a wider range of training and a more active membership. The insecure club may typically be suffering from lack of investment in facilities, an inability to launch gliders rapidly or consistently enough and difficulties in keeping new members, after they have had one or two trial flights.

The main physical site requirements are a flat and well-drained area of grass or a metalled runway located in an area suitable for lift from thermals or hills. The site should not be in the vicinity of any tall obstructions and preferably should have no local airspace restrictions. British Gliding Association advice *Starting a Gliding Club* identifies a minimally small club layout – allowing one 548 m (1800 ft) winch cable to operate in one direction only – as requiring approx 6 ha (13.8 acres) of land. A medium-sized club layout, with a 731 m (2400 ft) winch launch, and space for aero tow launching would require, at minimum, 33.3 acres.

However, a reasonable facility, allowing for storage of gliders, car parking and club house facilities suggests at least 20 ha (50 acres) are required, particularly if a choice of launch directions is to be achieved. The largest runway-based regional centres have sites of over 40 ha (100 acres).

In addition to launch facilities, a secure hangar and a club house are normal minimal requirements. Larger clubs may require a workshop, hostel type (bunkhouse) accommodation for those on courses, briefing and teaching rooms and offices for permanent staff. A number of clubs in remote sites noted for soaring will also require permission for the stationing of caravans or the erection of tents.

3 Parachuting

Parachuting is one of the oldest aerial activities and dates from the seventeenth century. It is the controlled descent usually from an aircraft to the ground, using a canvas or nylon canopy strapped to the participant's back to limit the speed of the fall and give directional manoeuvrability.

3.1 Sites and land use

A parachute operation requires the facility for an aircraft to land and take-off. Ideally, this should be a metalled, concrete runway with a flat well drained piece of grassed land. The site should comprise a drop zone which is sufficiently large (at least 24 ha (60 acres)) to allow it to be used safely by inexperienced novice parachutists. Both the drop zone and the immediate surrounding area should be clear of all obstructions and development, including housing. Any club which is involved in free fall parachuting should ideally be located within uncontrolled airspace to a height of at least 12,000 ft. Nearly all clubs fly from the area which they use as a drop zone and several clubs make use of more than one drop zone giving them flexibility in different weather conditions. A few clubs have preferred to negotiate for the use of farmers' fields as drop zones.

Clubs also require hangarage or secure parking for aircraft, accommodation for regular members and those on courses, and rooms and training facilities to instruct first time jumpers according to specifications laid down by the British Parachute Association (BPA) Safety and Training Committee. Most clubs also have a building or room which is used for the drying and re-packing of canopies.

Over 85% of clubs share the use of their site with other recreational and/or commercial activities. Over half of the parachute clubs share their site with recreational flyers or a flying club. The next most frequent uses of the same site are gliding, motor sports, parascending and microlight flying. Different orders of priority occur at different airfields.

A high percentage of airspace in the UK is controlled and 40% of parachuting clubs face restrictions on either when or where they can fly. Over half of these reported having restrictions placed on their use of airspace. The Oxon and Northants Parachute Centre, operating from Hinton-in-the-Hedges is sometimes limited during weekdays to a 3000 ft ceiling if the Upper Heyford military base is active. (The base of controlled airspace is at 5000 ft over the site.)

Noise can be a problem for parachute clubs, particularly if large, heavy aircraft are used. Most clubs operate voluntary codes of practice where possible so that residential areas are not overflown. However, unpredictable changes in wind direction mean it is not always possible to avoid residential areas.

4 Hang gliding

A hang glider is an unpowered aircraft which is capable of being foot launched by the pilot. Modern hang gliders are made from aluminium alloy tubing, wire rigging, and a special synthetic cloth called dacron or terylene. They are controlled by the shifting of the body weight in a full support harness to alter the centre of gravity in relation to the glider. This gives a high degree of manoeuvrability.

4.1 Sites and land use

Hang gliding is perhaps the least demanding of airsports in its site requirements. A participant needs a high take-off point sloping towards the wind, a space to park a car and to assemble the glider and a landing place equipped, ideally, with a wind sock. The best sites have space, in smooth air, to allow for top landings in an area adjacent to a take off spot. All take off and landing sites need to be relatively free from obstructions and buildings and can only be used when take-off can be effected into the wind. In a recent report, the Southern Council for Sport and Recreation notionally identifies a take-off area of about 45 m (49 yd) square and a landing area of about 0.4 ha (1 acre) as a minimum requirement. Such a facility would be suitable for a club event, when a number of pilots and motor vehicles would be likely to be present. Individual pilots, flying in smaller groups are able to make use of far smaller sites, often amounting to little more than a

clear take-off slope of approx 10 m (approx 33 ft) above an area of unobstructed or sharply falling land.

In attempting to define an ideal hill site, some of the most important factors are:

- The direction the hill faces (between north west and south are the most useful)
- Appropriate flying conditions (including a smooth airflow and enough lift for soaring)
- Easy physical accessibility reducing the amount of carry as much as possible
- Adequate capacity of the site, both on the ground, and in terms of uncontrolled airspace.

On any particular day a club may have only one or two sites that can be used, depending on the wind direction. Hill training sites require gentle slopes and space for landings which may be imprecise at first. Some sites may provide access to air that can be used to gain extra height. Most club sites have take-off points on slopes with gradients of at least 1:5 – many are steeper. Obstructions such as trees and buildings cause turbulence that is undesirable near take-off. Hang gliders are highly manoeuvrable and will change altitude and direction rapidly at the pilot's direction. If a hill has a wide ridge top it will reduce the risk of a pilot flying into the dangerous downdraughts of wind on the lea of the hill. If there is a sufficiently large space, the launch site should be moved periodically to prevent erosion at any one place.

5 Microlight flying

The first microlights were simply hang gliders with a small engine attached. These have been developed and now incorporate a sturdy structure suspended below the wing which includes the seats, wheels and engine. They are know as 'weight shift' microlights, but there is another type which looks and handles like a small aeroplane known as 'three axis' microlights.

5.1 Site and land use

A microlight can take off and land within 30–50 m (approx 33–55 yd). A landing space may be a concrete or grass runway, so microlights will often share sites with other airsports. The immediate surroundings should be unobstructed and consideration given to the presence of controlled airspace and any residential development in the vicinity. Basic requirements are therefore modest and many clubs may use a succession of privately owned fields to land or take off, so avoiding the need for planning permission.

6 Parascending

Parascending is the lifting of a person into the air by a parachute-type canopy, 1. Lift is created by the forward movement of a tow-line attached to a drive vehicle or boat. The sport embraces elements of both parachuting and hang gliding because long line descents can occur from over 2000 ft.

The majority of parascending launches are achieved by land based, auto-tow. Launching over land allows a participant to 'self-release' from the cable and float down unattached as would a parachutist. Once released, the parascender has the opportunity merely to descend or undertake some form of aerial activity using thermals and lift in the same way as a glider or hang glider pilot.

1

6.1 Sites and land use

Parascending basically requires an open site, free of all obstruction. Sufficient space is required to allow pilots to land safely. The length of a site determines the cable length that can be used for tows and so the height that can be achieved. It requires firm ground conditions throughout the year. Thus an airfield runway is ideal, as is a well drained field, agricultural land or public park.

Parascending can take place over land and water, thus it shares its sites with air, water and land based activities. There can be a conflict of interests with other land users such as motorcyclists, seasonal agricultural activities such as hay or silage making or pitch sports; secondly, airspace conflicts with model aircraft flying over launching points, or occasionally gliders; thirdly with landowners such as the MoD, where access may only be allowed to one type of recreational activity at a time.

7 Further information

This chapter has been based on information in *Providing for Air Sports*, by Martin Elson, Henry Buller, Ian Thorpe and Jon Lloyd and published by the Sports Council.

Part VI Water recreation

30
Rowing

Mike Earle and Nigel Weare

1 Water requirements

Competitive rowing and training can take place on rivers, lakes and with careful and proper management can share both water space and on-shore ancillary facilities with other activities such as sailing, canoeing, angling and sub-aqua.

International class racing is carried out over 2000, 1500 and 1000 m (2188, 1641 and 1094 yd) length courses, with buoys of the correct size and colour marking the lanes, **1**. Normal domestic competition courses however can be of any length but better if over 1000 m (1094 yd). It is possible to lay out a course around a bend but a straight course is preferred. A four-lane course requires a minimum width of 60 m (approx 66 yd) with approximately 100 m (approx 110 yd) for crews to slow down and return to the landing area.

It is desirable that the water is sheltered from the wind but not essential. At least one section of the water ought to provide shelter from the wind for training and when conditions are particularly difficult. Ideally the racing lanes should lie along the line of the prevailing winds. Wind breaks created by trees, shrubs, embankments and mounds can be beneficial. Spectator interest is focused on the finish line therefore it is advantageous to place the clubroom and social facilities opposite or overlooking a suitable position for the finishing line on the water.

Access to the water and boat launching and landing should be a minimum 15 m (approx 16 yd) wide but 40 m (approx 44 yd) is desirable and can be via non-slip steps, ramps or pontoons. The latter should take account of transverse stability, eg nine people standing on the edge holding a boat above their heads, **2**, and take account of tidal changes to the water level. Artificial lakes and gravel pits will experience seasonal changes in level due to evaporation and rainfall.

2 Boathouse

The boathouse should be sited on a lee shore close to the water but at least 18 m (approx 20 yd) from it to allow boats to be moved between the boathouse and water's edge, **3**.

The size of the boathouse will be dependent upon the size of the club and number of boats stored but

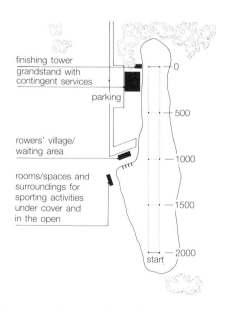

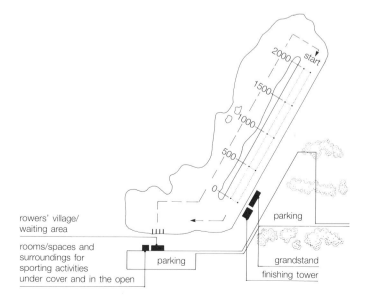

1 *Diagram of international class course*

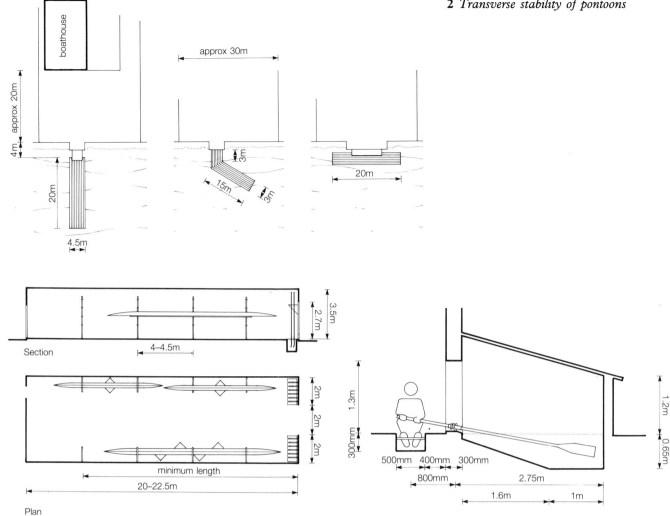

3 *Typical site plan*

5 *Rowing tank*

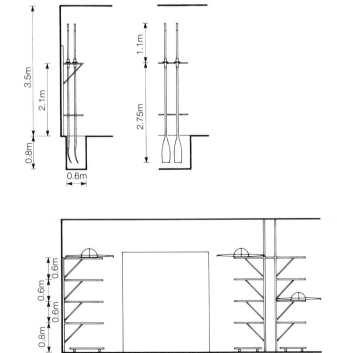

4 *Boat storage on racks*

the minimum dimensions are 12 m (39 ft) wide, 15 m (49 ft) long and an internal height of 2 m (6 ft 6 in) with 2 m (6 ft 6 in) wide access doors. It should be well insulated without windows or roof lights. This will help to minimise summer/winter temperature variations and help with security. A smooth non-slip concrete floor is preferred, laid to falls to the outside. Many clubs have developed ingenious ways of stacking their boats, oars and gear. **4** shows the recommended way of doing this.

3 Clubhouse

The clubhouse should have changing accommodation, toilets and hot showers, a social area, bar and storage and committee rooms. The facilities in the clubhouse will depend greatly on the size and finances of the club.

4 Weights room

A number of clubs have a weights room for training, preferably with free weights. It should be well ventilated in order to remove body odours and have a non-slip floor. Rowing and bicycle ergometers are best located in a separate space with controlled heating and ventilation as their use can generate strong air movements.

5 Rowing tank

An enclosed space for a rowing tank, 5, should have non-corrosive and impervious surfaces including a non-slip floor and background heating to 10-13°C. The tank will require drainage for emptying and cleaning. Noise control may be desirable.

6 Access and parking

Rowing trailers require a turning circle for an 11 m (36 ft) vehicle. Regattas can generate a strong following and a number of crews. Therefore adequate space should be available for boat trailers and the parking of cars.

31
Sailing

Robin Wilson

1 General

Sailing is a diverse activity, taking place on a wide range of waters and making use of craft from sailboards and small dinghies to large ocean-going yachts. Recently there have been some attempts to manage it as a commercially viable spectator sport, **1**. Since the 1950s the sport has grown in the UK, owing to a number of factors, including:

- New materials and construction techniques have allowed the development of a large range of comparatively inexpensive craft suitable for many types of water
- The opening up of inland waters has allowed people to take up the sport without travelling to the coast
- Small dinghies are easily transportable by trailer or roof top to a variety of sailing waters, **2**
- The emergence of sailboarding as a totally new sailing discipline with inexpensive and very portable equipment.

The rapid growth in the sport has led to increasing pressure on available resources. Many inland waters are fully used, resulting in congestion and conflicts with other users. In addition, land-based facilities such as car parks and launching facilities are often regarded as unsatisfactory or inadequate.

The types of location for sailing facilities are:

- Reservoirs, lakes and gravel pits
- Rivers
- Estuaries and sea/coasts

The main classifications of sailing are:

- Training
- Recreational/casual/pottering
- Racing

The factors affecting the suitability of water areas for sailing are:

- Depth of water (variations in depth owing to tide, water management, climatic conditions)
- Shape of water areas
- Size of water areas
- Water characteristics
- Wind characteristics
- Other users

1 *Indoor sailboarding. 'Funboard at Bercy' in France.*
Photo: James Bareham

2 *A massed-produced GRP dinghy transported on a car top.*
Photo: R Wilson

136

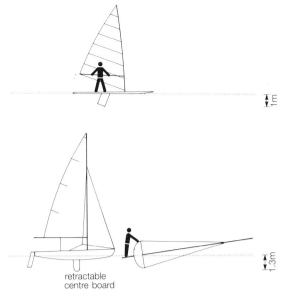

a

retractable
centre board

b

limited
cabin
accomodation

fixed keel

c

living accommodation

d

3 *Typical draughts of sailing craft (a) sailboards (b) dinghies (c) keelboats (d) cruisers*

4 *Water area used for fishing and sailing. Photo: R Wilson*

depth of water for sailboards is 1 m (approx 3 ft), dinghy sailing approximately 1.3 m (4 ft 3 in), for cruisers and keelboats 1.3–1.8 m (approx 4–6 ft) and for ocean-going boats, 4.5 m (approx 15 ft), **3**. Account should be taken of likely wave heights, variations in water level due to tides, water management, climatic conditions and other factors such as the flow of water in rivers.

It should also be noted that the area of water and associated facilities may have to cater for various other uses, including:

- Motorboats/hydroplaning/hovercraft racing
- Motor cruising
- Model boating
- Commercial user
- Water ski-ing
- Jet ski-ing
- Sub-aqua diving
- Canoeing
- Rowing
- Wild life
- Swimming
- Angling

Since a water area is in theory capable of such a multiplicity of differing activities, consideration should be given to zoning it or programming the times of use to allow the successful and non-conflicting integration of the different activities, **4**. Naturally, some activities are totally incompatible with others and in the UK advice should be taken from the regional and national Sports Councils.

- Accessibility
- Environmental factors
- Conservation factors

It is essential that expert advice is taken in assessing the suitability of a water area. In the UK, the Royal Yachting Association (RYA) will recommend classes of boats that are suitable for a specific stretch of water. The minimum

137

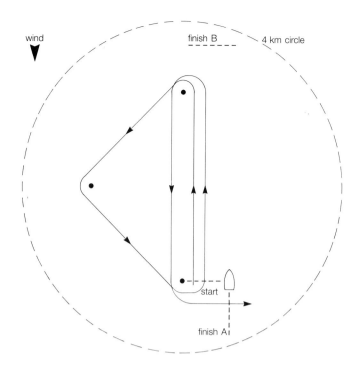

5 *A traditional Olympic course; the first leg is a beat to windward followed by two reaches; then a beat and a run; finally a beat to finish*

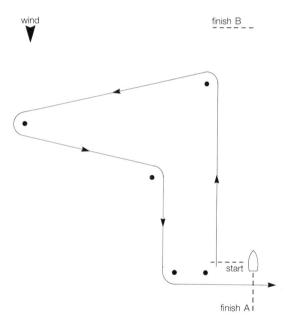

6 *New Olympic Course; first leg to windward followed by two reaches a run and a final reach*

2 Water areas and their selection

Sailing can take place on various shapes and sizes of water. There is a wide range of sailing boats available and it is likely that most water will suit some part of the range. Sailboarding in particular can utilise waters that previously had been unsuitable for traditional sailing. Training can take place on small areas of water such as gravel pits (say under 1 ha (approx 2.5 acres) and on rivers say 30 m (approx 33 yd) wide. The important consideration is the absence of such obstructions as moored boats and the conflicting presence of other users.

For those who require recreational sailing, the attractiveness of the water and its surroundings is probably the main consideration. A fairly large area of water such as a

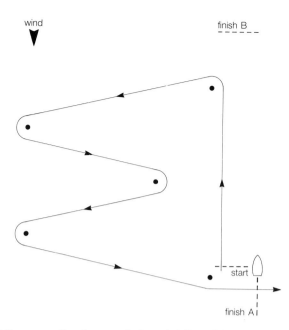

7 *'M' course; first leg to windward followed by four reaches.*

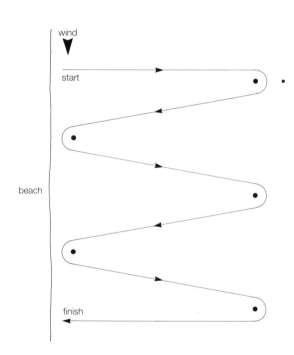

8 *Slalom Course: downwind*

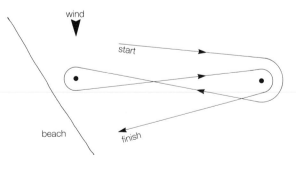

9 *Slalom course*

lake, a large gravel pit, a river 50 m (approx 55 yd) wide, or a sheltered estuary would be suitable.

Ideally, racing requires more space than other forms of sailing, with the larger and higher performance classes of boat requiring up to 800–1000 ha (approx 1977–2470

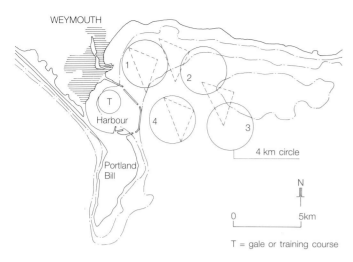

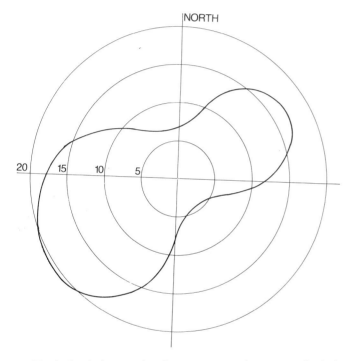

10 *Proposed National Sailing Centre at Weymouth, 1988*

11 *Typical wind rose, showing percentage frequency of wind direction for the UK*

Generally, in the UK the prevailing wind direction is from the south-west with the second most common direction being from the north-east.

2.2 Capacity

As a general guide to the capacity of an area of water a density of 2.5–5 boats/ha (1–2 boats/acre) may be taken. However, the capacity of an area will obviously depend on the individual situation with the size of boats, the competence of the helmsperson and the level of management being factors to consider. Where over-crowding has caused clubs to limit the numbers of dinghies on the water at any one time, a density of 3.3 boats/ha (approx 1.5 boats/acre) appears to be the maximum that is acceptable for boats of approx 4 m (13 ft) in length. In the case of sailboards a density of 6 boards/ha (approx 2.5 boats/acre) may be acceptable. However, such high densities are likely to be totally satisfactory only in racing situations or where the sailing is organised and relatively competent. Casual or training situations require the minimum possible density.

As a general guide the dinghy-parking capacity can be taken as being between 3–5 times the capacity of the water, since it is unlikely that all boats will be sailing at any one time. However, the population catchment of the facility should also be considered in assessing the necessary dinghy-parking provision. It would seem reasonable that a similar approach should be given to assessing the capacity of the car-park facility, although many factors might affect the number of people who travel by car. It has been suggested that the figure of 1.5 the boat capacity of the water can be taken as a general guide. If it is assumed that a club or facility supports a membership of 100 people who all own a boat, then a typical pattern might be as follows:

- 75 dinghies kept semi-permanently on site
- 10 dinghies towed down to the site each fine summer weekend
- 60 cars (10 towing dinghies) arriving on each day of a fine weekend.

The normal pattern at summer weekends might lead to a parking requirement for 85 dinghies and 60 cars. This figure might easily be doubled, however, if regattas for visiting boats are held. Where there is little local knowledge of use patterns a 'safe' provision might be 0.6 ha of parking space for each 100 sailing dinghies in regular use.

3 Locations

3.1 General

Generally, it is easiest to launch a sailing dinghy from a windward shore because the boat can be allowed to drift away from it. In cases where the prevailing winds are south-westerly and north-easterly, the ideal shore line for launching facilities is south-west, north-east, which allows boats to launch and land on a 'reach' (ie approximately at right-angles to the wind). This is particularly suitable for sailboarders. Where the geography of the water area does not allow this orientation, the use of pontoons, jetties and ramps can create suitable launching facilities, **12, 13** and **14**.

It can be a great advantage when organising racing if the sailing control is on a promontory. This allows races to be controlled from on shore and still allows the greatest possible number of start-line positions for racing to suit the wind direction. Such a position will also probably give a good all round view of the sailing area. In some

acres) of water. However, smaller craft can be raced on areas of water as small as 2 ha (4.9 acres) and as a general guide, an area of 200 ha (494 acres) of sheltered water will form a viable dinghy racing centre. An important consideration is the ability to set interesting courses for varying wind directions. At the top level of competition, racing is often over variations of an Olympic-type course which requires a clear water area of at least 2.4 km (2626 yd) in diameter, **5, 6, 7** and **8**.

2.1 Wind characteristics

The wind characteristics over an area of water are of primary importance for sailing and may influence the siting of launching facilities and associated facilities such as clubhouses and dinghy parks, **10** and **11**. Meteorological advice should be taken and the effect of the local geography on the area should be noted as hills and trees can disrupt the prevailing wind directions. Thick vegetation both in the form of weed in the water, and trees and bushes around it, may restrict the use of a water area during the summer but allow 'frostbite' sailing during winter months when seasonal growth dies away.

12 *Typical pontoon for temporary mooring and rigging of dinghies. Photo: R Wilson*

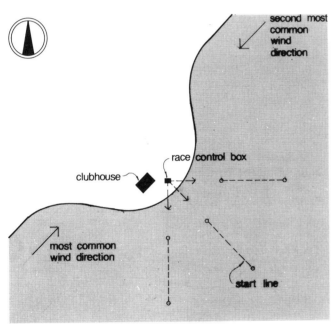

13 *Location of clubhouse and control box on a promontory allows a number of start line positions and a good view of the sailing area*

situations races can be controlled from 'committee' boats on the water. For high level competition this is essential. Such boats should be provided with radio links to the clubhouse or control box.

3.2 Supporting facilities
Factors to consider in the location of supporting facilities are:

● Access: vehicular, pedestrian and marine
● Aspect: views over and to water; views over and to dinghy park
● Landscaping: visual amenities

4 Site design
The relationship of car parking to dinghy parking and water should be carefully considered. It is often desirable to segregate cars from dinghies, both physically and

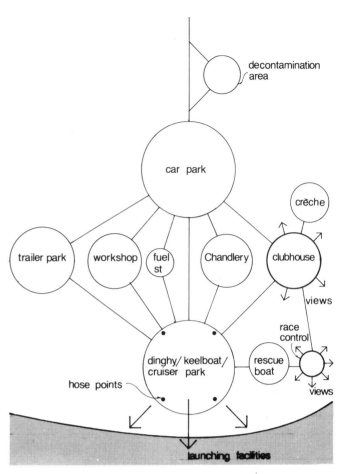

14 *Relationship diagram: primary elements on site*

Table 31.1: Facilities which may be required on site

		Minimum (1)	Desirable (2)
Car park		*	*
Decontamination area	(for reservoirs and lakes, etc)		
Boat park	dinghy		*
	keelboat		*
Board racks	dinghies or sailboards		*
Trailer park			*
Wash-down facilities			*
Moorings	pontoons (see also Chapter 34, Marinas)		
	buoys		
Boat launching	ramp	*	*
	slipway	*	*
	hard	*	*
	crane		
	winch		
	trolley		
Rescue boats	storage		*
	launching		*
	servicing		
Workshops	maintenance		*
	repair		
	recovery vehicle		
Storage	equipment (buoys, engines, etc)		
	winter storage		
Fuel storage			
Racing facilities	flag pole/signalling/boards		*
	cannon/hooter/bell/starter's box/buoys		
Chandlery			
Clubhouse	telephone	*	*
	toilets	*	*
	showers		*
	first aid		*
	lockers		*
	drying rooms		
	refreshment		*
	overnight accommodation		
	office/committee room/club room		
Landscaping	planting/screens/mounds/children's play/picnic area		

Note (1): Minimum facilities to provide access to water for the general public
Note (2): Desirable for typical club use

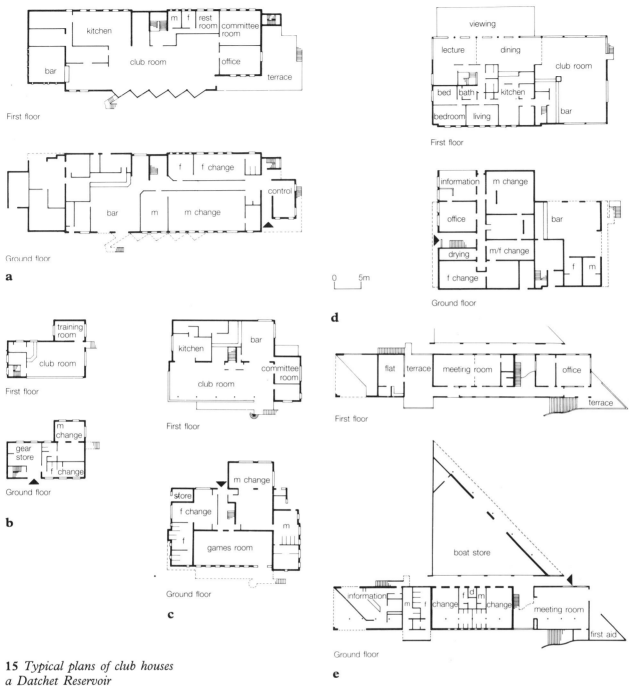

15 *Typical plans of club houses*
a Datchet Reservoir
b Weirwood Sailing Club – ground floor (above) and first floor (below)
c Queen Mary Reservoir
d Rutland Sailing Club – ground floor (above) and first floor (below)
e Sailing School, La Tranche sur Mer, France

preferably visually, by the use of planting and mounds. This segregation helps to stop the dinghy park being blocked by cars and also improves the visual appearance of the sailing club from the water. At the same time, yachtsmen often use their cars as storage for tools, equipment and clothes and would wish their cars to be parked as close as possible to their boats. In some situations trolleys have been provided to help overcome this problem while, for occasional large regattas, special arrangements might be made to allow car parking nearby or to be combined with the dinghy park, **12**. Adequate vehicular access to the dinghy park and launching facilities is required for delivery of boats and bulky items of sailing equipment. When an open meeting is put on by a club adequate unloading area and storage area for road trailers is required. Table 31.1 shows facilities which may be required on site.

Overhead electrical cables
Particular attention should be given to the danger of dinghy masts touching overhead cables both on land and over water. The local Electricity Board should be consulted to arrange for cables to be buried underground. Alternatively, cables may be raised well above the height of masts and warning notices displayed, but it should be noted that a height greater than the statutory minimum (5.2 m (approx 17 ft)) or that recommended by the IEE (5.8 m (approx 19 ft)) will be required.

5 Facilities
The various methods of operating a sailing facility may influence the detailed design of the building. The main areas required are discussed in turn below and illustrated by typical plans of existing facilities, **15a–e**.

141

16 *Rutland Sailing Club. (Architects: Eberlin & Partners). Photo: R Eberlin*

17 *Sailing School, La Tranche sur Mer (Architects Loïc Turpin). Photo L Turpin*

Although sailing is generally considered to be a club-based sport, with the clubs providing the organisation for racing, cruising and facilities such as rescue boats, slipways, boat parks and moorings, it is estimated that, in the UK, club membership accounts for less then 50% of the total number of sailors. Clubs also provide a social function, often throughout the year and for members no longer active in the sport. The range of private sailing clubs can stretch from those operating successfully with the barest of built facilities to those with a wide range of highly sophisticated amenities, **16** and **17**.

Sailing is also done on a more casual basis, by people who trail their boats to public launching facilities or sail from public moorings. Sailboarders in particular do not need special facilities and often operate from a beach with an adjacent car park. Local authorities may provide toilets, shower rooms and launching facilities for this group as well as for visiting yachtsmen. An example of a public 'pay as you play facility' provided by the Regional Water Authority is Datchet Reservoir where the clubhouse has been designed to be shared by all water users as club members or casual users.

5.1 Clubhouse facilities

The constitution and general disposition of the sailing club or promoting body will have an influence on the accommodation required and its design. If a full-time steward is to be employed by the club, for example, the catering facilities may be developed as a source of revenue. A steward's flat may also be required, along with overnight accommodation for visitors. Some clubs might specialise in hosting important regattas and see doing so as a way of off-setting running costs. At some clubs the facilities will be open on a daily basis with bars and restaurants in regular use, while in others these facilities will be open only at times of sailing. In some situations it will be possible for many of the facilities to be shared with other water recreation participants. In this way, amenities required by various water users, such as toilets, showers and refreshment facilities, can be provided in an economical way.

5.2 'Wet' and 'dry' zones

A feature of sailing-club buildings is that, after sailing, people will be using them in wet clothes, causing wetness or dirt to be 'walked' around the building. This should be considered when choosing finishes and planning the building. Generally, robust external floor surfaces such as paving slabs seem to be acceptable for wet areas. Drainage should be adequate for hosing down and heating and ventilating sufficient for evaporation of any water dripping from wet clothes. It seems to be impractical to organise the changing area plan into 'dirty' and 'clean' circulation areas. Duck-boards are commonly used to provide dry standing areas in changing rooms with wet and dirty floors and are particularly suitable where the internal environment of the changing area causes the floor constantly to be wet.

In some situations it may be appropriate to divide the accommodation into 'wet' and 'dry' zones. This will be particularly desirable where there are social or office facilities with soft furnishings. Generally, this is the solution adopted in the bigger establishments whereas smaller facilities tend to be designed with multi-purpose spaces used for different activities at different times. Much will depend on the particular situation. The factors to be taken into consideration will normally include the length of time a clubhouse is used, whether the sailing is seasonal or all the year around and the types of membership for which the club is catering.

5.3 Multi-use space

When considering the design of sailing buildings there may be scope to adopt a multi-use approach to the accommodation. For example, changing rooms which are not used in the winter months might become temporary boat storage or workshop areas for winter maintenance; or a multi-purpose club room can cater for a range of sailing, social or administrative uses such as the laying out of sails on a clear floor for measuring, briefing sessions for racing competitors or annual general meetings and a whole host of different activities. A larger space may be formed by drawing back removable screens normally used to provide a number of smaller spaces.

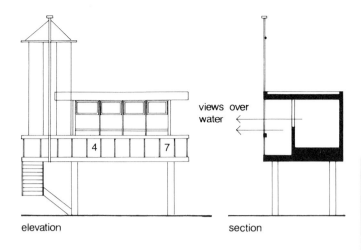

elevation   section

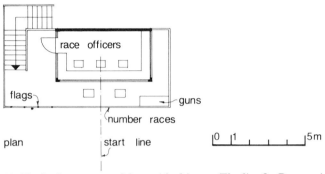

plan   start line   0 1   5m

18 *Typical race control box. (Architects: Eberlin & Partners)*

5.4 Phased development

It may be appropriate to plan the sailing accommodation so that it can be constructed in various phases. This will allow a clubhouse to expand in order to meet a growing demand, or be provided in stages as money becomes available. The initial provision should contain the basic accommodation and might be quite modest in scale. When improvements are made to existing sailing facilities, the long-term development ought to be considered in order to avoid piecemeal or wasteful improvements.

5.5 Outlook

In many cases it should be possible to design the building with views from the social and circulation areas over the sailing area and dinghy park.

5.6 Sailing/racing control

It is essential that the sailing control room is positioned with an adequate view of the sailing area. A typical control box is shown in **18** and **19** and may be separate from or incorporated into the main clubhouse. Also see **22**.

5.7 Check-list of racing facilities

Racing facilities may be required to some extent at almost any centre. They might consist of:

- Flag/signalling post or board
- Starting cannon, hooter or bell
- Rostrum for race officers with starter's box and stop clock
- Marks on shore and buoys to indicate starting lines, turning points and finishing lines
- Pontoons at which boats can be made ready and rigged for racing; they should be adjacent to the launching ramps and might also serve as temporary moorings
- Briefing area (see **20** and **21**)
- Measuring and weighing area for sails/boats/sailors

19 *Race control/safety box on raised ground to give a good view of the sailing area. Photo: R Wilson*

20 *Information area: notice board and race course board. Sufficient circulation space required for people to queue or study notices. Photo: R Wilson*

21 *Briefing session: race officers talking to the dinghy sailors prior to the start of a race. A suitable mustering area is required adjacent to the information room (area). Photo: R Wilson*

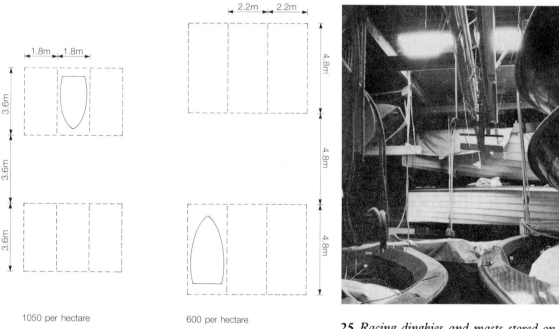

22 *Racing flags stored in marked rack in race control box*

flags stored in lettered racks folded ready for hoisting

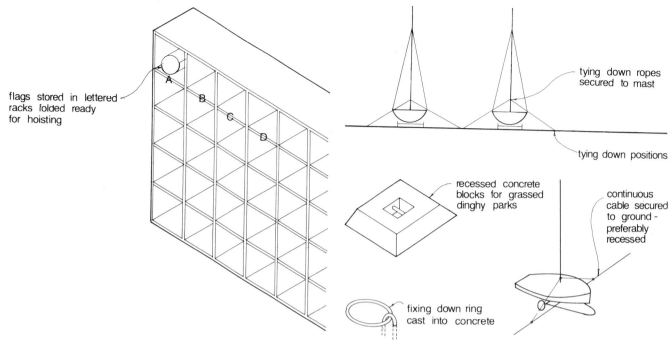

tying down ropes secured to mast

tying down positions

recessed concrete blocks for grassed dinghy parks

continuous cable secured to ground - preferably recessed

fixing down ring cast into concrete

24 *Tying down facilities in the dinghy park*

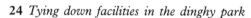

1.8m 1.8m

3.6m

3.6m

3.6m

2.2m 2.2m

4.8m

4.8m

4.8m

1050 per hectare

600 per hectare

23 *Dimensions for different densities of dinghy parking*

25 *Racing dinghies and masts stored on hoists in a covered boat shed. Photo: R Wilson*

5.8 The dinghy park

The organisation of the dinghy park will depend on the availability of land and the types of boat to be parked. Generally speaking, dinghies or trailers take up approximately the same space as cars although in some cases the stowage of masts, flat on top of the boats, can take up to 8 m (approx 26 ft) in length. Dimensions to achieve differing densities are shown in 23. Also see 24 to 31.

In the case of reservoirs and lakes, some water companies require grassed dinghy parks for amenity value. Concrete blocks can be set into the ground to secure the dinghies from being blown over in a wind. In general, hard smooth surfaces such as concrete are preferred for the main access routes in dinghy parks as they avoid problems with mud and allow the easy movement of boat trailers and trolleys.

Normal car parking construction is adequate for dinghy parks, providing it is recognised that vehicular traffic will take place whenever boats are collected or delivered. If the site is well drained a wearing course may not be required. Tarmac or bitumen should be avoided wherever possible because in hot weather these materials tend to adhere to dinghies, sails and equipment. The provision of secure racks for windsurfers may attract windsurfers to clubs. Ideally, they should be positioned close to the water.

5.9 Decontamination facilities

In the case of reservoirs and lakes the water companies may insist on careful decontamination of boats and equipment arriving at the club from other sailing waters, for example to prevent the spread of disease to fish

144

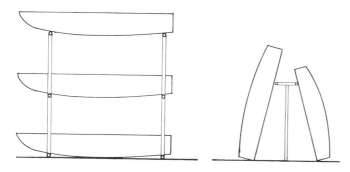

26 *Alternative storage arrangements where space is limited*

30 *Visiting boats rigging at a regatta. Ample space is required in a dinghy park for rigging/tuning/repair. Photo: R Wilson*

27 *Keelboats stored in the dinghy park on road trailers. Photo: R Wilson*

28 *Dinghies stored vertically on a raised platform on the foreshore. Photo: R Wilson*

31 *External staircase to a club building provides a useful raised platform for adjustment to the mast of the dinghy. Photo: R Wilson*

29 *Launching trailers and frames stored in a trailer park. The area can also be used for winter storage of cruisers and keelboats. Photo: R Wilson*

stocks. The water companies should be consulted on the extent and type of facilities required. They may be linked to the main entrance to the site or located centrally in the dinghy launching area.

5.10 Launching facilities

The construction of slipways should be a matter of detailed examination. Consideration must be given to the type of boats to be used, the fluctuation of water level, sub-soil

145

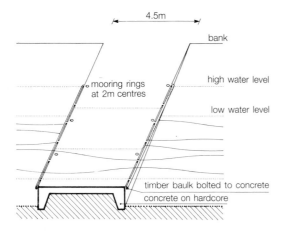

32 Typical slipway for a reservoir. (Architects: Eberlin & Partners)

33 Concrete hard with a profiled finish to give grip. Photo: R Wilson

34 Dinghy being recovered onto a launching trolley on a concrete hard. Photo: R Wilson

conditions and wave action. The load-carrying capacity of the slipway is also important since, in addition to sailing craft, the slipway may occasionally have to take motor vehicles. The number of slipways and their width depends on the maximum demand and should bear a relationship

both to the size of the dinghy parking area and how concentrated the demand will be. Consideration should be given to the total time it will take for necessary numbers of boats to launch. Cost may be a limiting factor where there is a large tidal range. A typical solution is shown in **32**.

Sailboards need more space for rigging and launching than dinghies. A grassed area or beach is suitable for this purpose along with a fairly wide expanse of beach with a gradual gradient for launching.

Various methods can be used for transporting boats in and out of the water, **33** and **34**. The most suitable method will depend entirely on individual circumstances and will be related to such things as the size and type of boats in common use, the range of tide conditions and the local water characteristics. Common types of launching facilities are:

- Dinghy ramp
- Dinghy stage (wide ramp suitable for launching a number of boats side by side
- Concrete hard or beach
- Slipway
- Crane

Sailing dinghies are normally taken down to the water's edge by trolley. Ideally, the slipway should be sufficiently wide to allow boats to pass in both directions. The minimum width for a single slipway to suit most dinghies is 3 m (approx 10 ft) and for a double slipway 4.5 m (approx 15 ft). A slipway 5 m (approx 16 ft 6 in) wide at water level will allow a dinghy to be launched over the side as well as off the end, thus increasing its capacity for use.

The length and gradient of the slipway depend on site conditions. Obviously the shorter the better, but the slope should not be steeper than 1:10 unless capstans, winches or other mechanical power units are provided for hauling out, 35. It may be convenient to have two gradients to assist landing and hauling out, for instance, 1:15 down to high-water level and 1:9 below high water. Often slipways will follow the natural beach slope. The siting and gradient depend on local conditions and advice on the best and most economical solution should be sought. The surface of the slipway should be as non-slip as possible. A coarse finish is usually satisfactory, while battens fixed to the surface of timber ramps will provide additional grip. An artificial beach may be created in situations such as a reservoir. This will allow a number of dinghies to be launched simultaneously.

Keelboats (and cruisers) require special consideration and a slipway should be constructed to suit a gantry for transferring boats from road trailers to launching trailers. The provision of a winch system is also necessary. It is an advantage if a jetty can be built alongside this slipway in order to help control the keelboats whilst they are being launched and allow them to be moored alongside the slipway for rigging and de-rigging, **36** to **42**.

5.11 Fuel storage

The storage of fuel for motor boats associated with sailing clubs needs to be considered in terms of convenient siting and as a possible hazard. The Fire Prevention Officer and Petrol Licensing Officer should be consulted on the location and design of the store. In addition, consideration should be given to visual aspects as it may be desirable to screen the facility with planting.

5.12 Changing rooms

It has been suggested that the proportion of male and female members of a typical club is about 60% men and

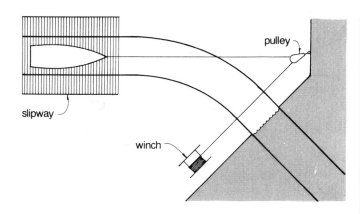

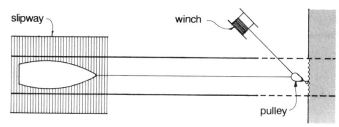

35 *Rail bound slipways with pulley and winch outside the work area*

36 *Motorised winch with a weather protection cover. Photo: R Wilson*

37 *Typical winch for launching and recovery of keelboats and cruisers. A warning notice draws attention to the hazard of the cable running across a pedestrian/car route. Photo: R Wilson*

38 *Keelboat being launched by winch and launching trolley from a slipway. Photo: R. Wilson*

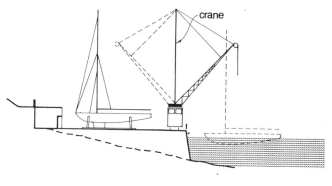

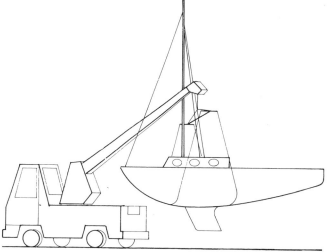

39 *Mobile or fixed crane for lifting out keelboats onto trailers or parking position*

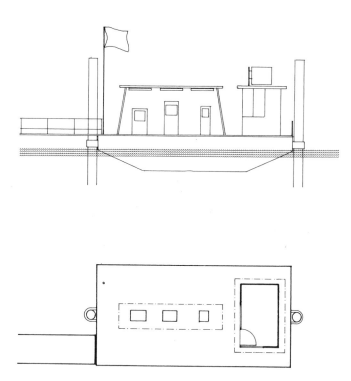

40 *Floating fuelling point for cruisers and power boats*

42 *External paving slabs used as the floor finish in the changing area. Photo: R Wilson*

41 *Space required for changing into bulky clothes while standing up. Ample space required for bags, boots, etc. Photo: R Wilson*

40% women and the changing facilities should be planned on the assumption that about 30% of members will be active. It would be prohibitively expensive, however, for the normal club to provide changing-room facilities based on the total number of active members and visitors. It must be assumed that changing needs will be staggered.

In club situations the most intense use of changing areas is before and after organised races. Where there are a number of class starts then the use will obviously be spread over a period of time. However, in the case of a large regatta, considerable pressure will be put on the changing facilities and this problem might be eased to some extent by providing temporary accommodation.

In the case of public 'pay as you play' facilities it has been suggested that a figure of 1.5 hours is reasonable for the turnabout time for sailing. The figure may be estimated more precisely by considering the hire time on which the sailing is based. The suggested changing time for a person changing before or after sailing is 15 minutes.

The changing rooms should be sized to allow for the bulk of wet suits and sail bags. A typical locker/changing seat is shown in **43**.

5.13 Drying room
This facility should be positioned near to the changing area (in the wet zone). There may be servicing reasons for locating the drying room near to the boiler room.

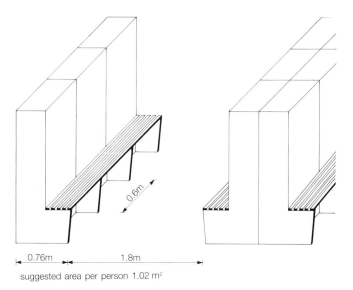

0.76m   1.8m

0.6m

suggested area per person 1.02 m²

43 *Changing room/locker layout. (Architects: Eberlin & Partners)*

44 *Children's playground adjacent to the clubhouse at Rutland Sailing Club. (Architects: Eberlin & Partners). Photo: R Eberlin*

5.14 Floor design

Good drainage is essential and the subfloor must be laid to good falls, with adequate channels and drain-aways. If ribbed floor tiles are specified, the direction of ribbing and adequate falls are critical: poorly drained floors remain damp and muddy, causing duckboarding to slip and become dangerous. Duckboarding should be hosed down regularly.

Non-slip permanent flooring is also essential, particularly if duckboards are to be laid loose (eg in lanes). Some types can be fitted with rubber anchor pads, but if this is done the floor must be flush surfaced (not ribbed) to ensure positive grip.

Monolithic, lower cost, floor finishes are adequate, for example granolithic flooring incorporating a non-slip finish and treated before use with a sodium silicate dust-retardant surface hardener. Such flooring could also take the form of an industrial-type plastic non-slip surface covering.

Wall to wall fitted areas have to be lifted occasionally to brush away dried silt and hairs which lodge between the extruded sections and the floor. Ribbed floor tiles offer a solution in areas where wall-to-wall duckboarding is to be fitted to give free cross drainage beneath the plastic extrusions. But, combined, this is an expensive floor.

Showers and wet areas on upper floors should incorporate tanking or other water-seal membrane under the subflooring or screed.

45 *Dinghy park surrounded by a high fence for security. Photo: R Wilson*

Duckboards

The use of duckboards should be considered in:

- Showers and dry-off areas
- Changing rooms
- 'Clean lanes' through dirty areas to help limit the spread of mud
- Other areas where users go bare-footed

5.15 Information

In larger sailing establishments, such as the Rutland Sailing Centre, an information room is included and becomes a key facility during busy weekends and regattas. The information rooms would normally contain:

46 *Lifebuoy positioned adjacent to launching facility. Photo: R Wilson*

149

- Notice boards
- Course boards
- Charts/boards
- Registration – sign off/on etc.
- Beach master

In other situations, where a separate information room is not provided, these elements are provided at convenient positions around the buildings. Often this is in the main multi-use room. Ideally the information room or area should be adjacent to the space where briefing sessions will take place, **20** and **21**.

5.16 Picnic facilities
Users coming for a day's sailing will probably wish to eat on the site. If no special provisions are made, they will probably use their cars or the car park. It may be worth providing a special area with outdoor seats and possibly a small shelter against the weather.

5.17 Play areas
A children's play area adjacent to the clubhouse will be a useful addition to the sailing facilities and will be used by younger children or those not interested in sailing. Such facilities should be carefully sited to achieve easy supervision and take account of possible hazards that may exist on the site such as the water's edge or car park. The area may be fenced off as in the example shown at the Rutland Sailing Club, **44**.

5.18 Rubbish
The measures required to control and contain rubbish will vary from site to site. Adequate numbers of disposal points with paper or plastic sacks on stands or other containers should be provided at appropriate points. It is also essential that clearance of these points takes place regularly and as soon after a weekend as possible.

5.19 Water supply
Piped water is required for washing down dinghies before and after use. This applies particularly at salt water locations where it might be regarded as an essential facility for washing down boats. A standpipe with a reasonable pressure should be provided near the top of the launching ramp. This can then be used to wash down the ramp as well. A hose pipe is also required, but on sites with little security owners may have to supply one themselves.

5.20 Security
Unless some effective form of security is provided, owners will be reluctant to leave their boats on site and the facility will consequently get used less often than it might be, **45** and **46**. Security measures can take many forms and will vary with the needs of each individual site. The more common measures are:

- A chain, secured firmly to the ground at each end, to which dinghy trailers and launching trolleys can be padlocked by owners' short lengths of chain. A common alternative is a single chain leading through all the trailers with one combination type padlock to the ground anchor.
- A 2.4 m (approx 8 ft) chain-link fence round the dinghy parking area
- Suitable overhead lighting.

32
Canoeing

Carel Quaife

1 General

Canoeing is probably the cheapest form of boating activity and can be pursued in one or more of its forms on almost any available waterspace. It is a healthy outdoor recreation attracting people of all ages from all walks of life.

In Britain, detailed information in relation to specific projects, including actual or potential participation levels, can be obtained from the British Canoe Union (BCU), its Water Facilities Technical Advisory Panel or its regional committees at the following address

The British Canoe Union
John Dudderidge House, Adbolton Lane,
West Bridgford, Nottingham NG2 5AS
Tel: 0602 821100 Fax: 0602 821797

2 Definitions

Canoeing: this generic term includes canoes, both open and decked, propelled by single bladed paddles and kayaks propelled by double bladed paddles.
Racing: racing over unobstructed still water courses of 500, 1000, 5000 and 10,000 m (547, 1094, 5470 and 10,940 yd).
Marathon: racing over courses where there may be obstacles requiring portage and may be on moving water.
Slalom: negotiation of a rapid river course, defined by gates, without fault in the shortest possible time.
Wild Water Racing: mastery of a competitor's boat in fast moving wild water, while running a prescribed course in the shortest possible time.
Canoe Polo: a five-a-side team ball game played in short kayaks.
Sailing: the BCU is the Governing Body for the IC 10 international sailing canoe, an advanced single handed sailing boat. Requirements as for dinghy sailing.
Surfing: competitive or recreational activities off surf beaches. (Analogous to board surfing or waveskiing.)
Rodeos: demonstration of acrobatic skills in sizeable but friendly hydraulic jumps (stopper waves).
Touring: making canoe journeys on any practicable waters.
General: basic instruction, fun events and pottering in canoes, usually at a single location.

3 Built facility requirements

The purpose built Worcester Canoe Club boathouse is shown in **2** and **3**. Designs must separate the dry social

1 *Holme Pierrepont NWSC Artificial Canoe Slalom Course.*
Photograph: Joe Mulholland

areas from the wet showering, changing and boat storage areas. Boat specifications vary so racking has to be designed to individual requirements; two examples are given in Table 32.1. Racks can be of tubular construction with cross bearers adjustable for height to permit changes in storage requirements. Boat weights vary from 12 kg (approx 26 lb) for a racing kayak to 40 kg (approx 88 lb) for a two man open canoe. Paddles stored vertically against a wall require a height of 2.3 m (7 ft 6 in) and location pegs. Buoyancy aids can be stored on 450 mm (18 in) long horizontal cantilever rods at 125 mm (5 in) horizontal centres three high at 600 mm (24 in) centres. Spray decks can be hung on hooks. There must be sufficient air circulation to enable equipment to dry out.

2 Worcester Canoe Club Headquarters

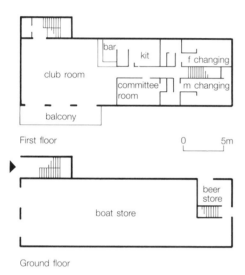

3 Headquarters of the Worcester Canoe Club: ground and first floor plans

Table 32.1: Examples of canoe storage

	Worcester CC	Nottingham KC
Floor	21.5 × 8 m (approx 70 ft 6 in × 26 ft)	27.4 × 6.7 m (90 × 22 ft)
Height	3.6 m (approx 12 ft)	2.4 m (approx 8 ft)
No. of boats high	11(1)	7
Rows across store	8	6
Boats down length (partial overlap)	4	6
Total capacity (boats)	352	252

Note (1): Access to upper racks by mobile steps

4 Site requirements

Site requirements are as follows:

- Secure boat storage area.
- 10 m (approx 33 ft) wide grassed area adjacent to water for boat parking. Vehicle and trailer parking adjacent to grassed areas.
- Platforms with unobstructed view for judges.
- Floodlighting to permit year round evening use.
- Provision for spectators.
- Landing stages/pontoons with deck 300 mm (12 in) above water level or slipways (max gradient 30°) with

transverse bars for grip or steps preferably 450 mm (18 in) wide with 300 mm (12 in) risers preferred.
- 'Danger Deep Water' and other standard safety signs.

5 Swimming pools

Swimming pools are important for training and for polo competitions. Access to the pool is required sufficient for boats 4 × 0.6 m (approx 13 × 2 ft) with facilities outside the pool to hose them down. There should be no breakable glass or low ceilings that are easily damaged. Pool tiles above the waterline should be rubber or other unbreakable material. Wall anchor points needed for polo goal supports. Secure boat storage is desirable.

6 Waterspace requirements

Newcomers are introduced to canoeing and competition at local fun events where any waterspace within reason can be used. Serious competition requirements are set out in Table 32.2. BCU regional officers can advise on potential uses of any given piece of water. A canoe can float in as little as 100 mm (4 in) depth and 250 mm (10 in) is sufficient for the paddle blade. Average depths greater than this are more suitable and reduce or eliminate riverbed drag on the canoe. Existing waterspace can be improved.

Table 32.2: Waterspace requirements (ideal minima)

Activity	Length	Width	Characteristics
Racing	1100 m (1203 yd)	35 m (38 yd)	Still and preferably sheltered water 2 m (6 ft 6 in) deep minimum
Marathon	6–20 km (3 miles 720 yd–12 miles 753 yd)	10 m (11 yd)	Still and moving water usually with obstacles requiring porterage
Slalom	600 m (656 yd) max	8 m (approx 9 yd)	Rough water
Wild water racing	3 km (1 mile 1408 yd)	8 m (approx 9 yd)	Rough water in part and navigable throughout
Canoe polo	30 m (approx 33 yd)	20 m (approx 22 yd)	Swimming pool or outdoor area with touchline pontoons/bank
Rodeo	20 m (approx 22 yd)	10 m (11 yd)	Rough fast moving water
Touring	5 km (3 miles 176 yd)	8 m (approx 9 yd)	All types of water
General	100 m (approx 109 yd)	10 m (11 yd)	Still or slow moving water

Where a river discharge is 3 cubic metres (approx 4 cubic yd) per second and it has a drop of 2 m (approx 6 ft) within about 200 m (656 ft) there is potential to construct an enhanced river slalom course or an artificial slalom course of regional significance. Examples are the Washburn and at Sowerby Bridge in Yorkshire and Cardington in Bedfordshire. Greater discharges permit courses of international standard such as at the Holme Pierrepont National Watersports Centre, Nottingham, England, **1**, the Afon Tryweryn in Wales and Augsburg, Germany. Courses can be constructed based on a pumped flow as for the 1992 Barcelona Olympics.

6.1 Weirs

Some designs of weir will throw a swimmer or canoeist clear if they fall in above or below. Other designs are very dangerous because the water configuration can trap and drown anyone falling in. The outflows from weirs can be designed or modified to produce excellent white water canoeing facilities. A vee shaped gauging weir is a suitable design. Detailed information can be obtained from the BCU Water Facilities Technical Advisory Panel.

6.2 Water quality

Waterways in which fish can thrive are generally considered safe. Canoeing is not an 'immersion' sport, although some forms are wetter than others. Deliberate immersion needed for training in some types of canoeing can be accommodated in a swimming pool whenever water of acceptable quality is not available.

7 References and further advice

British Canoe Union *Canoeing Handbook*, (1989).

Goodman, F and Parr, G, *Holme Pierrepont Artificial Slalom Course Users Guide*, (1986).

Goodman, F and Parr, G, *Weir Designs Suitable for the Canoeist*, (1988).

International Canoe Federation Competition Rules.

33
Angling facilities for people with disabilities

Bruno Broughton

Angling claims to have 3.8 million participants in the UK, making it one of the most popular participation sports. The majority are able-bodied, capable of carrying their equipment to a suitable swim selected by walking the bank and, if necessary, negotiating a steep slope down to the water's edge. Unless fishing from a river or canal towpath, anglers frequently have to set up their equipment on sloping banks which may be steep, soft, wet and covered in natural vegetation.

There are many people with a wide range of disabilities who are unable to gain access to suitable fishing stations and are therefore denied the opportunity of participating in this popular sport. Angling can provide disabled people with recreational opportunities which do not exist in most other sports. Good anglers learn to develop skills of patience, persistence and a philosophical response to both success and disappointment, rather than physical strength or speed. This helps to explain why angling suits disabled people so well. They are not necessarily more skilful, but they are more ready to recognise their mistakes and avoid repetitions in future.

On many fisheries, facilities for disabled anglers must be created to enable them to overcome the difficulties posed by the contours of the land surface. Usually, this will entail the construction of fishing stations or 'pegs' close to the water's edge, with suitable access to them. Where pegs have been sited sensibly and constructed to a high standard, they are valuable additions to on-site amenities. Too often, however, disabled anglers' pegs either have not been provided or are poorly designed or wrongly positioned and access to them may be inadequate, 1 and 2.

The minimum requirements for disabled anglers' pegs are:

- Position near car park/access point
- Sited in good fishing area
- Close to the water, on a stable bank
- Absence of dense vegetation in immediate vicinity
- Level surface from which to fish
- Raised kerb at the front
- Provision for placement of umbrella, bank sticks, and other equipment.

It is essential that pegs dedicated for use by disabled anglers are close to vehicular access points. Paths providing access to the water's edge must be negotiable by wheelchairs and the ambulant disabled using sticks or elbow crutches, with a minimum width of 1.35 m (4.5 ft) increasing to 1.8 m (6 ft) where two wheelchairs may need to pass. Angled access paths are suitable for gently-sloping banks; zig-zag paths of shallow gradients with intermediate, level landings, will be necessary on steeper banks. Upstands of 100 mm (4 in) should be provided at path edges where adjacent to steep downward slopes. A handrail or post and rail fence 1 m (3 ft) high should also be considered for such locations. Concrete and macadam are the most suitable construction materials.

Disabled anglers' pegs should not be sited away from areas used by other anglers. Many disabled anglers practise the sport with one or more friends who will wish to fish nearby. Pegs should be spaced at least 8–10 m (approx 26–33 ft) apart on well-fished venues, 15 m (approx 50 ft) or more on less intensively used fisheries. Each peg should be labelled clearly to ensure that disabled people have sole or priority use of these facilities.

Note should be taken of the direction of the prevailing wind. Pegs which face directly into the wind will be uncomfortable in breezy conditions.

On rivers, pegs should not be built where there are areas of very fast-flowing water. To enable right-handed anglers (the majority) to fish more effectively, it is preferable if the water flow is from right to left of the angler. The position of the pegs should be selected carefully to avoid areas where the bank is or could become undercut, or where very shallow water will reduce the chances of angling success. The water should be at least 1–1.5 m (approx. 3–5 ft) deep within 2–3 m (approx 6–10 ft) of the front of the peg.

Areas where large bankside trees or dense shrubs are growing close to the water should be avoided. This vegetation represents a potential obstacle in which the anglers' end tackle may become snagged. This is of particular importance on trout fisheries where, because of the need to keep the fly line airborne during casting, there should be at least 25–30 m (approx 80–100 ft) of open bank to the rear of each peg. However, low-growing shrubs, particularly evergreens, can provide useful windbreaks and cover when sited carefully.

Suitable disabled anglers' pegs can be constructed from a wide range of materials. It is vital that their finished surface is level, firm and does not slope towards the water. Wooden platforms which project into the water from the bank should be designed and constructed carefully so that the platform surface is no higher than 300–600 mm (1–2 ft) above the water surface. Where considerable fluctuations in water level are known to

154

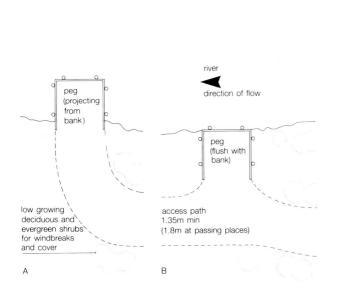

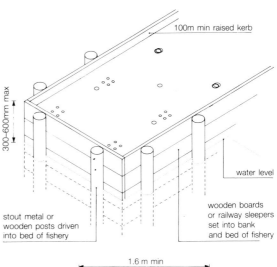

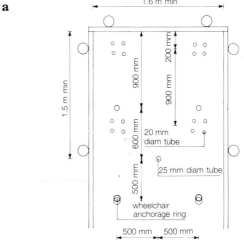

a

b

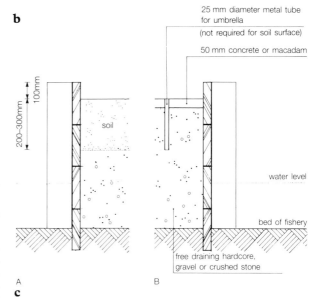

c

1 *Angling pegs for disabled anglers*

occur, the surface of the peg or platform may have to be positioned a little further above the average water level to prevent it becoming flooded too often.

The bank at the land/water interface should be strengthened to prevent erosion. One convenient means of achieving this is to install stout, horizontal wooden boards across the front of each peg, extending from the bed of the fishery to above the water surface – disused railway sleepers are ideal. They can be held in position with wooden or metal stakes driven vertically into the bed of the fishery.

Any soft or new wood should be pressure treated with a non-toxic preservative to prevent rotting. The area behind the front of the peg should be in-filled with suitable, free-draining material which is then fully compacted and levelled.

Each peg should be square or rectangular in shape, with minimum dimensions of 1.6 m (approx 5 ft) wide by 1.5 m (5 ft) long. If a kerb is created around the outside edges (the front and the sides), it should project above the peg surface by at least 100 mm (4 in). A low, horizontal rail could be installed across the front of the peg for additional security, but this is likely to hinder angling if it is higher than 300 mm (12 in) for coarse fishing pegs or 600 mm (24 in) for those to be used for game fishing.

It is important that the surface of the peg or the land immediately alongside is soft enough to accept metal rod rests, bank sticks and an umbrella pushed into the soil to a depth of 200–300 mm (8–12 in). If concrete or macadam is used to cover the peg surface, sections of 20–25 mm (0.75–1 in) internal diameter metal or plastic tubing 300 mm (12 in) long should be set into this material vertically, the upper end of each tube being flush with the surface, to accept these accessories.

To provide points for anchorage of wheelchairs, metal rings could be set in the surface of the peg on either side, towards the rear.

References and further advice

The Institution of Highways and Transportation, *Reducing Mobility Handicaps*. The Institution of Highways and Transportation, London (1991).

The Countryside Commission, *Informal Countryside Recreation for Disabled People*. The Countryside Commission (1982).

Thomson, N, Dendy, E and de Deney, D. *Sports and Recreation Provision for Disabled People*. The Architectural Press, London (1984).

Water Sports Divison of the British Sports Association for the Disabled. *Water Sports for the Disabled*. EP Publishing (1983).

2 *Detail of angling pegs*
(a) General view
(b) Vertical section
(c) Plan view

34
Marinas

Donald Adie

1 General

Marinas may be categorised by location, ownership and function as in **1** and **2**. Marinas on coasts and estuaries can be divided into four principal types shown in **3**, **4**, **5** and **6**:

- Offshore
- Semi-recessed
- Built-in
- Land-locked

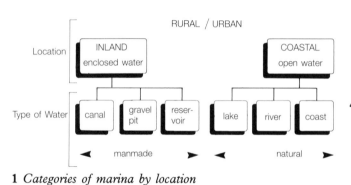

1 *Categories of marina by location*

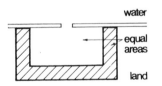

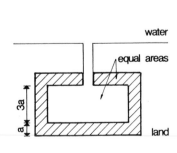

2 *Categories of marina by function*

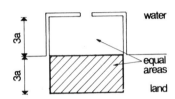

3 *The offshore marina*

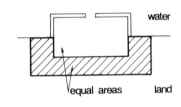

4 *The semi-recessed marina*

5 *The built-in marina*

6 *The land-locked marina*

The land-to-water area in each case remains equivalent and constant but the shapes and relationships vary as the land wraps around the water. The offshore marina has the shortest land/water interface but some land is 3 times further from the water than with the land-locked type.

1.1 The offshore marina
This has the advantages of a minimum bulkhead wall, minimum land take, and minimum dredging. It has the

disadvantages of being expensive in deep water, vulnerable to weather, currents and navigation hazards. It has minimum enclosure and is liable to silting by littoral drift.

1.2 The semi-recessed marina
This has the advantage of being good for cut and fill, and has the possible disadvantage of creating a navigation hazard.

1.3 The built-in marina
This has the advantages of uninterrupted shore line, a large land/water interface and considerable enclosure. These are counterbalanced by the disadvantages of a large land take, the long length of bulkhead wall, and a considerable amount of dredging.

1.4 The land-locked marina
This type has the advantages of maximum enclosure and minimum interruption of the shore line, balanced by the disadvantages of maximum bulkhead wall and the distance from open water.

2 Spatial requirements
A typical allocation of on and off-shore space, assuming a 50:50 land to water split, are given in **7** for the UK and **8** for American marinas. A guide to spatial requirements and likely sizes is given in Table 34.1. Section 2.1 gives a checklist of marina accommodation and services. Relationship diagrams of transportation, main activities and amenities are shown in **9, 10** and **11**.

2.1 Checklist of marina accommodation and services

Social activities
Clubhouse, boat owners' lounge, public house, bar, snack bar, restaurant, offices, committee rooms, starter's post, lookout, viewing terrace, sunbathing, reading room, navigational library, weather forecast board, chart room, television, children's play space, creche, paddling pool.

Table 34.1: Spatial requirements

	Minimum	Maximum
Land:water ratio	1:1	2:1
Density of boats (wet moorings)	62 per ha (25 per acre)	162 per ha (65 per acre)
Density of boats on hardstanding	25 per ha (10 per acre)	75 per ha (30 per acre)
Car:boat ratio	1:1	3:2
Density of cars 2.41 × 4.88 m (8 × 16 ft) bays	350 per ha (140 per acre)	520 per ha (140 per acre)
Boat length range	4.8–13.7 m (16–45 ft)	4.3–21.3 m (14–70 ft)
Boat beam	1.8–4.3 m (6–14 ft)	1.5–6.0 m (5–20 ft)
Boat draft – inboard	0.635–1.27 m (25–50 in)	0.483–1.65 m (20–65 in)
Boat draft – outboard	0.305–0.559 m (12–22 in)	0.203–0.635 m (8–25 in)
Sailing boats	1.14–1.77 m (45–70 in)	1.01–2.16 m (40–85 in)
Average boat length	5.48 m (18 ft)	9.14 m (30 ft)
Parking area:water area	1:5	1:1
Persons:boats	3:2	3:1
Persons:cars	1:1	9:2
Cars:boats	1:2	2:1

Shops
Food and general stores, tobacco, stationery, etc
Bookshop, chandlery, clothes
Hairdresser, beauty salon, barber shop
Sauna, masseur
Chemist
Launderette

Services and information
Marina office, information centre
Caretaker's maintenance workshop, storage and staff room
Banking
Post office, giro
Visitors' information service (eg doctors, restaurants, entertainment)
Flagpole, windsock
Weather and tides information
Kennels

Allied activities
Customs house
Harbourmaster's office
Coastguard, weather station and information
Radar, communications mast

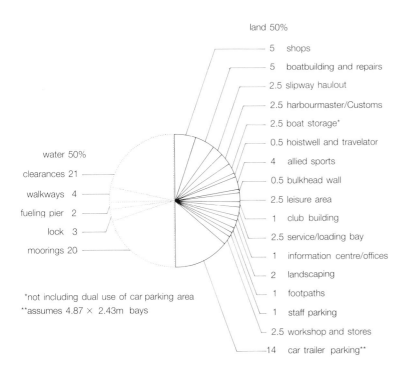

land 50%
— 5 shops
— 5 boatbuilding and repairs
— 2.5 slipway haulout
— 2.5 harbourmaster/Customs
— 2.5 boat storage*
— 0.5 hoistwell and travelator
— 4 allied sports
— 0.5 bulkhead wall
— 2.5 leisure area
— 1 club building
— 2.5 service/loading bay
— 1 information centre/offices
— 2 landscaping
— 1 footpaths
— 1 staff parking
— 2.5 workshop and stores
—14 car trailer parking**

water 50%
clearances 21
walkways 4
fueling pier 2
lock 3
moorings 20

*not including dual use of car parking area
**assumes 4.87 × 2.43m bays

7 Typical allocation of on and off-shore space for a UK marina assuming 50:50 land to water split with 4.8 × 2.4 m (approx 15 ft 6 in × 7 ft 6 in) parking bays

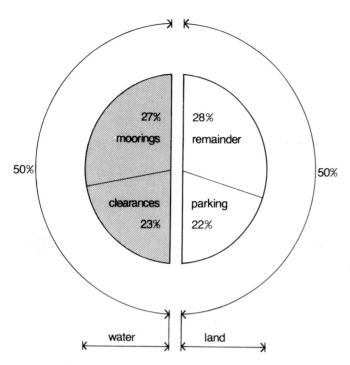

8 *Principal space allocations as percentages in ten American marinas with 5.8 × 2.7 m (approx 40 × 9 ft) parking bays*

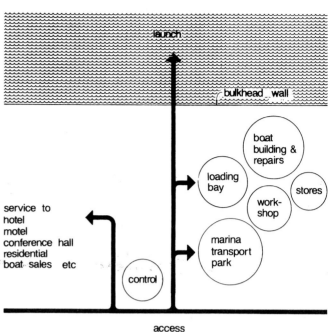

10 *The main activities of a marina*

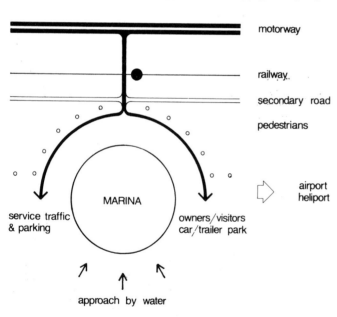

9 *Transport analysis*

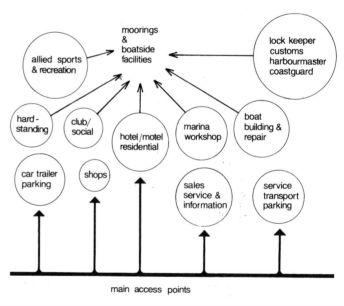

11 *Diagrammatic amenity layout*

Sea scouts
Lock-keeper's accommodation
Police, security station

Boatside facilities
Storage lockers, lavatories (public and private), showers, baths, drying rooms, cabinets
Bottled gas services, electricity, lighting and power, plug-in telephone service
Dockside laundry service
Tannoy system
Litter bins
Mail service

General services
Gas, main, bottled or in bulk storage
Electricity, lighting and power to piers and grounds (see

safety equipment)
Sewage and refuse disposal
Water supply
Telephones
Centrally controlled security system

Boat services
Boat building, repair, maintenance yard, material store
New and second-hand boat and engine sales and hire
Launching and hauling equipment (fixed and mobile)
Hardstanding
Launching ramps and slips
Dry storage of boats
Covered moorings (wet and dry)
Information board of local services
Brokerage, insurance, marine surveyors
Divers' service
Fuelling station or tender

Allied sporting activities: provision and instruction
Rowing
Scuba, skin-diving equipment and instruction
Water ski-ing, ski-kiting
Swimming
Fishing tackle (hire and sale of bait)
Sail training
Tennis, badminton and squash courts

Allied accommodation
Hotel, motel, holiday flats, public house, holiday inn

Transportation area and services
Car parking and service (fuel, repairs and hire)
Trailer bays and hire
Bus bay
Transport to and from local centres
Carts for stores and baggage
Motor cycle/bicycle sheds (open and covered)
Boat trips and coach tours
Marina staff electric runabout
Marine workshops and transport areas

Safety equipment
First aid post and observation platform
Fire-fighting equipment, fireboat
Life-saving equipment and instruction
Warning of flood lights to breakwaters, lock and harbour entrance
General security system, fences and lighting
De-icing or aeration equipment
Weather and tides information

Miscellaneous
Casual recreation area (eg picnic and kick-about area)
Swimming pool
Vending machine, ice dispenser
Paved and grassed areas
Landscaping
Gardener's stores and sheds

3 Maritime villages

The 1980s saw a move away from orthodox marinas toward maritime villages, ie residential, usually coastal, settlements where priority is given to sailing and water sports. Whilst it is related to the pure marina, the maritime village improves the economics by adding housing profit to the sometimes dubious return on berthing. It also dispenses with rows of identical walkways in a graph-paper layout and returns to the concept of the fishing village, the 'boat at the bottom of the garden' and the snug embrace of harbour walls.

The forerunner of this concept was Port Grimaud in the Bay of St Tropez, **12**. Other recent innovations in marina construction have been energy conservation, solar heating, improvements in water quality and long-term berth leasing which has revitalised marina economics.

4 Ancillary sports

One of the best recipes for success in marina operation is to attract a wide range of custom. All kinds of sports other than sailing may be encompassed, some of which – for example, golf, tennis, bowls and archery – are not water-oriented and may be quite land consuming. Others such as badminton, squash, deck games or trampolining are less so and may be accommodated fairly readily.

12 *Port Grimaud, St Tropez. Architect: Francois Spoerry, 1966*

Compatible Activities	angling	canoeing	rowing	sailing	sub-aqua	water skiing	hydroplane/motor boat racing	motor cruising	wildlife
angling	O	●	●	●	●			●	●
canoeing	●	O	●		●			●	
rowing	●	●	O		●				
sailing	●			O	●				●
sub-aqua	●	●	●	●	O				
water skiing						O			
hydroplane/motor boat racing							O		
motor boat cruising	●	●						O	
wildlife	●			●					O

13 *Compatibility of water sports*

Water sports are of course particularly suitable and fishing, swimming, water ski-iing and sub-aqua diving may be candidates for inclusion although water zoning may be required for safety. **13** gives details of activities which are likely to be compatible.

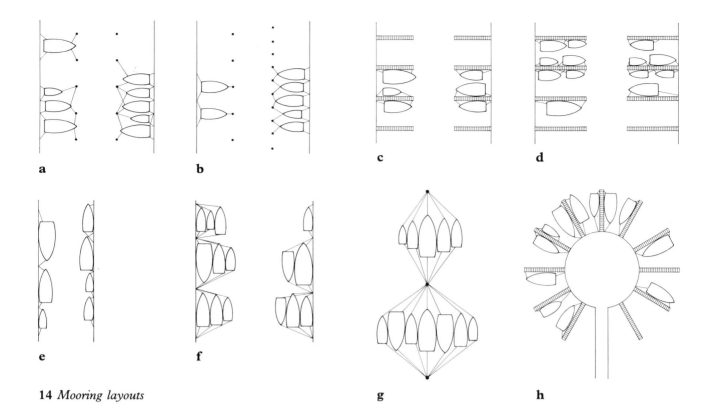

14 *Mooring layouts*

Table 34.2: Types of mooring

Type of mooring	Examples	Advantages	Disadvantages	Remarks
(a) Stern to quay, jetty or pontoon, bows to piles	Chichester Le Grande Motte Rotterdam Kristiansund	Jetty economy	Not as convenient for embarking alongside jetties or pontoons	
(b) Ditto but bows moored to anchors or buoys	Deauville and the majority of Mediterranean marinas	Jetty economy	Not suitable with large tidal range as excessive space required for head warps; danger of propellers being entangled in head warps	Particularly suitable for large yachts in basins with little tide range where gangways can be attached to sterns
(c) Alongside finger piers or cat-walks one yacht on each side of the finger	Cherbourg Larnaca (Cyprus) and many others	Convenient for embarking and disembarking		
(d) Ditto but more than one yacht on each side of the finger	Port Hamble Swanwick Lymington	Ditto and also allows flexibility in accommodating yachts of different lengths	Finger piers must be spaced wider apart than in (c) though this may be compensated for by the larger number of craft between jetties	Fingers may be long enough for two or three vessels. If more than three provision must be made for turning at the foot of the berths
(e) Alongside quays, jetties or pontoons single banked	Granville	Ditto		
(f) Alongside quays, jetties or pontoons up to 3 or 4 abreast	St Malo Ouistreham St Rochelle	Economical in space and pontoons	Crew from outer yachts have to climb over inner berthed yachts Loss of privacy	
(g) Between piles	Yarmouth Hamble River Cowes	Cheapest system as not walkways, also high density	No dry access to land; difficulty in leaving mooring if outer yachts are not manned Loss of privacy	Not recommended except for special situations such as exist in examples quoted
(h) Star finger	San Francisco	A means of accommodating large craft	Expensive circular deck area	

160

Sail training is sometimes included within the activities of the clubhouse or else set apart in a sailing school or separate club such as the Sea Scouts or some other youth organisation. Areas of more passive recreation are also included under the general heading of sitting areas or sunbathing and viewing terraces. However general or specialised their needs may be they will require thorough research to provide the necessary layout, buildings, equipment and staff. It is important in planning their accommodation that they are not cut off from the main harbour but keep contact with it in both a physical and social context. This provides both for those boat owners with a secondary interest and participants in these other activities who may wish the opportunity of becoming boat owners.

Water sports obviously need a waterside position; whether this is within the marina or not depends upon the sport and the circumstances. As well as providing links with the marina and clubhouse, allied sports will gain from some contact with each other and a good plan will provide for this social integration and probably gain in economy of layout. As with any hotel or residential element the inclusion of special sports will need land additional to the average of between 1:1 and 2:1 land to water ratio. Car parking may need to be separately annexed and additional to marina requirements.

In this part of the harbour there are opportunities in planning and architecture to provide an informal and relaxed atmosphere which is nevertheless efficiently designed for these specialised pastimes. While the buildings and active areas will need to be hard-wearing and rugged the quieter parts can be landscaped with planting and trees.

5 Catering for people with disabilities

Water sports are a valuable way of integrating people with disabilities into the life of the community. Water sports can contribute significantly to their quality of life and happiness.

6 Types of mooring

Details of the various optional types of mooring with their relevant advantages and disadvantages are given in Table 34.2. The various mooring layouts are illustrated in **14**.

7 References and further advice

Adie, D. *Marinas: A Working Guide to their Development and Design.* 3rd edition. Butterworth-Heinemann, Oxford (1983).

Blain, W R and Webber, N B, (ed), *Marinas. Volume 1: Planning and Feasibility. Volume 2: Design and Operation.* Computational Mechanics Publications, Southampton:.

35
Water skiing

Mike Earle and Barry Odell

1 Introduction
Over the past 15 years water skiing has been one of the fastest growing forms of water sport. It is both competitive and recreational. Competition may take three forms, known as 'tournament', 'barefoot' or 'racing'. In terms of use a division can also be made between coastal and inland water space. Water ski racing is mainly a coastal activity in GB with tournament and barefoot disciplines tending to be restricted to water-filled mineral extraction sites, inland lakes, reservoirs and rivers.

Most of the 150,000 to 400,000 people who are estimated to water ski at some time during a year do so only recreationally and outside any club structure. However, the competitive disciplines that have been developed are important for the specific water space demands they create. Tournament skiing involves three activities, slalom skiing around a course of six buoys, jumping from a ramp, and performing a range of turns and twists known as tricks.

Speed racing combines powerboats and water skiers in one team; barefoot is, as its name implies, skiing without skis. The use of the kneeboard (a board similar in shape to a small surfboard around one metre in length and on which the competitor kneels), is a recent development which further varies the experience of water skiing. Cable skiing is a significant related activity. Here the boat is replaced by a cable tow, similar to a drag lift used by snow skiers, which pulls the skier on a circuit around the water area. In West Germany, where the system was evolved, there are now nearly 30 installations and most water skiing takes place using this method.

2 Site requirements
Generally any rectangular area of water of over 4 ha (approx 10 acres) is suitable for competitive water skiing. Ideally the water area should be sheltered, have a reasonable minimum water depth and gently sloping banks (1:8 gradient) such that backwash and bank erosion are rendered insignificant. Space for reasonable car parking, a club house and changing facilities, boat storage and access are all desirable around the edge of the water area. For competition an area of up to 750 × 80 m (approx 820 × 88 yd) is required with slightly wider turning areas at each end. Areas of national importance for wildlife should be avoided and the presence of residential areas in close proximity is a disadvantage. Some clubs are fortunate enough to have both recreational and competition and training areas. These may usefully be separated by a peninsula of land from which judging may take place.

1 *Cable ski tow*

2.1 Characteristics of an ideal water ski site
1 One or more areas of water (separate, linked or continuous):
   - One area of up to 750 × 80 m (approx 820 × 88 yd) for competition and training, containing a slalom course and jumping ramp
   - One further area, minimum size 5 ha (approx 12 acres) – any shape – for recreational skiing.
2 Minimum water depth of 1.2 m (approx 4 ft).
3 Shelter from trees or surrounding high ground.
4 Gently sloping banks (1:8) to avoid backwash and bank erosion.
5 Unpolluted water.
6 Preferably constant availability – no other users or carefully organised sharing/zoning.
7 Launching slipway, jetties and/or rafts and/or pontoons for tying up boats.
8 Club house with facilities such as changing rooms, toilets, showers and car parking.
9 Boat house.
10 Access on shore around slalom course and jump for judging competitions.

3 Category of sites
The British Water Ski Federation categorises sites as suitable for different levels of competition as follows:

3.1 Category A: National Standard
The site will have a slalom course and a jump maintained to World Water Ski standards, and will be sheltered with

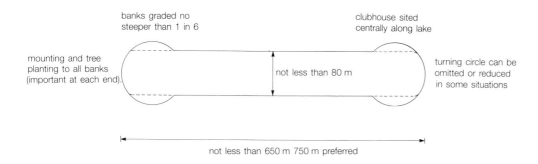

banks graded no
steeper than 1 in 6

clubhouse sited
centrally along lake

mounting and tree
planting to all banks
(important at each end).

not less than 80 m

turning circle can be
omitted or reduced
in some situations

not less than 650 m 750 m preferred

With careful planning, the preferred width of 80 m can be reduced at some points along the coarse.
Developers are advised to consult the BWSF before proceeding.

2

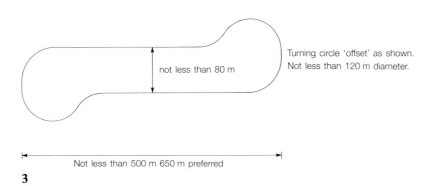

not less than 80 m

Turning circle 'offset' as shown.
Not less than 120 m diameter.

Not less than 500 m 650 m preferred

3

no backwash problems. Full competition boats will be available on the site at most times, with full-time staff available through the summer. Its minimum dimensions are as shown in **2**.

3.2 Category B: Regional Standard
The site will have a six buoy slalom course and a jump maintained to a good standard. The site should be sheltered with no backwash problems and full competition boats should be made available, **3**.

3.3 Category C: Sub Regional
The site will have a slalom course of six buoys preferably, but four would be acceptable, and a jump. The main purpose of the site will be for training and local competition. The skiing area should be a minimum of 400 m (approx 438 yd) long and a minimum of 80 m (approx 88 yd) wide; larger areas are needed for turning.

3.4 Category D: Recreational Standard
Almost any area of water over 300 m (328 yd) in length and 50 m (approx 55 yd) wide can be used at club level for recreational skiing. The larger the area of water the better, particularly for boat owning members. To prevent

wash problems, and to break up wind driven waves, it is advantageous for the water area to have central islands.

4 Cable tow skiing
Cable tow skiing makes use of the principle of the drag lift used at winter ski resorts. A cable is attached to five or six pylons around a lake and driven by an electric motor. Tow ropes are attached to the cable and up to 15 skiers can be accommodated at distances 100 m (approx 110 yd) apart around a circuit. The site can be as small as 2 ha (5 acres) of water. Ideal dimensions are 360 m (approx 394 yd) long by 120 m (131 yd) wide. The cable can be run at different speeds to cater for beginners or more advanced competitors including barefoot skiers. There were four installations in the UK in 1991 and more are planned. Cable tows have a number of important attributes:

- Low running costs
- A potential capacity of over 2000 tows per day
- Easy management, allowing small water areas to be used intensively
- Few environmental impacts, almost no noise being generated from the electric engines
- A non-intrusive appearance in the landscape.

36
Personal watercraft riding

Peter Cranstone

1 General

Personal watercraft (PWC) riding is a rapidly expanding watersport which takes place on coastal and inland waters. Gravel pits and inland water areas too small to accommodate waterskiing and windsurfing are ideal. Sites need to be carefully selected and take account of residential and existing amenities or sites inhabited by rare breeds of wildlife or waterfowl.

Impeller driven personal watercraft are fast and manoeuvrable and capable of speeds up to 50 mph (80 kph) and can carry one or two people.

At present much personal watercraft riding at inland locations operates on a hire basis. A typical hire operation running seven solo PWCs requires:

- Site: a secure area with lockable entrance gates.
- Access: PWCs are transported in lorries, vans or on trailers with an approximate vehicle length of 7 m (23.1 ft).

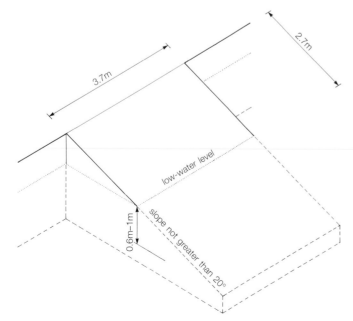

1 PWC launch area – recommended dimensions

- Parking: suggested minimum of 20 vehicles.
- Storage building: close to lake and large enough to accommodate, on racking, seven PWCs each measuring 2140 × 620 × 640 mm (approx 7 × 2 × 2 ft) and weighing 114 kg (approx 250 lb), plus wetsuits and buoyancy aids hung on rails. Non-slip floor.
- Workshop: to accommodate PWCs measuring 2140 × 620 × 640 mm (approx 7 × 2 × 2 ft) and weighing 114 kg (approx 250 lb). Non-slip floor.
- Changing rooms: preferably with warm showers.
- WC (both sexes).
- Petrol storage bunker, lockable and non-leakable; to meet fire regulations.
- Launch area: concrete ramp or hard grassy bank, 1. Account should be taken of seasonal variations in water levels due to evaporation and heavy rainfall.
- Resting area: hard bank or jetty on which to rest the craft when not in use. The slope should not exceed 15°.
- Lake: minimum size 6 ha (approx 15 acres) (eg 300 × 200 m (328 × 218 yd)). Minimum depth 1.5 m (approx 1.6 yd) to allow for seasonal changes. Weed presence to be minimal. Net matting, wooden boarding or a clay lining will reduce erosion of the banks. Earth mounds to reduce noise levels have been successfully introduced at a number of sites.
- Buoyed course: approximately 70 × 70 m (approx 77 yd) at least 3.5 m (approx 4 yd) from shore, oval or square in shape. Most people ride more naturally in an anti-clockwise direction.

2 Additional requirements for an owners' club

A club with 100 members will require:

- Car park, suggested capacity 100 cars. Many members will tow their own craft on trailers giving an approximate vehicle length of 7 m (approx 23 ft).
- Clubhouse with:
  - Bar/cafeteria
  - Changing rooms with warm showers
  - Manager's office
  - WCs
  - Extra storage for members' craft.
- Members' lake/course, separate from rental course. Minimum size 6 ha (approx 15 acres) (eg 300 × 200 m (328 × 218 yd)) and minimum depth 1.8 m (approx

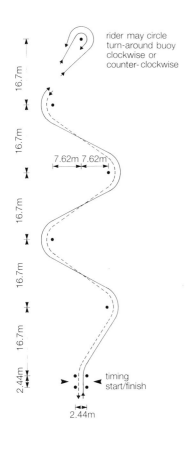

rider may circle
turn-around buoy
clockwise or
counter-clockwise

16.7m

16.7m

7.62m 7.62m

16.7m

16.7m

16.7m

2.44m

timing
start/finish

2.44m

*2 Suggested slalom
course layout*

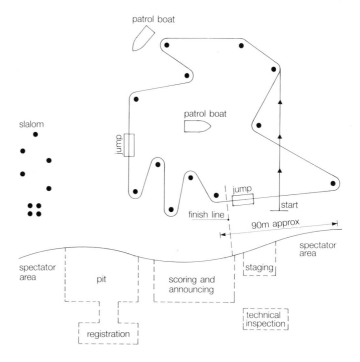

patrol boat

patrol boat

slalom

jump

jump

start

finish line

90m approx

spectator
area

spectator
area

pit

scoring and
announcing

staging

technical
inspection

registration

3 Suggested race site layout

4 Kawasaki X-4 Jet Ski

5 Kawasaki 550SX Jet Ski

2 yd) to accommodate freestyle manoeuvres; may also
include a slalom course (see **2**).

3 Additional requirements for a racing venue

See **3**.

4 References and further advice

More detailed advice can be obtained from the Personal
 Watercraft Association, Woodside House, Woodside
 Road, Eastleigh, Hants. Tel. 0703 616888

Part VII Sports data

37
Introduction

Peter Ackroyd

1 Introduction

In this Part, Peter Ackroyd and Maritz Vandenberg, with David Bosher (Floodlighting), Gordon Stables (Surfaces) and Ken Farnes (Cycle Racing), have compiled an A-Z of sports data in collaboration with the Governing Bodies of sports and many others.

2 Scope

The following chapters give fundamental technical information for over 50 sports and different disciplines based on standards used in Great Britain. Other sports may be played outdoors for recreation where conditions are suitable, **1**.

The minimum spaces required for relevant standards of play takes into account any necessary run-out or safety margins, team bench and officials' control spaces around the playing area. These together amount to the overall areas shown by a broken line surrounding the space diagram in each section. See also Marginal clearances and side movement below.

In answer to the frequent question 'How much land do we need?' the comparative areas of the most popular sports played on playing fields are shown in **2**. Overlaid

pitches are compared with an optimum area of 1 ha (approx 2.5 acres).

Readers should also refer to Volume 2 for details of indoor sports.

3 Metrication

In keeping with European practice imperial conversions are given following each metric dimension.

By far the majority of governing bodies now publish and mark-out using metric dimensions. Some have 'rounded off' dimensions; others have converted exactly. A few sports, such as rugby union football, have been faced with rephrasing traditionally known features of the pitch: for example the 'twenty-five' (yard line) was renamed the 'twenty-two' (metre line) to avoid distorting the proportions of the midfield area; the 10 yd line, however, remains the 10 m line.

4 Orientation

The limits of good orientation for a range of sports to avoid playing directly into the sun are shown in **3**. For the purpose of this chart the seasons for the various recreational facilities have been taken as:

1 *Volleyball outdoors is a growth activity, given suitable ground and climatic conditions. Photo: S C Publications Unit*

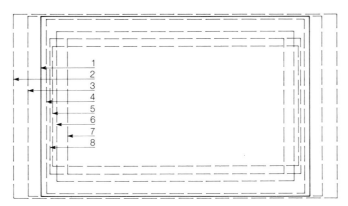

2 Winter games pitches compared with a 1 ha (approx 2.5 acres) area. 1 1 ha area of 125 × 80 m (10000 m²) (solid line) compared with full size pitch areas: 2 Rugby Union pitch 156 × 80 m; 3 Rugby league 134 × 80 m; 4 Association Football (senior pitch) 118 × 77 m; 5 American Football 113 × 52 m; 6 Soccer junior area 108 × 67 m; Hockey 100 × 61 m; 8 Lacrosse 116 × 61 m. NB: All sizes include the safety margins surrounding the pitch; ie the overall maximum area. TUS diagram

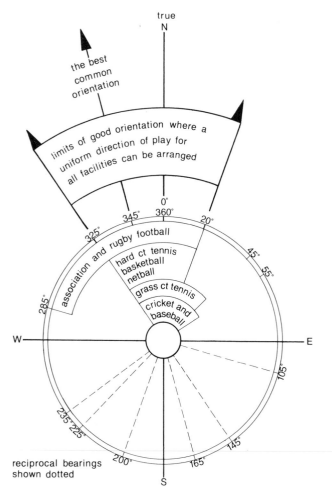

3 Orientation diagram. National Playing Fields Association

Association Football and Rugby Football	From September to April 30
Hard court tennis, Basketball, Netball	All the year round
Cricket, Baseball, Grass court tennis	From May 1 to September 15

Hockey pitches may be sited in any direction as in this game the ball seldom rises sufficiently for the sun to be a nuisance.

5 Marginal clearances and side movement

The dimensions of end and side margins are intended as a guide to the minimum distances between pitches. Where pitches are sited next to boundaries, roads, buildings or other fixtures discretion should be used as to whether the clearances prescribed are sufficient, having regard to the type of game and the nature of the adjoining property. Thus an association football pitch with a main road behind the goal, or property on which damage or trespass might be caused, would probably require an end clearance of 12–15 m (40–50 ft) to avoid risk of accident or complaint. Alternatively, as a protective measure, high chain link fencing could be erected along the boundary behind the goal.

Where overplay of winter games pitches is likely to occur, adequate allowance should be made for end or side shifting to permit the reinstatement of worn areas. Unfortunately, in practice the necessary space for this purpose is seldom available. The game most likely to require this extra space is Association Football and to be effective the pitch should be moved each year a distance of at least 9 m (29 ft 6 in) either endways or sideways. Where, however, space is restricted a lesser distance than this is better than no shifting at all.

6 Acknowledgements

We would like to thank the following for their help: Sports Council for Wales, Scottish Sports Council and Sports Council for Northern Ireland; the Governing Bodies of sport (named in References for each sport) with contributions from many officials; National Playing Fields Association; the Sports Council's Development and Facilities Units and also Information and Publications Units; the sports equipment trade; recreational consultants, architects and many others who have supplied illustrations.

7 Further advice

An updated directory and guide to Governing Bodies of sport is available from the Sports Council's Information Unit.

38
Archery – target and clout

Peter Ackroyd

Target archery

The marking-out sequence of official Round distances has been reversed since the first edition of this Handbook so that the archers now remain on the shooting line whilst the targets are moved for a change of distance. Additional lanes for press, waiting archers and spectators are set out behind the shooting line.

Critical factors

- Overall area of the shoot including the revised shaped surrounding safety zones
- The lanes behind the shooting line
- The alternative sets of distances to imperial or metric measurements.

Space

2 shows the layout and dimensions of an outdoor archery shooting range and the surrounding safety zone. In the northern hemisphere archers should shoot towards the north or north-east.

Targets must be spaced at least 2.5 m (8 ft 2 in) apart when two archers are shooting at once, as is normal; and 3.66 m (12 ft) apart when three archers are shooting at once. Archers remain on the shooting line throughout and the targets, 4, are moved towards them for succeeding rounds.

The shoot is dimensioned in yards; but the target lines can also be spaced in metres. The alternative sets of dimensions are given in Table 38.1.

Table 38.1: Alternative target line distances for target archery

Measured in yards	Measured in metres
	10 m (10 yd 34 in) (Junior events)
20 yd (18.28 m)	20 m (21 yd 32 in) (Junior events)
30 yd (27.43 m)	30 m (32 yd 30 in)
40 yd (36.58 m)	40 m (43 yd 27 in)
50 yd (45.72 m)	50 m (54 yd 25 in)
60 yd (54.86 m)	60 m (65 yd 23 in)
80 yd (73.15 m)	70 m (76 yd 21 in)
100 yd (91.44 m)	90 m (98 yd 17 in)

Markings

The shooting line and target lines, as also the various lines behind the shooting line, must be clearly marked out on the grass by white lines or tapes. All lines are set out from the shooting line.

Surface

Normally, the preferred surface is natural grass; but mineral or synthetic surfaces may be used for practice or club events. For general information see Part III.

Clout archery

In clout archery arrows are shot high in the air to fall on targets consisting of concentric circles marked out on the ground in white lines, or circular white cloths pinned down. In the northern hemisphere, archers should shoot towards the north or north-east.

Critical factors

- Overall area of space including the wide surrounding safety margins
- Clear height, free of obstructions and cables.

1 *Photo: James Dunlop*

171

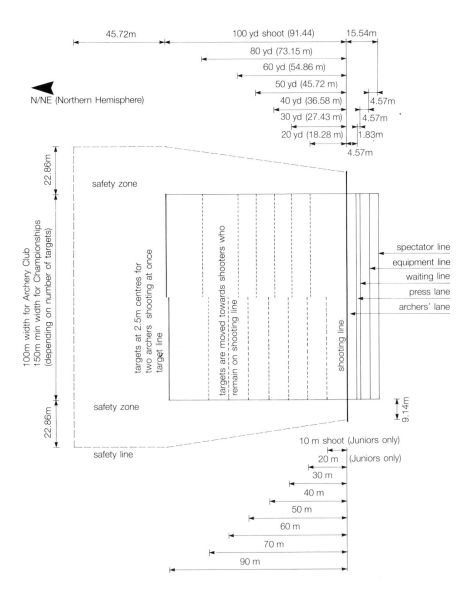

45.72m   100 yd shoot (91.44)   15.54m

80 yd (73.15 m)

60 yd (54.86 m)

50 yd (45.72 m)

40 yd (36.58 m)   4.57m

30 yd (27.43 m)   4.57m

20 yd (18.28 m)   1.83m

4.57m

N/NE (Northern Hemisphere)

22.86m

safety zone

100m width for Archery Club
150m min width for Championships
(depending on number of targets)

targets at 2.5m centres for
two archers shooting at once
target line

targets are moved towards shooters who
remain on shooting line

shooting line

spectator line

equipment line

waiting line

press lane

archers' lane

22.86m

safety zone

9.14m

safety line

10 m shoot (Juniors only)

20 m   (Juniors only)

30 m

40 m

50 m

60 m

70 m

90 m

2 Space diagram for target archery. In addition to the UK imperial distances, eight international distances in metric measurements are listed in Table 38.1. Archers now remain on the original shooting line and at the change of distance the targets are moved

Space

Overall field length, from the shooting line to the safety line beyond the 164 m (180 yd) target, is 233 m (255 yd), **3**.

Shooting distances for male and female participants are as in Table 38.2.

Table 38.2: Target line distances for clout archery

Males	Females
180 yd (164.59m) adult	140 yd (128.02m) adult
140 yd (128.02m) under 18	120 yd (109.73m) under 18
120 yd (109.73m) under 16	100 yd (91.44m) under 16
100 yd (91.44m) under 14	80 yd (73.15m) under 13
80 yd (73.15m) under 12	

Markings

The shooting line is the only marking, but it is advisable to mark or peg the outline of the target locations. The surrounding safety zone should be roped off and supervised.

Targets are 7.3 m (24 ft) in diameter.

Floodlighting

For details of requirements and recommendations refer to Chapter 18 and the CIBSE Lighting Guide: LG4 – Sports. See also Volume 2, Chapter 17, Indoor Archery.

References and further advice

The Grand National Archery Society.

See also Volume 2, Chapter 17, Indoor Archery.

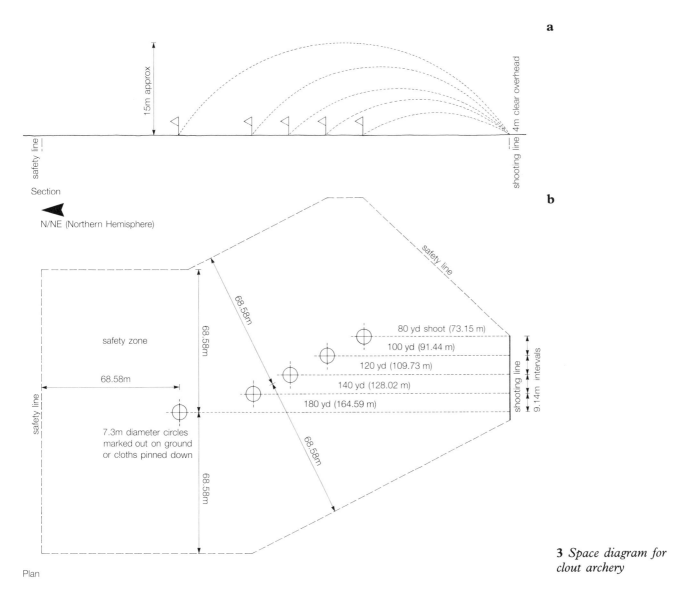

a

15m approx

4m clear overhead

safety line

shooting line

Section

N/NE (Northern Hemisphere)

b

safety line

68.58m

68.58m

safety zone

68.58m

68.58m

68.58m

7.3m diameter circles
marked out on ground
or cloths pinned down

80 yd shoot (73.15 m)

100 yd (91.44 m)

120 yd (109.73 m)

140 yd (128.02 m)

180 yd (164.59 m)

shooting line

9.14m intervals

Plan

3 *Space diagram for*
clout archery

4 *Photo: Sports Council*

39
Athletics – track and field

Peter Ackroyd

Introduction

It is essential at the earliest stage that anyone considering the provision of any new athletics facility in the UK should consult the facilities officer of the British Athletics Federation (BAF) for advice on the type of facility required and its situation. In Great Britain the future needs of the UK as a whole are kept constantly under review and up-to-date information will be supplied by the BAF. Early consultation should also take place with the appropriate Sports Council or its Regional Office; see also 'Further references and advice' at the end of this chapter.

Grades of track

Regional, area and club use
If primarily for local club use and training, the track should be situated in the best position to serve the needs of the local community and the schools in the area, **1**.

1 *Photo: Haringey Athletics Club and Wood Green School, London. The closest possible co-operation between local authorities, clubs and schools is vital for the development of athletics. Economy of provision can be more readily effected where a track and indoor training area are provided as a combined joint provision facility. These can be used by both school and club athletes out of school hours, as at this exemplary centre which has significantly contributed to British athletics' success. Prototype development by The London Borough of Haringey, Sports Council and Southern Counties AAA; see also Volume 2, Chapter 70. Photo: LMGT Consultants, Harlow*

For public tracks at area and club level, requirements should be governed by the needs of the local situation. The funds available are likely to determine whether the track and runway surfaces should be synthetic or hard porous (waterbound). Wherever possible, the runways at least should be synthetic and to help keep down costs, combined runways and reduced runway widths are sometimes acceptable. The safety radii for the throws may be less than those required at national level and might be reduced. However, safety arcs must remain constant.

The site selection for a regional or sub-regional track requires more careful planning to decide which location is most conveniently situated to serve the catchment area. It is essential to take into account existing and proposed sports facilities, particularly a well-equipped centre where use can also be made of a training hall and other amenities. See also Number of Lanes below.

For locations where there is not a track consider the development of school-based basic training facilities for sprint and field disciplines, **3**.

Major tracks, **4**, should be close to a motorway and the rail network. Where the need to attract maximum spectator support is a vital consideration, ease of access to a stadium is likely to be a major factor in determining its popularity.

Critical Factors
- Consultations regarding grade and location of proposals
- The whereabouts of prospective partnership facilities
- Provision of outdoor and indoor training facilities
- Orientation
- Overall area of track and field including safety measures
- A natural turf surfaced central area is fundamental
- The sole recommended siting for hammer and discus events
- Ample storage and separate fire resistant storage for foam filled soft landing areas
- Tractor and maintenance storage.

The final layout should be decided only after close consultation with local athletic clubs, schools and other interested bodies. Providers are also strongly advised, before the plans are finally approved, to submit detailed proposals to the national governing body of athletics for comment.

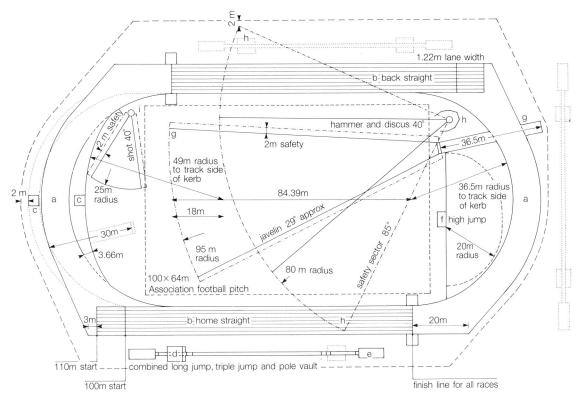

2 *Layout guide for 400 m (approx 438 yd) running tracks and field events. This layout, with alternative sitings for field events, is based on NPFA Diagram 13b. Different arrangements are possible to suit particular circumstances. For high level competition, however, alternatives for the siting of the throwing circles are limited if maximum distances are to be thrown safely. Where a wider or narrower track, or a different length, is required, the appropriate dimensions can be calculated from the following formula:*

$$L = 2P + 2pi \ (R + 300 \ mm)$$

where L = *Length of track in metres (yards)*
P = *Length of parallels or distance apart of centres of curves in metres (yards)*
R = *Radius to track side of inner kerb in metres (yards)*
pi = *3.1416 (not 22/7)*

It is recommended that the radius of the semi-circles should not normally be less than 32 m (35 yd) or more than 42 m (approx 46 yd) for a 400 m (approx 438 yd) circuit.

Detailed diagrams of track and field event spaces, for example steeplechase jump water pit and throwing cages, can be referred to in IAAF and NPFA publications (see References). Where a temporary track is marked out on a grass, hard porous (waterbound) or a synthetic play area without a raised or flagged border, the track length must be measured along a line 200 mm (8 in) instead of 300 mm (12 in) from the track side of the inner edge.

Orientation

It is often difficult to reconcile the requirements of wind direction and the need to avoid an approach into the setting sun. Where possible, provide alternative directions for running, jumping and throwing, **2**. For essential detailed guidelines concerning evening sun and prevailing winds, refer to NPFA Drawing 13b Notes (see References). See also Straights below.

If the central winter games pitch is for football, its long axis should if possible be within the arc 285 to 020°.

Space requirements and layout details

Space requirements
A 400 m (438 yd) 6 to 8 lane running track including the central area, requires a minimum area of the right shape of about 2 ha (5 acres). In addition, a minimum width of about 6 m (20 ft) is allowed around the circuit of the track for circulation and additional standing spectators. These requirements might take up a further 0.5 ha (1.2 acres) approx. A track of regional or national status may need an increased space allowance according to the nature of the accommodation to be provided.

Great emphasis is placed on the need for taking adequate safety measures at all times. This applies particularly to throwing events. Further details are obtainable from the governing bodies of athletics.

The following recommendations, relating to the lettered references on **2**, explain briefly some essential considerations when assessing possible alternative layouts of facilities for track and field events.

Track events

a: Number of lanes
The fundamental question is usually 'how many lanes should be provided?' The 'best buy' simple answer in

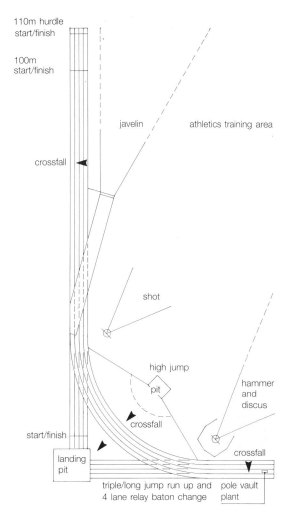

110m hurdle
start/finish

100m
start/finish

crossfall ◄

javelin   athletics training area

shot

high jump
pit

hammer
and
discus

crossfall ►

start/finish   crossfall

landing
pit

triple/long jump run up and   pole vault
4 lane relay baton change   plant

3 *Layout of an outdoor training development at Balbardie, West Lothian, Scotland*

the UK is generally a six lane, 400 m (approx 438 yd) track, together with indoor training facilities (for data, refer to Volume 2). New eight lane tracks should be located and planned only with the full agreement of the athletics Governing Bodies (see Introduction). The general scale of provisions of lanes is set out in Table 39.1. Lanes are always 1.22 m (4 ft) wide to the centre of markings.

Table 39.1 General scale of lane provisions

Standard of use	Synthetic all-weather surface	Hard porous (waterbound) surface
Competition to international minimum standards, BAF Areas and Regional competition and below	6 lanes 7.32 m (24 ft)	7 lanes 8.54 m (87 ft 3 in)
International competition	8 lane straight	8 lanes 9.76 m (32 ft)
Full standard		9 lanes on straight(s)
Major international competition	8 lanes 9.76 m (32 ft) 10 lane straights	—

b: Straights

Where there will probably be considerable use by the public, local clubs and particularly schools, or for competition at national and international level, it is desirable for the 'home' and 'back' straights to have an extra two lanes and both to have the same number of lanes. Events with

a large number of 'heats' (eliminating rounds) then take less time to finalise in a full programme.

The advantages of providing a 'back' straight as well as a 'home' straight are that sprint and hurdle events can be held simultaneously and the direction of running can be changed to suit wind conditions.

c: Steeplechase and water jump

In the UK it is normal practice to site the water jump inside the track circuit. The measurements shown will give a steeplechase lap of 394 m (431 yd) (via water jump). Alternatively it is permissible to site the water jump outside the track (as shown dotted on diagram). For lap length and other dimensional implications, refer to NPFA publications.

The water jump must measure 3.66 m (12 ft) in width internally and 3.66 m (12 ft) from the approach side of the hurdle to the top of the slope. The depth slopes from 0 to 700 mm (0 to approx 28 in).

Field events

The layout for field events can be varied to suit particular local requirements. Normally a winter games pitch has to be included in the layout. Where this can be omitted a more suitable arrangement may be possible, (eg Putting the shot, see below) and the range of facilities improved.

For training purposes, **2, 3**, it is an advantage, where space is available, if additional throwing facilities can be sited outside the track. There must be due regard, however, to the need for proper control and supervision to ensure the safety of other users and the public including additional safety throwing cage(s).

d: Pole vault

The pole vault runway is combined with that of the long and triple jump, utilising removable take off boards/blanking boards to maximise the runway's use and provide the best spectator viewing for all three events. The runways are double ended, allowing satisfactory siting of the pole vault soft landing units. Provision for an alternative siting (shown dashed on **2**), enables an approach from the opposite end of the runway.

Runways should never be sited within the central arena parallel to the home or back straights, owing to the possibility of a discus or hammer rebounding off them.

Where a hard porous (waterbound) surface is used, a separate pole vault runway should be installed with the soft landing unit centrally positioned to allow athletes to approach from either direction.

Only a soft landing area should be used. The international rule requires the size to be not less than 5 × 5 × 1.2 m (16 ft 6 in × 16 ft 6 in × 4 ft) thick. For safety, the pole vault box should not be nearer to the track or other adjacent facility than 6 m (approx 19 ft), the length of the full size pole.

e: Long and triple jump

If pole vault, long and triple jump practice and competition are to take place at the same time, separate runways and landing areas must be provided as shown in **2**.

The landing areas for the long jump and the triple jump should each measure not less than 9 × 2.75 m (29 ft 6 in × 9 ft) wide or a maximum of 3 m (approx 10 ft).

f: High jump

The use of a soft landing area 5 × 3 m (approx 16 ft × 10 ft) is essential (see also Storage space for athletics

4 *Don Valley Stadium Sheffield. Built for the World Student Games 1991 and now to be used as a Regional track.* *Photo: DBS Graphics*

equipment). The length of runway should not be less than 20 m (approx 65 ft), preferably 25 m (82 ft), by installing a removable kerb, thereby allowing use across the track. With a synthetic surface, the high jump area and javelin runway is usually surfaced in one piece, called the Dee, right up to the inner edge of the track.

g: Javelin
The main runway should be 36.50 m long × 4 m (approx 120 ft × 13 ft) wide and the secondary runway (shown dotted on **2**) not less than 30 m (98 ft) long, with a recommended minimum of 33.50 m (110 ft). The runway should extend 600 mm (24 in) beyond the throwing arc. The arc may be painted on a synthetic surface. For national and regional tracks, the layout of the javelin arc must allow for the increasing length of throws and maintain safety distances from the track.

Space must be available outside the 29° throwing sector to enable the area to be roped off for a distance of 2 m (6 ft 6 in) outside the sector lines.

h: Hammer and discus
International and national rules require that all hammer and discus throws shall be made from an enclosure or cage to ensure the safety of spectators, officials and competitors. The diagram position shown is the *sole*

recommended siting position within the central arena. It should be noted that the safety sector extends onto the home straight (right handed throwers) and over the back straight and secondary combined pole vault long and triple jump runway (left handed throwers).

Throwing circles: hammer 2.135 m (7 ft) diameter (+ or – 5 mm (0.2 in))
discus 2.50 m (approx 8 ft) diameter (+ or – 5 mm (0.2 in))

Hammer throwers prefer a smoother finish to the concrete surface than discus throwers. For this reason, separate circles are generally preferred. Both circles may, however, be placed in a single cage, the discus circle being at the rear. However, owing to safety factors in conjunction with the practicalities of installation within the central arena, it is considered that the only acceptable solution is for a concentric circle to be provided and sited within a hammer and discus cage provided with extension wings.

Sufficient space must be left between cage and track to permit free circulation of athletes and officials.

i: Putting the shot
The provision of two permanent shot circles is advisable. The primary one should be sited adjacent to the entry to

177

the water jump from the back straight, the landing area being provided with a non-turf surface capable of retaining shot imprints. The secondary shot circle utilising a turf landing area is indicated with a dotted line. This shot circle should be positioned to give sufficient space to permit the free circulation of officials for the 100 m (109 yd) and 110 m (120 yd) events. Portable shot circles complying with the ruling bodies' tolerances are permissible for competition purposes and may be sited within the central arena.

The throwing circle is 2.135 m (7 ft) diameter (+ or – 5 mm (0.2 in)). For club and training tracks, a safety radius of 22 m (approx 72 ft) should be adequate. Space must be available outside the 40° throwing sector to enable the area to be roped off for a distance of 2 m (6 ft 6 in) outside the sector lines.

Changing and other accommodation

This is an essential part of track provision. It should be planned alongside the home straight, preferably near to the finishing line. Wherever possible, the changing rooms should be combined with the requirements of other games and activities and include provision for social and refreshment facilities, club and lecture rooms, a training hall, first aid and possibly doping control. Standards of space for changing, showers and other accommodation are given in NPFA and Amateur Athletics Association (AAA) references at the end.

Storage space for athletics equipment

Ample secure storage space for a huge amount of bulky equipment is essential, and should be additional to any storage accommodation provided for groundsmen's equipment. Storage should be light, airy, temperate and dry. A dark, damp corner under the stand, as in many stadia, is not satisfactory and significantly reduces the life of the equipment. For new provision the minimum ceiling height should be 4 m (approx 13 ft). Spaces required for storing listed equipment are also specified in NPFA/AAA publications. Accommodation for tractor and other maintenance machinery, equipment and materials is also essential.

Training items should be kept separate from competition equipment and issued accordingly.

The high jump and pole vault soft landing mattress contain foam filling which is a fire hazard. Refer to Volume 2, Chapter 55 and to the References concerning the need for separate storage for foam filled equipment.

Surfaces

For general information see Part III. The following is an outline guide only:

- Synthetic materials provide a consistently good surface capable of continuous and unlimited use in most weathers. Maintenance consists of regular sweeping/vacuuming, occasional hosing down, repainting when necessary of line markings and the occasional repair.
- Hard porous (waterbound) surfaces require considerable maintenance by a skilled groundsman every time the track is used. The surfaces are not all-weather and

seldom provide a consistently good running surface but are much cheaper to construct and suitable for club use and training.

- On hard porous (waterbound) tracks, an extra lane is necessary so that sprint and hurdle events can be run on the six outer lanes to avoid the inner lane which is subject to heavy use during long distance events.
- The central area must have a natural grass surface because artificial grass or synthetic materials are unacceptable for field throwing events. A winter season sports pitch is often marked out: dimensions are given in datasheets in Part VII. See also Chapter 22.
- Temporary tracks may be marked out on natural grass.
- Paved areas, j on 2, are useful to allow stands to be placed on both the inside of the track (for judges) and the outside (for timekeepers) unless the latter can be satisfactorily seated in the spectator stand. Where encroachment on to a winter games pitch is unavoidable, temporary wooden platforms should be used.
- Hard standings should be provided for steeplechase and other hurdles when not in use.
- If the steeplechase water jump is sited inside the track circuit, the kerbing at the entry and exit points for the water jump approach must be removable.

For further details of gradients, kerbs, surface construction, jumpboards and markings for other track and field events and manholes to access communications, photofinish, electronic timing and surface watering systems, refer to current publications and consult the governing bodies for athletics.

Markings

The setting-out of track and field event facilities with their various multi-coloured line marking is a highly specialised service which requires very experienced consultants, contractors and operatives. For track grading certification and for events where record times are recorded, markings are surveyed and rechecked for accuracy.

Barrier fence

Where spectators have access to the track area, it may be desirable to erect a protective barrier around the track. This should not be nearer than 1.5 m (5 ft) to the track and ample space should be left at the end of the straights for runners to pull up after passing the finishing line. It should be 1.1 m (3 ft 6 in) high, strong enough to take the weight of spectators leaning on it and designed to prevent small children and dogs wandering onto the track.

Spectators

The main seating should be as close as possible to the finish on the home straight. Spectators in the main stand should not have to look towards the setting sun. For sightlines, seating, spectators' amenities and circulation, including those for people with disabilities, refer to Chapter 22.

Floodlighting

Floodlighting is essential for the maximum use of tracks and training areas to enable training and competition to be carried out during the hours of darkness.

For details of requirements and recommendations, refer to Chapter 18 and to CIBSE Lighting Guide: LG4 – Sports.

References and further advice

International Amateur Athletes Federation

The British Athletics Federation

The National Playing Fields Association

NPFA, March 1992. *Drawing 13b: Layout guide for 400 m running tracks*. Notes refer to important layout changes and recommendations (especially on hammer and discus safety sectors). An essential reference to amplify this chapter.

Sports Council 1988 *Fact Sheet: Foam based sports, recreation and play equipment* and Home Office Fire Services Circular No. 1/1988 (FSCI/88) 'Fire hazards associated with the use of cellular foam in sports and recreational facilities'.

Scottish Sports Council, 1986: Information Digest FD 20: *Athletics training area: Balbardie, West Lothian.*

IAAF and BAF Annual Handbooks

IAAF Technical Committee, *Track and Field Facilities* publication being prepared, including regulations and guidelines for locating, planning, constructing, equipping and maintaining facilities, will become the standard international sources of reference.

Indoor training facilities – see Volume 2, Chapter 70

Indoor competition facilities – see *Arenas: a planning design and management guide*, Sports Council, 1989

40
Baseball

Peter Ackroyd

Baseball developed in America from the English games of cricket and rounders. It is played by two teams of nine men (plus reserves who wait on the sidelines) on a level, reasonably smooth grassy field in the centre of which is the diamond, **1**.

Critical factors
- A well drained surface for the diamond
- The pitcher's mound and home base must be carefully prepared
- Maintenance of home base and base paths
- Drainage of non-grass areas
- Anchorage of bases
- Safety cover for exposed sprinklers in the outfield
- Line markings must not use hot lime
- Height of back-stop fencing
- Baseball expresses weights and measures in imperial units

1 *Photo: Ian Weigtman*

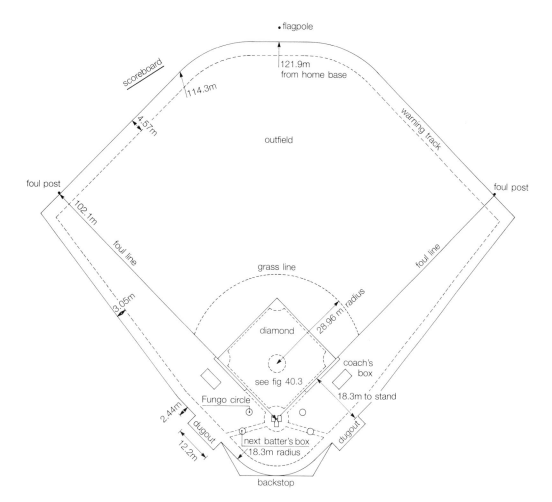

2 *Baseball field. All lines shown in solid should be marked with 127 mm (5 in) wide lines. The diamond area is detailed in 3. A complete facility includes dugouts, backstop netting, fences and stabilised areas on deck circles, fungo circles and coaches' boxes, located above. The safety these provide is important. Dugouts protect players from weather, fans and (if properly guarded) from errant baseballs. Bat boys and ball boys also should be provided with protected areas*

Playing space dimensions

The total area required is at least 100 × 100 m (approx. 330 × 330 ft), **2**, within which is the diamond – actually a square, with lengths approximately 27.4 m (specified as 30 × 30 yd by the American rules). Field dimensions can vary depending upon players' age groups. Layout and dimensions of the diamond are also shown on **3**.

Surfaces and plates

The diamond and infield surfaces

A grass or synthetic turf (non-sand filled) diamond is required, **3**. It must have a good surface which is not bumpy or damaged and be well drained. For general information see Part III.

Watering is extremely important in dry periods with weekly deep-watering preferable to a daily sprinkle. Any non-grassed areas of the infield also should be well-drained, to avoid the soil becoming waterlogged after rain or densely compacted over a period of use.

Pitcher's mound

The mound is a circular earthen knoll 5.5 m (18 ft) in diameter, sloping as shown in **3**. At its crown is a flat area 1.53 m (5 ft) wide and 0.86 m (34 in) deep, on which is mounted the pitcher's plate or 'pitching rubber', in

exactly the position shown on **3**. In front of the rubber is a second rubber plate at a lower stepped level to protect the earth from repetitive spike action of the pitcher pushing off during delivery of the ball. The mound should be made of a clay loam consisting of 40% clay, 20% silt and 40% coarse sand; and never of clays which become greasy when wet. It may be covered with a tarpaulin or mat, spiked down at the corners, during practice sessions to reduce wear and tear.

Home base

This is a very heavily used area, needing careful maintenance, **3**. Its composition may be the same as that of the pitcher's mound, to which coarse sand may be added if the surface becomes too compacted or additional clay if it becomes too loose. The area in front of the plate, towards third base, should have a layer of fine soil to provide safe, non-injurious sliding. The actual plate must have a bevelled edge and be firmly secured on a wooden or concrete base. Non-slippery mats may be used during practice to reduce wear and tear on the earthen surface.

Base paths

These intensively used dirt paths or 'running alleys', **3**, tend to get trodden out, hardened and hollowed, leading to water entrapment which can cause game cancellation.

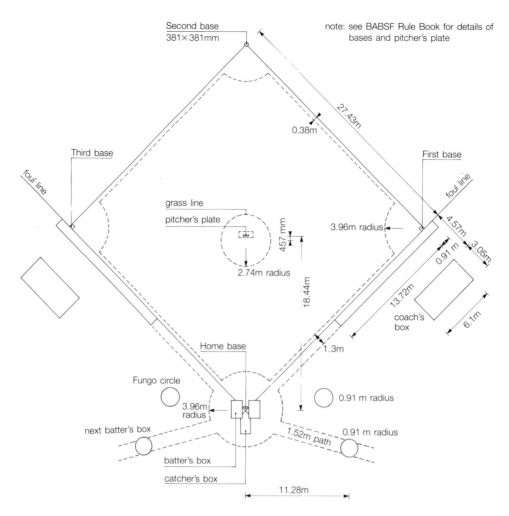

Second base
381×381mm

note: see BABSF Rule Book for details of
bases and pitcher's plate

27.43m

0.38m

Third base

First base

foul line

foul line

grass line

pitcher's plate

457 mm

3.96m radius

4.57m

3.05m

0.91 m

2.74m radius

18.44m

13.72m

coach's
box

6.1m

Home base

1.3m

Fungo circle

3.96m
radius

0.91 m radius

next batter's box

1.52m path

0.91 m radius

batter's box

catcher's box

11.28m

3 *Space diagram of full-size diamond*

They should regularly be refilled with loose soil and raked level with the infield.

Bases
All bases should be securely anchored and the Hollywood type, fixed by a peg set in concrete, is the best.

Outfield surfaces
The outfield, **2**, needs less maintenance than parts close to the diamond; but potholes, exposed sprinkler connections and other potentially injurious features must be covered and the surface kept reasonably level.

Markings
All lines, shown in solid on **2** and **3**, should be marked in 127 mm (5 in) wide white bands on the field. The playing areas are measured to the outside of lines (ie the playing area includes the lines). If limed, use only dehydrated and not hot lime. Marking chalk, manufactured for this specific purpose, is excellent but expensive. All lines should be straight and true.

Fences and safety barriers
Fencing or ball-arrest netting is needed behind the batter's box and adjacent to public areas, **2**. Minimum height at the backstop position is 9.2 m (30 ft), elsewhere 2.4 m (8 ft). A batting cage is expensive, but highly recommended.

Changing facilities
Accommodation is required for 44 players (including substitutes) and four officials per field.

Floodlighting
For details of lighting requirements and recommendations refer to the national Governing Body of the sport.

References and further advice
British Baseball Federation.

41
Basketball

Peter Ackroyd

The English Basket Ball Association continues to encourage the development of basketball as an outdoor activity. A number of local authorities have been encouraged to provide outdoor basketball facilities in public playgrounds and recreational areas, **1**.

Critical factors
- To develop basketball as an outdoor recreation on suitably surfaced areas.
- In restricted spaces, to develop half court play areas.

- Full size free throw lanes(s) must be provided.
- Colour of line markings must contrast with surface and other sports markings.
- Goal post locations and fixings.

Space
The alternatives are to provide:

- A full basketball court with two goals. Court dimensions are set out in **2**. Where the facility shares a hard

1 *The EBBA is developing basketball as an outdoor recreation by encouraging the provision of more casual pass-around and shooting practice areas. Photo: Sports Council and KH Action Sport*

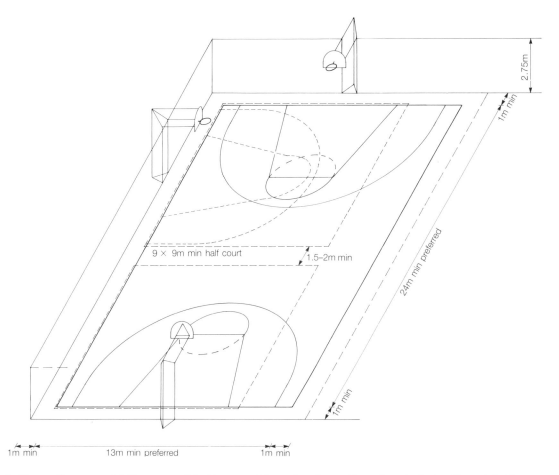

2.75m

1m min

24m min preferred

9 x 9m min half court

1.5-2m min

1m min

1m min   13m min preferred   1m min

2 Space diagram of full court and half courts. Note also the outline of a single backboard half-court option for restricted sites. Detailed dimensions of the free throw lane are as for indoor basketball and shown in Volume 2, Chapter 20

play surface with other activities such as tennis, it is suggested that the court dimensions could be extended to enable a basketball installation to be set up so that it does not interfere with other sports. On tennis courts the basketball backboard support could be positioned in the stop netting.

● A single backboard used for half court play. For the half court, **2**, almost any piece of flat ground may be used, provided there is a total uninterrupted space of at least 9 x 9 m (approx 10 yd) with a one or two post supported goal, or a well mounted backboard. A nationwide 3 versus 3 outdoor competition is being established.

Markings

When marking any outdoor basketball play area, it should be remembered that although the outer court dimensions (measured to the inside of perimeter lines) may be varied to suit the space available, the marking of the free throw lane should not be changed and the free throw line should be marked 4.60 m (approx 5 yd) from the front face of the backboard, **2**.

Where single installations are made, two of these can be set up side by side, if the play area is too small to accommodate a full size court. The colour of lines must contrast with the surface and with other sports on a multi-games area.

Equipment

Low cost basketball posts with backboards are now available. Fan shaped boards have been developed for permanent outdoor installation, **1**. Another development has been the use of steel and fibre glass to produce vandal proof installations. Where the backboard is being situated as part of a boundary fence, the posts supporting the boundary fence can also be used to support the backboard.

Safe mobile backboard units are very expensive and will require suitable storage space. Removable socketed posts can present storage and erection problems due to weight or the fact that the sockets can get lost or become difficult to replace flush with the surface.

Surfaces

Outdoors the game may be played on bound and unbound mineral or in-situ synthetic surfaces. The surface should preferably be permeable and meet the requirements of BS 7044 Part 4. For general information see Part III.

Floodlighting

For details of requirements and recommendations refer to Chapter 18, and to CIBSE Lighting Guide: LG4 – Sports.

Changing

Allow for 20 players and two officials per court.

References and further advice

The English Basket Ball Association.
Multi-use games areas in Chapter 28.
Surfaces for Outdoor Sport in Part III.
Basketball – Indoors in Volume 2, Chapter 20.
Tennis Courts in Chapter 65.

42
Bicycle polo

Peter Ackroyd

Bicycle polo is a form of polo (see Chapter 68) adapted to the use of bicycles instead of ponies. The European version of the game – played mainly in Britain, Ireland, Belgium and France – uses a smaller grass pitch. The teams of both men and women contain six players (one of them a reserve) who carry long-handled mallets, the object being to drive the ball upfield and strike it into the opposing goal, **1**.

Critical factors
- A grass-surfaced pitch of the overall dimensions shown in **2**, including surrounding safety margins.

Playing space dimensions
Dimensions are still laid down in yards, though metric equivalents are given here for convenience and are variable. Minimum size is 82.3 x 54.9 m (90 × 60 yd); and maximum size 100.6 x 73.2 m (110 × 80 yd).

Goalposts are 2.74 m (9 ft) high, and set 3.66 m (12 ft) apart, all of these being inside dimensions.

End and side margins
An obstacle-free zone of 2–3 m (approx 7–10 ft) is required at each end of the pitch, and one of at least 1.5 m (5 ft) at each side.

Surface
Grass only. The various kinds of synthetic surfaces are either untried or regarded as possibly dangerous. For general information on grass surfaces see Part III.

Markings
Lines should be 51 mm (2 in) wide, preferably in white. The playing area is measured to the inside of the perimeter lines (ie the playing area excludes the lines).

1 *Photo: Michael Steele*

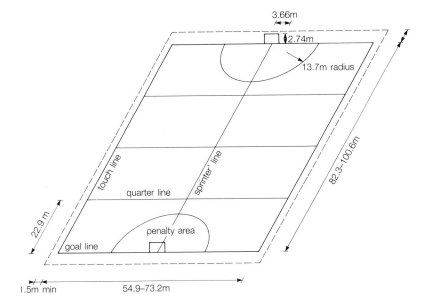

3.66m

2.74m

13.7m radius

touch line

quarter line

sprinter line

82.3–100.6m

22.9 m

penalty area

goal line

1.5m min

54.9–73.2m

2 *Space diagram of bicycle polo pitch*

Fences and safety barriers
There are no specific requirements, but a roped-off area behind the goals is desirable at exhibitions.

Changing facilities
Changing accommodation is required for 12 players (including two reserves) and five officials per pitch.

Floodlighting
This sport is not commonly floodlit and therefore no specific recommendations are provided. For general recommendations for floodlighting outdoor sports refer to Chapter 18, and the CIBSE Lighting Guide: LG4 – Sports.

References and further advice
The Bicycle Polo Association of Great Britain.

43
Bowls: Lawn Bowls

Peter Ackroyd

This is an ancient game, dating back to the thirteenth century or earlier. It is played on a smooth grassed surface by two to eight players at a time, **1**. Each player rolls his wood – a heavy ball of 120 to 130 mm (approx 5 in) diameter, with a built-in bias to take a curved path when rolled on a flat surface – towards a small white ball known as the jack. Points are scored by finishing closer to the jack than one's opponents. The winner is the player, or team, with most points after an agreed number of ends.

Critical factors

- A very smooth and regular-surfaced flat green
- No markings are required
- Under floodlights, lighting must be highly uniform, shadow-free and without glare so that players can judge the positions or trajectories of balls accurately and without visual stress.

Playing space dimensions

The green, **2**, should form a square of not less than 36.58 m (120 ft) and not more than 40.23 m (132 ft) per side. It must be surrounded by a holding ditch and beyond that a bank. The ditch must have a width of 203 mm (8 in) to 381 mm (15 in), and a depth below the playing surface of 51 mm (2 in) to 203 mm (8 in). The bank must be at least 230 mm (9 in) above the level of the green; preferably upright, or alternatively at an angle of not more than 35° to the perpendicular, **2**.

The green is divided into individual rinks for play by means of wooden pegs driven in on the perimeter at specified intervals. As these are not part of the permanent design, details are not given here.

Surfaces

Refer to Chapter 14 for details of natural and synthetic turf surfaces. Recreational bowls has been tried on sand-filled synthetic turf, **3**.

Changing facilities

Changing spaces should be provided for 52 players and two officials.

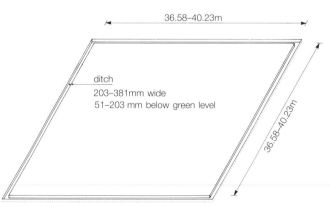

2 *Bowling green*
A rink width is 5.49 m (18 ft) minimum and 5.79 m (19 ft) maximum. The minimum distance from the outside rink to the ditch is 610 mm (24 in). The maximum height of the ditch bank is 230 mm (9 in) and the angle not more than 35° from the perpendicular. An upright bank is recommended. Construction details are available from the NPFA. Permissible variations in size allowed by the Laws include greens not shorter than 30.2 m (33 yd) in the direction of play. For domestic play a rink may be not less than 4.3 m (14 ft) wide

1 *Photo: R Gardner*

3 *A recreational game on sand-filled synthetic turf at Worthing Leisure Centre. Photo: Peter Ackroyd*

Floodlighting

For details of floodlighting requirements and recommendations refer to Chapter 18, and CIBSE Lighting Guide: LG4 – Sports.

References and further advice

English Bowling Association.
Bowls halls and clubs, Volume 2, Chapter 72

44
Camogie

Peter Ackroyd

Camogie is based on the ancient Irish sport of hurling (see Chapter 61), but modified to suit girls. In Ireland it is their most popular participant sport and organised at all levels of education. County and Provincial Championships, and all-Ireland Championships, are established for Club and County teams, **1**. While local authorities and universities provide dedicated pitches, few if any Camogie clubs possess their own facilities: they tend to share pitches with Gaelic Football or Hurling clubs.

There are two teams of 12 girls who play with crooked broad-bladed sticks made from ash and a ball (sliothar) covered with leather. If the ball passes above the opponent's crossbar one point is scored, and if it passes below it, 3 points are scored.

1 *Photo: The Sports Council for Northern Ireland*

190

Critical factors
● Space dimensions and safety margins.

Playing space dimensions
The size of pitch is not fixed, **2**. The minimum size is 95 x 60 m (104 × 65 yd), and maximum size 110 × 70 m (120 × 76 yd). The goal area at each end is 9 × 4 m (approx 10 × 4 yd); and goalposts are spaced 4.5 m (approx 5 yd) apart. Goal posts are 6 m (approx 20 ft) high with a crossbar 2 m (6 ft 6 in) above the ground. A margin of 5 to 10 m (approx 5 × 11 yd) is required at each end of the pitch, and one of 3 m (approx 3 yd) at each side.

Markings
Lines should be 50 mm (2 in) wide, marked in white even on shared pitches. The playing area is measured to the outside of the perimeter lines (ie the playing area includes the lines).

Surface
The regulation surface is grass but synthetic sand-filled turf is used for practice. Shale is acceptable for schools' play. For general information see Part III.

Fences and safety barriers
Fencing or ball-arrest netting of at least 6 m (19 ft 6 in) height is required adjacent to public areas.

Floodlighting
Competitive games are not usually floodlit. For supervised training and practice requirements refer to Chapter 59.

Changing facilities
Accommodation is required for a total of 30 players (including substitutes) and five officials per match.

References and further advice
The Sports Council for Northern Ireland.
The Camogie Association.

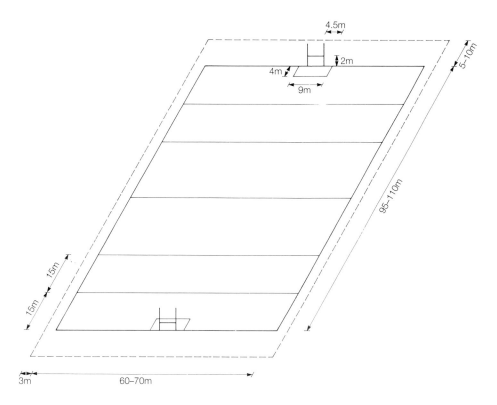

2 *Space diagram of a camogie pitch*

45
Cricket

Peter Ackroyd

Critical factors
- Orientation of the cricket table
- Number of wicket strips across the table between layout of winter games pitches
- Drainage and siting of manhole covers
- Watering and location of hydrants
- Quality and texture of the surface topsoil.

Orientation
Cricket tables and wickets should be sited more or less north to south in order to minimise blinding or distraction of batsmen and bowlers by low sun. Orientation inside 325 to 55° N and 145 to 235° S is strongly recommended, **1**. The location of a pavilion, from where the majority of spectators view the game, is another determining factor.

Playing space dimensions
Generally, a cricket table is constructed approximately 27 m (30 yd) square to accommodate the 22 yd long pitch (a cricket strip in play) and any peripheral drainage scheme, but width is often dictated by the number of matches expected to be played and may be considerably increased where seniors and juniors share the same table. For example, to allow a rotation of 18 positions for a 20.12 × 3.05 m (22 yd × 10 ft) wide pitch, plus a spare pitch for practice or wet weather, would need a table of ten pitch widths approximately 27 × 30.5 m (90 × 100 ft).

The overall dimensions of table and out-field are set out in Table 45.1 and 2 and 3, as reaffirmed by the NCA.

Changing facilities and clubhouse
For recommendations and examples, refer to Chapter 24

1 Photo: Photocall Features

Table 45.1 Overall dimensions
Cricket only

No of Pitches	Rotation	Width A	Width 1	Length	Approx area
Seniors with 46 m (approx 50 yd) boundary					
9	17	27.44 m (30 yd)	125 m (approx 137 yd)	119 m (130 yd)	1.5 ha (3.7 acres)
6	11	18.29 m (20 yd)	116 m (approx 127 yd)	119 m (130 yd)	1.4 ha (3.4 acres)
Juniors with 37 m (approx 40 yd) boundary					
9	17	27.44 m (30 yd)	107 m (117 yd)	99 m (108 yd)	1.1 ha (2.7 acres)
6	11	18.29 m (20 yd)	98 m (107 yd)	99 m (108 yd)	1 ha (2.4 acres)

Cricket and winter games

Cricket square	Senior football	Junior football	Width 2	Length	Approx area
27.44 × 27.44 (30 × 30 yd)	100 × 64 m (109 × 70 yd)	90 × 55 m (98 × 60 yd)	164 m (179 yd)	118 m (129 yd)	2 ha (approx 5 acres)
27.44 × 18.29 (30 × 20 yd)	96 × 60 m (105 × approx 66 yd)	82 × 46 m (approx 90 × 50 yd)	142 m (155 yd)	114 m (approx 125 yd)	1.6 ha (approx 4 acres)

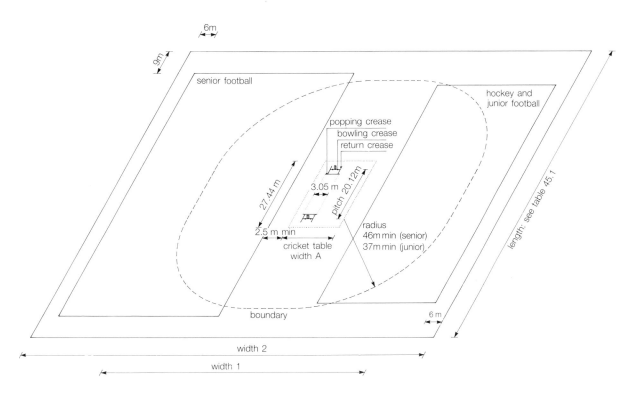

2 Layout of cricket field and winter games pitches. To be read with Table 45.1

and to the essential technical references at the end of that chapter.

Surface
For natural turf and non-turf synthetic surfaces refer to Chapter 15 and to the essential technical References at the end of that chapter.

Floodlighting
This sport is not commonly floodlit and therefore no specific recommendations are provided. For general recommendations for floodlighting outdoor sports refer to Chapter 18, and the CIBSE Lighting Guide: LG4 – Sports.

References and further advice
The National Cricket Association.
The National Playing Fields Association.
The Sports Turf Research Institute (STRI), *Cricket Grounds – the evolution, maintenance and construction of natural turf cricket tables and outfields*, 1991.
For other natural turf and non-turf surfaces references see Chapter 15.
Indoor cricket in Volume 2, Chapters 23 and 74.

46
Croquet

Peter Ackroyd

Croquet originated in France in the 13th century as Paille Maille. A modified form of this game reached England, via Ireland, under the name croquet, and achieved very great popularity in the Victorian era.

The game is played by one or two players at a time on a court (or lawn) on which iron hoops are set. The object is to drive balls through these hoops using a long-handled mallet, **1**.

There are two variants:
- Association croquet, played at international level and at most clubs. This requires a full-sized court.
- Short croquet, meant for beginners but becoming increasingly popular, and played on a smaller court

(see below). Many clubs now have one or more short lawns in addition to their full-sized courts.

Critical factors
- Overall area of space including the surrounding safety margins.

Playing space
Standard dimensions are still laid down in yards, but metric equivalents from the Laws are given here for uniformity.

1 *Photo: Sports Council*

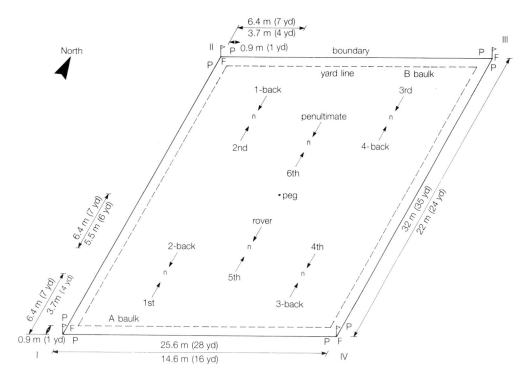

2 *Space diagram and layout of a croquet court or lawn. The dimensions for Association Croquet are given above the arrowed distance lines. Those below the lines are for Short Croquet. Corner pegs are located at (P) and flags at (F). A recommended size for a short croquet lawn is 22 × 14.6 m (24 × 16 yd)*

The standard-sized playing space, normal for international matches and championships, is 32 × 25.6 m (approx 35 × 28 yd) overall, including the yard line – see **2**. These dimensions result from the setting-out formula of five 6.4 m (approx 7 yd) modules for the length, and four modules for the width. For other standards of play smaller courts are permitted, provided they retain the length-to-width proportions of five to four. A gap of 1.8 m (approx 2 yd) between adjacent courts is recommended.

A recommended minimum size for a Short Croquet court is 22 × 14.6 m (approx 24 × 16 yd). Below this size, so little skill is required that the appeal of the game is diminished.

Surface
A grass lawn is at present the only recommended surface. However, synthetic carpets with non-directional pile have been used successfully and the Croquet Association is keen to develop the use of outdoor artificial surfaces. For general information see Part III.

Markings
Boundary lines as on **2** should be marked in white. While there are no rules governing width, lines wider than 50 mm (2 in) would probably look out of place and are not recommended.

Fences
A check-fence about 150 mm (6 in) high may be placed around the boundary, and about 0.9 m (1 yd) outside it. This may be made of wire netting, or wooden laths. Where a croquet ground is exposed near to a public way, secure fencing is advisable to protect the condition of the lawns.

Changing accommodation
For big championship events there may be up to eight players and substitutes per court; and up to four officials in total.

Floodlighting
This sport is not commonly floodlit and therefore no specific recommendations are provided. For general recommendations for floodlighting outdoor sports refer to Chapter 18, and the CIBSE Lighting Guide: LG4 – Sports.

References and further advice
The Croquet Association.
Indoor Croquet, Volume 2, Chapter 24.

47
Crown green bowls

Peter Ackroyd

Each player has two bowls, known as woods. The object of the game is for players to bowl their woods as near as possible to a jack bowl marker, which can be delivered in any direction across the green. Unlike lawn bowls (see Chapter 43), crown green bowling is not confined to rinks.

Critical factors
- A smooth, well drained and correctly contoured surface.

Playing space dimensions
The green must be a minimum of 25 m (27 yd) square, and preferably 37 m (approx 40 yd) square. There is no maximum size. The surface must be cambered and a recommended profile is given in Table 47.1 below, to be read in conjunction with **2**. The heights given are measured above the corners of the green.

Table 47.1 Details of camber formation

	Circle radii	Circle heights
A	0	254 mm (10.0 in)
B	3.05 m (10 ft)	248 mm (9.75 in)
C	6.10 m (20 ft)	235 mm (9.25 in)
D	9.14 m (30 ft)	216 mm (8.5 in)
E	12.19 m (40 ft)	190 mm (7.5 in)
F	15.24 m (50 ft)	165 mm (6.5 in)
G	18.29 m (60 ft)	127 mm (5.0 in)

Surface
Either natural grass or synthetic turf. There are no markings. For specific and more general information see Part III.

1 Photo: Gordon Stables

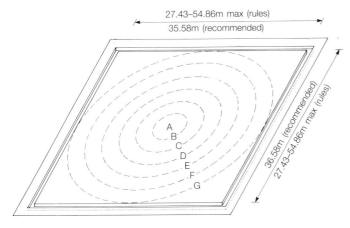

27.43–54.86m max (rules)
35.58m (recommended)

36.58m (recommended)
27.43–54.86m max (rules)

A
B
C
D
E
F
G

2 *Space diagram showing preferred contours of crown above corners of the green. Radii and heights A-G are given in Table 47.1. The crown can be higher than 254 mm (10 in) and it need not be central. The green could have two crowns. It is unlimited in shape or size and need not be square. If rectangular or trapezoidal the shortest side should be longer than 25 m (82 ft)*

Floodlighting

A player must be able to see the jack and the lie of the woods around it, and to follow the run of the live wood. The player's judgement must not be impaired by harsh shadowing even when both jack and wood are closely clustered. The bowling green should appear to be uniformly bright from all playing ends, whilst maintaining low glare to participants and spectators.

For details of requirements and recommendations refer to Chapter 18, and CIBSE Lighting Guide: LG4 – Sports.

References and further advice
British Crown Green Bowling Association Official Handbook.
Indoor Crown Green Bowls, Volume 2, Chapter 72.

48
Curling

Peter Ackroyd

The origin of curling is unknown, but old stones have been unearthed indicating that the game in Scotland goes back at least to the early 16th century. It is also referred as the "roarin' game", because of the noise the stones make as they move across the ice. For a fuller history and description of the game, refer to Volume 2, Chapter 144. Outdoors the game is played on frozen lochs (lakes) or on purpose-made curling ponds which freeze naturally in cold weather.

Critical factor
● Test the thickness of the ice for safety.

Playing space dimensions
The longitudinal dimensions are fixed: 34.75 m (38 yd) from tee line to tee line; with hog lines, back lines, and foot lines positioned as shown on 1; giving an overall length from foot line to foot line of 42.06 m (46 yds).

Width is not fixed, but recommended to be 4.75 m (approx 5 yd) minimum. It is also recommended that an additional 1.22 m (4 ft) be added to the length of the rink, behind each foot line, thus giving an overall length of approximately 44.50 m (48 yd).

Space between adjoining rinks
None required.

Surface and markings
An ice surface is required, marked as shown in 2 by means of blue or black lines between 5 mm (0.25 in) and 25 mm (1 in) in width. Dimensions are to the centres of lines.

Fences and safety barriers
None required.

1 *Photo: Scottish Sports Council*

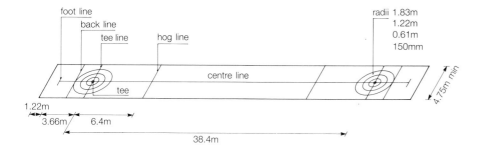

foot line
back line
tee line
hog line
radii 1.83m
1.22m
0.61m
150mm
centre line
tee
1.22m
3.66m
6.4m
38.4m
4.75m min

2 Space diagram. Rink markings are measured to the centre of lines. Side and end safety surround margins are not required

Floodlighting

This sport is not commonly floodlit and therefore no specific recommendations are provided. For general recommendations for floodlighting outdoor sports refer to Chapter 18, and the CIBSE Lighting Guide: LG4 – Sports.

References and further advice

The Royal Caledonian Curling Club (RCCC).

Constitution and Rules 1990–91, published by the RCCC.

Design of ice rinks and other ice facilities in Volume 2, Part 6.

49
Cycle racing

Ken Farnes

Introduction

Cycle racing incorporates a number of disciplines, the principal ones being road racing and track racing, staged in velodromes.

Road racing

Whilst the majority of road racing takes place on the open road, a number of races are held on closed circuits. Traditionally these circuits have been in parks or aerodromes but more recently circuits designed particularly for cycle racing have been constructed.

This chapter identifies the key elements to be considered when designing a closed road circuit for cycle racing and the buildings associated with the circuit to facilitate its ready use for cycling. By their nature, circuits designed for cycle racing will also be attractive for a variety of other uses.

Circuit sponsors should be prepared to make their facilities available for cycle race coaching, cycling proficiency courses for young riders, pleasure riding and, when the cycling programme permits, other uses such as roller skating, race walking, road running and training. The use of the circuit for powered traction such as motor bikes or go-karts should be avoided, however, because they tend to drift on corners and drag the road surface. This can result in punctures for cycle race competitors.

There are no fixed dimensions for cycle racing circuits but the minimum length of the shortest circuit should be 3 km (approx 1.9 miles) while 5 km (approx 3 miles) is probably a sensible maximum length.

The circuit should normally be cambered roadway with at least 6 m (approx 20 ft) width for most of its length. In limited areas the width can be reduced to 4 or 5 m (approx 13 or 16 ft) if space requires. If width constrictions are frequent this will limit the number of competitors permitted in each race. Ideally the finishing should be straight for at least 200 m (approx 220 yd) and preferably 8 m (approx 26 ft) wide with a similar width run-on for at least 100 m (approx 110 yd) past the finish line. The design of bends should be relatively free flowing although one or two tighter corners and chicanes to test the bike handling ability of competitors can be included in the circuit. The circuit should take advantage of natural contours and wherever possible have short hills and descents incorporated to test the capabilities of the competitors. Designers should also take advantage of cut and fill to form climbs and descents.

The road surface will probably be tarmacadam and should be cambered to provide drainage run-off and assist the competitors to follow the course. Circuits should be well drained but not have raised kerbs so that competitors can run off onto grass at the sides should an accident occur. Equally the grassed areas should be level with or fall gently away from the road to avoid earth and grit being washed onto the road surface causing punctures and accidents. In areas of cut at least 1.5 m (approx 5 ft) level ground and adequate land drainage must be included in the design adjacent to roads.

Where space permits, alternate courses should be incorporated to allow a variety of courses to be followed and avoid boredom to competitors who use the circuit regularly.

The circuit should be supported by a building located outside it containing changing accommodation for up to 150 competitors. Further rooms for first aid personnel, massage and medical control facilities should also be incorporated. The circuit can provide a focus for clubs and coaching activity in the locality and therefore a club room and facilities for weight training and coaching should also be incorporated where possible. The building will also accommodate the circuit manager and any maintenance equipment and staff.

The circuit should be equipped with public address equipment. Sufficient parking for competitors, officials and spectators should be provided, again located outside the circuit so they do not have to cross the circuit while racing is taking place.

The use of the circuit as a local focus for cycling will be enhanced if circuits for cyclo cross and BMX racing can also be included in the planning and design of the circuit.

Outdoor velodromes

The first cycle tracks, in the 1860s, were big, flat and with a dirt surface similar to horse racing circuits. The modern velodrome is a complete venue for track cycling, with a banked track allowing speeds of up to 110 km/h (68 mph), surrounded by a complex of spectator and support facilities.

Track cycling is practised in indoor arenas and on outdoor velodromes, 1, and the UCI recognises records for indoor and outdoor tracks. Most of the requirements for indoor tracks (see Volume 2, Chapter 75) apply equally to open air velodromes.

The British Cycling Federation (BCF) considers that in the North European climate tracks for national or international use should be indoor and preferably of 250 m (approx 273 yd) size.

1 *Pedal Power. Photo: Chris Smith (Sunday Times) from a winning portfolio in the Sports Photographer of the Year Competition, 1988*

There is little distinction between a cycle track for competition and training because the track must fulfil the same design requirements. There is little benefit in building tracks for training only unless a country has well developed facilities for competition.

Critical factors
- Location: in the UK consult the BCF
- Siting
- Circumference of track
- Relationship of track and track centre to existing ground levels
- Whether a canopy over the track and/or spectators is incorporated in the design
- Surface of track and markings
- Construction on supporting structure or prepared base
- Extent of spectator facilities.

Siting and construction
The track should be designed and constructed under the supervision of a specialist who is experienced in track

building and the procurement of the appropriate materials. Failure to use experienced designers and constructors has on occasions resulted in poor installations which become unpopular with riders and promoters and quickly fall out of use.

Because the spectator and ancillary accommodation does not necessarily have to fit into a regular building envelope designers will have more freedom in planning the accommodation.

The orientation of an outdoor track should take account of the sun's position in the afternoon and early evening to ensure that cyclists and spectators are not affected by strong sunlight or shadows. In the northern hemisphere this suggests that the long axis of the track should be approximately north-south with the home straight on the western side. Shelter from strong and prevailing winds should be incorporated into the landscaping of more open velodromes.

The siting of the track in relation to topography is of fundamental importance. Many tracks are constructed in natural or excavated bowls. Careful planning can achieve cost and functional benefits. Designers should consider the benefits of constructing tracks above ground level or

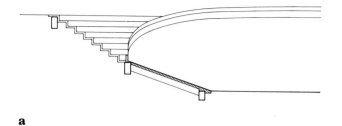
a

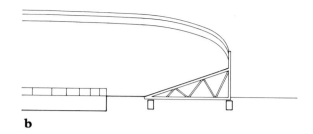
b

2 a and b: Tracks constructed in natural or elevated bowls; the principal alternative cross-sections. Note also the possibility of lowering the central area to benefit sight lines. Diagram based on IAKS Design Guide

partially or fully below ground level. 2 shows the principal alternatives.

Constructing a track above ground level will probably be the least expensive for the track itself, but other facilities and grandstands may be more expensive unless the space underneath can be utilised for changing and ancillary accommodation.

A partially sunken track excavated approximately to the level of the track in the straights can be cost-effective. Excavated material can be used to form terraced embankments for spectators.

Where excavation will not be affected by the water-table, it is possible to excavate to the height of the bankings (approx 5 m or 16.5 ft) provided that it is not proposed to locate accommodation under spectator areas. Seating can be located on the terracing formed from the excavation and any ancillary facilities located around the spectator areas.

Several major tracks feature a central area approximately 1–1.5 m (approx 3–5 ft) lower than the inner track perimeter, 2. This has the advantage of reducing obstructions for spectators' sight lines. Such a feature should be considered for outdoor tracks staging major international competitions. A suitable safety barrier with netting must be included to prevent riders and officials falling into the central area. Although such a feature reduces the space available for other sports, tennis or basketball courts can be incorporated in the infield area.

Outdoor tracks are constructed in concrete, wood or tarmacadam. Concrete and wood are much faster surfaces and are appreciated by the riders, but in the UK the BCF considers that concrete is acceptable for tracks designed for local or regional use. Selected hardwood is preferred for major tracks. These three options and constructions are discussed in Track Surface and Construction below.

Many outdoor tracks in Europe feature continuous canopies which extend over the spectators and track, 3. Designers should take account of wind patterns to ensure suitable cover to the track.

Because a track with a canopy is generally unaffected by weather conditions, the facility can achieve projected usage targets and will establish a reputation for programme reliability. The incorporation of a canopy in any outdoor velodrome is therefore a preferred solution in Northern Europe and areas with frequent rainfall. The BCF considers than an outdoor track without a canopy is acceptable for local use.

Track dimensions

The BCF encourages the construction of 333.33 m (approx 365 yd) and 250 m (approx 273 yd) outdoor tracks giving 3 or 4 laps for 1 km (1094 yd). The final choice will depend upon the land available and other sports uses in the track centre. Whilst tracks with circumferences between 200 m (219 yd) and 485 m (530 yd) have been constructed in the last 20 years the BCF is reluctant to agree dimensions other than 333.33 m (approx 365 yd) (without a canopy) and 250 m (approx 273 yd) (with canopy for regional track) for outdoor tracks because they do not reflect current international trends and are less popular with riders and coaches.

4 shows the space requirements for a 333.33 m (approx 365 yd) track and the profiles of banked straights and bends are shown in **5**. The geometry of a 250 m (approx 273 yd) track is given in Volume 2, Chapter 75. Shorter tracks are considered to be more spectator-friendly because spectators are closer to the action. Smaller tracks are also more convenient for intensive training and teaching riding techniques.

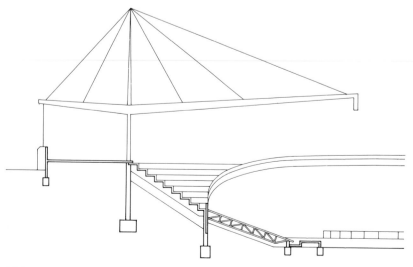

3 A cross-section of a canopy over spectator areas and track. Diagram based on IAKS Design Guide

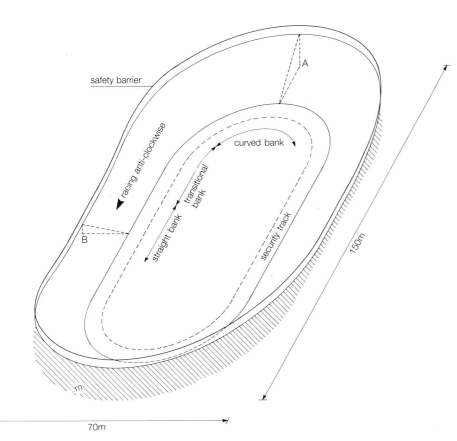

4 *Space diagram. Outdoor tracks should preferably be of 250 or 333.33 m (approx 274 or 365 yd); 285.714 m (approx 313 yd) is a less acceptable alternative. If the track is to be provided with a canopy the BCF recommends the 250 m (approx 274 yd) size. If it is to be provided outdoors without cover then the 333.33 m (approx 365 yd) size is recommended, as shown here and in 7*

Safety zones

There is not an outer safety margin surrounding the track, but care must be taken in detailing the outer perimeter of it to ensure that water run-off and debris from spectator areas does not run onto the track surface. Safety on the outside of the track is provided for by the safety fence (see the IAKS Project Guide). In order to ensure good sight lines the first row of seats should be situated directly at the balustrade.

A band 600 mm (approx 2 ft) wide, known as the Cote d'Azur, is constructed inside the racing surface as a slow running area. A further safety zone should be left inside the Cote d'Azur not less than 2.5 m (approx 8 ft) wide on the straights and 3.5 m (approx 11 ft) in the curves, **1** and **5**. Where motor-paced racing is anticipated the width should be increased to 3.5 m (approx 11 ft) and 4.5 m (approx 15 ft) respectively. In outdoor velodromes the surface of the safety zone is frequently grass but soft synthetic surfaces might also be used. The safety zone can coincide with safety margins along a pitch within the track centre.

Track centre uses and access

A 333.33 m (approx 365 yd) track will allow a hockey or football pitch for local use to be planned in the inner area; whilst smaller circumference tracks, or where the centre is lowered, can successfully accommodate tennis and basketball courts. Nets or boards must be provided to prevent balls passing onto the cycle track during training periods on the cycle track.

The most appropriate access to the infield for cycles, competitors and officials is by tunnel. The ideal location for the tunnel is between the changing rooms and the area of one of the curves exiting well inside the safety zone, **4**. The minimum cross-section of the tunnel should be 2.5 × 2.5 m (approx 8 × 8 ft). Steps with a central ramped section are the preferred entrance and exit of the tunnel. Access to the track centre by means of a bridge

affects sight lines and presents a safety hazard. Bridges are not therefore recommended for track centre access.

It will be necessary to incorporate an access with gate for small maintenance vehicles to the track centre at a convenient point in the back straight. Designers may find on smaller tracks that the angle of the track makes access for vehicles difficult. In this case the tunnel should be ramped and large enough for maintenance and team equipment.

A further small gate will be required near the finishing line for officials and VIPs. All openings in the balustrade must, when closed, match the profile and performance of the safety fence construction.

A clearly defined riders' area will be required for the preparation and recuperation of competitors. This is normally located in the semicircular area furthest away from the finishing line and incorporates bench seating and cycle stands, arranged in areas for separate teams, possibly with a weatherproof cover. The area should be equipped with power-points, air compressor, water supply, a first-aid post and a catering point. Where the riders' quarters are below track level a ramp should connect the track centre to the area adjacent to the starting lines.

The track centre may be grass, concrete or synthetic material. Grass is not favoured since it causes dirt and grit to get onto the racing surface. A synthetic surface suitable for other games is preferable since it allows the cyclists to warm up in the track centre before races and warm down after them.

Track surface and construction

Volume 2, Chapter 75, Indoor Velodromes, discusses the racing advantages of various surfaces and the design speeds which must be considered in the design of the tracks and illustrates design details. There are three options for track construction and surface which are described below.

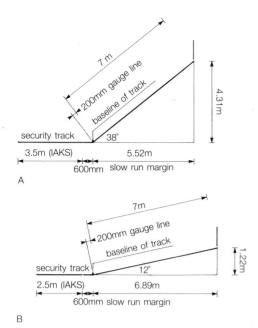

5 *Sections through the banking along straights and around bends. BCF*

Whatever the surface, a continuous drainage gully must be incorporated in the design around the inner circumference of the track to take run-off from the track and track centre. This must be carefully detailed because it will be located in the Cote d'Azur adjacent to the racing surface (see safety zones above).

Concrete tracks

When competently constructed, a concrete track has good durability. The shape of a concrete track will be similar to a wooden track but the formation of the sophisticated transitions will be more difficult. The finished surface can, however, be very fast as at the Olympic Centre, Mexico, where many world records have been established.

The surface will be either directly finished concrete or a layer of cement or resin-based mortar over a base slab formed on well packed earthworks, or onto a reinforced slab spanning between supports.

To reduce stress in the base slab and to avoid surface cracking, expansion joints should be incorporated laid at right angles to the direction of the racing. Joints following the direction of racing must be avoided. Expansion joints should be filled with a mastic which will remain level with the surface.

Wooden tracks

The surface of wooden tracks should be formed with selected hardwood, which is the preferred choice of the BCF for tracks in the UK. Well selected West African Afzelia has proved particularly successful. Care should be taken if considering other types of wood because weathering has caused splintering of many apparently suitable hardwoods.

Where a wooden track is planned, or when resurfacing a concrete track with a timber surface, it should be constructed to enable adequate ventilation to the underside of the surface. Most wooden tracks are therefore constructed on a flat base on a trussed structure or with supporting beams.

Tarmacadam or asphalt tracks

Although tarmacadam or asphalt has been used for several tracks in the UK this has been on tracks with a larger circumference than 333.33 m (approx 365 yd) and with bankings below 25°. Tarmacadam or asphalt surfaces have proved difficult to lay and satisfactory maintenance has proved particularly difficult. They should therefore be avoided.

Markings

The multi-coloured markings for the track are carefully specified by the Union Cycliste Internationale (UCI) and BCF. Designers should refer to their National Federation for the specifications for track markings on new and repainted tracks. The paint used should be durable non-glossy and not so thick as to produce a raised surface. See also Maintenance and painted advertising panels on the track surface below.

Fences and safety barriers

Volume 2, Chapter 75, Indoor Velodromes, describes the characteristics of the balustrade around the outer perimeter of the track.

Changing accommodation

See Volume 2, Chapter 75, Indoor Velodromes, for descriptions and plans of changing and support facilities.

Floodlighting

For details of requirements and recommendations refer to Chapter 18, and the CIBSE Lighting Guide: LG4 – Sports.

Maintenance

Maintenance should be undertaken by a specialist who understands the critical geometry and surfaces required for top class cycling. In northern European climates it will be necessary to sand the surface of wooden tracks every 2 or 3 years to eliminate raised grain.

Many tracks feature advertising panels painted onto the track surface. Care must be taken to use a non oil based paint for both advertisements and track markings because water will stay on the surface of certain paints. If the remainder of the track is dry this results in delay to the racing.

References and further advice

British Cycling Federation (BCF) Handbook, published annually by the BCF.

International Working Group for Sports Facilities and Equipment, *Installations de Sports Cyclistes – Elements de Planification*, IAKS, Köln (1980).

International Working Group for Sports Facilities and Equipment, *Working Group Cycle Sports Facilities: Velodromes*, IAKS, Köln (1988).

Impianti per il ciclismo: Dossier. A whole issue devoted to the history development and design for all cycling disciplines, particularly indoor velodromes. *Spaziosport*, Vol VI No 3, Italian National Olympic Committee, September (1987).

Cycling, indoor velodromes, Volume 2, Chapter 75.

50
Cycle speedway

Peter Ackroyd

Cycle speedway is a bicycle version of the motorcycle racing which developed in the 1940s, **1**. There are now a number of purpose built tracks where the sport is very popular. Normally four racers compete in a race class.

Critical factors
● The safety margin and barrier surrounding the track
● The quality and maintenance of the surface

● An obstruction free centre of track
● Floodlighting can be important.

Track dimensions
Inside circumference of track is 64 to 91.4 m (210 to approx 300 ft); and the recommended track width is 5–6 m (approx 16–20 ft). Bends and/or straights may be banked, but the degree of banking should be checked with the Governing Body, **2**.

1 *Photo: Roger Nicholson by courtesy of The Cycle Speedway Council*

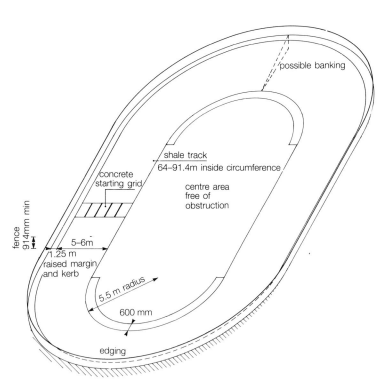

possible banking

shale track
64–91.4m inside circumference

concrete
starting grid

centre area
free of
obstruction

fence 914mm min

5–6m

1.25 m
raised margin
and kerb

5.5 m radius

600 mm

edging

Surface and markings

The recommended track surface is shale and no markings are required. The central area should preferably be grassed, and must contain no obstructions.

Fences and safety barriers

A barrier at least 914 mm (3 ft) high is required all round the outer perimeter of the track, at a minimum distance of 460 mm (18 in) from the track edge.

Changing facilities

Accommodation is required for 16 cyclists and one official per event.

Floodlighting

Floodlit racing is an integral part of the sport, and the vast majority of tracks have floodlighting facilities. There are no recommended standards but a similarity with cycle racing may be made as a guide; requirements and recommendations are given in Chapter 18, and CIBSE Lighting Guide: LG4 – Sports.

References and further advice

The Cycle Speedway Council.
Cycle speedway indoors in Volume 2, Chapter 25.

51
Eton fives

Peter Ackroyd

1 *The old fives court at Eton, c 1870. A hand-ball game played by pairs in a three-walled court, Eton fives is played at over 50 centres throughout England, mainly in London, the Midlands, and the south-eastern counties, and in Australia, Malaysia, West Africa, and Europe. It is one of the three versions of the game, each named after the public school of its origin (see also Rugby Fives in Volume 2, Chapter 77). This data is re-published from the 1st Edition and not updated. Further information possibly may be obtained from the Eton Fives Association. Photo: Country Life*

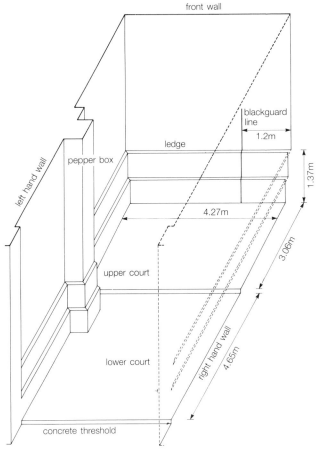

2 *Space diagram of an Eton fives court. Courts vary in dimensions, but all have a ledge running across the front wall making a horizontal line 1.37 m (approx 4 ft 6 in) from the ground. Running across the court is a shallow step 3.05 m (10 ft) from the front wall, dividing the court into an inner or upper court and an outer or lower court. The lower court is 4.65 m (15 ft) in depth and 4.27 m (14 ft) wide. At the end of the step, projecting from the left-hand wall, is a buttress known as the pepper box. The upper court slopes downwards approximately 125 mm (approx 0.5 in) in 3 m (approx 10 ft) from the front wall to the step.*

52
American Football

Peter Ackroyd

American football is a variant of British Rugby Football. Its rules crystallised in the early 1900s, but the game's massive rise to popularity did not start until about 1921. It is now the great American sport of the autumn season, as is baseball in summer, **1**. The game is played on a field termed a gridiron (owing to the parallel lines marked across it, along its entire length), normally by two teams of eleven-a-side on the field with twenty or more substitutes per squad in the team box. There are two forms of the game, 'professional' and 'collegiate' football, whose rules now differ only slightly.

Critical factors
- The required width of the field of play, **2**.
- Overall area of space including the minimum safety margins within the 'limit lines', **2**
- End zones must be of identical size

- Coaches' areas distinctly marked between sidelines and the coaching line/box are strongly recommended
- 4.5 m (5 yd) line markers along the limit and coaching lines are required for reference points
- A set of 9 m (10 yd) chain markers and a down-box are essential equipment at any field
- Last but not least, for players safety on multi-sports grounds, any solid surfaces, posts or protrusions within the limit lines must be adequately padded.

Playing space dimensions
The Rules specify imperial dimensions, **2**, and approximate metric equivalents are also given here for convenience.

The standard playing surface is 91.4 × 48.8 m (300 × 160 ft) with two 9.15 m (30 ft) end zones added to the length as shown on **2**. Where these dimensions cannot be

1 *Giants vs St Louis. Photo: Colorsport*

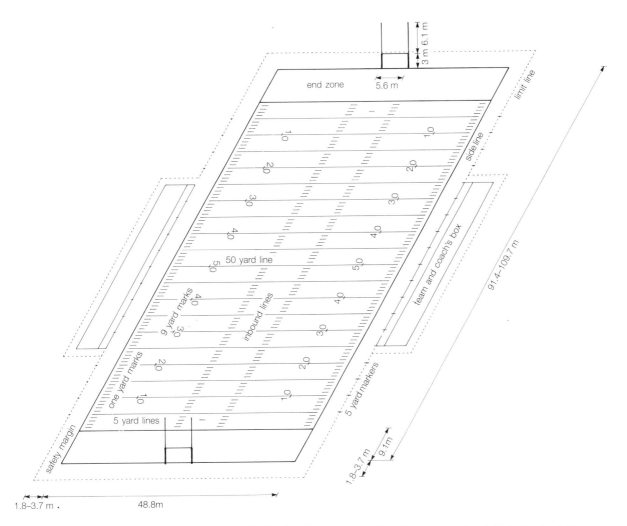

2 *Space diagram of American Football field. Broken line surrounding the rectangular field is the limit line 1.8 m (6 ft) minimum outside the playing area. Goal posts 5.6 m (18.5 ft) apart are at least 9.1 m (30 ft) high; the top of the crossbar is 3 m (10 ft) above the ground. Also note the coaching areas must be distinctly marked and other requirements listed in critical factors. If a full sized field is not possible the equal length of both end zones preferably should not be reduced. Dimensions of detailed mid-field markings are not given here for reasons of clarity; details are given in Section 2 of Rule 1 in the Rules of American Football (see References)*

obtained the playing surface length may be reduced. Minimum length is 73.2 m (240 ft) plus 9.1 m (30 ft) end zones. Critical dimensions are noted above.

Safety margins

A minimum 1.83 m (6 ft) wide safety margin must be maintained all round the field. Where space allows, twice this width is recommended around the field. It is marked by dashed limit lines consisting of 300 mm (12 in) dashes at 600 mm (24 in) intervals outside the side and end lines. The limit lines and safety margins are marked out around the outside of team areas and coaching boxes.

Surface

Both natural grass and synthetic turf are acceptable. For general information see Part III.

Markings

The field must be marked in a non-toxic material by 100 mm (4 in) wide lines, preferably in white but failing that

in yellow. Goal lines may be of contrasting colour. Measurements shall be from the inside edge of the side lines, but the entire width of each goal line shall be within the end zone (the playing area excludes the side lines but includes the end lines).

Dimensions of detailed midfield markings can be found in Section 2 of Rule 1 of the rules of the game (see References).

Fences and safety barriers

A fence is required all round the field at a distance of 6.1 m (20 ft), with a minimum height of 9.1 m (30 ft).

Changing

Changing spaces are required for 30 to 40 players plus four to six officials.

Storage

Secure storage is required for a set of 9 m (10 yd) chain markers plus a down box.

209

Floodlighting

For details of requirements and recommendations refer to Chapter 18, and the CIBSE Lighting Guide: LG4 – Sports.

References and further advice

The British American Football Referees Association.
The Rules of the Game, particularly for detailed markings.

53
Association football and five-a-side

Peter Ackroyd

Association Football, more usually known as just 'Football' or 'Soccer', is now widely played by both sexes, 1. A miniature version is called 'five-a-side' and is included at the end of this chapter. 'Soccer six' is another indoor game, referred to in Volume 2, Chapter 27.

Association football

Critical factors
- Varying space dimensions for grades of play
- Varying widths of surrounding safety margins for natural or artificial grass or other surfaces
- Sightlines and resultant margin widths in the design of a stadium
- Choice of surface and early consultations
- Stability of ball arresting, high fencing behind the goals
- Consultations for floodlighting

Space and dimensions of the field of play

Dimensions of the pitch, 2, vary for different standards of play, for grades of competition, for age of players. An outline of these are given in the space Tables 53.1 and 53.2 below. For others, consult regional or local competition organisers. In the design of a new Stadium, also refer to Table 53.2 and Chapter 22 regarding the width of space surrounding the pitch related to other essential matters of sightlines and changes in horizontal ground levels. Table 53.3 shows dimensions for artificial surfaces.

For matches played by women, pitch dimensions are the same as for men but the size, weight and material of the ball and duration of the periods of play are different.

Detailed setting out dimensions of the various areas of the field of play are published in the Laws of Association Football (see References). Metric conversions are those authorised by the International Football Association Board.

1 *Synthetic all weather pitch at Alleyns School. Photo: Taylor Alden Ltd*

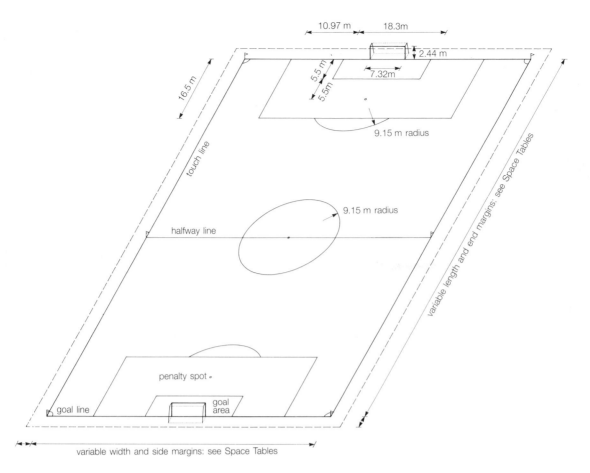

Dimensions shown on the diagram:

10.97 m   18.3m
2.44 m
7.32m
5.5 m
5.5 m
9.15 m radius
9.15 m radius
16.5 m
touch line
halfway line
penalty spot
goal line   goal area
variable length and end margins: see Space Tables
variable width and side margins: see Space Tables

2 *Association football pitch. Dimensions of the areas and lines within the pitch are given in the Laws of the game*

Table 53.1 Dimensions of natural turf multi-pitch facilities for regional, county or lesser competitions

NPFA recommendations based on normal practice

	Length m (yd)	Width m (yd)	End margin (1) m (yd)	Side margin (1) m (yd)	Length overall m (yd)	Width overall m (yd)
Senior (18 years & over)	96–100 (105–109)	60–64 (65–70)	9 (10)	6 (10)	114–118 (125–129)	72–76 (78–83)
Juniors (under 18 years)	90 (98)	46–55 (50–60)	9 (10)	6 (10)	108 (118)	58–67 (63–73)
5th year & older pupils	91–96 (100–105)	50–59 (54–64)	6 (7)	4.5 (5)	103–108 (113–118)	59–68 (64–74)
3rd & 4th year pupils	82 (90)	46 (50)	6 (7)	4.5 (5)	94 (103)	55 (60)
1st & 2nd year pupils	73 (80)	41 (45)	6 (7)	4.5 (5)	85 (93)	50 (54)
Primary schools, 9–13 year olds	70–80 (76–88)	40–50 (43–54)	6 (7)	4.5 (5)	82–92 (90–101)	49–59 (54–65)

Note (1): Margin widths allow for shifting and remarking pitches to spread the wear of goal areas. See also Note (1) in Table 53.2 below regarding the design of a new local stadium.

Table 53.2 Dimensions of single pitch or new stadia

	Length m (yd)	Width m (yd)	Safety Margins (1) end m (yd)	side m (yd)
International matches and FA UK Senior matches	100–110 (109–120)	64–75 (70–82)	4 (4)	2.75 (3)

Note (1): in the design of a new stadium, refer also to Chapter 22.

Table 53.3 Dimensions for artificial surfaces including synthetic turf

	National (from Table 53.2) m (yd)	Regional/county/club (from Table 53.1) m (yd)	Recreational (1) m (yd)
Length of pitch	110–100 (109–120)	100–91.4 (1) (109–100)	91.4 min (100 min)
Width of pitch	75–64 (82–70)	64–55 (1) (70–60)	55 min (60 min)
End safety margin	4 min (4 min)	4 min (4 min)	4 min (4 min)
Side safety margin	4 min (4 min)	3 min (3 min)	2 min (2 min)
Overall	118 × 83 (129 × 91)	108 × 70 (118 × 77)	99.4 × 59 (1) (109 × 65)
Minimum size	to 108 × 72 (118 × 79)	to 99.4 × 61 (109 × 67)	

Note (1) The minimum dimensions are based on the recommended size of an artificial turf hockey pitch: refer to Chapter 59.

3 *Late play at Mansfield Town FC. Photo: Taylor Alden Ltd*

It is recommended that the pitch size requirements and other technical data for any of the particular standards of competition play (mentioned above and in Table 53.1) should generally apply to both natural turf pitches, or those surfaced with one of the artificial surfaces mentioned below. The exception to this recommendation concerns the width of the surrounding safety margins, which should be the same as the widths specified for hockey on a multi-sports synthetic grass surface (see data in Chapter 59).

Therefore, safety margins should be 4 m (approx 13 ft) wide behind the goal line and 3 m (approx 10 ft) wide along the side touch lines. Any obstruction within these widths should be padded. The grass surface should extend beyond the touch lines, by a minimum of 3 m (approx 10 ft) and 2 m (approx 6 ft 6 in) respectively.

For recreational or training games, a hockey pitch sized field of play is satisfactory, plus a minimum club-standard surrounding safety margin of 2 m (approx 6 ft 6 in) width along both side touch lines and 4 m depth behind both goal lines.

Surfaces

Natural turf grass is recommended by the football governing bodies and is the only surface allowed for some competitions. Early consultations are advisable to clarify whether an artificial surface is acceptable; and if it is, then to choose between mineral or synthetic turf surfaces, **1**. For general information see Part III.

Where drop-in goal posts are proposed, blanking caps must be provided for hockey or other games. Part III gives details of the design and construction of outdoor sports surfaces.

Markings

The field of play, **2**, shall be marked with distinctive lines not more than 120 mm (5 in) in width, although 76 mm (3 in) is normal, the longer boundary lines being called the touch lines and the shorter the goal-lines. V-shaped ruts are not acceptable instead of lines. The goal-line must be marked the same width as the depth of the goal-posts and the cross-bar so that the goal-line and the goal-posts conform in the same interior and exterior edges. Dimensions include the width of the touch lines; that is, the lines are included in the size of the pitch. The space within the inside areas of the field of play includes the width of the lines marking these areas.

Line markings are normally white. On multisports areas, a light colour is preferred, depending upon the surface colour and other markings.

Goal-posts

Goal-posts and cross-bars must be made of wood, metal or other approved material as decided from time to time by the International FA Board. They must be either square, rectangular, round, half round, or elliptical in shape, and of white colour. Net supports and fixings must not protrude in any way likely to cause injury to a player colliding with the goal unit.

Changing spaces

Allow for 13–16 players per team, plus three or four officials per match, depending upon the standard of play.

Fencing

Where a pitch is close to a building or a site boundary fence, then it is advisable to increase the height of the security fencing adjacent to the goal areas to approximately 8–10 m (approx 26–33 ft) for the length of the penalty area (approx 28 m (approx 30 yd)) and therefore also its strength and stability. Where pitches are sited next to boundaries, roads, buildings or other fixtures, discretion should be used as to whether the end and side margins in the Tables are sufficient, having regard to the type of game and the nature of the adjoining property on which damage or trespass might be caused. An end clearance of 12–15 m (approx 13–16 yd) would probably be required to avoid risk of accident or complaint.

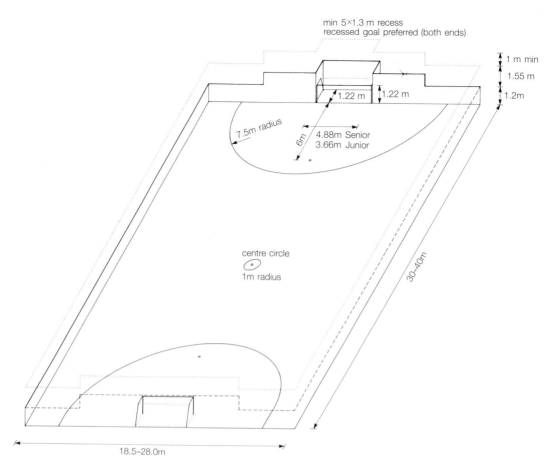

min 5×1.3 m recess
recessed goal preferred (both ends)

1 m min
1.55 m
1.2m

7.5m radius

4.88m Senior
3.66m Junior

6m

1.22 m   1.22 m

centre circle
1m radius

30-40m

18.5-28.0m

4 *Layout of five-a-side pitch, showing alternative positions of portable goal units or built-in recessed goals. The dotted line indicates the high level enclosure above the rebound wall*

Alternatively, as a protective measure, high chain link fencing could be erected along the boundary behind the goal.

Alternatively, to reduce weight and ball impact, nylon arrester netting may be used in place of wire netting but the wind stability of the support framework is still of critical importance.

Floodlighting
Refer to Chapter 18 and the CIBSE Lighting Guide: LG4 – Sport. It is advisable to consult local leagues and local authorities at any early stage in proposals to floodlight a ground. Some football leagues have specific minimum standards for lighting with ground inspection controls. Some leagues require annual checks to verify that lighting levels are being maintained.

Five-a-side football
Five-a-side play is mostly recreational, with games played lengthwise or across the width of multi-use games areas, **3**: see also Chapter 28. The Rules available from the Football Association (FA) are for guidance only. Rules compiled and published by the National Association of Boys' Clubs, London, have been approved by the FA and adopted by various national organisations. For other competitions, dimensional rules and other space requirements should be obtained from the organisers.

Critical factors
● This game must be played off a rebound barrier, or boards; there is no safety margin space surrounding the

pitch, **2**.
● Changes to markings and colour.
● Completely flush, non-abrasive surfaces for players' safety.
● Recessed goal space and high fencing along goal-lines.
● Access gates must open away from and not onto the pitch and be faced with rebound panels.
● Stop nets above a barriered perimeter.
● Stability and safety of goal units.
● Storage space for goals off the pitch and clear of safety margins around other court markings.
● Floodlighting, **4**.

Space
This game can be played anywhere on a playground or multi-games area having a minimum area of approx 30 × 18 m (approx 33 × 20 yd), **4**. There is no free space around the pitch as a feature of the game is the use of the surrounding enclosure as a rebound surface. In a shared area, where the end or side lines are not wall surfaces, a portable barrier must be provided between pitches to complete the enclosure of each pitch. Goals preferably may be recessed between the barrier units along the end line, as shown in **3** and **4**, or placed against end fencing and protrude onto the pitch.

Other recommendations are similar to or adapted from those in Volume 2, Chapter 27, Five-a-side soccer, and Chapter 28 of this volume.

Floodlighting
Refer to Chapter 28; also Chapter 18 and the CIBSE Lighting Guide: LG41 – Sports.

References and further advice

The Football Association

The National Association of Boys Clubs

The National Playing Fields Association

Pan Books (1990/91) *Referees' Chart and Players' Guide to the Laws of Association Football.*

Sports Council, TUS Datasheet 29 *Multi-use Games Areas and Five-a-side Soccer.* Also Chapter 27.

FIFA *Technical Recommendations and Requirements for the Construction of the New Stadia.*

Chapter 22, including Football Stadia Advisory Council publications.

Five-a-side indoors, Volume 2, Chapter 27.

54
Australian football

Peter Ackroyd

The game is immensely popular in Australia where it evolved from a mixture of rugby and Gaelic football rules, 1. Until recently it was played nowhere else, but teams are now developing in Britain, Canada and the US.

Australian football is played on an oval ground by two teams of 22 players each, and lasts 100 minutes, divided into four 25-minute quarters plus extra time. To score a goal, worth six points, the ball must be kicked between the goal posts. If the ball is touched by another player before crossing the scoring line, hits the goal posts, passes over the goal posts or passes between the goal and behind (actually 'a side') post a 'behind', worth one point, is registered. If the ball is rushed over the scoring line no goal is scored, just a behind. Opponents may be tackled by 'bumping' or 'holding' to prevent them scoring, or to get the ball away from them.

Critical factors
- The oval shaped pitch
- A correctly spaced and dimensioned set of goal posts at each end.

Playing space dimensions
There are no set dimensions for the playing surface although the recommended size is between 150–185 m (493–607 ft) in length and between 130–150 m (428–493 ft) in width. The ideal playing surface is 165 m long by 150 m wide (540 × 493 ft). The minimum for junior games is 130 × 110 m (427 × 360 ft). Goal positions are marked by a set of four posts 6.4 m (21 ft) apart at each end of the field. The two centre poles are the 'goal posts' and must be at least 6 m (19 ft 9 in) high; the outer ones are the 'behind posts' and must be at least 4 m (13 ft 2 in) high, 2.

End and side margins
There is no fixed rule, but a surrounding gap of 3 m (10 ft) is generally required between spectators and the oval boundary line.

Surface
The game is played on grass only. For details of grass pitches see Chapter 8.

Markings
The oval boundary, the bounce circle, and the square surrounding the bounce circle, must all be marked in 100 mm (4 in) wide white lines. The playing area is measured to the outside of the perimeter lines (ie the playing area includes the lines).

Changing spaces
Allow for 44 players and six officials for each pitch.

1 *Photo: British Australian Rules Football League 1990*

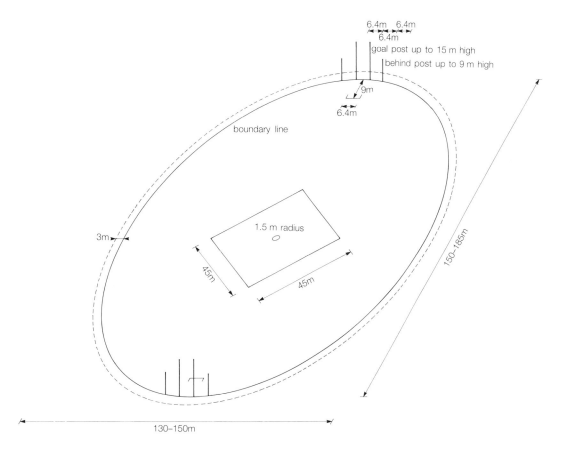

2 Space diagram of playing field with team formation, Australian football. Goal posts (G) and behind posts (B) are 6.4 m (21 ft) apart; goal square is 9 m (approx 30 ft) deep

Floodlighting

This sport is not commonly floodlit and therefore no specific recommendations are provided. For general recommendations for floodlighting outdoor sports refer to Chapter 18, and the CIBSE Lighting Guide: LG4 – Sports.

References and further advice

The British Australian Rules Football League.

Australian Football, a fundamental guide to the game (available from the above League).

55
Gaelic football

Peter Ackroyd

Gaelic football looks rather like a compromise between Association and Rugby Football and is played almost exclusively in Ireland although British and American teams compete in the All-Ireland championships. There are two teams of 15 players each, **1**.

Critical factors
● Overall area of playing space including the surrounding safety margins.

Playing space dimensions
Pitch size is not fixed. The minimum size is 128 × 77 m (420 × 253 ft) and the maximum 146 × 91 m (480 ×

300 ft), **2**. For under-twelves, the pitch length should be 26 m (85 ft 4 in) less. The goal area known as the 'parallelogram' at each end is 13.7 × 4.5 m (45 × 15 ft) and around it is an outer 19 × 13 m (62 ft 6 in × 42 ft 9 in) parallelogram. Inside this larger parallelogram a penalty is awarded for a personal foul only, whereas any foul within the inner parallelogram area concedes a penalty. The goalposts are spaced 6.4 m (21 ft) apart and are 5 m (16 ft 6 in) high, with a crossbar 2.4 m (8 ft) above ground.

End and side margins
A margin of 1.5 m (5 ft) is required on all four sides of the pitch.

1 *Photo: Hugh Brady*

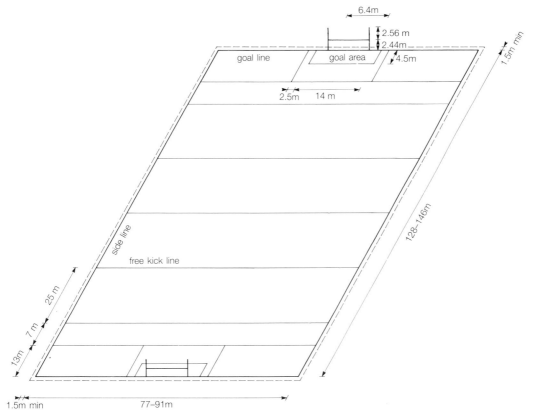

2 *Space diagram of Gaelic football pitch.*

Surface

Grass, synthetic turf (sand-filled grass) or shale. For general information see Part III.

Markings

Lines should be white and 50 mm (2 in) wide. The playing area is measured to the outside of the perimeter lines (ie the playing area includes the lines).

Fences and safety barriers

Fencing or ball-arrest netting is required adjacent to public areas, of minimum height 6 m (20 ft).

Changing facilities

Accommodation is required for 42 players including substitutes and five officials per match.

Floodlighting

This sport is not commonly floodlit and therefore no specific recommendations are provided. For general recommendations for floodlighting outdoor sports refer to Chapter 18, and the CIBSE Lighting Guide: LG4 – Sports.

References and further advice

Sports Council for Northern Ireland
Chapter 61

56
Rugby league football

Peter Ackroyd

Rugby League was founded in Northern England as a breakaway from Rugby Union Football (see Chapter 57). Unlike Rugby Union, which is exclusively amateur, professionalism is allowed. The game is played between two teams of thirteen-a-side, using an oval leather-covered ball. At each end of the field is an H-shaped set of goal posts, 1.

Critical factors
- A level, well-maintained grassed field of the overall dimensions given below, including the surrounding safety margins
- A correctly positioned and dimensioned set of goal posts at each end.

Playing space dimensions
Minimum dimensions of the playing area are 88 × 55 m (96 × 60 yd) and maximum dimensions 100 × 68 m

(110 × 75 yd). Each goal is formed by two upright posts 5.5 m (18 ft) apart and at least 4 m (13 ft) high, with a crossbar 3 m (10 ft) above the ground. These are inside dimensions, 2.

End and side margins
There should be a margin of at least 6 m (20 ft) at each end of the pitch, and at least 2 m (7 ft) but preferably 6 m (20 ft) at each side.

Surface
Natural grass only. For information on grass pitches see Chapter 8.

Markings
Lines should be 76 mm (3 in) minimum width and preferably in white, failing that in yellow. The pitch is

1 *Photo: Butterworth-Heinemann Ltd*

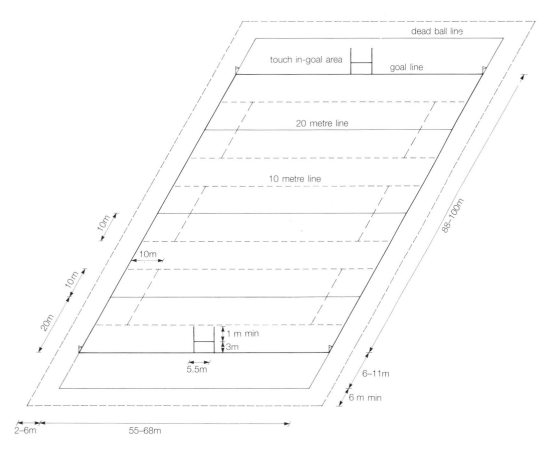

dead ball line

touch in-goal area

goal line

20 metre line

10 metre line

10m

10m

10m

20m

88–100m

1 m min

3m

5.5m

6–11m

6 m min

2–6m

55–68m

2 *Space diagram of a rugby league football pitch*

measured to the inside of the perimeter lines (ie the playing area excludes the lines).

Changing facilities
Changing accommodation is required for 30 players and three officials per pitch.

Floodlighting
For details of requirements and recommendations refer to Chapter 18, and to the CIBSE Lighting Guide: LG4 – Sports.

Further advice
The Rugby Football League and the British Amateur Rugby League Association.

57
Rugby union football

Peter Ackroyd

Rugby Union is an amateur game played with an oval leather-covered ball by two teams of 15 players, **1**. At each end of the field is an H-shaped set of goal posts and the object of the game is for each team to score points by carrying the ball across the opponents' goal line and placing it on the ground (thus scoring a 'try'). After each successful try the scoring side kick the ball towards the same set of goal posts from a defined position on the field and if the ball passes between the posts and over the cross-bar (called a 'conversion'), it scores further points. During the course of the game the ball may be kicked, carried or thrown; and opposing players may be physically 'tackled' by gripping round the legs or body to prevent them gaining ground or passing the ball.

Critical factors
● A level, well-maintained grassed field of the dimensions given below, including surrounding safety margins.

Playing space dimensions
Maximum dimensions of the ground, **2**, are defined in Law 1 of the game. School pitches may be smaller, as shown in Table 57.1 below. Goal posts must be at least 3.4 m (11 ft) high and the crossbar must be at least 3 m (10 ft) above the ground. Corner posts have a minimum height of 1.2 m (4 ft).

End and side margins
There should be a reasonably clear area (the outer broken line on **2**) surrounding the playing area, with no obstructions within at least 5 m (approx 16 ft 5 in) of the touch lines.

Surface
Natural grass only, except that surfaces of rubber-crumb or synthetic turf are acceptable for training. For general information on all these surfaces refer to Part III.

1 *Photo: Sports Council*

Markings
The lines shown in solid on **2** must be marked in white. The pitch is measured to the inside of the perimeter line (ie the playing area excludes the lines).

Fencing
The only requirement is that there should be no obstruction within at least 5 m (approx 16 ft) of the touchline.

Changing facilities
Accommodation is required for 42 players (21 per team room) and three officials. An acceptable floor area would

Table 57.1 NPFA recommended pitch sizes for schools

Age group	Field-of-play length	In-goal-depth	Width	End margin	Side margin
1st & 2nd year	73 m (approx 80 yd)	6.5 m (7 yd)	46 m (50 yd)	3 m (approx 10 ft)	4.5 m (approx 15 ft)
3rd & 4th year	82 m (approx 90 yd)	6.5 m (7 yd)	50 m (approx 55 yd)	3 m (approx 10 ft)	4.5 m (approx 15 ft)
5th year and older	91-96 m (approx 100–105 yd)	9 m (approx 10 yd)	55-59 m (60–approx 65 yd)	3 m (approx 10 ft)	4.5 m (approx 15 ft)

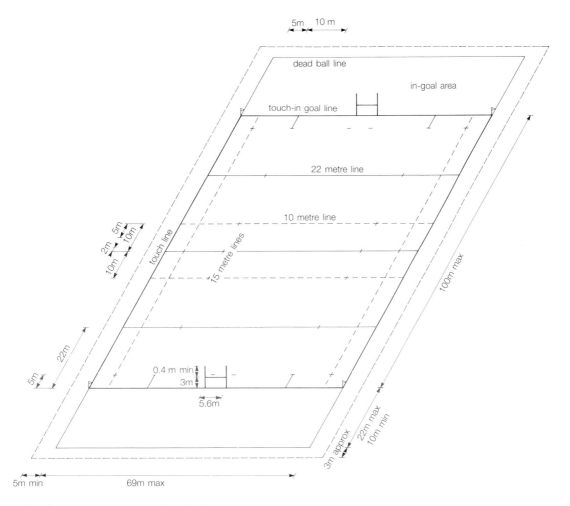

5m 10 m

dead ball line

in-goal area

touch-in goal line

22 metre line

10 metre line

15 metre lines

touch line

2m 5m
10m
10m

100m max

22m

5m

0.4 m min
3m

5.6m

3m approx

22m max
10m min

5m min   69m max

2 *Rugby union football pitch. The field-of-play is the area as shown on the plan, bounded by, but not including, the goal lines and touch lines. The playing area is the field-of-play and in-goal. The playing enclosure is the playing area and a reasonable area surrounding it. Goal post uprights must exceed 3.4 m (11 ft). Height from ground to crossbar is 3 m (approx 10 ft). Corner posts have a minimum height of 1.2 m (approx 4 ft)*

be 1 sq m (approx 11 sq ft) per player. All players with a skin cut or abrasion should use a shower, not a communal bath. If, in the course of time and the rebuilding of clubhouses, it may be considered that communal bathing is not entirely hygienic, individual baths or showers may be preferable.

First aid room

A small, warm, clean space is required where a player can rest while waiting for an ambulance, recover from a shock, or be treated by a doctor or paramedic. It should be equipped with a couch, some blankets, pillows and a medicine cabinet. A stretcher and first aid kit should always be readily available.

Floodlighting

Refer to Chapter 18, and to the CIBSE Lighting Guide: LG4 – Sports.

References and further advice

Rugby Football Union (RFU), Twickenham
Injury Prevention Pamphlet 7, RFU

58
Handball

Peter Ackroyd

Handball is a no-contact game played with one or two hands by catching, interpassing and throwing the ball, **1**, **2** and **3**. There are two outdoor versions of the game:

- Handball played by teams of seven-a-side on a court of the same size as indoor handball, shown in Volume 2, Chapter 30; but preferably on a synthetic surface, tarmacadam or asphalt.
- Field handball played on grass by teams of eleven-a-side and the original game developed in the 1900s. It

is still played in Central Europe, but in most countries it has now given way to the Olympic indoor game.

For general information on these surfaces see Part III.

Floodlighting
This sport is not commonly floodlit and therefore no specific recommendations are provided. For general recommendations for floodlighting outdoor sports refer to Chapter 18, and the CIBSE Lighting Guide: LG4 – Sports.

References and further advice
British Handball Association.
Handball indoors, Volume 2, Chapter 30.

1 *In Swedish schools handball is a major sport. Photo: Norman Mortimer*

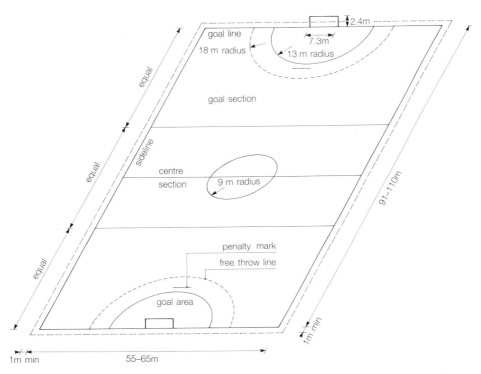

2 *Space diagram of a field handball pitch. In this eleven-a-side game, the goal is an exact replica of the Association Football goal*

3 *Handball on synthetic sand filled turf in Holland. Photo: Sports Council*

59
Hockey

Peter Ackroyd

Hockey is a hard-ball game, played by men or women on a grass or non-turf pitch, **1** and **2**. There are a number of variations played on pitches of different sizes and markings:

- Hockey, or field hockey as it is sometimes known, is played by teams of eleven players, on a full-size pitch of the dimensions given in diagram **3**.
- The seven-a-side game is played on a half-size pitch as shown in **4**. The markings are scaled-down from the full game and two pitches can be marked out side-by-side on the area of a full-sized pitch. Competitions are normally restricted to teams of under 14 year-olds.
- Mini-hockey is also played by teams of seven players on a half-sized pitch, but with quite different markings as shown in **5**. Competitions are normally restricted to teams of under 12 or 10 year-olds.
- A six-a-side game is another version which is either a scaled-down seven-a-side pitch, or, more often, the indoor game played recreationally outdoors on a multi-use games area **4**. (See also Chapter 28).

Critical factors
- Orientation and ground contours
- A smooth and level pitch of the dimensions shown

1 *Photo: Mike Brett Photography*

2 *Photo: Hockey Field*

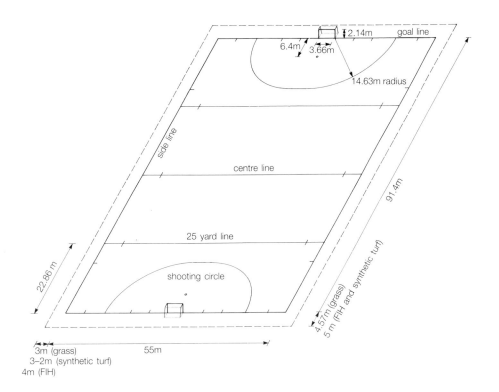

goal line

2.14m

6.4m

3.66m

14.63m radius

side line

centre line

91.4m

25 yard line

22.86 m

shooting circle

4.57m (grass)

5 m (FIH and synthetic turf)

3m (grass)
3–2m (synthetic turf)
4m (FIH)

55m

3 *Space diagram of hockey pitch. The widths of the surrounding safety margins can be reduced for synthetic pitches as set out in Table 59.1. Details of the goal units are given in* **6**

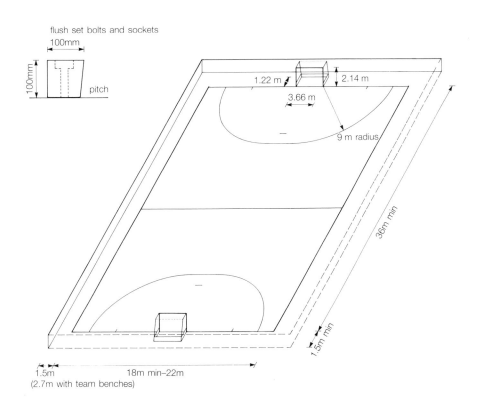

flush set bolts and sockets

100mm

100mm

pitch

1.22 m

2.14 m

3.66 m

9 m radius

36m min

1.5m min

1.5m
(2.7m with team benches)

18m min–22m

4 *Six-a-side hockey pitch. Note the need for side-boards as shown in the detail alongside. These are flush bolted down into sockets set flush with the pitch surface. For details of multi-use games areas refer to Chapter 28*

in the diagrams, with adequate surrounding safety margins
- Choice of surface

The layout and design of an artificial surface pitch also needs to take into account:

- Alternative sports uses, for example, see Chapters 28 and 53
- Division and markings for smaller games, see Chapter 60.
- Siting of fencing posts and floodlighting columns
- Any permanent obstacles or protrusions, within the clear width of safety margins, must be well padded
- Space for other goal units and equipment to be stored or parked beyond and clear of hockey safety margins, **6**
- Additional changing spaces to serve intensive use of pitches
- Wide access for maintenance equipment
- Pitch watering
- Provisions for spectator and advertising boards.

Playing space dimensions

The playing area of a hockey pitch is shown in **3**. End and side margin dimensions are explained below. Dimensions of a synthetic grass pitch are also set out in the following Table 59.1 and in **3**.

Table 59.1 Dimensions of a synthetic grass pitch

	FIH	Club/recreational
Length of pitch	91.44 m (100 yd)	91.4 m (approx 100 yd)
width of pitch	54.86 m (60 yd)	55 m (approx 60 yd)
End margins		
minimum width	5 m (16 ft 5 in)	5 to 4 m (16 ft 5 in to 13 ft) (3)
Side margins		
minimum width (1)	4 m (13 ft)	3 to 2 m (9 ft 9 in to 4 ft 9 in)
Minimum overall area (1)	101.44 × 62.86 m (approx 111 × 69 yd)	101.4 to 99.4 × 61 to 59 m (approx 111 to 109 yd × 67 to 64 yd)
Minimum area of synthetic grass (2)	97.44 × 60.86 m (approx 107 × 67 yd)	97.4 × 59 to 57 m (approx 106 × 64 to 62 yd)

Note (1): Clear widths are free of any obstruction and inside of fencing. For club level pitches the NPFA considers that the FIH overrun widths could be reduced to a total of 3 m (approx 11 ft) (2 m (6 ft 6 in) of synthetic turf plus 1 m (approx 1 yd) of another surface material) at sides.
Note (2): Plus outer-margin surround of another surface material. May be increased for officials, see text below.
Note (3): 5 m is now recommended wherever possible.

End and side margins

For a natural grass pitch the NPFA recommends as a guide the following minimum margin widths between pitches: 3 m (10 ft) along both sides and 4.57 m (15 ft) at both ends. Because grass is vulnerable to wear, where possible it is an advantage to provide wider margins to allow groundsmen to shift the pitch from time to time. Overall minimum size is therefore 100.54 × 61 m (110 × 67 yd), as shown in **3**.

For a synthetic pitch, the FIH specifies a minimum safety margin surrounds. The potentially most dangerous area for players running off the pitch at high speed is behind the goals. There must be a minimum of 5 m (approx 16 ft 5 in) between the end line and any (permanent) obstruction, with the synthetic grass extending a minimum of 3 m (approx 10 ft) around the pitch. The overrun provisions are designed to safeguard players, umpires, ball attendants and other officials against injury. See also Surfaces below.

The Sports Council considers that a decision may be taken at club level to relax FIH recommendations. The side lines margins, however, should not be less than 2 m (6 ft 7 in) of which at the very least 1 m (approx 3 ft) should be synthetic grass (but see Table 59.1 Note (1) which considers wider side margins). The design will depend, however, on the numbers of spectators being catered for. Margins must be wide and clear enough for players safely to run out beyond the pitch, without risk of having to pull up violently or dangerous collision with a solid obstruction such as a soccer goal unit, **6**. Occasionally, smaller items do encroach into these margins (eg advertising boards, substitute benches) but they should be so designed or padded to minimise the risk of injury to players.

Table 59.1 sets out the absolute minimum area of synthetic grass and overall clear area within a fence. Many tournaments and leagues now require the provision of an officials' table for which at least 1 m (3 ft) outside the 2 m (6 ft 6 in) safety margin is ideally required. Similarly additional space should be provided (outside the minimum width of margins) to store bulky soccer goals which could be hazardous to the hockey players, **5**.

Surfaces

- Natural grass surfaces should follow guidance in Chapter 8.
- For all-weather mineral or synthetic non-turf surfaces, refer to Chapters 9 and 10
- For synthetic turf pitches, refer to Chapter 11 and see References at the end of this chapter for Sports Council and FIH essential references
- The FIH 1991 list of approved surfaces also contains sand-filled surfaces for major international tournaments. For national, county, club and school levels, there are other suitable synthetic grass systems available. The governing bodies of hockey and the Sports Council's regional officers should be consulted regarding current specifications.

The following detailed requirements for synthetic grass surfaces should also be noted:

Surrounding safety margins: the FIH revised standard requires that, surrounding the pitch, the surface shall continue with the same qualities of material, slope and smoothness for a minimum distance of 3 m (10 ft) before any change in that surface occurs and for a further minimum distance of 2 m (6 ft 7 in) at each end and 1 m (3 ft 3 in) along each side before any obstruction is encountered. Only the prescribed side line flags should obstruct this area and they, as well as the corner flag, should be capable of bending to the horizontal without injuring any person.

It is important that the primary overrun of 3 m is an extension of the synthetic playing surface. The outer 1 m (3 ft 3 in) of side overrun or 2 m (6 ft 7 in) of end overrun can be constructed from a number of alternative materials provided it is level, is not dangerous to fall on and provides a smooth transition with the grass at which point a drainage channel may be provided. Also, such needs as drain covers or covered reticulation channels

5 *Weld-mesh fencing and ball boards at Clarence Park, St Albans. Note that the football goal is inadvisably standing partly within the hockey safety margins. Photo: Peter Ackroyd*

may be accommodated. These should be designed so as not to cause players to trip.

Pitch watering and porosity: non sand-filled surfaces need large capacity water hydrants, at two positions at the pitch, to allow for pitch watering or a pop-up sprinkler system. Consult widely at an early stage, as considerable quantities of water may be necessary. Refer also to the FIH standards and recommendations for watering and pitch porosity, including sand-filled surfaces.

Leaves cause a maintenance problem: it is important to keep synthetic pitches clean and free of debris which interferes with the roll of the ball and becomes trodden into the surface.

Markings

Markings should be in white, or yellow, and 75 mm (3 in) wide. The pitch is measured to the outsides of perimeter lines, ie the playing area includes the lines.

Markings may either be painted on or integrated in manufacture, but care must be taken with the durability of painted lines since repeated applications might destroy the smoothness of the surface. A danger also exists with integral lines since any significant stretch of the surface may cause dimensional inaccuracies.

Goals

These large items of equipment need to be robustly manufactured and fitted with ballboards. See also Storage and equipment below.

Fences and safety barriers

Fencing is useful to keep balls within the playing area (particularly at night, when stray balls may not easily be found) and to discourage unauthorised encroachment onto the playing field. If fencing is provided, the recommended height is 3 m (10 ft) above the playing surface, except in the areas within 10 m (33 ft) on either side of the goals, where it should be 4.5 m (15 ft) above playing surface. A 150 mm (6 in) high chamfer edged rebound skirting board along the bottom is advisable. Weld-mesh is preferable to chain link fencing which is liable to damage from hockey balls.

If fencing is provided, there must be entry gates for players/spectators and maintenance machinery, the latter requiring one extra-wide set of double gates. Gates should have 150 mm (6 in) high ball boards along the base.

Changing and team facilities

Because synthetic pitches allow several games to be played consecutively, team rooms and lockers for several teams may be necessary – probably for a minimum of four to six teams, comprising 12 to 16 people each. For club matches there should be provision for 24 to 28 players and substitutes to change at one time; and for national and county matches, 32 or more. In addition, changing accommodation must be provided for at least three and sometimes eight match officials per game.

Team benches and officials' areas are needed alongside each pitch, preferably under shelter; and a clock and public address system. Refer also to End and side margins.

6 *Goal unit detail. Photo Richard Gardner*

Storage and equipment

Equipment storage should be provided close to the field for items such as benches, line marking equipment, maintenance machinery, litter bins, hose-reels for pitch watering, advertising boards, balls and the like. If the field may be used for other games (such as tennis or soccer) from time to time, storage space should also be provided for the removable goals, nets, posts and flags etc. required for all of these. (See also safety caution given in End and side margins above).

Floodlighting

For details of requirements and recommendations refer to Chapter 18, and the CIBSE Lighting Guide: LG4 – Sports.

References and further advice

The Hockey Association and The All England Womens' Hockey Association.
'The Rules of the Game of Hockey' 1990, published by the Hockey Rules Board.
Sports Council (1990) *Artificial Turf Pitches for Hockey: A planning, design, construction and management guide.* This ringbound publication also includes the next two publications:
● Sports Council TUS Datasheet 57, *Hockey* (1990)
● International Hockey Federation (FIH), *Handbook of Requirements for Synthetic Hockey Surfaces Outdoor* (Revised 1991)
Indoor Hockey, Volume 2, Chapter 31.

60
Mini hockey and six- or seven-a-side hockey

Peter Ackroyd

Both mini hockey and seven-a-side hockey are played on a half-sized pitch, with seven players per team; but they are played to different rules.

Seven-a-side hockey is very like true hockey, except that it is played on a half-scale pitch, with markings similarly scaled down, and it is meant for under-14 year olds.

Mini hockey is restricted to players aged ten, or under-twelves. Just as in true hockey, the players propel the ball along with curved sticks, aiming to strike it into the opponents' goal. Pitch markings are quite different from those of true hockey or seven-a-side hockey.

A six-a-side game is another version which is either a scaled down seven-a-side pitch, or, more often, the indoor game played recreationally outdoors on an MUGA: see Chapter 28.

Critical factors
- A smooth and level field of the specified dimensions as shown in **1**, with correctly positioned and sized goalposts
- The pitch markings are different for each version of the game
- Rebound boards at ground level around the goals.

Playing space dimensions
The UK Governing Bodies still refer to dimension in yards, with metric equivalents given in the Rule Book in line with metric dimensions as used by the FIH:

- For seven-a-side hockey, playing field length is 50.3 to 54.86 m (55 to 60 yd), and width 41.15 to 45.7 m (45 to 50 yd), **2**.

1 *Photo: Hockey Digest*

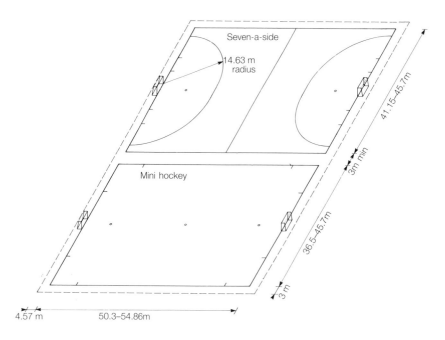

2 *Space diagrams of an outdoor seven-a-side pitch (**a**) and mini-hockey pitch (**b**). For comparison the pair are shown drawn to the same scale as, and overlaid within, a full-size pitch area (**1**). Note the differing pitch markings and different minimum widths, with a constant maximum of 45.7 m (50 yd)*

● For mini hockey, playing field length is as above, but width need only be 36.5 to 45.7 m (40 to 50 yd).

In both cases, the intention is that two of these reduced pitches may be fitted into one full-sized field, **2**.

Each goal structure consists of two upright wooden posts 2.14 m (7 ft) high and 3.66 m (12 ft) apart, joined at the top by a crossbar – all of these being inside measurements. Wooden rebound boards are essential where the netting meets the ground.

End and side margins
As for hockey; but if two half-sized pitches of the above dimensions are laid out within a full-sized hockey field, the size of the latter will determine the space between, which should not be less than 3 m (approx 3 yd).

Surface
As for hockey (see Chapter 59).

Markings
See **1** for the different line markings, which should be in white, or failing that in yellow, and 75 mm (3 in) wide. The pitch is measured to the outsides of perimeter lines, ie the playing area includes the lines.

Fences and safety barriers
As for hockey. Any obstructions or projections within the safety margins must be padded to a height of at least 2 m (6 ft 6 in).

Floodlighting
For details of recommendations refer to Chapter 18, and the CIBSE Lighting Guide: LG4 – Sports.

References and further advice
The Hockey Association.

61
Hurling

Peter Ackroyd

Hurling, one of the fastest of all team games, is still the national game in Ireland where in places the style of play has affinities with the Shinty of the Scottish Highlands. The game is also played in England, USA and Australia and has been demonstrated in Europe. There are two teams of 15 players, each with a with crooked, broad-bladed stick, and a ball, **1**.

Critical factors
- Overall area of the playing space including surrounding safety margins.

Playing space dimensions
The pitch size is not fixed but is very similar to Gaelic Football. The minimum size is 128 × 77 m (420 × 253 ft) and maximum 146 × 91 m (480 × 300 ft). For under-twelves, the pitch length should be 26 m (85 ft 4 in) less. The goal area at each end is 13.7 × 4.5 m (45 × 15 ft) and the goalposts are spaced 6.4 m (21 ft) apart. They are 4.88 m (16 ft) high with a crossbar 2.44 m (8 ft) above the ground, **2**.

End and side margins
A margin of 4.57 m (15 ft) is required at each end of the pitch and at least 3 m (10 ft) along each side.

Surfaces
The regulation surface is grass, but as for Camogie sand-filled synthetic turf is used for practice and shale is acceptable for school play. For general information see Part III.

1 *Photo: Robert McNiece*

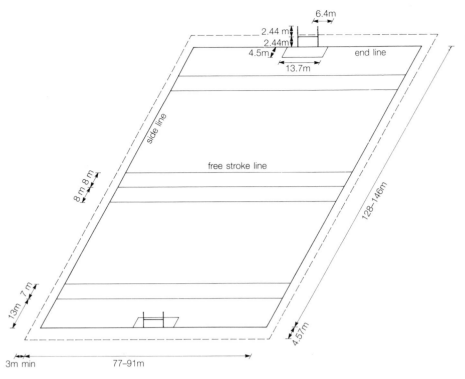

2 *Space diagram of a hurling pitch. Dimensions and line markings are very similar to Gaelic Football*

Markings

Lines should be white and 50 mm (2 in) wide. The playing area is measured to the outside of the perimeter lines (ie the playing area includes the lines).

Fences and safety barriers

Fencing or ball-arrest netting at least 6 m (20 ft) high is required adjacent to public areas.

Changing facilities

Accommodation is required for 42 players including substitutes and five officials per match.

Floodlighting

This sport is not commonly floodlit and therefore no specific recommendations are provided. For general recommendations for floodlighting outdoor sports refer to Chapter 18, and the CIBSE Lighting Guide: LG4 – Sports.

References and further advice

Sports Council for Northern Ireland.
Chapter 55.
Chapter 73.

62
Korfball

Peter Ackroyd

Korfball is a ball-handling game of Dutch origin played by mixed eight-a-side teams comprising four men and four women, with the rules designed to give equal opportunities to both sexes, **1**. The techniques are similar to those used in netball, handball and basketball (see Chapters 41, 58 and 66) except that dribbling with the ball is not allowed. It should be noted that the original form of the game ('field korfball') was played on a larger field than that given below, with twelve players split equally into three divisions. This version still survives in London and in Holland.

Critical factors
- Overall area of space including the surrounding safety margins

1 *Korfball is a ball-handling game of Dutch origin. Photo: British Korfball Association*

- Well-kept, well-drained pitch with a hazard-free surface
- The goal structures must have no protrusions, such as fixings, which could cause injury to players.

Playing space dimensions
The ideal size is 60 × 30 m (197 × 98 ft 6in). For recreational play this can be reduced to 50 × 25 m (164 × 82 ft), and for very young children to 40 × 20 m (131 × 65 ft 6 in), **2**.

The goals are baskets 450 mm (approx 18 in) in diameter, fixed at an overall height of 3.5 m (11 ft 6 in) above ground, mounted on sturdy poles. The latter are mounted on flat plates fixed to the ground by means of a central spike. Posts are 10 m (33 ft) from the end of the pitch, with penalty spots 2.5 m (8 ft 5 in) in front of the posts.

End and side margins
There must be a clear margin of 1.5 m (approx 5 ft) all round the playing area.

Surface
A well-drained flat surface of natural grass, cut short and sharp, is preferred. Artificial surfaces of tarmac, concrete or dry synthetic grass may be acceptable. The chosen surface must be free of all hazards such as unevenness, drain covers, stones or frozen patches, which could cause injury in this very fast and vigorous game. For general information see Part III.

Markings
Lines as shown on **2** are marked on the pitch by means of 30 to 50 mm (1¼ to 2 in) wide white-coloured removable tapes held down by pins, whereby pitches can be readily shifted about on a grass field. The pins holding down the tapes must not project dangerously above the surface; and penalty spots must not be marked out with any hard object such as a metal disc. Dimensions are measured to the insides of perimeter lines (ie playing area excludes the lines).

Equipment
A first-aid kit and mobile field-hospital for dealing with concussion, sprained ankles, dislocated or swollen fingers,

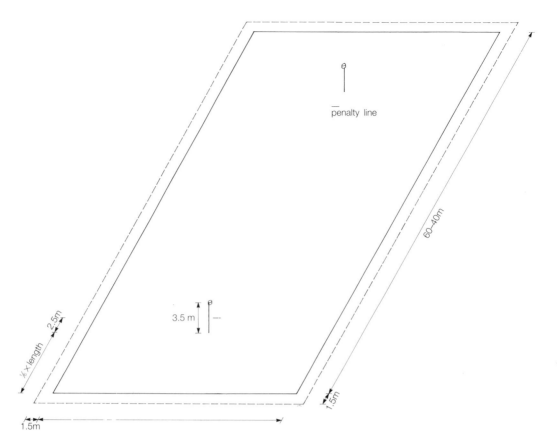

penalty line

60–40 m

2.5 m

⅙ × length

3.5 m

1.5 m

1.5m

2 *Space diagram of the pitch. The ideal overall playing area is a rectangle 63 × 33 m (approx 207 × 108 ft) level and of short, sharp grass. If necessary, smaller sizes are permitted for young players or where the available area does not allow for a full-size pitch*

trodden feet or blisters; and a supply of cold water or ice. The telephone number or location of the nearest doctor or hospital should be posted where officials can see it.

Changing facilities
Changing spaces for twelve men and twelve women are required, plus three officials.

Floodlighting
This sport is not commonly floodlit and therefore no specific recommendations are provided. For general recommendations for floodlighting outdoor sports refer to Chapter 18, and the CIBSE Lighting Guide: LG4 – Sports.

References and further advice
The British Korfball Association.
Korfball indoors, Volume 2, Chapter 35.

63
Lacrosse: men

Peter Ackroyd

Lacrosse derives from a game originally played by North American Indians, which was introduced to Britain via Canada in 1867. It is played by two twelve-a-side teams and unlike women's lacrosse (see Chapter 64) the pitch is bounded, **1**.

Critical factors
● Overall area of space including the surrounding safety margin.

Playing space dimensions
Pitch length is not fixed, and depends on the space available; but a length of 100 m (109 yd) and a width of 55 m (60 yd) is recommended. Distance between the goal and the end line is fixed, **2**.

Space between pitches
Clear space between adjoining pitches must be 6 m (20 ft). A 3 m (10 ft) margin must therefore be added to each pitch all round.

Surface
Traditionally the game is played on natural grass, but synthetic surfaces (including sand-filled and non sand-filled grass) are also used. For general information see Part III.

Markings
The centre line is 100 mm (4 in) wide and all other markings 50 mm (2 in) wide. White is the preferred colour, failing that yellow.

Fences and safety barriers
None are formally required, but if used fencing should be 3 m (10 ft) high to be effective.

Changing facilities
Changing spaces are required for 26 players (52 in the case of international matches); and for two officials (four in the case of international matches).

Floodlighting
This sport is not commonly floodlit and therefore no specific recommendations are provided. For general recommendations for floodlighting outdoor sports refer to Chapter 18, and the CIBSE Lighting Guide: LG4 – Sports.

References and further advice
English Lacrosse Union.

1 *Photo: Roger Price*

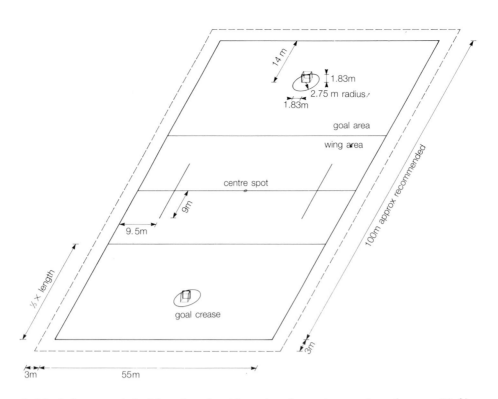

2 *Men's lacrosse pitch. Note that the side and end margins are 3 m (approx 10 ft) on all four sides, thus adding a total of 6 m (approx 20 ft) to the recommended playing space length and width*

64
Lacrosse: women

Peter Ackroyd

Lacrosse derives from a game originally played by North American Indians, which was introduced to Britain via Canada in 1867. It is played by two twelve-a-side teams on a field with a goal some distance from each end. Each player has a 'crosse' – a hickory stick, framed and strung at the far end with leather thongs to form a triangular net – which is used to catch, pass and throw a solid rubber ball of about 240 mm (8 in) diameter, **1**.

Critical factors
● New marking of the pitch, July 1991

Playing space dimensions
Pitch length is not fixed, and depends on the space available; but a length of 110 m (360 ft) and a width of 60 m (197 ft) is the minimum area recommended. Distance between the opposing sets of goalposts is 92 m (302 ft). Each goal consists of two perpendicular posts 1.83 m (6 ft) high and the same distance apart, **2**.

Surface
Traditionally the game is played on natural grass, but synthetic surfaces such as rubber-crumb or synthetic turf are also used. For general information see Part III.

Markings
Each goal is surrounded by a circle of 2.6 m radius (8 ft 6 in) known as 'the crease', beyond which new rules require a half-circle 15 m (49 ft 3 ins) radius from the goal. In the centre of the field is a circle of 9 m (29 ft 6 in) radius (the 'centre circle'). All markings are 50 mm (2 in) wide, in white. Note that boundary lines are not to be marked.

Changing facilities
Changing spaces are required for 32 players and three officials.

Floodlighting
This sport is not commonly floodlit and therefore no specific recommendations are provided. For general recommendations for floodlighting outdoor sports refer to Chapter 18, and the CIBSE Lighting Guide: LG4 – Sports.

References and further advice
All England Women's Lacrosse Association (AEWLA).

1 *Photo: Phil Sheldon*

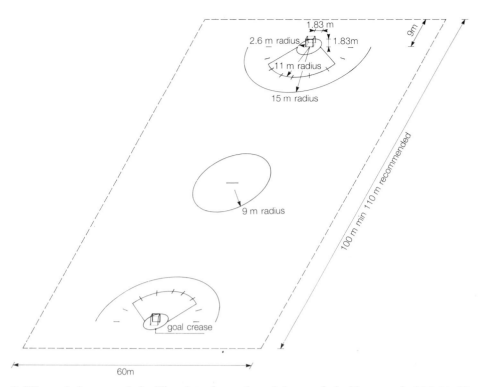

2 *Women's lacrosse pitch. The plan shows the minimum desirable area, ie 110 × 60 m (360 × 197 ft). The boundary lines are not to be marked in. The women's indoor seven-a-side game has been superseded by Pop-Lacrosse*

65
Lawn Tennis

Christopher Harper

The modern game, **1**, developed from real tennis (see Volume 2, Chapter 83). Field tennis, played on grass, became popular in the last century, but it was the promotion of the game with standardised rules in the 1860s and 70s that paved the way for tennis as it is played today. All weather court surfaces further increased interest as did the eventual development of indoor courts for club use and some major tournaments, **3**.

Critical factors
- Safety margins around the court (and clear, unobstructed height)
- Orientation: courts must be aligned on or close to a north/south axis. This is a major consideration in site suitability and layout.

Space and layout
Court and overall dimensions for both one and a series of courts are given in **2** and Table 65.1 below.

Court markings
The Rules of tennis state that the centre service line must be 50 mm (2 in) in width and other lines, with the exception of the base line, are not less than 25 mm (1 in) or more than 50 mm (2 in) wide. The base line may have a width of 100 mm (4 in). Court markings are white.

1 *Photo: Richard Gardner*

Table 65.1 Tennis space requirements

Marked out playing area	International and National Championships m	ft	Club and County m	ft	Minimum recreational standard m	ft
Court length	23.77	78	23.77	78	23.77	78
Court width	10.97	36	10.97	36	10.97	36
Length of net (doubles)	12.80	42	12.80	42	12.80	42
Runback at each end	6.40 (1)	21 (1)	6.40	21	5.49	18
Side run out, each side	3.66 (1)	12 (1)	3.66	12	3.05	10
Side run between aligned courts without separate enclosure	ND	ND	4.27	14	3.66	12
Overall size of enclosure(s)						
Length	36.58 (1)	120 (1)	36.58	120	34.75	114
Width for one enclosed court	18.29 (1)	60 (1)	18.29	60	17.07	56
Width for 2 courts in a single enclosure			33.53	110	31.70	104
Width added for each additional court			15.24	50	14.63	48

Note (1): May need increased overall dimensions for court officials, furniture and sponsorship boards

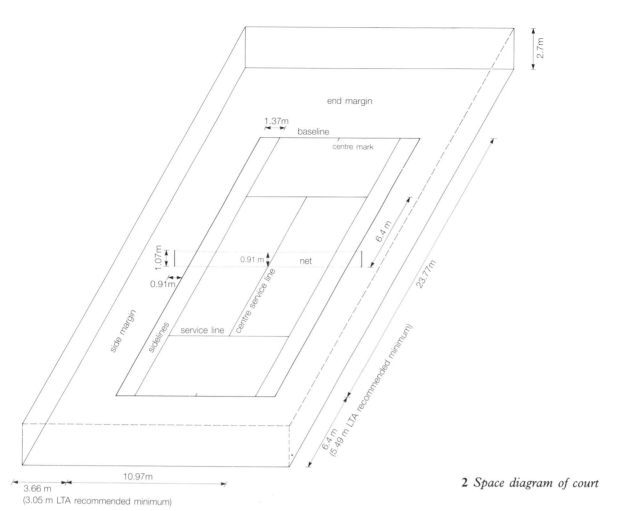

2.7m

end margin

1.37m

baseline

centre mark

1.07m

0.91 m

net

6.4 m

0.91m

side margin

sidelines

service line

centre service line

23.77m

6.4 m
(5.49 m LTA recommended minimum)

6.4 m (5.49 m LTA recommended minimum)

10.97m

3.66 m
(3.05 m LTA recommended minimum)

2 *Space diagram of court*

3 *Aerial view of Federation Cup Site, Nottingham 1991. Photo: Martin Ellis Associates*

Surface selection

See Chapter 16.

Floodlighting

For details of requirements and recommendations refer to Chapter 18, and the CIBSE Lighting Guide: LG4 – Sports.

Water supply

Water services will be required for essential maintenance of certain types of tennis surface.

Fencing

Courts must be fenced to a minimum height of 2.75 m (9 ft) with steel posts, rails and steel mesh netting coloured black/green. Side netting can be dropped to 1.2 m (approx 4 ft) height for all but the end two post bays and court division nets will also be 1.2 m (approx 4 ft) height.

The lowest level of specification which should be considered is for painted steel angle posts with lateral stabilisation supporting plastic coated 45 or 50 mm (1¾ or 2 in) mesh. Galvanised steel supports are preferable and, in vulnerable locations, galvanised (and decorated) weld-mesh can be considered. A steel top rail connecting uprights provides a neater appearance than a top straining wire and restraint must be provided along the base of the netting where distortion can occur. Fencing design should take account of applied wind break fabric, 2 m (approx 6 ft 6 in) height, to the end netting.

Access gate widths must be sufficient for maintenance machinery and gate design and thresholds should permit easy entry of wheelchairs. There should be no dangerous projections and gate handles and latches should be recessed.

Changing requirements

Ideally, four changing spaces should be provided per court with a percentage of additional spaces for overlap.

It may be assumed that male/female use is on a 50:50 basis. In practice, and with the majority of players arriving at Tennis Centres and clubs by car ready changed, facilities can be underutilised, so provision should be carefully assessed according to location and predicted use. (For details of changing design, showers and clothes storage refer to Chapter 23)

Tennis tournaments

Tournament venues must be designed to accommodate occasional spectator events which will require considerably enhanced facilities **3**. These will include:

- A Centre Court: this principal court will normally be surrounded with banks of permanent spectator seating which can be augmented by additional temporary terraces set up on designated land around the perimeter.
- Court number 1 and additional spectator courts: each court must leave space for a bank or banks of temporary seating. It should be noted that end of court seating provides the best viewing of tennis.
- Enhanced dimensional requirements may be needed for court furniture and sponsorship boards.
- Inter-court access malls and assembly areas to cater for peak time spectator admissions.
- Adequate car parking and land for overspill parking.
- Temporary accommodation for stewards, officials, the press, extra changing accommodation for players, hospitality suites and bars and refreshments area. There should be sufficient enclosed or partially enclosed accommodation to provide shelter in inclement weather.
- Services for both permanent and temporary accommodation, and a computerised events scoreboard.

References and further advice

The Lawn Tennis Association's Facilities Department. References under 'Indoor Tennis' Volume 2, Chapter 100.

66
Netball

Peter Ackroyd

Netball is a popular game for girls and women, played by two teams of seven-a-side. There is a goalpost at each end of the court, with a metal ring at the top. The ball (about 700 mm (27 in) in circumference) may be passed from one player to another, but running with the ball, or kicking it, is not allowed, 1.

1 *Photo: Brian Worrell*

Critical factors
● Overall area of space including the surrounding safety margins.
● A non-slip playing surface.
● Type of goalpost support and its location – see Equipment.

Playing space dimensions
Playing area is fixed at 30.5 × 15.25 m (100 × 50 ft) for all standards of play, 2. For National standards of play, each of the four surrounding margins must be 1.5 to 2 m (4 ft 11 in to 6 ft 6 in) wide. For Regional, County and Club levels, all surrounding margins are a minimum of 1.2 m (3 ft 11 in); and for Recreational play 0.75 m (2 ft 6 in).

Overall areas are therefore as shown in Table 66.1.

Markings
Lines as shown on 2, of not more than 50 mm (2 in) width, are marked on the court in white, or (if white markings for other sports are already present) in yellow or red. Dimensions are measured to the outsides of perimeter lines, ie playing area includes the lines.

Surface
A well-drained non-slip surface is a critical requirement. Uncoated open textured macadam is preferable until a non-slip colour coating is developed, proven and readily available. Research is being broadened to investigate other synthetic surfaces with better shock absorbing properties for improved under foot comfort and reduced risk of injury. Surface slopes should not be greater than 1 in 100 and across the line of play where the area is also used for tennis. For general information, see Part III.

Table 66.1 Space requirements for various standards of play

	International/National	Regional/County/Club	Recreational
Playing space court dimensions	30.5 × 15.25 m (100 × 50 ft)	30.5 × 15.25 m (100 × 50 ft)	30.5 × 15.25 m (100 × 50 ft)
Safety margins	1.5-2 m (approx 5–6 ft 6 in)	Minimum 1.2 m (approx 4 ft)	Minimum 0.75 m (approx 2 ft 6 in)
Overall length (including margins)	33.5-34.5 m (110–112 ft)	Minimum 32.9 m (100 ft)	Minimum 32 m (105 ft)
Overall width (including margins)	18.25-19.25 m (60–63 ft)	Minimum 17.65 m (58 ft)	Minimum 16.75 m (55 ft)

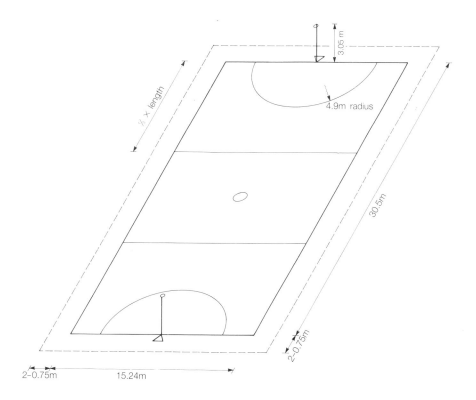

2 *Space diagram of netball court. Two transverse lines drawn parallel to the goal lines divide the court into three equal parts (from the outside of the goal lines to the centre of the dividing lines). Note the new ruling, given in Equipment, for critical location of goalposts and supports.*

Fences and safety barriers

Fencing of 2.8 m (9 ft) height is recommended all round, with a height of 3.8 m (12 ft 6 in) behind and approximately 3 m (10 ft) both sides of the goalposts.

Equipment

The goalposts may be round or square, are 3.05 m (10 ft) high and 50 to 100 mm (2 to 4 in) in diameter. The metal rings at the top are 380 mm (15 in) in diameter. The new ruling from July 1991 is that the goalpost at the mid-point of each goal line shall be placed so that the back of the goalpost is at the outside of the goal line. Posts may be inserted into a socket in the ground or supported by a metal base which shall not project on the court (which includes the goal line – see Markings above). For international matches the goalposts should preferably be inserted into a socket in the ground. For other matches each post may be supported on a metal baseplate, but which, owing to the locational constraint above, must be situated behind the goal line (off the court) but with a forward mounted post on the line. This poses goalpost stability and safety problems for equipment manufacturers, and for players.

Changing facilities

Changing spaces should be provided for twenty players (including substitutes) per match plus ten officials.

Floodlighting

For details of requirements and recommendations refer to Chapter 18, and to CIBSE Lighting Guide: LG4 – Sports.

References and further advice

The All England Netball Association Limited. Netball indoors, Volume 2, Chapter 37.

67
Petanque

Peter Ackroyd

Petanque (the proper name for the French game of boules and pronounced 'peyt-onk') became established in Britain in the 1970s. The rules are simple, a very inexpensive 'terrain' or 'piste' (as the outdoor pitches are called) will do, and an uneven surface is definitely preferred to a smooth one. Petanque is therefore easily catered for and a game for everyone from the family enjoying a day out to dedicated competition players.

Many public houses have provided pitches, often on existing car parks or gravel drives, **1**; local authorities have started to put down terrains; and television coverage of international competitions is anticipated, which will no doubt boost the game enormously.

Because of the wide appeal of the game, installation of a terrain at (for instance) a pub, a stately home or a motorway rest area may well generate income from the hire of boules and the sale of food and drink to players and spectators. Stately homes which are open to visitors seem a particularly appropriate location. They often have large gravelled areas very suitable for the game, provide an impressive setting, offer visitors an enjoyable non-strenuous activity, and are likely to have the catering and other facilities to cater for 200 spectators and players.

The game is most commonly played by six people (two three-a-side teams) using metal boules weighing 0.5 kg (approx 1 lb) each. The diameter is 70 to 80 mm (approx 2.75 to 3 in). The object is to roll the boule as close as possible to a smaller ball, the jack or 'cochonnet', across an undulating surface.

Critical factors
- The terrain surface should not be too smooth and, unlike most other outdoor games, it should not be grass
- The piste should be of the dimensions given on **2**; and have a safety upstand all round
- The number of pistes required, and therefore overall area, is controlled by the fact that each individual piste can accommodate a maximum of six players.

Playing space dimensions
Each piste should be at least 12 × 3 m (approx 40 × 10 ft) and preferably 15 × 4 m (approx 50 × 13 ft), which is the required size for national competitions with a 1.5

1 *Photo: Pic Photos*

Table 67.1 Overall dimensions

Number of pistes	*Size of each piste and height of upstand around*	*Approx overall area of pistes (not including side or end margins)*
Recreational or club (minimum size)		
6	12 × 3 m (approx 40 × 10 ft) piste 230-300 mm (9–12 in) upstand	216 sq m (2325 sq ft)
8	12 × 3 m (approx 40 × 10 ft) piste 230-300 mm (9–12 in) upstand	288 sq m (3100 sq ft)
Club or national (maximum size)		
6	15 × 4 m (49 × 13 ft) piste 300 m (12 in) upstand	360 sq m (3875 sq ft)
8	15 × 4 m (49 × 13 ft) piste 300 m (12 in) upstand	480 sq m (5167 sq ft)
Inter-club or national competitions		
32	15 × 4 m (49 × 13 ft) piste 300 mm (12 in) upstand	2000 sq m (21,528 sq ft)

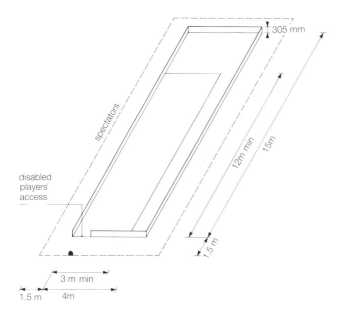

2 *Space diagram. Additional space is needed for competition officials and players' sitting out*

m (approx 5 ft) wide walkway between adjacent pistes. Each piste will cater for a maximum of six people, the usual number for each game. Most clubs aim to cater for up to 36 or 48 players at a time, and must therefore provide six or eight pistes. Overall size is therefore as shown in Table 67.1.

Surface

Very regular, smooth surfaces are inappropriate. The skill of 'reading' an undulating surface to decide the line to be taken to the jack contributes strongly to the appeal of the game. So does the element of unpredictability, which gives the beginner a sporting chance against the expert.

The requirement is therefore a dry, somewhat uneven surface which will provide the boule with some grip on landing, but not so loose or deep as to hinder its progress. The ideal is a base of asphalt (eg a car park or drive) or well-tamped hardcore, to drain away water, on top of which is spread 6–15 mm (approx 0.25–0.6 in) of top-dressing. The cheapest dressing is sand or gravel, the ideal is '4 mm (approx 0.16 in) to dust' pea, beach or granite chippings.

Markings

None required.

Safety kerb or barriers

The boules may travel with considerable force, and spectators need protection. Upstand kerbs all round the piste are therefore required, preferably of timber. Minimum heights are given in Table 67.1 and in **2**; but some clubs provide barriers up to 900 mm (approx 3 ft) high, which may then carry advertising boards, providing a source of revenue to help maintain the terrain. Railway sleepers, being heavy, make excellent kerbs. Scaffolding boards are also suitable, but they must be well-supported to withstand the impact of boules.

There should be an access opening in the barrier for players, and a ramp if necessary to cater for disabled players.

Equipment

Basically the only equipment required by each player is a set of boules. For competitions a scoreboard, benches and officials table, are required.

Spectators

Spectators usually form an impromptu 'couloir' corridor around an interesting game but for an important competition, such as the very big 'Marseillaise' in France, banked seating is necessary.

Floodlighting

This sport is not commonly floodlit and therefore no specific recommendations are provided. For general recommendations for floodlighting outdoor sports refer to Chapter 18, and the CIBSE Lighting Guide: LG4 – Sports.

References and further advice

The British Petanque Association.
The Sports Council, TUS Datasheet 58: *The Design, Management and Promotion of Petanque Terrains* The Sports Council (April 1989).

68
Polo

Peter Ackroyd

Polo came to the West from India, where it was popular among British army officers in the mid 19th century. Rules were drawn up by the Hurlingham Polo Committee (now the Hurlingham Polo Association) in 1875 and still form the basis of the game today. It is played on a grass field by two four-a-side teams mounted on ponies. Each player is equipped with a long-handled polo-stick comprising a mallet-like head of bamboo or willow, and a 1.3 m (4 ft 3 in) malacca shaft, which is used to drive along a ball made of willow or bamboo-root, 1.

A variant called Arena Polo is becoming popular, played outdoors or indoors on an artificially-surfaced field, either three-a-side or two-a-side. This requires a smaller field, surrounded by a boarded wall. See Volume 2, Chapter 84.

Critical factors

- Polo requires a regular-surfaced grass field of the dimensions shown in 2, including the increased size of the surrounding safety area
- Arena polo requires an artificial equestrian surface.

Playing space dimensions

In the rules, all dimensions are specified in yards, as the sport has not yet gone metric; but equivalents are given here for convenience.

For regular polo, played on an open-sided field, dimensions are as shown in 2. There is no minimum width. The minimum distances between adjoining pitches is 54.8 m (60 yd) between goals and 18.2 m (20 yd) along the sides.

1 *Photo: Neilson McCarthy*

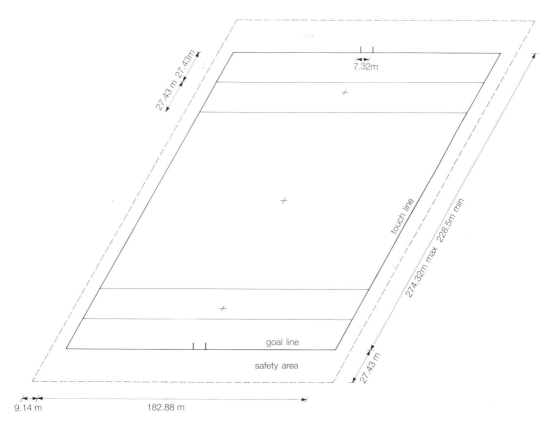

2 *Polo ground. Dimensions shown are those of a full-size ground including the safety area, which should be at least 4.5 m (5 yd) beyond the touch lines and 18.3 m (20 yd) at either end*

If the ground is boarded, maximum width is reduced to 146.30 m (160 yd). Each goal is formed by two posts 3.05 m (10 ft) in height, spaced 7.32 m (8 yd) apart.

Floodlighting
This sport is not commonly floodlit and therefore no specific recommendations are provided. For general recommendations for floodlighting outdoor sports refer to Chapter 18, and the CIBSE Lighting Guide: LG4 – Sports.

References and further advice
The Hurlingham Polo Association.

69
Riding and equestrianism

Peter Ackroyd

There are many outdoor riding and competition disciplines for which facilities are needed. These include at least four distinct types of equestrian establishments:

- Livery stables that provide facilities for general recreation (where access to countryside is important), training for competition and possibly hunting.
- Riding Centres or schools that cater for either basic riding school customers, career training or training for top competition standards in various riding disciplines.
- Trekking Centres with an outdoor manège for initial tuition.

- Competitive Centres including major showgrounds and local show grounds where events are held outside. These are often combined with one or more of the above types.

This chapter mostly outlines the latter of these four types, but includes elements common to all types of outdoor spaces.

The British Horse Society (BHS) requirements for a riding centre include:

- Covered riding school
- Stables, 1

1 *Before showing, Essex County Show. Photo: Kicksports Foto*

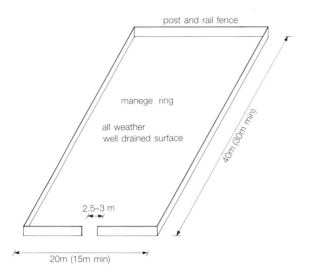

2 *An outdoor schooling manège should be provided at riding schools and stables (see Chapter 19). An all-weather surface is important, surrounded by post and rail fencing, 3.*

3 *All weather surfaced manège. Photo: Sports Council*

- Saddle or tack room
- Forage and general stores
- Manager's office
- Lavatories and washing facilities
- Canteen with clubroom
- Living accommodation
- An outdoor manège, **2 & 3**
- A dressage arena, **4 & 5**
- A show jumping arena, **6 to 8**
- Cross country fences
- Hacking paths, bridleways or tracks giving access to the countryside
- Horse box and trailer park, **9**
- Separate car parking.

For advice on livery stables, riding centres and trekking or for details of ring or course building, consult early with the organisations listed in References.

Critical factors

- Site location and size.
- Early and full consultations, particularly with landowners and for planning permission. NB: consult Structure and Local Plans in relationship to land use policies for horse based activities, landscape quality and proximity of local community.
- Well drained land, protected from prevailing winds.
- Access to bridleways.

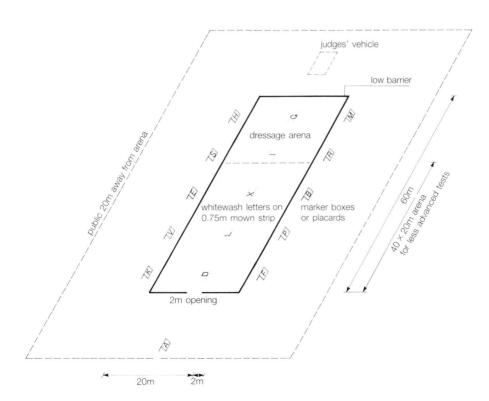

4 *Dressage arena. The broken line indicates that spectators and cars should be at least 15–20 m (approx 49–66 ft) away from the arena, 5*

5 *Pony Club area qualifiying dressage multi-ring competition. Photo: SGL Corporate Ltd*

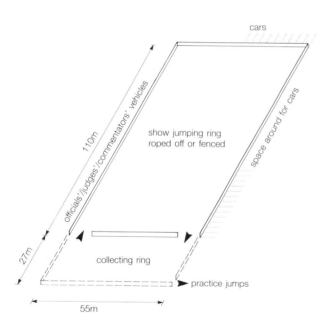

6 *Show jumping ring, 7 and 8*

- Suitable approach roads and site access with adequate parking and turning for large vehicles.
- Safely modified natural obstacles, **12**.
- Safety distance between parked vehicles and horse lanes between rings, **9 & 10**.
- Collecting rings or area for each show or competition ring, **4 & 6**.
- Warm-up areas, **15**.
- Overnight stabling for major event venues

7 *Junior Jumping. Photo: Dominic Savill*

Space

The following diagrams show the rings and large spaces required for some of the showing and competitive disciplines listed in References. For cross country courses consult the relevant Governing Bodies.

At local shows, the number and shape of rings will be determined by the nature of the event and the space avail-

able. One or two showjumping rings can be needed depending upon the classes and entries. For affiliated British Show Jumping Association (BSJA) events, two to four rings may be needed, **8**. If space is tight, the officials and commentary point can share one end with a smaller collecting ring. A warm-up and at least one practice jump ring is needed, **15**. A clear-round (beginners') jumping

8 *BSJA affiliated show jumping at Potton Equestrian centre, Cambridgeshire. Photo: John Bull Photography*

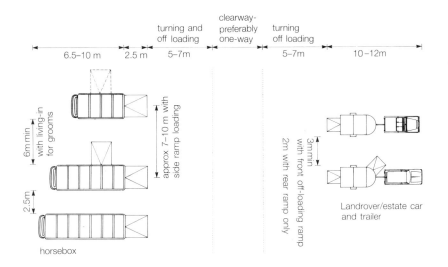

9 *Parking and loading spaces for horse vehicles. Live-in boxes or caravans should be spaced 6 m (approx 20 ft) apart for public health standards, 10*

ring is a useful addition. A separate gymkhana area and two or three showing class rings complete the typical scene. Space is required nearby for catering tents, portaloos, trade stands or mobile suppliers, St John's Ambulance, veterinary, and horse box lines **10** and **11**. These can total about 5–10 ha (approx 12–25 acres) of land.

There must be adequate space allowed for horse lanes to and from rings and the warm-up and collecting areas.

Permanent stabling and other indoor accommodation and facilities are outlined in Volume 2, Chapter 00. For major events at venues without permanent stabling, temporary stabling may be required. For detailed advice contact BHS.

Surfaces

For intensive exercising and schooling a manège is required, **2, 3**. The ground forces (shear and point load) under horses' hooves repetitively pounding and circling the same area of surface day upon day, year upon year in all weathers, must not be underestimated. In addition to having suitable load bearing characteristics, the surface also needs to be serviceable in extremes of weathers. This is a civil engineering problem which requires specialised constructions designed for short term (up to 5 years) or long term (over 5 years) use. For short term use an organic surface may be satisfactory but for longer use an inorganic material on a free draining macadam base should be considered. The alternative types of all weather surface are:

10 *Horse box lanes at a show ground. Photo: Peter Ackroyd*

- Organic surfaces, such as wood fibre or chips
- Inorganic sand, or a fibre and sand mix
- Granulated PVC/sand mix
- Other inorganic proprietary surfaces

It is strongly recommended that qualified independent advice should be sought at the outline design stage. See also References.

For competition rings and courses natural field turf or stubble fields are normal. Artificial all-weather surfaces are gaining ground, following those developed for racing. Consult with organisations and the trade.

Markings

Dressage is one of the few marked out to a standard format, **4 & 5**. Most other courses or rings use numbered obstacles and flag markers. Start and finish 'lines' are usually mobile electronic timing beams.

Fencing

Competition rings are usually roped off, but permanent rings may be railed.

At permanent sites, horse 'health and safety' fencing should be provided set back at least 1.5 m (5 ft) from trees and hedges (some are poisonous) and adjoining property. Post and rail hardwood or tanalised fencing is strongly recommended. Alternatively, economical fencing consists of larch posts and top rail infilled with 2/3 strands of wire. Avoid barbed wire. Never strain a fence off a gate post, always use a separate strainer post. Gates should swing freely, have catches that cannot be 'fiddled' open by horses and have a means of being fastened in an open position.

11 *After showing, Essex County Show. Photo: Kicksports Foto*

12 *Cross country hunter trials. Photo: Richard Gardner*

13 *Junior eventing. Photo: Nicholas Meeks*

14 *Carriage driving. Rings are also provided for showing, scurry, road driving and other competitions on dry land. Photo: Mark Shearman*

Floodlighting

Outdoor shows take place in hours of daylight. However, floodlighting is required where there is regular use after dusk for schooling or warm-up and practice jumping at indoor shows.

Lighting is provided to enable the safe movement of both horse and rider appropriate to the standard of participation. The actions of both must be clearly seen by other riders, officials and trainers.

The lighting must be adequate to enable the safe progress of both horse and rider over the jumps. It is important that a high degree of lighting uniformity is achieved with sufficient floodlighting positions to remove shadowing. The eye level of a rider is typically between 2 and 2.5 m (approx 6 ft and 8 ft) above ground level and may significantly increase when jumps are taken. This should be considered when determining a suitable mounting height for floodlighting. Glare to both horse and rider should be limited as much as possible.

The lighting installation should provide even illumination over the total ground area. Shadows should be avoided as they may cause horses to shy. In many cases, the most cost-effective lighting solution would be provided by a side-lighting system similar to those used by a minor sports ground or multi-use sports area. Table 69.1 shows recommended illuminances

Table 69.1 Recommended Illuminances

Application	Illuminance (lux) E_m	Plane of measurement	Uniformity ratio	Mounting height (m)
Schooling (supervised practice and training)				
Showjumping	150	Horizontal on ground	0.5	10 (min)
Dressage	100	Horizontal on ground	0.5	10 (min)
Warm-up outdoors for indoor competition				
Showjumping	300	Horizontal on ground	0.5	10 (min)
Dressage	200	Horizontal on ground	0.5	10 (min)

Refer to Chapter 18 and CIBSE Lighting Guide: LG4 – Sports for further details regarding Floodlighting.

References and further advice

Biathlon: Modern Pentathlon Association of Great Britain.
    Showjumping and one sport from pentathlon elements.
Bridleways The British Horse Society (BHS).
Carriage driving British Driving Society, BHS.
Cross country, eventing and horse trials BHS.
Dressage BHS.
Endurance or long distance riding BHS.
Gymkhanas or mounted games The Pony Club (PC), BHS
Modern Pentathlon Modern Pentathlon Association of Great Britain. The five sports are showjumping, shooting, running, fencing and swimming.

15 *Popping over the practice jump in a set aside warm-up area. Photo: Adrian Spaldin*

Polo Hurlingham Polo Association and also refer to Chapter 68.

Riders with disabilities Riding for the Disabled Association

Riding establishments, schools and stables BHS

Show jumping British Show Jumping Association and PC

Showing classes BHS, British Show Pony Society and breed associations.

Tetrathlon PC. Requires showjumping facilities within reasonable distance for cross-country running, swimming and shooting elements: BHS for adult events of different disciplines.

Trekking BHS.

Vaulting BHS.

BHS publications, including *Notes on the Construction of all-weather arenas and surfaces*. Published by F D Lovatt Smith and BHS, 1988.

Riding and equestrianism indoors, see Volume 2, Chapter 84.

70
Roller hockey

Peter Ackroyd

Roller hockey, adapted from field hockey and ice hockey is a fast, keenly contested game in which sprint speeds of around 48 km/h (approx 30 mph) are achieved; but serious injuries are rare. It is played by two teams of five players each wearing roller skates with up to five reserves per team, 1. One referee assisted by two goal judges superintends a match.

The game is played on a rectangular, flat and level surface. The necessary equipment is a ball, roller hockey sticks and two goal cages. Matches can be played in the open air under most weather conditions, either by day or under artificial lighting by night; or indoors as shown in Volume 2, Chapter 85.

Critical factors
- A rink is required always with a length-to-width ratio of 2:1, marked out as on 2

- Goal cages of the required specification
- Smooth but non-slippery surface finishes
- A perimeter barrier all around the rink
- Location of publicity panels clear of the rink surface and not behind goals
- Contrasting colour of ball, rink surface, line across goal mouth and barrier.

Playing space dimensions
Sizes of penalty area (12.15 × 5.48 m (approx 13 × 6 yd)) and goal cages (1.7 m (approx 2 yd) internal width × 0.95 m (approx 1 yd) internal base radius) are constant; but overall rink size is not fixed. In all cases the ratio between length and breadth must be 2:1, with a tolerance of plus or minus 10%. A reasonable playing area would be 40 × 20 m (approx 43 × 22 yd), and 34 × 17 m (approx 37 × 19 yd) is an absolute minimum

1 *Photo: National Roller Hockey Association of England*

258

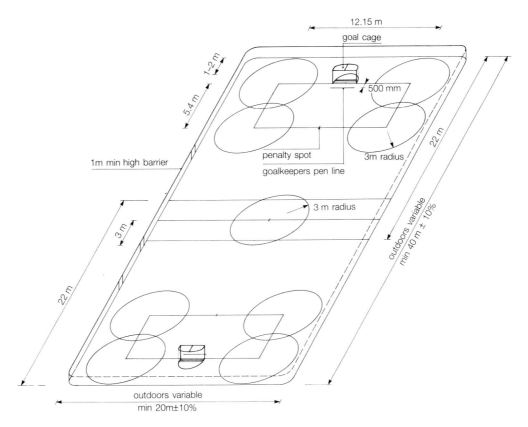

2 *Space diagram of a roller rink. Owing to the varying sizes of roller skating rinks it is not practicable to lay down a hard and fast rule for the overall dimensions of the playing area, but the size of the penalty areas and goal cages are constant. A reasonable playing area would be 40 × 20 m (approx 43 × 22 yd), with a tolerance of plus or minus 10%. There is a 1 m (approx 3 ft) high barrier around all sides*

for official matches. All four corners should be rounded to a radius of 1 m (approx 1 yd). To the above rink dimensions should be added end margins of at least 1 m (approx 1 yd), but not more than 2 m (approx 2 yd), behind the goals. Side margins are not necessary.

The goal

The goal is a cage to the dimensions in **2**, with a wooden frame firmly fastened at the joints and very strong white string netting able to withstand the most powerful shots. Metallic netting is definitely not allowed. The rear net must be suspended from the top rail, trail on the ground and not be fixed at the bottom to prevent the ball from rebounding. The internal face of the base frame should be padded, the padding to commence 200 mm (8 in) from the vertical posts of the goal mouth. The front frame must be 80 mm (3 in) in width and painted white.

The goal must not be covered or lined with any material likely to impede the sight of the goal judge, who stands on a platform fixed to the back of the goal on the lower transverse bar. Neither the goal judge nor the platform (which must be not more than 200 mm (8 in) wide) must impede or cause danger to the players.

The distance behind the goals must be at least 1 m (approx 1 yd), and not more than 2 m (approx 2 yd).

Surface

A stiff, smooth-finished, non-slippery bound surface, such as wood, asphalt, concrete or synthetic material. For general information see Part III.

Markings

Lines to the exact dimensions shown in **2** should be marked out preferably in white, alternatively in yellow, and in all cases 80 mm (3 in) wide. The line across the goal mouth must be of a different colour from that of the ball being used. The pitch is measured to the inside of the perimeter lines (ie the playing area excludes the lines).

Fences and safety barriers

The rink must be surrounded on four sides by a barrier 1 m (approx 3 ft) high, which must have planks of wood at the base to a minimum thickness of 20 mm (0.75 in), and a height of 200 mm (8 in).

If publicity panels are displayed inside the barrier, they must be placed at least 300 mm (12 in) above the base and must leave a clear 200 mm (8 in) band all round the rink, this band to be painted a neutral colour to contrast with the colour of the ball.

There must be no publicity panels within 2 m (approx 2 yd) of either side of the goal (measured from the outside of the goal); and no inscriptions of any kind behind the goal.

Floodlighting

For details refer to Chapter 18 and the CIBSE Lighting Guide: LG4 – Sports.

References and further advice

Rules of the Game, published by the National Roller Hockey Association

259

71
Roller skating and speed skating

Peter Ackroyd

Free skating and artistic skating are fairly informal activities and do not require a marked rink of precise dimensions, **1**. Speed skating is more formal, and requires a track of particular layout and dimensions.

Critical factors
- A smooth, level floor with as few, unlipped joints as possible
- A barrier to separate skaters from viewers or passers-by.

Playing space dimensions
There are no fixed dimensions for Free Skating and Artistic Skating generally; but 40 × 20 m (131 ft × 65 ft 6 in) minimum is necessary for national competitions, and 45 × 25 m (148 × 82 ft) minimum for championships, **2**.

For Speed Skating, dimensions depend on number of skaters using the track simultaneously – see **3**.

Surface
A concrete substrate, either with a smooth self-finish, or topped with macadam or some other stiff, smooth and unjointed material. Where joints are unavoidable, great care must be taken to avoid lipping. Grass is not suitable. For general information see Part III.

Markings
White (or black, if this would be more visible against the surface colour) lines of between 13 and 32 mm (0.5 and

1 *Photo: Richard Wilding Journal Photos.*

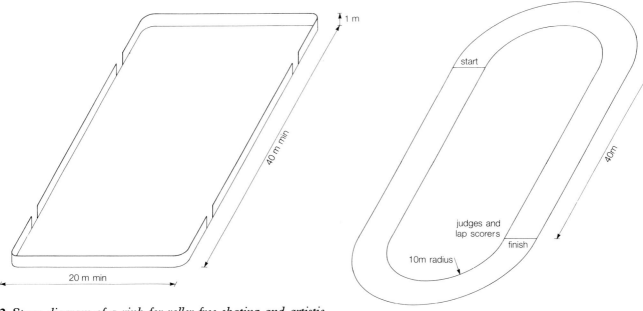

2 *Space diagram of a rink for roller free skating and artistic skating*

3 *Space diagram of speed roller skating rink. The width of the track limits the number of racing skaters in each heat: 2.44 m (8 ft) = 2 skaters, 3.66 m (12 ft) = 3 skaters, 4.57 m (15 ft) = 4 skaters, 5.49 m (18 ft) = 5 skaters, 6.10 m (20 ft) = 6 skaters*

1.2 in) width. The skating area is measured to the inside of the perimeter lines (ie the skating area excludes the lines).

Fences and safety barriers
There should be barriers all round, minimum height 1 m (approx 3 ft), to separate skaters from viewers or passers-by.

Ancillary facilities
Changing accommodation for 30 skaters and ten officials. Where competition or championship skating is involved, a judges' room where calculations may be done is also needed. For artistic skating, music facilities are required.

Floodlighting
This sport is not commonly floodlit and therefore no specific recommendations are provided. For general recommendations for floodlighting outdoor sports refer to Chapter 18, and the CIBSE Lighting Guide: LG4 – Sports.

References and further advice
Federation of Roller Skating, England.

72
Rounders

Peter Ackroyd

The game is played between two teams of between six and nine players. The batter stands with both feet within the batting square, holding a round wooden bat 460 mm (18 in) long, and attempts to strike balls bowled from the bowling square. After a successful strike the batter runs to first post and may attempt a complete circuit of the track (thus scoring a 'rounder') before the opposing team can retrieve the ball and return it, **1**.

Critical factors
● The compulsory markings, distances and pegs, **2**

Playing space dimensions
Pitch size and layout are fixed, as shown in **2**, with an outfield radiating approximately 50 m (approx 55 yd) from peg 1. Solid lines are compulsory markings, broken

1 *Photo: Alan Edwards*

lines are peg setting-out lines. The simplest way of marking the pitch is by using lengths of string as follows:

Post positions
Put Peg 1 (which must be on the right-hand front corner of the batting square) in the ground and directly opposite that peg 2, the second post, at a distance of 17 m (approx 56 ft). Take a 24 m (approx 79 ft) length of string and tie a knot in the middle (each half 12 m (approx 40 ft)). Fix one end of the string to each peg and carry the centre knot out to the right until the string is taut. At the knot put in peg 3 at the first post; then repeat the operation to the left and put in peg 4 at the third post. Now take a 17 m (approx 56 ft) length of string with a centre knot (each half 8.5 m (approx 28 ft)) and fix one end to peg 4 and the other to peg 1. Carry the knot to the left until the string is taut, and this gives the position of peg 5, the fourth post.

Bowling square
Stretch the 17 m (approx 56 ft) string from peg 1 to peg 2, then measure 7.5 m (approx 24 ft 6 in) along the string. The front of the bowling square can now be marked 1.25 m (approx 4 ft) either side of the string and parallel to the front line of the batting square. The other three sides of the square can now be marked. It will be found that if the string is stretched between pegs 3 and 4, it cuts the side lines of the square 1 m (approx 3 ft) from the front line.

Batting square
Make a line extending 2 m (6 ft 6 in) from peg 1 towards peg 5 to form the front line of the batting square. The remaining three sides can now be marked.

Space between adjoining pitches
10 m (approx 33 ft) between outfield boundaries, which are circles of approximately 50 m (55 yd) diameter (not compulsory) centred on peg 1.

Surface
Natural grass or synthetic turf. For general information see Chapters 8 and 11.

Markings
The front line of the batting square is extended in both directions for at least 12 m (approx 39 ft) in solid lines.

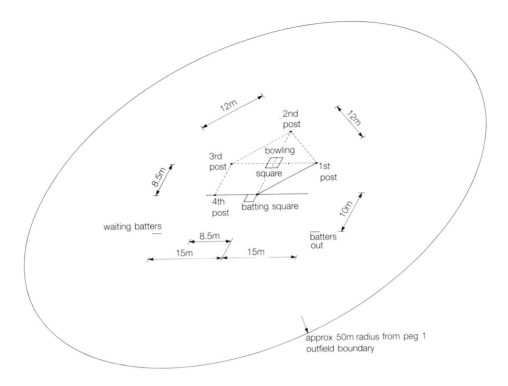

2 *Diagram of rounders field. Dark lines and pegs are compulsory markings. Broken lines are peg setting out lines. Space between adjoining fields is 10 m (33 ft) between outfield boundaries, which are circles of approximately 50 m (165 ft) diameter centred on peg 1*

A line is also marked connecting peg 1 with peg 3. A 2 m (6 ft 6 in) line is marked from peg 5 into the 'backward area'. All distances are to the outside edges of perimeter lines (ie the playing area includes the lines). Lines are 50 mm (approx 19 in) wide, preferably in white; second choice is yellow.

Changing facilities
Changing spaces for 22 players and two officials per pitch would be desirable.

Floodlighting
This sport is not commonly floodlit and therefore no specific recommendations are provided. For general recommendations for floodlighting outdoor sports refer to Chapter 18, and the CIBSE Lighting Guide: LG4 – Sports.

References and further advice
National Rounders Association (NRA)
Rules of the Game and Hints to Umpires 1990, published by the NRA.

73
Shinty

Peter Ackroyd

The game of Shinty goes back to the roots of Gaelic Scotland and the even earlier heritage of the Celtic race and bears a family resemblance to the Irish stick-and-ball game of Hurling (see Chapter 61). Originally the two games were identical but over the centuries they have drifted apart in development and technique.

Today Shinty (or Camanachd, as it is popularly known in Scotland) is played twelve-a-side, using crooked, broad-bladed sticks and a ball, 1.

Critical factors

● Overall area including the surrounding safety margins.

1 *Photo: Donald Mackay*

Playing space dimensions

Pitch size is not fixed. Minimum size is 128 × 64 m (140 × 70 yd) and the recommended ideal size 155 × 73 m (170 × 80 yd). Goal posts are spaced 3.66 m (4 yds) apart, with cross bars at a height of 3.05 m (10 ft) above ground. For under-fourteens, the pitch should be 91 × 46 m (100 × 50 yd) and the crossbar on the goals lowered to 2.44 m (8 ft), 2.

Surface

Natural grass. For information on grass pitches see Chapter 8.

Markings

Lines should be marked in white. All lines (except the goal-line, between the goal posts) should be 40–75 mm (1.5–3 in) wide; those between the goal posts should be between 75–100 mm (3–4 in) wide. The playing area is measured to the outside of the perimeter lines (ie the playing area includes the lines).

Fences and safety barriers

The field shall be fenced off at a distance of not less than 1.8 m (6 ft) outside the bye-lines and side-lines, to a recommended minimum height of 1.1 m (3 ft 6 in).

Changing facilities

Accommodation is required for 28 players and seven officials per match.

Floodlighting

This sport is not commonly floodlit and therefore no specific recommendations are provided. For general recommendations for floodlighting outdoor sports refer to Chapter 18, and the CIBSE Lighting Guide: LG4 – Sports.

References and further advice

The Camanachd Association, Scotland.
Scottish Sports Council.

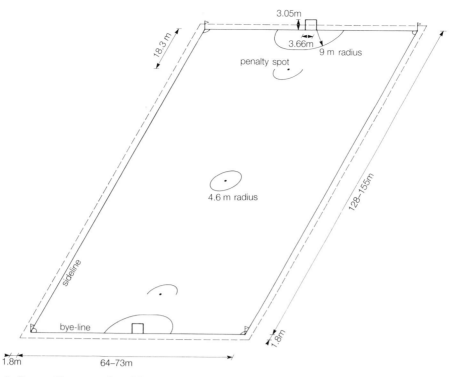

3.05m

3.66m

9 m radius

penalty spot

18.3 m

4.6 m radius

128–155m

sideline

bye-line

1.8m

1.8m

64–73m

2 *Space diagram of a shinty pitch. The ideal size is 140 × 73 m (170 × 80 yd): Further details can be obtained from the Scottish Sports Council*

74
Softball

Peter Ackroyd

Softball is a member of the baseball family of games (see Chapters 40 and 72) and there are two main varieties, Fast Pitch and Slow Pitch, played by both men and women. Participants range from primary school children to senior citizens and teams can comprise any mix of age and gender; softball can be a very pleasant recreational game. Players use a bat similar to that for baseball and a ball which is larger but not soft. The ball is pitched under-arm and two teams take turns to bat through seven innings. The aim is to score runs by completing a circuit around the bases without being 'put out'. Most of the action takes place around the bases in the area known as the infield, **1**.

Critical factors
- Overall area of space including the surrounding safety margins
- The safety fencing along three sides
- If floodlighting is provided, it should be bright enough to permit sight of balls hit in the air, but without discomforting glare

1 *Photo: National Softball Federation*

- Purpose-built pitches should have properly prepared mineral surfaced infields.

Playing space dimensions
The game is played on a smaller field than baseball, with varying field dimensions depending on the age and gender of players. Distance from home plant to outfield fence (see **2**) varies from 85 m (275 ft) for adult male players to 55 m (175 ft) for under-twelve players. Recommended principal dimensions are given in Table 74.1 below. Also see **3**.

Table 74.1 Recommended dimensions

Adult Softball Game	Division	Bases m	ft	Pitching m	ft	Fences m	ft
Fast pitch	Female	18.29	60	12.20	40	60.96	200
	Male	18.29	60	14.02	46	76.20	250
Modified	Female	18.29	60	12.20	40	60.96	200
	Male	18.29	60	14.02	46	80.80	265
Slow pitch	Female	19.81	65	15.24	50	76.2	250
	Male	19.81	65	15.24	50	83.82	275
	Co-ed	19.81	65	15.24	50	83.82	275
	Super	19.81	65	15.24	50	91.44	300
16 inch	Female	16.76	55	11.58	38	60.96	200
slow pitch	Male	16.76	55	11.58	38	76.20	250

Youth Softball Division	Bases m	ft	Pitching m	ft	Fences Minimum m	ft	Fences Maximum m	ft
Girls – Slow Pitch								
10-under	16.76	55	10.67	35	45.72	150	53.34	175
12-under	18.29	60	12.20	40	53.34	175	60.96	200
15-under	19.81	65	14.02	46	68.58	225	76.2	250
19-under	19.81	65	15.24	50	68.58	225	76.2	250
Girls – Fast Pitch								
10-under	16.76	55	10.67	35	45.72	150	53.34	175
12-under	18.29	60	10.67	35	53.34	175	60.96	200
15-under	18.29	60	12.20	40	53.34	175	60.96	200
19-under	18.29	60	12.20	40	60.96	200	68.58	225
Boys – Slow Pitch								
10-under	16.76	55	10.67	35	45.72	150	53.34	175
12-under	18.29	60	12.20	40	53.34	175	60.96	200
15-under	18.29	60	14.02	46	76.20	250	83.82	275
19-under	19.81	65	15.24	50	83.82	275	91.44	300
Boys – Fast Pitch								
10-under	16.76	55	10.67	35	45.72	150	53.34	175
12-under	18.29	60	12.20	40	53.34	175	60.96	200
15-under	18.29	60	12.20	40	53.34	175	60.96	200
19-under	18.29	60	14.02	46	60.96	200	68.58	225

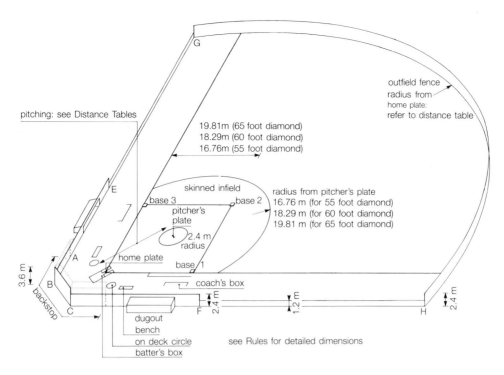

pitching: see Distance Tables

outfield fence radius from home plate: refer to distance table

19.81m (65 foot diamond)
18.29m (60 foot diamond)
16.76m (55 foot diamond)

skinned infield

base 3
base 2

pitcher's plate

radius from pitcher's plate
16.76 m (for 55 foot diamond)
18.29 m (for 60 foot diamond)
19.81 m (for 65 foot diamond)

2.4 m radius

home plate

base 1

3.6 m

backstop

A

B

C

coach's box

dugout bench

on deck circle

batter's box

F

see Rules for detailed dimensions

E

G

H

2.4 m

1.2 m

2.4 m

2 *Space diagram of a softball field, including the three alternative sizes of diamond. The recommended minimum of fencing shown is intended to meet most safety requirements, but not contain every batted or thrown ball in play. Note also the location of team 'dugouts'*

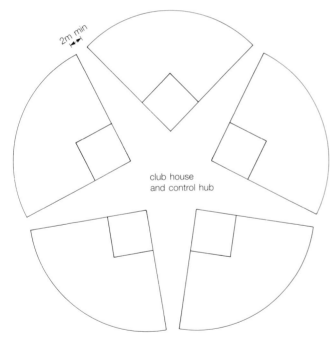

2m min

club house and control hub

3 *A 'wagon-wheel' fiveplex layout of five fields with suggested hub site for match control point and possible clubhouse with elevated commentary/control box overlooking the fields*

End and side margins

There must be a clear space of 18 m (60 ft) between pitches on all sides.

Surface

Natural grass is recommended for outfields. If this is impossible, synthetic turf (either sand filled grass or non-

sand filled) may be considered. Infields should be of finely compacted mineral material. For general information see Part III.

Markings

Lines as shown on **2** are marked on the pitch by means of 75 m (3 in) wide white lines. The size of the pitch is measured to the outside of the perimeter lines (ie the playing area includes the lines).

Barriers and fencing

A basic backstop is obligatory for regular Fast Pitch playing, **2**, and highly recommended for Slow Pitch playing. Its central section, diagonally across the corner behind the home plate, is at least 3 m (10 ft) long and 3.6 m (12 ft) high; with an additional wing on each side of 3 m (10 ft) length and 2.4 m (8 ft) height. Particularly in cases where the pitch backs onto pedestrian ways or adjoining pitches, there should be continuation fences (containing gates) from these barriers to points 3 m (10 ft) beyond the 1st and 3rd bases; and these fences should be at least 2.4 m (8 ft) high. If it is desired to enclose the pitch completely, they may then be linked with the curved outfield fence by means of 1.2 m (4 ft) high fences. The outfield fence should be 2.4 m (8 ft) high.

Team dugouts

These two areas house the teams during the game. One is on the first base line side (away team), the other on the 3rd base side (home team). They are most usually at ground level and take the form of lean-to sheds with the roof sloping away from the fence. Dimensions should be 1.25 m (4 ft) deep, 2 m (6 ft 7 in) high and 6 m (20 ft) long. The main fencing provides the front wall looking out onto the playing area with a fixed wooden bench along the back wall. Access must be from the playing side only via a gated opening at one end.

Changing facilities

Changing spaces for 28 to 40 players (including substitutes), plus two to four officials, per pitch.

Floodlighting

This sport is not commonly floodlit and therefore no specific recommendations are provided. For general recommendations for floodlighting outdoor sports refer to Chapter 18, and the CIBSE Lighting Guide: LG4 – Sports.

References and further advice

The National Softball Federation.
Softball indoors, see Volume 2, Chapter 39.

75
Stoolball

Peter Ackroyd

1 *Photo: Sports Council Publications*

Stoolball is more than 500 years old and the forerunner of modern cricket, being played with similar (but simpler) rules and equipment on any suitable surface, **1**.

The game is played largely by junior schools in southeast and southern England, having the big advantage that it is comparatively cheap and does not need an immaculately maintained pitch. There are 13 leagues and Associations affiliated to the National Stoolball Association.

Stoolball is usually played by eleven-a-side teams, either 'ladies' or 'mixed', with one side fielding and the other batting. Bowling is underarm and the ball, aimed at the wickets, does not pitch. The bat is in the shape of a table tennis bat, made of willow with a long, sprung and spliced handle. Balls are solid and covered in kid leather.

Critical factors
● The field surrounding the pitch

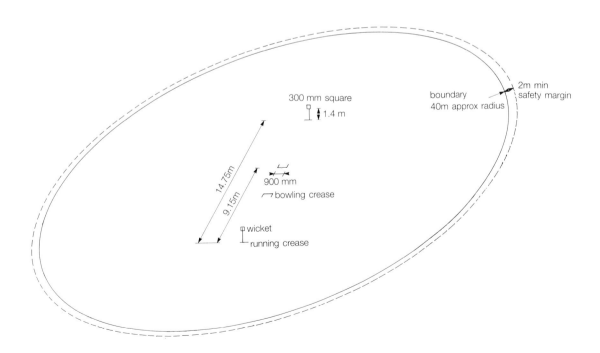

2 *Diagram of a stoolball pitch. The striker at the top wicket (ie stake, and face board) faces bowling from the bottom bowling crease, and vice versa. The running creases need only be dabs of whitewash to show where the wicket is locate*

Playing space dimensions

Pitch length and width as shown on **2** with an outer boundary 40 m (45 yd) radius from the centre point between wickets. The wickets are wooden stakes, painted black at the bottom up to a height of 300 mm (approx 12 in) from the ground, which have mounted upon them 300 mm (approx 12 in) square wooden faceboards as shown in **1**, each such board being 13 mm (approx 0.5 in) thick and protruding 6 mm (0.25 in) from the stake.

Surface

Natural or synthetic turf. For general information see Part III.

Markings

Bowling creases are marked in 40–50 mm (1.5–2 in) wide white lines; running creases need merely be marked by a dab of whitewash to show the location of the wicket.

Changing spaces

Allow for 24 players per pitch

Floodlighting

This sport is not commonly floodlit and therefore no specific recommendations are provided. For general recommendations for floodlighting outdoor sports refer to Chapter 18, and the CIBSE Lighting Guide: LG4 – Sports.

References and further advice

National Stoolball Association.

76
Tchouk-ball

Peter Ackroyd

Tchouk-ball is a relatively new game devised by the Swiss biologist, Dr Hermann Brandt, which developed during the 1970s. It requires dedication and the development of skill, but intentionally excludes adversarial play and personal competitiveness. The rewards of the game lie in co-operation, **1**. Tchouk-ball became accepted first in schools (still the major focus of activity), colleges and universities and is now quite widely played, particularly in Britain but also in Europe and the Far East.

The game is played by two teams of between six and 15 players, using a round leather-covered ball of 540 to 600 mm (approx 22 in) circumference which is thrown at the 'rebound net' (a framed sprung net at each end of the field) to bounce back in various trajectories. A point is scored when the rebounding ball falls into unoccupied court, where the opposing team is unable to prevent it touching the floor. Apart from well-judged 'shooting' at the net, the key skills are fast and accurate passing and catching of the ball between team members.

Critical factors
- A grass or other soft outdoor surface
- Firmly anchored rebound net.

Playing space dimensions
The recommended playing area is 40 × 20 m (approx 131 × 66 ft) with a minimum of 30 × 15 m (approx 98

1 *Photo: Eamonn McCabe*

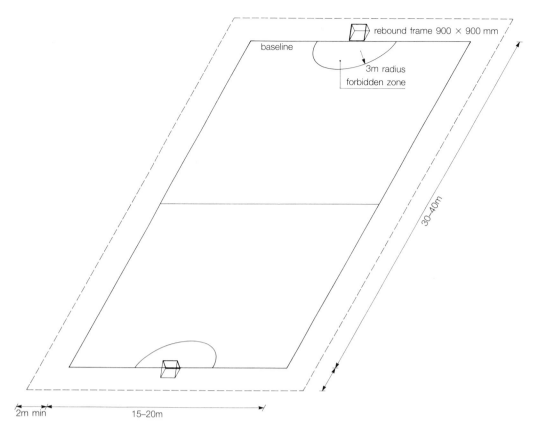

rebound frame 900 × 900 mm

baseline

3m radius
forbidden zone

30–40m

2m min

15–20m

2 Space diagram

× 49 ft) for two full teams. A clear area of 2 m (approx 7 ft) is recommended all round the playing area, **2**.

Rebound net frames
At each end of the playing area is an all-steel frame, painted blue, measuring 900 × 900 mm (3 × 3 ft). Each frame is set at an angle of 60° to the ground and is strung with a very highly tensioned synthetic fibre net of 40 mm (1.5 in) mesh which will give powerful rebound of the ball and withstand all-weather use. The steel frame folds flat for easy transport, weighs about 18 kg (40 lb), and is ready-drilled to allow pegging down on a grass field.

Surface
Preferably grass; but as the ball should not touch the ground, virtually any soft level, flat surface will do. For general information see Part III.

Markings
All markings, as shown on **2**, are 50 mm (2 in) wide and areas are measured to the outsides of lines (ie the lines form part of the areas they delineate).

Changing facilities
Allow for 24 players and three officials per playing area.

Floodlighting
This sport is not commonly floodlit and therefore no specific recommendations are provided. For general recommendations for floodlighting outdoor sports refer to Chapter 18, and the CIBSE Lighting Guide LG4: Sports.

References and further advice
British Tchouk-Ball Association Handbook.
Indoor Tchouk-ball: see Volume 2, Chapter 41.

77
Tug of war

Peter Ackroyd

Tug-of-war is a sport for both sexes and all ages. Two opposing teams of six to eight-a-side (see below) grip a 32 m (approx 105 ft) length of rope and try to pull the other side in their direction, the winning distance for a pull being 4 m (approx 13 ft). All competitions are held under the rules of the Tug of War Association, and a permit is issued for each competition, **1** and **4**. The weight classes are shown in Table 77.1.

International tug-of-war is pulled at the weight classes shown in Table 77.2.

Critical factors
- A roped-off pulling area is required, on level ground, to the dimensions shown on **2**, including any safety margins around
- A rope of 100–123 mm (4–5 in) circumference.

Pulling area dimensions
The fixed length of pitch is 60 m (approx 66 yd), and width 20 m (approx 22 yd). A winning line is marked

1 *Photo: The Tug of War Association*

Table 77.1 Weight classes (Tug of War Association)

Youths (15 to 17 years of age)		Senior men (over 17 years of age)	
460 kilos (72 stones 7 lb)	six-a-side	560 kilos (89 stones 7 lb)	eight-a-side
560 kilos (89 stones 7 lb)	eight-a-side	600 kilos (94 stones 7 lb)	eight-a-side
		640 kilos (100 stones 10 lb)	eight-a-side
		680 kilos (107 stones)	eight-a-side
		720 kilos (113 stones 7 lb)	eight-a-side
		Catchweight	eight-a-side
Women			
460 kilos (72 stones 7 lb)	eight-a-side		
560 kilos (89 stones 7 lb)	eight-a-side		

Table 77.2 Weight classes (international)

Youths (15 to 17 years of age)		Senior men (over 17 years of age)	
560 kilos (89 stones 7 lb)	eight-a-side	560 kilos (89 stones 7 lb)	eight-a-side
		640 kilos (100 stones 10 lb)	eight a-side
		720 kilos (113 stones 7 lb)	eight-a-side
Women			
460 kilos (72 stones 7 lb)	eight a-side		
560 kilos (89 stones 7 lb)	eight a-side		

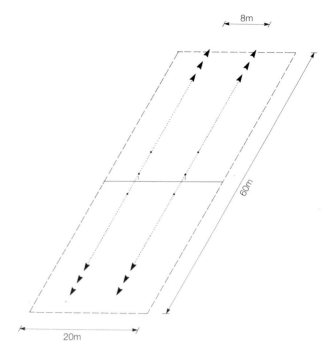

3 *Diagram of an international pulling area*

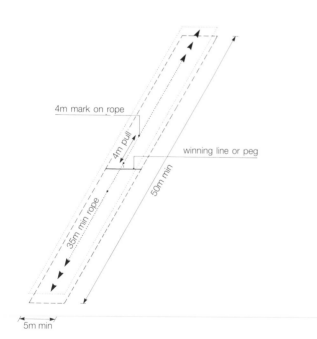

2 *Space diagram of a single pulling area*

4 *Photo: Stuart Hollis*

across the centre. A 3 m (approx 3 yd) wide safety distance is required between roped off pulling areas, **2** and **3**.

Surface
Natural grass only. For details see Chapter 8.

Ancillary facilities
A public address system, which can be used to keep spectators informed of the progress of the competition, is an advantage. Changing rooms or tents should be nearby.

Floodlighting
This sport is not commonly floodlit and therefore no specific recommendations are provided. For general

recommendations for floodlighting outdoor sports refer to Chapter 18, and the CIBSE Lighting Guide: LG4 – Sports.

References and further advice

The Tug of War Association.
Tug of war indoors, Volume 2, Chapter 43.

Index

Access
 disabled people, 10, 72, 73
 multi-use games areas, 126
 stadia, 74, 75, 76, 83–5
Accommodation
 golf clubhouses, 107–11
 pavilions, 96–9
 stadia, 74–5
Acrylic surfaces, 64
Adams and Stewart Soil Binding Test,
 50
Ageing of surfaces, 27
Air sports, 128–30
Alarms, 100–1
All England Netball Association, 245
All England Women's Hockey
 Association, 230
All England Women's Lacrosse
 Association, 239
Amateur Athletics Association (AAA),
 174
American football, 208–10
Amphitheatres, 67–8
Ancillary facilities, 21
 stadia, 91–2
Angling by disabled people, 154–5
Ann Arbor Stadium, 80
Archery, 171–3
Arena trial motorsports, 120
Arsenal football ground, 71
Artificial surfaces see synthetic surfaces
Asphalt surfaces, 37, 204
Association croquet, 194
Association Football, 211–15
Athletics, 174–9
 stadia, 77
 surfaces, 25, 45–6, 178
Australian football, 216–17
Autocross, 119–20
Autotests, 119–20

Babycare facilities, 10
Balbardie athletics track, 176
Ball/surface interaction, 26–7, 50
Barcelona Olympic stadium, 69
Baseball, 180–2
 softball, 266–8
Bases
 cricket pitches, 50, 51–2
 multi-use games areas, 125
 synthetic surfaces, 42–3, 45
 see also foundations; substrates
Basketball, 183–5
Berlin Olympic stadium, 69

Bicycle polo, 186–7
Bituminous surfaces, 53
Blind people, 10
BMX racing, 200
Boathouses, 133–4
Boats see canoeing; rowing; sailing
Boules, 246–7
Bounce from surfaces, 26
Bound mineral surfaces, 37–8
Bowling greens, 47–9, 188
Bowls
 crown green, 196–7
 lawn bowls, 188–9
 pavilions, 99
Bridleways, 256
Bristol football grounds, 71
British Amateur Rugby League
 Association, 221
British American Football Referees
 Association, 210
British Athletics Association (BAF),
 174
British Australian Rules Football
 League, 217
British Canoe Union (BCU), 151, 152,
 153
British Crown Green Bowling
 Association, 197
British Cycling Federation (BCF), 200,
 201
British Gliding Association, 128
British Handball Association, 224
British Horse Society (BHS), 250, 253,
 256, 257
British Institute of Golf Course
 Architects (BIGCA), 105
British Korfball Association, 236
British Parachute Association, 129
British Petanque Association, 247
British Show Jumping Association
 (BSJA), 252, 253, 256, 257
British Show Pony Association, 257
British Sports Association for the
 Disabled, 9, 155
British Standards (BS) see standards
British Tchouk-Ball Association, 272
British Water Ski Federation, 162–3
Building Regulations, 9, 10, 72, 73
Building services
 golf clubhouses, 111, 112
 stadia, 75–6

Cable tow skiing, 163
Calgary stadium, 85

Camanachd, 264–5
Camogie, 190–1
Canoeing, 151–3
Cantilevered roofs for stadia, 71, 86
Car parking see parking
Cardiff Arms Park, 80, 82
Carriage driving, 256
Cash flows, 7–8
Cast elastomer surfaces, 46
CEN see standards
Central Council of Physical Recreation,
 30
Chairlifts for ski slopes, 116
Changing rooms, 91, 96, 97, 99–100
 for disabled people, 10
 multi-use games areas, 126
 see also individual article for each sport
Chartered Institute of Building Services
 (CIBSE), lighting, 28, 60
Chelsea football ground, 82
Children Act (1989), 55
Children's play facilities, 30, 55–6
CIE (Commission Internationale de
 l'éclairage), 61
Cincinnati stadium, 84
Circulation space in pavilions, 98,
 99–100
Clay tennis courts, 54
Clout archery, 171–3
Clubhouses, 94–101
 golf, 106–12
 rowing, 134
 sailing, 140, 141, 142
Coated macadam surfaces, 37
Codes of practice
 floodlighting, 28, 59–61
 planning negotiations, 19
 surfaces, 25
 see also standards
Colour
 line markings, 28
 seating, 82–3
 surfaces, 27, 40
 tennis courts, 53
Colour coated macadam surfaces, 53
Columns of roofs, 86
Comfort of seating, 83
Comfort of stadia, 85–6
Community use of facilities, 71
Compaction of grass pitches, 33
Compactness of design of stadia,
 78–81
Competitive sports, 20–1
Composite surfaces, 46

Concrete surfaces, 37
    cycle racing tracks, 204
    tennis, 53
Costs, 6–8
    of surfaces, 25, 49
Countryside Commission and disabled
        people, 155
Countryside sports, 4–5
Covered accommodation, 85–6, 87
    see also roofs
Covered stadia, 88–9
Cricket, 192–3
    surfaces, 50–2
Croquet, 194–5
Crown green bowls, 196–7
    surfaces, 47–9
Cruisers (sailing boats), 137
Crystal Palace stadium, 86
Curling, 198–9
Cycle Speedway Council, 206
Cycling
    bicycle polo, 186–7
    racing, 200–4
    speedway, 205–6
Cyclo cross, 200

Deaf people, 9–10
Decontamination of sailing boats, 144–5
Decoration of golf clubhouses, 111–12
Design of stadia, 73–6, 77–82
Development briefs, 18–19
Development plans, 18
Dinghies, 137
Directors' boxes, 91
Disabled people
    angling, 154–5
    facilities for, 9–11, 72–3
    riding, 257
Discus, 177
District Sport and Recreation Strategies,
        13, 18
Ditches for bowling greens, 47
Doping control, 92
Dortmund Stadium, 81
Double-decker surfaces, 46
Drag lifts for ski slopes, 117
Drainage
    bowling greens, 47
    cricket pitches, 51
    golf courses, 104
    grass pitches, 30, 32–4
    multi-use games areas, 125
    recreation sites, 31
    ski slopes, 115
    stadia pitches, 91
    synthetic turf pitches, 42
Dressage, 251, 256
Driving see horse riding; motor sports
Driving ranges for golf, 105
Drugs see doping
Dry zones in sailing clubs, 142
Drying areas, 98, 148–9
Durability of surfaces, 27
Dusseldorf stadium, 72, 80, 87

Emergency services, 91
EN see standards
Enduros, 119–20
English Basket Ball Association, 183
English Lacrosse Union, 237
Environment, Dept of, Planning Policy
        Guidance Notes (PPGNs), 18
Environmental effects of countryside
        sports, 4–5

Equestrianism see horse riding
Ethylene propylene diene modified
        (EPDM) rubber surfaces, 46
Eton fives, 207
European standards see standards
Evenness of surfaces, 25–6, 50
Exits from stadia, 84

Federation of Roller Skating, 261
Fences and fencing, 62, 89–90
    multi-use games areas, 126
    see also individual article for each sport
    see also walls
Fertilization of grass pitches, 34
Field event athletics, 176–8
Field korfball, 235
Field tennis, 241
FIFA (Fédération Internationale de
        Football Association), 215
    access to ground, 84
    fences and moats, 90
    lighting, 61, 87
    spectator accommodation, 80
    World Cup requirements, 92
FIH see International Hockey
        Federation
Film crew accommodation, 91
Filter membranes for pitches, 35
Finland, Olympic stadium, 69
Fire resistance of surfaces, 27
Fire safety
    seating, 82
    standards, 92–3
Fire Safety and Safety of Places of
        Sport Act (1987), 93
First aid, 91, 98
Fishing by disabled people, 154–5
Five-a-side football, 211, 214
Fives, 207
Flat green bowls, surfaces, 47–9
Flexibility of stadia, 86–7
Floodlighting, 21, 28, 59–61, 87
    multi-use games areas, 121–2, 124
    see also individual article for each sport
Floors of sailing clubhouses, 149
Football
    American, 208–10
    Association, 211–15
    Australian, 216–17
    five-a-side, 211, 214
    Gaelic, 218–19
    rugby league, 220–1
    rugby union, 222–3
    safety, 93
    stadia, 69, 77, 89
        as multi-sports complexes, 71–2
    synthetic surfaces, 41
    World Cup requirements, 92
Football Association, 215
    crowd safety, 93
Football League, synthetic surfaces, 41,
        43
Football Spectators Act (1989), 93
Football Stadia Advisory Design
        Council (FSADC), 9, 93
Footpaths for disabled people, 10
Force reduction of surfaces, 27
Foundations
    floodlights, 61
    waterbound surfaces, 38
    see also bases; substrates
Fuel storage for motor boats, 146

Gaelic football, 218–19
Gangways, 81
Gliding, 128–9

Goal areas, 126
Goal posts, 213
Golf
    clubhouses, 106–12
    courses, 102–5
Governing bodies, 170
Gradients
    playing fields, 32, 33, 35, 38
    ski slopes, 114
    stadia pitches, 91
    synthetic pitches, 42, 46
Grand National Archery Society, 172
Grass bowling greens, 47
Grass pitches, 30–6
Grasstrack racing motorsport, 119–20
Greece, stadia, 67, 68
Grey-green bituminous surfaces, 53
Gritted bituminous surfaces, 53
Guest boxes, 91
Guide to Safety at Sports Grounds, 93
Gymkhanas, 253, 256

Hammer throwing, 177
Handball, 224–5
Hang gliding, 129
Hard porous waterbound surfaces,
        37–8
    athletics, 178
    tennis, 54
Haringey Athletics Club, 174
Hearing impaired people, 9–10
High jump, 176–7
Hill climb motorsports, 119–20
Hillsborough Stadium, 71, 93
Hockey, 226–30
    mini-hockey, 226, 231–2
    roller hockey, 258–9
    six/seven-a-side, 226, 231–2
    surfaces, 41, 42, 43, 226, 228–9
Hockey Association, 230, 232
Hockey Rules Board, 230
Home Office, Guide to Safety at Sports
        Grounds, 93
Horse riding, 250–7
    polo, 248–9
Hospitality boxes, 91
Hurling, 233–4
    see also camogie; shinty
Hurlingham Polo Association, 249

IAKS, 202, 203, 204
Ice rinks for curling, 198–9
Illumination see lighting
Impact absorption of surfaces, 27
Impervious acrylic surfaces, 64
In-situ synthetic surfaces, 40, 46
Indicator boards, 91
Indoor skiing, 113
Informal recreation, 20
Information centres in sailing clubs,
        149–50
Inlaid line markings, 27–8
Institution of Electrical Engineers, 59,
        60, 61
Institution of Highways and
        Transportation, 155
Institution of Lighting Engineers, 60
Intensity of use, 20–1
International Amateur Athletics
        Federation (IAAF), 25, 179
    synthetic surfaces, 46
International Hockey Federation (FIH)
    lighting, 61
    synthetic surfaces, 41, 42, 43, 228,
        230
International Olympic Committee, 87

International Tennis Federation, 61
International Working Group for
    Sports Facilities and Equipment,
    204
Irrigation
    bowling greens, 47
    covered stadia, 88
    cricket pitches, 51
    hockey, 229
    ski slopes, 117–18
    waterbound surfaces, 38
Islington open space, 43

Javelin, 177

Kart racing, 119–20
Keelboats, 137
Korfball, 235–6

Lacrosse
    men, 237–8
    women, 239–40
Land requirements, 169–70
Landfill sites, 31, 32
Launching sailing boats, 145–6, 147
Lawn bowls, 188–9
Lawn tennis, 241–3
    pavilions, 99
    surfaces, 53–4, 64
Lawn Tennis Association, 54, 243
Laws and regulations
    Building Regulations, disabled
        people, 9, 10, 72
    Children Act (1989), 55
    Fire Safety and Safety of Places of
        Sport Act (1987), 93
    Football Spectators Act (1989), 93
    lighting, 61
    Local Government Acts
        (1982/1990), 17
    Local Government and Housing Act
        (1989), 17
    Planning Act (1990), 18
    Planning and Compensation Act
        (1991), 17
    Safety of Sports Grounds Act
        (1975), 93
    Seeds Regulations, 34
    Town and Country Planning Act
        (1971), 17
Learning difficulties, people with, 10
Levelness of surfaces, 25–6, 47
Life cycle costing, 6–8
Lighting
    illumination levels, 60
    laws and regulations, 61
    and orientation, 80
    pavilions, 101
    ski slopes, 116
    of stands, 91
    and TV, 88
    see also floodlighting
Lighting Guide (CIBSE), 28
Line markings see marking
Live-in accommodation, 99, 110
Livery stables, 250
Local Government Acts (1982/1990),
    17
Local Government and Housing Act
    (1989), 17
Local plans, 18
London Olympic stadium, 68
Long jump, 176

Lords Cricket Ground, 70
Louisiana Superdome, 89
Lubrication of ski slopes, 117–18

Macadam surfaces, 37
    cycle racing, 204
    tennis, 53
Manèges, 251, 253
Marinas, 156–61
Maritime villages, 159
Marking pitches and tracks, 27–8
    synthetic surfaces, 40
    synthetic turf, 43
    waterbound surfaces, 38
    see also individual article for each sport
Melbourne Olympic stadium, 69
Metrication, 169
Mexico City stadia, 79
Michigan University stadium, 80
Microlight flying, 129–30
Milan football stadium, 71, 88
Mineral surfaces, 37–8
Mini-hockey, 226, 231–2
Minneapolis Metrodome, 88
Moats, 90
Modern Pentathlon Association, 256
Moorings in marinas, 160, 161
Motocross, 119–20
Motor boat fuel storage, 146
Motor sports, 119–20
Multi-sports complexes, 71–2
Multi-tiered stadia, 82
Multi-use games areas (MUGAs),
    121–7
Multi-use stadia, 86–7
Multi-use water areas, 137
Munich Olympic Park, 69, 80, 81, 85

Naples Stadium, 85
National Association of Boys Clubs,
    215
National Cricket Association (NCA),
    193
    pitch tests, 50
National Playing Fields Association
    (NPFA), 35, 36, 38
    athletics tracks, 175, 179
    cricket, 193
    floodlighting, 60, 61
    football, 215
    gradients, 35, 38
    multi-use games areas, 127
    orientation recommendations, 95,
        170
    rugby union, 222
    space requirements, 30, 35
    surfaces, 36, 38
National Roller Hockey Association,
    259
National Rounders Association, 263
National Softball Federaton, 268
National Stoolball Association, 269,
    270
Natural surfaces, 25
Natural turf, 35
    bowling greens, 47
    cricket pitches, 50–1
Netball, 244–5
Non-competitive sports, 20
Non-particulate filled synthetic turf,
    54
Nottinghamshire County Council
    cricket pitches, 50, 52
Nylon synthetic turf, 41

Off-road motorsports, 119–20
Olympic sailing, 138
Olympic stadia, 67, 68, 69
Orientation, 169–70
    athletics tracks, 175
    cricket, 192
    and lighting, 80
    pavilions, 95
    pitches, 80
Outdoor playing space, 30
Outdoor sports, 3–5

Painted line markings, 28, 38
Par in golf, 102–3
Parabolic spectator tiers, 81
Parachuting, 129
Parascending, 130
Parking
    for disabled people, 10
    at sailing clubs, 144
    at stadia, 83–5, 91
Partially sighted people, 10
Participation in play, 56
Participation standards, 20, 21
Particle size in hard surfaces, 37
Particulate filled synthetic turf, 54
Pavilions, 94–101
Pedestrian access, 85
Performance of cricket pitches, 50
Perimeter fences, 89–90
Permeability of grass pitches, 33
Person/surface interaction, 27
Personal Watercraft Association, 165
Personal watercraft (PWC) riding, 164–5
Petanque, 246–7
Photographer accommodation, 91
Pipe drainage of playing fields, 32
Pitch and putt golf courses, 105
Pitches
    grass, 30–6
    orientation, 169–70
    size, 169–70
    see also individual article for each
        sport
Planning, 12–13, 17–19
    agreements, 18
    air sports, 128
    floodlighting, 59
    grass pitches, 30–1
    multi-use games areas, 122
    obligations, 17–19
    pavilions and clubhouses, 94–5
    permission, 9, 17
Planning Act (1990), 18
Planning and Compensation Act
    (1991), 17
Planning Policy Guidance Notes
    (PPGNs), 18
Plastic line markings, 28
Plastic surfaces, 39, 54
Platter lifts for ski slopes, 116
Play facilities, 30, 55–6
Playboard Ltd, 127
Playing Pitch Strategy, 13, 18, 30
Playing space see space
Playing surfaces see surfaces
Playwork, 55–6
Pole vaulting, 176
Polo, 248–9
    bicycle polo, 186–7
Polymeric synthetic turf, 41–2
Polymeric tennis surfaces, 54
Polyurethane (PU) surfaces, 39, 40, 46
Pontiac Silverdome, 88
Pony Club (PC), 256, 257

279

Porous surfaces
  athletics, 178
  tennis, 53, 54
Portable pavilions, 96
Portable surfaces, 28
Powder line markings, 28
Prefabricated sheet surfaces, 45–6
Press facilities, 83, 91–2
Professional's accommodation in golf
    clubhouses, 108, 110
Public transport to site, 10

Quality control of synthetic surfaces,
    40

Racing
  canoes, 151
  cycles, 200–4
  motorsports, 119–20
  sailing boats, 139–40, 143
Radio crew accommodation, 91–2
Rake of spectator tiers, 81–2
Rallycross, 119–20
Rallying (motorsports), 119–20
Ramps for disabled people, 10, 73
RAPRA Technology Ltd, 50
Rebound from surfaces, 26, 50
Rebound walls, 62, 125
Reclamation sites, 31, 32
Regional Councils for Sport and
    Recreation, 13
Regional Recreation Strategies, 13
Regulations see laws and regulations
Reinforcement of turf, 35
Resin-bound rubber crumb surfaces,
    46
Riding see horse riding
Riding for the Disabled Association,
    257
Riser heights of spectator tiers, 82
Road racing
  cycling, 200
  motorsports, 119–20
Rodeo canoeing, 151
Roller hockey, 258–9
Roller skating, 260–1
Rolling resistance of surfaces, 27
Rome
  Coliseum, 81
  Olympic stadium, 68, 69
  stadia, 67–8
Roofs of stadia, 71, 85–6, 87–9
Rootzone drainage, 34
Rounders, 262–3
Rowing, 133–5
Rowing tanks, 135
Royal Caledonian Curling Club, 199
Royal Yachting Association, 137
Rubber surfaces, 39, 45, 46
Rugby Football League, 221
Rugby Football Union, 223
Rugby league, 220–1
Rugby stadia, 77
Rugby union, 222–3
Rural areas, synthetic pitches, 43

Safety, 93
  moats, 90
  perimeter fences, 89–90
  seating, 82
  stadia, 70–1, 73, 77, 83–90
  see also individual article for each sport
Safety of Sports Grounds Act (1975),
    93
Sailboards, 137
Sailing, 136–50

Sailing canoes, 151
San Diego stadium, 82, 84
Sand for pitch drainage, 34
Sand racing motorsport, 119–20
Sandwich surfaces, 46
Scottish Sports Council, 264, 265
Scratch scoring in golf, 102
Seating for spectators, 82–3
Security
  pavilions, 100–1
  sailing clubs, 150
Seeding of grass pitches, 34
Seeds Regulations, 34
Seven-a-side hockey, 226, 231–2
Sheet rubber surfaces, 39, 45
Sheet synthetic surfaces, 39–40, 45–6
Sheffield stadia, 71, 72, 88
Sheltering bowling greens, 49
Shinty, 264–5
Shock pads for synthetic turf surfaces,
    42–3
Short croquet, 194
Shot putting, 177–8
Show jumping, 252, 253, 257
Showers, 98, 99
  for disabled people, 10
Sight lines, 78, 81–2
Signs for disabled people, 10, 11
Site selection, 30–1
Six-a-side hockey, 226, 231–2
Size of pitches, 169–70
Skating
  roller hockey, 258–9
  roller skating, 260–1
  speed skating, 260–1
Ski slopes, 113–18
Skiing, 5
  artificial ski centres, 113–18
Slip resistance of surfaces, 27
Slit drainage, 31, 33–4
Soccer, 211–15
Softball, 266–8
Soil Science Research Unit, 50
Soils
  bowling greens, 47
  cricket pitches, 50
  grass pitches, 32–3
Space availability, 30
Space requirements, 169–70
  see also individual article for each sport
Spain, stadia, 67
Specialist surfaces, 44–54
Specification for Artificial Sports Surfaces,
    26, 27, 52
Spectators
  accommodation, 77, 78–83, 85–6
  fences and moats, 89–90
  see also individual article for each sport
  see also viewing
Speed skating, 260–1
Speedway cycling, 205–6
Spin of ball, 26, 50
Split (Yugoslavia) stadium, 89
Sponsors' facilities, 91
Sport for All, 12
Sport in the Community, 13
Sports Council
  air sports, 130
  athletics tracks, 174, 179
  clay tennis courts, 54
  District Sport and Recreation
      Strategies, 13, 18
  hockey, 230
  multi-use games areas, 127
  petanque, 247
  Pitch Prototype Panel, 34, 35

Sports Council (cont.)
  Playing Pitch Strategy, 13, 18, 30
  sailing, 137
  ski centres, 118
  Specification for Artificial Sports
      Surfaces, 26, 27, 52
  Sport in the Community, 13
  synthetic surfaces, 26, 27, 41, 52,
      127, 230
  walls and fencing, 62
Sports Council for Northern Ireland,
    190, 219, 234
Sports Turf Research Institute (STRI),
    33, 34, 35, 49, 50, 193
Sprinklers see irrigation
Sprint motorsports, 119–20
Stability of surfaces, 50, 51
Stadia, 67–93
Stairs, 81
Standard scratch scoring in golf, 102
Standards
  BS3621, 100, 101
  BS4737, 101
  BS5588, 92–3
  BS5649, 60, 61
  BS5669, 125, 126
  BS5696, 38
  BS5810, 10
  BS7044, 25–6, 27, 38, 40, 43, 50
  BS8203, 50
  European standards, surfaces, 27
    alarms, 101
  fire safety, 92–3
  grass seed, 34
  lighting, 59–61
  locks, 100, 101
  outdoor playing space, 30
  particleboard, 125, 126
  of participation, 20, 21
  for surfaces, 25–6, 27, 34, 38, 50
  synthetic surfaces, 40, 43, 126
  see also codes of practice
Statutes/statutory instruments see laws
    and regulations
Steeplechase athletics, 176
Stiffness of pitches, 50, 51
Stoolball, 269–70
Storage, 98–9
  multi-use games areas, 126
  see also individual article for each sport
Structure Plans, 18
Structures for floodlights, 60–1
Subsoil of grass pitches, 32
Substrates, 25
  see also bases; foundations
Sun effects on stadia, 88
Supplementary Planning Guidance,
    18–19
Surfaces, 21, 25–56
  artificial see synthetic surfaces
  athletics, 25, 45–6, 178
  bowls, 47–9
  cricket, 50–2
  evenness, 25–6, 47
  grass pitches, 32–5
  interaction with, 26–7
  markings see marking
  mineral, 37–8
  multi-use games areas, 125
  performance, 26–7
  portable, 28
  qualities, 26–7
  selection, 26
  specialist, 44–54
  stability, 50, 51
  synthetic see synthetic surfaces

Surfaces (*cont.*)
  tennis, 53–4, 64
  texture, 27
  see also individual article for each sport
Surfing canoes, 151
Synthetic surfaces, 21, 25
  athletics, 45–6, 178
  bowling greens, 47–9
  cricket pitches, 51–2
  and equipment, 63
  hockey, 41, 42, 43, 226, 228–9
  in-situ, 40, 46
  sheet, 39–40
  tennis, 53–4
  see also individual article for each sport
Synthetic turf, 35, 41–3
  tennis courts, 54
System buildings of pavilions, 95–6

Tape line markings, 28, 38
Target archery, 171–2
Tarmacadam racing tracks, 204
Taylor Report, 93
Tchouk-ball, 271–2
Television
  crew accommodation, 91–2
  and lighting, 88
Tennis *see* lawn tennis
Textile surfaces, 39
Texture of surfaces, 27
Tiered spectator accommodation, 81–2
Toilets, 91, 97–8, 99
  for disabled people, 10
  golf clubhouses, 108

Tokyo stadia, 69, 88
Topsoil of grass pitches, 32–3
Tournaments, tennis, 243
Town and Country Planning Act (1971), 17
Toxicity of surfaces, 27
Track athletics, 174, 175–6
Track cycling, 200–4
Traction coefficient of surfaces, 27
Trail riding, 120
Training and pitch wear, 21
Translucency of stadium roofs, 87–8, 89
Transport, Dept of, 38
Transport to site, 10
Trekking, horse, 250, 257
Trials, motoring, 119–20
Triple jump, 176
Tug of war, 273–5
Turf
  bowling greens, 47–9
  cricket pitches, 50–1
  reinforcement, 35
  synthetic, 35, 41–3
Turfgrass Seed, 34
Twickenham Football Ground, 87, 89

Unbound mineral surfaces, 37–8
Unitary Development Plans (UDPs), 18
Uplift for ski slopes, 116–17

Velodromes, 200–1
Viewing
  distances, 78

Viewing (*cont.*)
  locations, 77, 78–80
  sight lights, 78, 81–2
Visually impaired people, 10

Walls, 62
  multi-use games areas, 125
  see also fencing
Water jumps in athletics, 176
Water quality, 153
Water recreation, 133–65
Water skiing, 162–3
Water supply to sailing clubs, 150
Waterbound surfaces, 37–8
  athletics, 178
  tennis, 54
Watering *see* irrigation
Weather protection
  of pavilions, 95
  of stadia, 85–6, 88
Weights rooms for rowing, 134
Weirs, 152–3
Wembley Stadium, 69, 79
Wet areas, 98
Wet zones in sailing clubs, 142
Wheel/surface interaction, 27
Wheelchair access, 9, 10, 72–3
Wind effects
  on pavilions, 95
  and sailing, 138–9
  on stadia, 88
Winter sports, 5
Winterbottom Report, 41, 43
Wooden cycle racing tracks, 204

Zones of stadia, 77–8